RATTLING THE CAGES

Oral Histories of
North American Political Prisoners

edited by Josh Davidson, with Eric King

AK PRESS

Praise for *Rattling the Cages*:

"*Rattling the Cages* brings the term 'political prisoner' into sharper focus by providing outstanding oral accounts from a wide range of North American political prisoners. In the finest tradition of oral history—'the poetry of the everyday,' the literature of the streets—this book takes us to the source, and shines a bright, illuminating light into the shadowy world of our peculiarly American gulag. *Rattling the Cages* dives head-first into the wide world of direct personal experiences and human meaning-making, offering an important antidote to propaganda, dogma, and stereotype."
—**Bill Ayers**, author of *Fugitive Days* and *Public Enemy*

"*Rattling the Cages* has more wisdom, harder-earned, per page than any other book I've ever read. It is the kind of wisdom most people hope to never know, the kind of wisdom that comes from facing the true nature of our state and what it does to those who resist its power. The lessons of this book force those of us on the outside to ask whether we are walking the way we believe. *Rattling the Cages* will be essential reading for years to come."
—~~Baynard Woods~~, author of *Inheritance: An Autobiography of Whiteness*

"Prison can't win, Huey Newton famously said, because walls and bars cannot hold back ideas. And this book is brimming with ideas from survivors of political repression. *Rattling the Cages* is an intimate intergenerational dialog with movement activists representing sixty years of struggle and too many years of incarceration. In conversations both hopeful and heartfelt, intense and inspiring, they share how they live to fight another day."
—**Dan Berger**, author of *Stayed on Freedom: The Long History of Black Power Through One Family's Journey*

"As a collection of oral histories, Davidson's *Rattling the Cages* provides an essential archive on both the breathtaking cruelty of American prisons and on the courage and humanity of those locked away. To heed the critiques of its contributors is to accept that all imprisonment is political. But something in these pages throbs even louder than critique. Here, too, one finds love and the joy born from struggle. Those serve as the foundation of this book's brilliant contributions, of the world they—and we—hope to build."
—**N. D. B. Connolly**, Johns Hopkins University

"*Rattling the Cages* pulls off a virtual prison break. It brings so many of my favorite people together, all in one place, to share their incredibly powerful perspectives on life, politics, and dynamics as political prisoners, and to talk about what the future holds."
—**Leslie James Pickering**, author of *Mad Bomber Melville*, former Earth Liberation Front spokesman, and co-founder of Burning Books bookstore

This book is dedicated to all the young radicals and revolutionaries growing up today. Knowing this history will help us create a better tomorrow.

This book is in memory of all the political prisoners, current and former, that we have lost. And specifically to those who died while this project was being completed: Russell Maroon Shoatz, bo brown, Romaine "Chip" Fitzgerald, Thomas "Blood" McCreary, Kathy Boudin, Albert Woodfox, Marshall "Eddie" Conway, and Dr. Mutulu Shakur.

Rattling the Cages: Oral Histories of North American Political Prisoners

© 2023 Josh Davidson and Eric King

This edition © AK Press (Chico / Edinburgh)

ISBN: 978-1-84935-521-6
E-ISBN: 978-1-84935-522-3
Library of Congress Control Number: 2023935612

AK Press
370 Ryan Ave. #100
Chico, CA 95973
www.akpress.org
akpress@akpress.org

AK Press
33 Tower St.
Edinburgh EH6 7BN
Scotland
www.akuk.com
ak@akedin.demon.co.uk

The above addresses would be delighted to provide you with the latest AK Press distribution catalog, which features books, pamphlets, zines, and stylish apparel published and/or distributed
by AK Press. Alternatively, visit our websites for the complete catalog, latest news, and secure
ordering.

Cover design by Josh MacPhee
Printed in the USA on acid-free paper

"It is an irony that the political prisoner sees the broadest strokes of the political life of the society by peering through a narrow window on the world. . . . They challenge us to understand that the struggle for power is not a far-off goal of some future insurrectionary period, but a strategic concept that informs how we build our movement, choose our tactics, and confront the enemy every day."

—Alan Berkman, Holmesburg Prison, foreword to *Build a Revolutionary Resistance Movement: Communiques from the North American Armed Clandestine Movement, 1982–1985*

"Neither imprisonment nor threats of death will sway me from the path that I have taken, nor will they sway others like me. . . . More powerful than my fear of the dreadful conditions to which I might be subjected in prison is my hatred of the dread conditions to which my people are subjected outside of prisons throughout this country."

—Jamil Abdullah Al-Amin (formerly H. Rap Brown), "Statement in Washington, July 26, 1967," in *SNCC Speaks for Itself*

"Nobody is going to give you the education you need to overthrow them. Nobody is going to teach you your true history, teach you your true heroes, if they know that that knowledge is going to set you free. . . . As long as we expect amerika's schools to educate us, we will remain ignorant."

—Assata Shakur, in *Assata Shakur: An Autobiography*

"Josh, things are dismal, but I do find moments of joy. But real joy comes from resistance, struggle, striking a blow against the system. I don't know how to do anything else. I don't desire to do anything else."

—Michael Kimble, March 2022, letter to editor Josh Davidson

Contents

Interviews

Foreword

The contributors to this volume belong to a long lineage of resistance movements that have produced radical critiques and fundamental political challenges to government and society. From struggles against colonialism mounted by Indigenous people and slave rebellions during past centuries to contemporary antiracist mobilizations and unmitigated refusals to normalize violences inflicted on the environment and on women and nonbinary people, these and other forms of resistance have defined the subjugated histories of North America. These and other collective repudiations of class, race, gender, sexual, and other hierarchies are linked to global efforts to guarantee more habitable and mutualistic futures for plant life and for animal life, including the humans who have been the source of so much destruction.

Rattling the Cages calls upon us to imagine agents of history very differently from the ways we have been encouraged to think of powerful individuals as the motors of change. This collection of oral histories helps us to see political prisoners—past, present, and future—as representing the collective movements that imagine and fight for worlds with more expansive promises of freedom. They are our messengers, our dreamers, and our pioneers. They teach us that we do not have to accede to existing modes of organizing our collective existence. They remind us that there is life beyond racial capitalism, beyond heteropatriarchy, beyond the terrible web of carcerality, which they boldly critique even as it has captured their bodies. They are harbingers of the freedom to come. Let us celebrate those who have been able to join the ranks of those who are resisting outside the walls; let us redouble our efforts to bring the others home so that they may join us in our quest to banish prisons and police from our world to come.

Angela Y. Davis

Angela Y. Davis is Professor Emerita of History of Consciousness and Feminist Studies at UC Santa Cruz. An activist, writer, and lecturer, her work focuses on prisons, police, abolition, and the related intersections of race, gender, and class. She is the author of many books, including *Angela Davis: An Autobiography*, *Are Prisons Obsolete?*, and *Freedom Is a Constant Struggle*.

Preface

"I want to really capture what their prison experience was like, what they really feel about support, so the next generation (god willing there will be a next generation) will know what their mothers and fathers went through. We cannot let those experiences go to waste. We cannot turn our backs on these people with apathy or indifference. We need to love them the way they loved the world enough to fight for it."

—Eric King

This book is the result of years of correspondence and conversation with anarchist political prisoner Eric King. While he was confined in some of the most brutal federal prisons across the US, Eric and I found comfort and affinity in reading books and discussing them. It was one way of building a relationship through prison bars. We were reading *Say Nothing* about the IRA, the Troubles, and former combatants sharing their stories, when he came up with the idea of interviewing political prisoners in order to bring voice to the experiences they endure in struggling to create a better world.[1]

As we began this project, Eric had been held in solitary confinement for several years, facing an additional twenty years in prison after being assaulted

---

1. The Irish Republican Army (IRA) was an Irish paramilitary organization that fought for a united Ireland. Their battles with the British state were most intense in the 1970s and 1980s, a period commonly referred to as the Troubles. Patrick Radden Keefe, *Say Nothing: A True Story of Murder and Memory in Northern Ireland* (Anchor Books, 2020)

by a guard and defending himself. He was eventually acquitted of "assaulting" an officer in a jury trial. Prior to all this, Eric had been held for a brief time at United States Penitentiary (USP) McCreary, where he was forced to face off against a violent white supremacist. Also at McCreary, Eric had the opportunity to share a cell for a few days with longtime political prisoner and anti-imperialist freedom fighter Jaan Laaman.[2] The stories and experiences shared between the two during that short time were mutually enlightening. That brief time of solidarity in struggle between two committed political prisoners was an early impetus for this project.

I reached out to as many current and former political prisoners and anarchist prisoners as I could find to understand why they were imprisoned and how they maintained their political convictions behind bars. This primarily included those confined for their politically motivated actions and a few who have become more politically conscious while imprisoned. As Sean Swain said in the pages that follow, "There's no such thing as an apolitical prisoner. The state is a political construct; judges hold political office; prosecutors make political choices; criminal laws are passed by politicians. The act of caging a human being is a political one. To violate law, to say, 'I am above the state rather than the state being above me,' is a political act. All prisoners are political. Some are more consciously so."[3]

Those currently being held within the many prisons that cover these stolen lands were easier to locate than some of those who have since gained their freedom. Some did not want to talk about the time they did—or are continuing to do—behind bars. Some did not want their experiences shared publicly. Others were more than happy to share their stories of what they learned in prison.

The conversations that follow show resilience, determination, and an unswerving commitment to the struggles for which these freedom fighters continue to fight. The principled resistance in the face of the unimaginably cruel and tortuous conditions they survive speaks volumes to their character. From former sixties and seventies radicals and Black Liberation Army (BLA)

---

2. Jaan Laaman was a political prisoner for over forty years due to his involvement in direct actions carried out by the anti-imperialist underground organization the United Freedom Front (UFF). Jaan's story is included here.

3. Sean Swain is an anarchist prisoner, writer, and organizer who has been wrongly imprisoned since 1991. Sean's story is included here.

militants to current antifascists, from nonviolent Catholic activists to Animal and Earth Liberation Front (ALF/ELF) saboteurs, those interviewed in the following pages continue to fight for something better, whether on this side of the prison walls or the other.[4]

Their stories and experiences also serve as shining examples of the inhumanity of the carceral system and the depravity that the state embraces to maintain power. The interviews here cover half a century of confinement in some of the most brutal, dehumanizing prisons on the planet. Some of those interviewed spent months or years confined in such places, while others spent decade after decade shipped between one hellish prison to another. Some of those included here may never return to life outside. The fact that these interviews are filled with love, compassion, concern, empathy, and hope—with humanity itself—shows that no level of carceral torture can kill the revolutionary hope for a better world.

As we began this project, Eric was visited by his attorneys at the time. This is a brief snapshot of their dispatches from that visit:

> Eric is an antiracist, antifascist anarchist serving a ten year federal sentence for an act of protest over the murder of Michael Brown, an eighteen-year-old Black man who was killed by police in Ferguson, Missouri, in 2014. He is scheduled to be released in 2023. In a federal prison system filled with racial segregation, white supremacist gangs, and brutal violence, Eric's time locked up has been the stuff of activists' nightmares. Some prison guards and "white power" prisoners work together to exact vengeance on prisoners like him—"race traitors," LGBTQIA individuals, and smaller-framed people who are visibly proud of standing against fascism, as evidenced by their tattoos.
>
> Eric has been left in a cage by guards to be beaten or killed by the leader of an infamous white supremacist gang; framed; seriously beaten at least a dozen times; had his head split open by a guard and rendered unconscious; and was taken into a mop closet and punched

---

4. The Black Liberation Army (BLA) was an underground, revolutionary Black nationalist organization in the 1970s and 1980s that fought back against the institutional racism and violence of the US government. The Animal Liberation Front (ALF) and the Earth Liberation Front (ELF) are international direct action movements that operate clandestinely in support of animal liberation and the earth, respectively (and collectively). See glossary.

multiple times in the face by a Bureau of Prisons [BOP] Lieutenant who screamed "terrorists killed my daughter" before throwing the first punch. Eric was then strapped to a metal bed in four-point restraints while multiple guards beat him, and a captain used a shield to smother him while hissing, "I hope you get raped or beaten up at your next institution." And, sure enough, he did get beaten . . . while guards watched. Eric currently faces a federal criminal assault prosecution for allegedly punching the BOP Lieutenant in self-defense. He has been waiting for a trial on the charge for almost three years now. If he is convicted, this hell may be prolonged for several more years.

To those not familiar with the trials and tribulations of political prisoners, this sounds shocking. For those locked up—especially those incarcerated for political reasons—and their loved ones on the outside, the inhumanity of the prison system is all too familiar. Individually examined, these instances of abuse and assault may appear to be the result of "bad apples" within the prison system. But viewed collectively—as this volume attempts to do—you see that the very system itself is a bad apple, rotten to the core.

In the initial stages of this project, Eric wrote to me, "I want to dig deep and ask the questions . . . that I think would be helpful to those in the future and [have experienced political prisoners] teach us how they've navigated this shitty world." Here are those answers.

Josh Davidson
Eugene, 2023

Josh Davidson is an abolitionist involved in numerous projects, including the Certain Days: Freedom for Political Prisoners calendar collective and the Children's Art Project with political prisoner Oso Blanco. Josh also works in communications with the Zinn Education Project, which promotes the teaching of radical people's history in classrooms and provides free lessons and resources for educators. He lives in Eugene, Oregon.

Acknowledgments

Eric's Acknowledgments

This book was a labor of love and also risk. I thank all those inside (who are not included here) who showed solidarity. Their stories may never be in print, but they suffered all the same.

I can't fully describe the amount of work Josh put into this book; he carried so much of the work that it probably reinjured his ankle. He took my dream and created a reality. I am blessed to have such great pals and comrades.

I want to also give gratitude to my wife, who has been a constant source of love and happiness. And also those comrades who assisted in other ways, helping to locate contact info, helping with interviews (Danielle), and so on. Thank you to everyone who supported our project in any way.

The life of the political prisoner is often categorized into two different topics—what their "crime" was and how bad they've suffered—almost fetishizing the horrors those inside have had to live through and with on a daily basis. One of the goals of this project was to look beyond that. What were birthdays like? What were friendships like?

We wanted to honor the fact that life doesn't stop when you're inside; there are still joys and disappointments, heartbreaks and victories. We also wanted to give those political prisoners a chance to tell it in their words, to represent their lives however it felt best. Prison is a really shitty place, and it felt really important to document how ethical people navigated such an unethical environment.

I'm inspired by the people inside these pages, and I am extremely grateful that they've shared their time and experiences with us. There will be future political prisoners and abolitionists who will benefit greatly from the stories inside, and hopefully many others will be moved to join the liberation struggle.

Our goal was to honor the lives of those inside. To hold their experiences for future generations, to show that not only does what they went through matter, they too matter. Solidarity to all inside, those who made it out and those who didn't.

Thank you. Until all are free. Anarchy always, ✓✓✓ everywhere.

Eric King
from a cage at Florence ADX, 2022

Josh's Acknowledgments

This project would not have been possible were it not for the participation of many willing, generous, and radical people. First and foremost, love and solidarity to Eric King for the idea, the inspiration, and the continued friendship.

Love and solidarity also to David Gilbert, not only for his participation in this project but also for introducing me to the world of political prisoner support. I've been involved ever since knocking his book *No Surrender* off the shelf at the recently opened Red Emma's Bookstore & Coffeeshop in Baltimore in 2006 and proceeding to sit there and read it all afternoon. His friendship and unrelenting encouragement has transformed my life and made possible so many treasured relationships. Welcome home, brother!

The connections and affiliations that allowed this project to bloom deserve tremendous gratitude here. While I write to many, many people locked up behind bars, I relied on several people's personal and professional contacts in order to get the participation of a wide array of political dissidents.

Thank you to Ashna Ali, Dan Berger, Frida Berrigan, susie day, Rog, Jason Hammond, Walidah Imarisha, Naomi Jaffe, J. "g." J., Bonnie Kerness, Elisa Lee, Daniel McGowan, Luis Alejandro Molina, Bill Ofenloch, Leslie James Pickering, Cassandra Shaylor, Donna Willmott, and the Fire Ant Collective for making connections and encouraging your contacts to consider participating in this project. Thank you too to Farhan Ahmed, Sandra Freeman, Aric McBay, Josh MacPhee, Hector Rodriguez, and ~~Baynard Woods~~ for your help and encouragement along the way.

A big thank you to my fellow Certain Days collective members for your constant inspiration and for your continued support of this project. My heartfelt appreciation to each and every one of the amazing contributors included here, not only for your tireless commitment to struggling for something better but also for trusting me and allowing me to help amplify your voices.

I am forever grateful to AK Press for their encouragement of this project from the beginning and for bringing Eric's idea into fruition. The support of Eric's partner, Rochelle, and the Anarchist Black Cross folks have also been instrumental in realizing this book. I cannot thank Pat Corekin and Amy Schwartz enough for their expert editing, and for having the patience and taking the time to provide insights on bringing this all together.

My deepest gratitude and love to Sara Falconer for writing the introduction and to Angela Y. Davis for writing the foreword. Their words not only provide context but offer decades of experience in combating incarceration and supporting those still behind bars.

I want to thank my family and friends, my mom and my sister particularly, for their continued support and reassurances along the way. And, last but not least, to Danielle: this book would not have been possible without you. Thank you for your zealous encouragement, for jumping into the tedious work of transcribing interviews, for helping me conceptualize what stories and what experiences needed to be shared, and for listening to my ramblings and ideas over the several years it took to make this anthology you're now holding in your hands. And to Miles, our feline friend and constant coconspirator, who sat by my side through each of the interviews but didn't make it long enough to lay upon the finished book.

Any errors, inconsistencies, or omissions are mine and mine alone.

None are free until all are free!

Josh Davidson
Eugene, 2023

Introduction

I first read the words of people in prison in the pages of the punk zine *Maximumrocknroll*. I felt the spark of humans seeking connection with the world outside, and I wrote back.

Around the same time in 2001, a renewed movement was growing against capitalism and towards a better world. I saw activists arrested during protests, from the World Trade Organization in Seattle to the Summit of the Americas in Québec. When friends were helped by an ABC (Anarchist Black Cross) chapter in Genoa, Italy, I learned about the group and their work to support political prisoners being held around the globe.

It was those early letters that drew me into a conversation that has lasted for decades—about how to fight repression, learn the lessons from our histories, and contribute to a different vision of society. I felt that spark again, the excitement of hearing back from people I'd read about, and getting to know them. I realized that I could play a small part in raising their voices.

Those letters helped shape my political development. I was hearing about the history of civil rights movements from the people who had led them—members of the Black Panther Party, American Indian Movement, antiracist and antiwar organizers, and more.

And that's the beauty of the book you're holding now: You will hear firsthand from people who have participated in struggles for social justice throughout generations.

I love that it's an oral history, because it feels like a conversation. It's an eye-opening glimpse of the day-to-day realities of people inside. It's a powerful call to action. As political prisoner Eric King, who helped lead these interviews from prison, says: "I realize how important outside support is more and more every day. With every new restriction, I see why the Bureau is so terrified of seeing people backed by real support.... Even though I haven't had mail in over a year, some folks really turned up for me ... refusing to let me be buried and forgotten."

Throughout the years, I worked with many people across North America to disseminate the words of prisoners. We found many ways to collaborate: by mail, over the phone, over a shared bag of salty chips during a prison visit.

We worked together on wonderful projects and events, from Prison Radio in Montreal to demonstrations outside of jail walls to festive holiday card writing parties. The Certain Days: Freedom for Political Prisoners calendar gave me a chance to work with Herman Bell, David Gilbert, and Xinachtli (who you'll learn from in the following pages), and Robert Seth Hayes (rest in power). As Herman often reminds us, "If you don't have a Certain Days calendar in your home or in your office or wherever you happen to be hanging out, consider yourself a square."

With editor Jaan Laaman, I helped to produce *4strugglemag*, a print and online zine for prisoners and outside supporters. Jaan's idea was to create an outlet for political prisoners on themes including capitalism, racism, war, and imperialism. We ended up with thousands of prison subscribers across the US and Canada who contributed to the dialogue in unexpected and inspiring ways, bringing questions of feminism, hip-hop, and more to our readers.

Whether the people you'll hear from in this book went inside as political prisoners or became engaged while imprisoned, they are organizers, contributing to ongoing struggles and sharing radical critiques. They know too well the lengths the state will go to maintain control. They often need help with resources, combating censorship, and finding platforms for their words— which is something many of us on the outside can give. As abolitionists, we have an opportunity to bring them into our everyday lives and organizing, not just into prison solidarity groups and publications.

Beyond the political lessons, the accounts in this book are so important to read as testimonies to life in prison. Almost every person in this book reflects on the importance of outside support, in helping them to stay connected to their families and communities, and even to stay alive. It's important on an individual level, but also as part of larger abolition movements. Former political prisoner Donna Willmott puts it well: "The fact that the movements for abolition—to defund the police, to end mass incarceration, to abolish ICE—are gaining so much strength opens up possibilities to strengthen the work to support folks inside."

Most of the people featured in these pages are based in the US. Here in Canada, Black and Indigenous people are incarcerated at higher rates, with inhumane conditions throughout the system. The First Nations people of Wet'suwet'en and other nations have been targeted for protecting their land from exploitation.

Prisoners' Justice Day has been observed since August 10, 1976—a hunger strike and a day of mourning starting with Eddie Nalon, who died in prison in Millhaven, Ontario, while in segregation. Today in Ontario, we are facing a prison expansion that calls for strong action. We need to support and amplify these struggles.

Ann Hansen's chapter offers a unique perspective on Canadian prisoners and in particular the situation for women in prison. She says, "Having support is one of the main reasons that people don't get abused.... It is important to try to develop direct communication with prisoners."

I do feel that we have a responsibility to support people in prison and to work to dismantle this unjust system. But beyond that, we also gain so much from the relationships we build with each other. At times I have felt even more supported by my friends inside than the other way around. This work is tangible. It keeps me grounded and keeps me committed to struggle even when I'm feeling frustrated and burned out.

To this day, I still feel the spark of connection—often when I need it most. While being interviewed with my dear friend Daniel McGowan—who served seven years as part of the "Green Scare" cases and is featured in this book—on the *Which Side Podcast*, we were referred to as "elders." We laughed; it was surprising to hear but sort of true. But if we have wisdom to impart, it's because we've had many years of working together with the elders from our own movements.

This book is so important, bringing together perspectives from different generations, movements, places, and lives. I hope you'll feel moved to pick up a pen, because there's no replacement for that direct conversation.

Thank you to all of the contributors and to Josh and Eric for the years of dedication and work to collect all of these stories, even in the midst of abuses and barriers to communication.

We must let our friends inside know that they're not forgotten and that we're here to fight for them.

Sara Falconer
Hamilton, Ontario, 2022

Sara Falconer is a writer, editor and digital strategist who works with nonprofits. She has been creating publications with prisoners since 2001. Sara lives with her awesome family in Hamilton, Ontario—the traditional territories of the Erie, Neutral, Huron-Wendat, Haudenosaunee, and Mississaugas.

Donna Willmott

Donna Willmott has been intimately involved in radical causes since a young age. In 1969, she traveled to Cuba as part of the first contingent of the Venceremos Brigades.[1] Donna worked with numerous groups to implement revolutionary change and was supportive of political prisoners before her own arrest. In 1985, Donna and others were arrested in connection with a planned escape attempt of Puerto Rican political prisoner Oscar López Rivera.[2] In 1994, after spending nine years underground, she and her codefendant turned themselves in, and Donna subsequently served twenty-seven months in prison at MCC Chicago and FCI Dublin, followed by six months in a halfway house in San Francisco. Since her release, she has worked tirelessly to abolish solitary confinement and ensure that younger generations continue efforts for radical change. She is a mentor with the Anne Braden Anti-Racist Organizer Training Program and a member of the Catalyst Action Fund, which promotes racial justice through elections and civic engagement.

---

1. The Venceremos Brigades are an international solidarity effort first orchestrated between Students for a Democratic Society (SDS) and the Cuban government in 1969. Volunteers labor alongside Cuban workers as an act of solidarity to combat US embargoes.

2. Oscar López Rivera is a Puerto Rican freedom fighter who was a political prisoner for over thirty years due to sedition charges for his involvement in the Fuerzas Armadas de Liberación Nacional Puertorriqueña (FALN), a clandestine paramilitary organization that fought for Puerto Rican independence. Oscar's story is included here.

Prison Life

When I first arrived in prison, I was mentally prepared on some level—I was clear about my political stance and had a lot of support from my family and political community. I had a lot of anxiety about what it would mean to leave my four-year-old daughter, and that was certainly the most difficult part of my experience. The early days of separation from her were particularly hard until I was able to see her on a regular basis.

Adapting to a prison routine itself wasn't especially difficult, but the structure of "controlled movement" was quite challenging. The misogynistic culture of the prison was hard emotionally—routinely being called "bitches" and "whores" by the guards, getting pat-searched by male guards after every meal, having a light shined in my face in the middle of the night every night and knowing male guards had access to my cell, getting strip-searched after every visit—these were some of the hardest day-to-day things that I never got used to. They were designed to humiliate you and wear down your spirit.

The most helpful routines for me were centered on walking the yard every day before going to my job and participating in yoga and meditation classes, as offered. I usually wrote letters, read, made phone calls, or visited with other prisoners in my unit after dinner.

I had a very short sentence, so I can't say I ever lost hope about my personal situation of incarceration. Which is not to deny the struggle against hopelessness I sometimes feel when I think of climate catastrophe, the violence of white supremacy, unending wars, the tremendous suffering people experience all over the world—the things that call us to the movement in the first place. I have a Post-it over my desk that says, "How can I be a good ancestor?" which helps me deal with feelings of hopelessness. Knowing that I likely will not live to see so many of the things I hope for, but, in the scheme of things, that doesn't matter. Being in the struggle, doing what I can from where I am is what I can do right now.

My happiest moments were in the visiting room, especially with my partner and daughter. I'll always remember the day she came to visit and showed me that she was learning to read. It was incredibly emotional—I was so proud of her, and I also felt that I was missing so much of her day-to-day growth. I loved it when she could meet some of the other women I was doing time with; it seemed to make prison seem less scary for her, knowing that I had friends inside. It's also worth noting that the happiness of those visits was followed by emotional wipeouts. I'd go back to my cell and sleep for a very long time. And my partner said our daughter would often throw up as soon as they left the prison, then sleep all the way home.

I learned to type! I learned to crochet so I could make things for my daughter. I learned to make enchiladas out of Doritos and fry onions on an iron!

I had one friend inside who was dying—we had an informal healthcare team of fellow prisoners who brought her food, massaged her, wrote letters for her, helped her with hygiene, and so on, until she was too ill to stay in the unit. Being able to support her in a collective way was really important to her and to all of us. But no one should have to die in prison away from family and friends outside—it's inhumane and heartless.

My sentence was short, but, even in that time, things got worse. It seemed that whenever there was a new warden they had to make their mark and let everyone know there was a new sheriff in town. When I first arrived at FCI Dublin, we were allowed to wear some of our own clothing. Then that was taken away and we all had to wear these hideous uniforms. Then there were more restrictions regarding phone use. Important programs like meditation and yoga were canceled for being "too soft" on criminals. The prison was really overcrowded. Long-termers I knew had it the hardest—they went from having single cells to being three people in a cell built for one. That was hard enough if you were doing a short sentence and really awful for people who were doing decades inside.

Many of the long-term prisoners talked about the negative effects of a criminal injustice system based on people testifying against each other in court—the way that it breaks an older code of conduct in which snitching was not accepted. It makes it so much harder for prisoners to trust each other in big and small ways.

When a young woman in the cell next to me committed suicide after learning that her boyfriend gave evidence against her, I was shocked to my core. I don't think I was prepared for the level of psychological violence of the whole system—not only imprisonment but also the whole criminal injustice system.

Seeing a young woman who had just given birth returned to her cell wearing a hospital gown and slippers, no baby in her arms, looking like the world had ended for her . . . this is one of those images that stays with me years later, the utter cruelty of it.

Organizing with other women inside kept us connected to our communities outside and was one of the things I felt best about. Organizing around HIV/AIDS, supporting women inside who were recently diagnosed, and organizing education and prevention efforts. Another example: in 1995, there was a period of white supremacist attacks on Black churches in the South. Many were burned and reduced to rubble. Led by the Black women inside, we were able to have a faith-based event in the chapel. Then we organized a walkathon in the prison yard to raise money to rebuild the churches. We were able to raise money from family and friends outside as well as getting contributions from each other inside. People were extremely generous; we raised thousands of dollars. It was so important that we could do something concrete to connect people inside with the struggle of the Black community outside—one struggle, one fight.

Politics and Prison Dynamics

I think that racial violence per se is much less common in women's prisons than in men's. Some white women tended to keep to themselves, but interracial friendships were common, and I never had a problem with my friendships with women and trans folks of color.

I don't think I was aware of the level of white privilege I would still have inside. It was not a case of all of us being in the same oppressive boat. Very soon after I arrived, the unit manager wanted to change my job from working in the kitchen to being a tutor because I had been to college. It became clear that almost everyone who worked in education was white. After talking with my comrades, I asked to finish my three-month kitchen duty that everyone was required to do. And while some of the guards clearly disliked those of us who were political prisoners, I know that some of the staff, particularly in the education department, treated me more respectfully than they did the women of color.

I was fortunate to be able to do my time with several other political prisoners. At Dublin, I was with Puerto Rican freedom fighters Lucy Rodriguez, her sister Alicia Rodriguez, Carmen Valentín Pérez, Dylcia Pagan, Haydee

Torres, Ida McCray from the Black liberation struggle, and anti-imperialist prisoners Marilyn Buck, Laura Whitehorn, and Linda Evans.[3] They were all doing very long sentences, some sentenced to eighty years or more. I was able to develop friendships with some of them that have lasted to this day. The prison administration was very wary of the political prisoners and our impact on other prisoners, but we found a way to do organizing that benefited fellow prisoners, like the creation of PLACE (Pleasanton AIDS Counseling and Education), started by Linda Evans. After my release from prison, I was not able to visit them, but I was able to participate in the campaign to free the Puerto Rican political prisoners, and I helped start a support committee for Marilyn.

Looking Forward

I've been really fortunate to have support from most of my family and my political community. That support, especially from comrades who invited my partner and daughter to live with them during my incarceration, was essential to my ability to do my time. Honestly, I don't think I realized how much my family and other supporters gave of their time and energy until I was released and started to undertake support for both political and social prisoners myself. How much energy went into every visit, taking phone calls, raising money for commissary, responding to requests for this book or that article, legal help. It's easy for people to underestimate how central it is to support the families of incarcerated people as well as the incarcerated person. Loved ones really do the time as well, and it's not easy to grasp that for lots of people.

  While there always is a core of people who support political prisoners, I think largely our movements have failed to build the same kind of strong support that you see in many places—for instance, the Palestinian struggle

3. Lucy Rodriguez, Alicia Rodriguez, Carmen Valentín Pérez, Dylcia Pagan, and Haydee Torres are Puerto Rican freedom fighters who were political prisoners for decades due to sedition charges based on their involvement in the FALN. Ida McCray was imprisoned for her involvement in a plane hijacking in 1972, and after her release she founded Families with a Future, an organization devoted to providing support for the children of incarcerated mothers. Marilyn Buck, Linda Evans, and Laura Whitehorn are anti-imperialists who were imprisoned as part of the Resistance Conspiracy Case. See glossary. Laura and Linda's stories are included here.

or the Irish struggle. In those movements, support for political prisoners is seen as totally central. There are many reasons for this. The lack of clarity about the nature of the state and the necessity of resistance is certainly one reason.

I also think the divide between supporting those who go to prison for political reasons and those who are inside because of capitalism, colonialism, misogyny, et cetera, has not been helpful to us. I think we should be making those connections to shine light on the nature of the system as a whole. The fact that the movements for abolition—to defund the police, to end mass incarceration, to abolish ICE—are gaining so much strength opens up possibilities to strengthen the work to support folks inside.

I also think making intergenerational connections is so important. There are still many political prisoners who have been inside for decades who we have not been able to get released. And there is a new generation of political prisoners, and there will be more. While people come out of different movements, it's important that we see the connections, the legacy of resistance. No movement can grow if it can't support the people who are willing to take risks to change things.

I think one of the most important things for surviving and thriving in prison is to keep coming back to who you are and why you're committed to a vision of a different world. Prison is designed to crush your spirit, so trying to find small daily acts that help you resist the ways the state tries to get inside your mind is so important. I'm not suggesting that people won't get depressed, won't have really difficult periods of time; that's human. Try to remember that you're not alone, that people before you have taken this path that involves sacrifice, and more people will. That people all over the world have given so much to birth a more humane world. As Marilyn Buck said, "They call me an enemy of the state, so I know I must be doing something right."

I keep thinking about the number of political prisoners who have died inside these last few years, feeling those tremendous losses, and feeling deep gratitude for those who support political prisoners and work tirelessly for their release.

James Kilgore

James Kilgore was a member of the Symbionese Liberation Army (SLA) and was indicted along with other members for participation in a bank expropriation in which a person was killed.[1] He evaded arrest and spent the next twenty-seven years underground, mainly living and teaching in Zimbabwe and South Africa with his wife and two children. He was arrested in 2002 in South Africa, extradited to the US, and subsequently spent six and a half years behind bars. Before being extradited to the US, he spent six weeks in jails and prisons in South Africa. Jim then spent nineteen months in federal pretrial custody at FCI Dublin, another nineteen months at USP Lompoc, and then was transferred to the California prison system, where he served the remainder of his sentence at Deuel Vocational Institute (sometimes called Tracy) and High Desert State Prison in Susanville, California. Since his release, he continues to be involved in social justice and abolitionist causes. He is the director of the Challenging E-Carceration project at MediaJustice and the codirector of FirstFollowers reentry program in Champaign, Illinois. Jim has published two nonfiction books since being released— *Understanding Mass Incarceration: A People's Guide to the Key Civil*

---

1. The Symbionese Liberation Army (SLA) was an underground paramilitary organization founded by an escaped Black prisoner, Donald DeFreeze, and white coconspirators in the Bay Area in the early 1970s. Their most widely publicized action was the kidnapping and ransom of media heiress Patty Hearst. The majority of the original members were murdered by the Los Angeles Police Department (LAPD) and the FBI in a massive attack in Los Angeles in 1974.

Rights Struggle of Our Time (New Press, 2015) and *Understanding E-Carceration: Electronic Monitoring, the Surveillance State, and the Future of Mass Incarceration* (New Press, 2022). He also wrote three novels while imprisoned—*We Are All Zimbabweans Now* (Ohio University Press, 2011); *Prudence Couldn't Swim* (PM Press, 2012); and *Freedom Never Rests: A Novel of Democracy in South Africa* (Jacana Media, 2012).

Prison Life

I became politicized in 1969 and 1970 at UC Santa Barbara, the time of the national strike around the invasion of Cambodia and local students strikes around the firing of a professor. That culminated in the burning of the Bank of America in Santa Barbara, which I didn't actually participate in. I was there earlier in the evening as part of the demonstrations, but then I went home, and later that night they burned down the bank.

What ensued after that was really the imposition of some kind of martial law, state of emergency in the student community. We ended up having the National Guard going up and down our streets in armored personnel carriers and so forth. We had a curfew, and that was really a game changer for me in terms of giving me an understanding of how the state was prepared to engage with protesters who sort of went beyond the boundaries that they felt were acceptable. This direct confrontation with the armed might of the state was a really big turning point for me.

After I graduated in 1969, I bounced around in different kinds of political stuff. I stayed in Santa Barbara for a little while, then moved to Los Angeles for about a year and a half, and then I went and lived in Berkeley and North Oakland from 1971 to 1975. A couple people from my neighborhood in North Oakland were involved in a group called the Revolutionary Army.[2] They did bombings of antiwar targets, and I let them use our address for their fake IDs and stuff, but I wasn't involved directly in their activities. They got arrested

---

2. The Revolutionary Army was a militant Bay Area underground group founded in the early 1970s by Willie Brandt, Wendy Yoshimura, and others. They planted bombs and planned other actions to protest the Vietnam War, and members sometimes worked in solidarity with the SLA.

in 1972, and I visited them a lot in prison. So this was a connection between me and people who were engaging in armed struggle.

I had kind of a political blank spot there in late 1972, 1973. I was doing a little work at the Berkeley Tenants' Union and Free Clinic, but the movement was receding then, and I was trying to figure out my next steps. Then we had the kidnapping of Patty Hearst in 1974. I knew one of the people that was involved in that, Angela Atwood, who was a friend of my partner at the time, Kathleen Soliah. When Angela and the five others got burnt alive by the police in LA on May 17, 1974, the three remaining members of the SLA—Bill and Emily Harris and Patty Hearst—came to my partner's workplace and asked for help. They had something like $70 and an old car, and we basically started doing whatever we could to raise resources for them, to help them survive what was certainly at the time the most intense person-hunt in memory.

Now I don't want to go into a whole lot of details of what happened there, but I ended up getting involved in some bank robberies, in one of which a woman was killed. Then, in September 1975, Bill and Emily and Patty Hearst, along with a couple of other people involved, were arrested. But I was actually working at the time, so I managed to escape, and I went underground for what turned out to be twenty-seven years.

I spent a lot of that time living in Seattle, in Milwaukee, and Minneapolis. I was involved in aboveground activities in those cities under pseudonyms. I was involved in the anti-apartheid movement, in particular, and that led me to make friends with a lot of people from Zimbabwe. So when Zimbabwe became independent in 1980, they invited me to come and live in Zimbabwe and teach in the schools there. I had some forged documents and I managed to get in and teach school there, basically from 1982 to 1991. Then I moved to South Africa, where I worked in a school that provided support for people who had been involved in the political struggle, who were trying to get into historically white universities. Then, later on, I became involved in doing a lot of education for trade unions. Up until 2002, the time when I was arrested, I was married, and I had two kids—one born on the day Nelson Mandela came out of prison in 1990 and the other one was born in 1994.[3]

---

3. Nelson Mandela was a political prisoner for twenty-seven years in South Africa because of his involvement in the African National Congress (ANC) and its militant wing, uMkhonto we Sizwe (MK), and the fight against apartheid. After his release from prison, Mandela served as president of South Africa from 1994 to 1999.

I always had support. I was lucky. I got arrested in South Africa. In South Africa, half the government of South Africa at that time had been in prison, so the idea that I had taken up arms in the US—I mean that was kind of a plus. I can still remember in the jail there seeing these guys at the other end of the hallway. They looked at me, and they gave me a fist, and they said, "All of South Africa supports you." Since I was politically involved in South Africa, I had tremendous support, and my family had tremendous support, from the people that I worked with, people in the unions, people in the community, and from personal friends. One of the national cabinet members whom I knew made a statement to the press calling me a hero of the poor. We also had a lot of friends who we shared childcare with. So there was an incredible network of support for my partner and my kids. To show you how different the tone was there, the principal of the school where our youngest son went sent a letter home to all the parents in the school when I got arrested saying, "Lonnie's father's been arrested. This is a very hard time for him. Show him all the love you can."

I'd been on the run for twenty-seven years, so it was not a surprise to get arrested. I mean, it's almost like death: you know it's going to come but you don't know when. So, when it comes it's not like, "Oh gee, I'm arrested, what a surprise." No. I had a certain mental preparation for it. Plus I had a lot of support, and my family had a lot of support, so that wasn't too traumatic.

What was traumatic was landing in High Desert State Prison and getting acquainted with the system of racial segregation and white supremacy in the California State Prison System. That was the most traumatic part of my prison incarceration—the shock of the dominance of white supremacy in those prisons. It's terrible. Because everything in the California State Prison System is racially segregated, including cell assignments, you're forced to just engage with these white supremacists and find ways to coexist with them and to follow some of the insane rules of the prison. Like not sharing food with people of so-called other races. You can't sit at certain tables. You can't use certain cell phones. You can't use certain showers. All that kind of stuff. It was just terrible. I figured out how to buy a little bit of space, how to navigate the segregation, and how I could connect to Black, Latinx, and other people of color in the population. But it was always tense and problematic.

The worst part about that was when I landed in High Desert; I came on the bus, and I got put in a gym with a bunch of people, including these two guys that came on the bus with me. We kind of struck up a friendship on the bus ride, and I sat at a table with them, so I started telling them I had been in South Africa. They were kind of interested in that. Then they said, "Is your wife white or Black?" and I said, "My wife is Black." They both said, "We didn't have this conversation. Don't ever tell anybody that here. You will be killed if they find out." That was incredibly traumatic. I couldn't have my family come and visit. It was just a horrible, horrible kind of feeling of powerlessness, betrayal, and feeling like I was forced to make these brutal compromises. I was unsure whether I should just go ahead and do it and take what came. That was the worst part about prison by far. That was the California State Prison System.

I wouldn't say I lost hope. Because I had a [release] date, right, and the day wasn't that far away. When I was in the feds, I was walking down the hallway, talking to one of the guys who was in the unit across from me and he said, "You know I've got thirty-one years, and I got the shortest sentence in my unit." I sat there going, "Oh shit, I'm not gonna whine about this six and a half that I've got." So I didn't lose hope. I had a history. I had all those years of being educationally and politically involved, so I had a determination that I was gonna get out and was going to fight the system that was keeping everybody down. I also had my family to look forward to, spending time with my children, my mother, and my partner—experiencing the love I knew they had for me and giving it back. Besides, I was determined when I got out that I would keep being a fighter. That's how I lived my life for all those years, so I knew how to do that. And now I had this other experience, so I had to figure out how to process that experience to turn it into some kind of capital that I could use in terms of organizing.

There were few moments of happiness inside, but there is one [moment] that sticks out. When I was in High Desert, I worked as a teacher's aide. Basically what that usually means is that you get to grade all the papers. The teacher that I worked under was okay. I think she had an interest in trying to see people get some form of education. I had a lot of conversations with her, and she recognized that I had some educational experience. So one day she was teaching math, and she was a shitty math teacher. She wasn't one of those mathematically minded people. She just stopped in the middle of the lesson and said, "Mr. Kilgore, why don't you come up and teach the rest of the math class?" So I got up there, and I had fun with it. This was around the 2008 economic crisis. When I was in South Africa, I did a lot of popular education for unions and committee organizations around issues of political economy, what was happening with the World Bank and structural adjustment, and so on. I did a lot of workshops on free trade and privatization and intellectual property rights. I was used to breaking it down, because in South Africa and especially for the working classes, English is a third or fourth language. If you're gonna talk academic English, nobody's gonna understand a word you're saying. I asked the teacher if I could do some kind of workshop here, some stuff on economics and the economic crisis. And she said, "Yeah, okay."

I proposed doing a basic presentation and then breaking the groups up into four groups. One was the officials of the World Bank, the second one was heads of African states, the third was some global corporate body, and the fourth one was the US government. I wanted to set up a debate. A pseudo-UN General Assembly discussion with each of those groups presenting their position around the economic reforms that were coming up and trying to fight for their position; a role-play activity. She told me, "Yeah we can do that, but when you do these groups, you know you've got to break them up by race." And I said I wasn't going to do that. Then she talked about some of her experiences of trying to do something like that on another yard, and how they threatened to kill her, and all that kind of shit. I said, "I'll tell you what, I'm going to go around to everybody in this class and I'm going to tell them what I'm going to do. I'm going to get them to agree to have these groups." So I did, and everybody agreed to it.

Then we just had this amazing workshop where people really got into it. We had this great debate, where you had these white supremacists acting as if they were the head of some African nation and arguing convincingly for their position. Then one of these white supremacist guys told me the following week, "I had a visit this week, and my family started talking about the economy. I started explaining to them how the economic crisis came up, and who was benefiting from it, and how all that worked. They just sat there and looked at me, like, 'How the hell did you learn all this shit in prison?'" That was a pretty good moment as a popular educator. The name of the college I used to work at was called Khanya College—so I just said I took the kind of Khanya College methodology into the prison in High Desert, and it worked.

I never wrote fiction before I went to prison. I basically taught myself how to do it. When I was in the prison in Lompoc in the library, they had a series of books from *Writer's Digest* on how to write fiction. There was a volume on character development, one on setting, one on plot structure, et cetera. I had written a draft of a novel, and I sent it off to a friend of mine who had just finished a PhD in literature, and I asked her to respond to it. When she responded to it, she said, "This isn't a novel. The characters are flat, your plot doesn't work," blah blah blah. Everything was totally wrong with it. So, I hated on her for a few days, and then I decided, well, maybe I better try to figure out how to do this better. I found these books in the library and read them all from cover to cover. By the time I finished reading those, and also read a lot of other novels, I began to think like a novel writer, rather than a nonfiction writer. That's really what I learned.

I think what I was prepared for the least was how passive people were and how few critical thinkers there were in the population. There were very few people who engaged in any kind of critical, intellectual life, or even really stood up to authority. I was pretty shocked at how compliant most people were. I felt a lot of them had really reactionary positions in regard to prison. There was a lot of blaming other people in the population, rather than being at all sympathetic to the fact that this is a structural issue. You're in these fucking hellhole prisons, and people do weird shit, so why do you want to make fun of them or blame them for being weak or some shit when really it's the whole system that's the problem? I mean, maybe I still had some romantic George Jackson visions or something when I landed in prison, but I didn't find that to be much a part of the reality.[4] I think it's probably a little bit different now, as of the past few years, but, of course, the racial shit was absolutely horrific.

Probably the proudest thing I had was just the fact that I developed this capacity to write and was able to keep writing. The situation wasn't very conducive to doing it. I think that would be it. I mean, I wish I could say that I organized strikes and did all kinds of shit like that to mobilize people, but the tenor wasn't there. The political consciousness wasn't there to make that shit happen. The racial divisions were so intense in the state that you couldn't really bridge that gap. I think if I had been doing a longer sentence, I might

---

4. George Jackson was serving a one-year-to-life sentence in California state prisons when he joined the Black Panther Party (BPP) and cofounded the Black Guerrilla Family (BGF) in the late 1960s. He wrote two highly publicized books while incarcerated and garnered international support prior to being killed by guards in a supposed escape attempt in 1971. See glossary.

have had a different attitude toward it, but my position really was: I know myself, I know when I get out of here I'm going to do something useful, and I'm not going to let myself get all fucked up in here over some bullshit that I can't change, especially when I'm just reacting to stuff out of frustration rather than in a way that's going to have an impact on the way things are run. It's also a rationalization for not doing certain things, but I feel like there's an element of realism to it. That's the way it was. Since then, with the hunger strikes and popular awareness about the prison industrial complex, things are different. When I was locked up, we didn't even know the term "mass incarceration." Michelle Alexander hadn't written *The New Jim Crow* [yet]. We had Critical Resistance and Jericho and a few others, but they were small and didn't have the influence or presence that the movements for prison reform and abolition have today.[5] No Black Lives Matter. Most importantly, formerly incarcerated people were just beginning to organize in the early 2000s. We were still calling ourselves "convicts." All that has come a long way, but, of course, there's still a long way to go.

Politics and Prison Dynamics

You have to build your self-discipline to figure out: "what are the moments that I'm going to push back, and how am I going to push back?" For me, education and being an educator was a way of pushing back. That was a way of saying to the people that were in my classes, "You all have potential. You can do this shit." When I was teaching math, everybody in the class said, "I'm no good at math." And I said, "Bullshit. It's not that you're no good at math. If you're selling drugs, you can count the money, right? You can do math. But the way they teach math, and the way they treat you, you internalize the fact that you think you're dumb and you can't do this math. Now if you want to do this, I'm going to show you how to do it."

There was one guy, Angel Martinez, in Lompoc. He was doing the math classes, and we were doing simultaneous linear equations on the board. He looked at that and he said, "That's it. That's the moment where I walked out

---

5. Critical Resistance was founded in 1997 and has worked ever since to eliminate the prison industrial complex. The Jericho Movement was founded in 1998 to raise awareness and seek the freedom of US-held political prisoners. See glossary.

of high school math and never went back. If only I knew how interesting and exciting this was, I never would have done that." That's a great moment.

You're not standing next to me, but when I come onto the prison yard it's not like everybody says, "Oh, we better stay out of his way. He's gonna kick our ass." I had to figure out how I was going to survive when everybody else weighs fifty pounds more than me, is doing thirty pull-ups at a stretch and then taking a two-minute break and doing twenty more. How am I going to not get into shit here and not get my ass beat right, left, and center? Nobody ever laid a hand on me, and obviously some of that is white privilege. Some of that is being older. But I think some of it is also being able to read the tea leaves and figuring out how to keep your ass out of trouble.

I had some fights with guards. When I first landed at High Desert, they all pulled me aside. There were about six or eight of them in a circle and they said, "You're not making it out of here. Who do you think you are?" I'm just sitting there saying, "Okay, well, whatever." But you learn how to carry yourself as if you are fearless, but not in a macho way, not in a fighting way. You have to have a character that's not going to get caught up in bullshit.

Whenever there were discussions about police and guards, I was always taking the most radical positions. People respect that, but they don't expect it from somebody that looks like me. By doing that, and also because I can articulate my positions in ways that other people couldn't necessarily, you gain some respect. I also gained respect by helping people with legal papers, and so on. I can remember doing math in the dirt. People wanted to do GED [General Educational Development] math, so I'd be out there in the dirt doing "x + 3 = 7. We bring the three over to this side, subtract it." Doing that in the dirt. But by doing that, you build a base, and people will defend you. People will tell other folks, "Leave him alone. He's all right." One time I had a white supremacist Hells Angel shot caller on the yard at High Desert who pulled me aside and pointed out some young guy who just came on the yard, and he said, "I want you to teach that guy. I don't want him to end up doing thirty-five years here. Teach him and get him his GED so he can get out of here and do something for himself."[6] So I said, "Okay, I gotcha. I can do that, yeah." Compared to all the other shit he might want me to do, that was easy.

---

6. The Hells Angels Motorcycle Club (HAMC) is a nationwide outlaw motorcycle organization founded in 1948. Known to be involved in organized crime, the Hells Angels are often violent and racist in their actions.

In terms of racism, you just kind of learn how to navigate the terrain. I mean, I never in my life had a conversation with somebody who had a swastika tattoo on their forehead [before prison]. But I learned how to talk to somebody like that with respect. Fortunately, I'm a sports fan, and that's a great, saving conversation-maker in prison. I could talk football, I could talk basketball, not so good on baseball. But football and basketball are enough to get you through. I did a lot of that. I played a lot of basketball, which was a way of earning respect. Even though I was old, I was still pretty good. I stopped playing when I was sixty, but I was playing fairly competitively. In my late fifties, I was on the unit team. Out of sixty people, we would form a team of four players, and I was one. I could play, and that was useful as well as fun. It was useful in terms of establishing myself. I think it was a connector with Black men, but also it was about me not being a big strong guy, but showing that I have athletic capacity as a way of keeping people away. Because we're dealing with toxic masculinity in one of its highest forms. So, how do you navigate that toxic masculinity without totally capitulating? I'm not going to go around using homophobic language; I'm not going to go around using racist language. I'm going to call people out when they do it, when I can. But it's just moment by moment because it's always there. In the California State Prison System, it's never not there. Every minute of your day is structured around that segregation.

I remember one time there was a guy on the yard who was about eighty-three years old, and he had deep dementia, and he could barely move around. But he would come out in the yard, and we would walk him around. We had tables, like five or six tables around the yard at various points. But the tables were segregated. So, we're walking around the circle, and we get to a Black table, and the old man says, "I want to sit down." I go, "Fuck, no." So, then I go to the two guys that are there, and I say the old man's got dementia, and ask if he can just sit here for a second. The guy says, "You've got to go ask *your* own people." You've got to go ask *your* people. All of a sudden, I look down at the white table and here comes one of these white supremacist guys running at full speed down toward the table. He can see that there might be trouble brewing, so he comes down, and he says, "No, the old man can't sit here, we will take him down here" [to the white tables], and they whisk him away. It was crazy shit, man.

There's so much of it. Like I say, every minute of every day, it's like that.

People have this idea that nothing happens in prison. That people sit in their cells all day and look at the walls. But I describe prisons as a hive of activity. I mean, it's different kinds of activity than you might find on the outside, but when you look out, you see what's going on. If you've been there, you know there's a lot of shit happening. And people are trying to survive. People are trying to do what they can to recapture whatever humanity is lost. Whether that means doing drugs, or making wine, or whatever it means, reading the Bible or the Koran, that's what's going on.

[If I could change anything about my prison time, it would be] not being able to have a visit from my family. The alternative to that was going into protective custody in California. They've got PC—protective custody—yards for people who are considered not suitable to be on the main line, either because maybe they informed on somebody, maybe if they're gay, transgender, if they've left a gang and the gang's got a hit out for them, they go into what they call protective custody. When I landed at High Desert, the lieutenant told me, "I want to put you in protective custody. To everybody on the yard, you look like a child molester. And child molesters don't last very long in these places." I was kind of like, "Fuck you. I'll take my chances with them rather than take your offer," which for me was like being a snitch.

In California, a lot of the people who are in protective custody are there because of the viciousness of the population, the gang discipline, the homophobia, the transphobia. People just not wanting to be told what to do or being given an instruction to go hit somebody and refusing. To the mainstream population and to me coming into this with this kind of political framework, I'm looking at the people in protective custody as people I don't want to have anything to do with or be associated with. In hindsight, I'm not so sure that's really the correct perspective. It might make more sense to look at that being another group of the prison population that is criminalized and victimized by the institution, and this is what happens to them. My decision not to go there was more based on, "Well, those are a bunch of rats and this and that, and I'm not like that." Maybe in hindsight, if I had gone there, it would have been a different kind of situation in terms of visits from my family, visits from my Black friends, and all that sort of thing.

Looking Forward

When I came out of prison, my focus was to work on the system of mass incarceration. I felt like a movement against mass incarceration would be a really important force in terms of trying to free political prisoners. I still think that's true. I think that all the people who have gotten out have done so because there's been a whole lot of work, not only around political prisoners, but around incarceration itself, and how fucked up the US criminal legal system is in terms of how it treats people. That's provided some space for some people to get out or get a hearing that they wouldn't have had before. But what can you say? There's never enough that can be done. There is no magic bullet for any of this shit. People dealing with the prison-industrial complex keep coming up with the magic bullet: ending cash bail, progressive prosecutors, letting out people who have nonviolent convictions; it's bullshit, you know. It's all systemic. You can't carve anything out. You have to fight to get rid of the system. But you have to figure out, at any given moment, where the pressure point is where you can make a win, where you can make a gain without compromising everybody else. I'm never going to say let's let all the nonviolent drug dealers out and let's give everybody that's got a murder conviction an extra ten years. No, fuck that. You've got to have a systemic perspective.

There's also a danger of abolitionist purism and what I call abolitionist fluffism. Abolitionist purism, to me, is saying, "Well, if we're not abolishing prisons, I'm not doing anything." Anybody who's been incarcerated knows fucking well that getting somebody out of solitary and getting them into a medium security institution—where they can have visits, where they're going to programs, where they can have access to better commissary, better medical—all that is vitally important. That is something that you have to fight for. You can't say "that's not abolitionism." That's a wrong understanding of how the system works, and particularly a wrong understanding of how it impacts the people who are directly affected, who have that lived experience. I'm an abolitionist, but I'm a cautious abolitionist about what reforms I support.

I'm not as quick as some abolitionists are to condemn a lot of reforms. I'm also really not down for what I call fluff abolitionism, which says, "We need a world without prisons. Oh, what a wonderful place that would be."

We forget that between us and that world without prisons, there's the state, the military, the police, the guards, and you've got to be ready to struggle against all of them and move them out of the way before you're going to get to your world without any prisons. If you're not ready to do that, if you just want to sit in restorative circles and talk about your feelings, that's not fighting for abolition. And I'm not making fun of restorative circles, they're important, they can play a function, but people confuse that with fighting for abolition, with being the ultimate tactic to fight for abolition. It's one tactic, a reformist tactic, a very useful tactic. But to fight for abolition, you've got to mobilize a political movement that's capable of taking on the powers that be, and that's the biggest piece.

I'm pretty cautious about giving people advice about coming into prison because it's been twelve years since I've been in prison. It's changed a lot. It depends on who you're talking about. Are you talking about somebody coming into prison as a political prisoner, or are you talking about somebody who's got five years to do on a drug beef? I would talk to those two people in different ways. People with a drug beef, I'd say, "Well, what do you want to do? Do you want to do your time, do you want to get out, what's your situation? Stay out of trouble, try to learn, try to educate yourself, make the most of your time." If you're a political prisoner, [I'd say] "Try to build yourself a network of allies on the outside and see if there are opportunities to politicize or have political discussions inside the prison. There may be, there may not be. It varies from prison to prison, from population to population. You might be able to do some of that, you might not. Be careful. Don't be too quick to put your politics out on the table. It can be used against you in a lot of ways."

We clearly have to recognize the ways in which white privilege affects political prisoners. I mean, if I was Black, I'd be doing life. I have no doubt. Or I could be dead. The fact that we, as a group, were able to get a lenient judgment from a liberal judge in Sacramento, who told me to do three years on a bank robbery where someone was killed—that's just not going to happen today. Of course, part of that had to do with the fact that it's old law, but you can't help but think that there's that white privilege piece. I think it's important to acknowledge that. At the same time, it's not like we want white political prisoners to volunteer to do more time because they're going to get let out. So how do you navigate that? How do you make sure that people know that even inside prison there is white privilege? It's far less than it is on the outside, in day-to-day life. But in terms of how the system sentences you, and the way they treat your cases, it's very, very real and very, very strong. I think that's something not to forget.

I feel that in a lot of ways, for me to do my time was easier than for my family to do my time. When you're in prison, you don't have responsibilities. You don't have to worry about paying the bills, about what's happening to your kids, what's happening to your mother. You worry about it, but you can't do anything about it, so it doesn't absorb your daily life. You don't have all those responsibilities that you have when you're out, and you don't have to deal with the trauma that your incarceration inflicts on your kids, on your family, and so forth. Your network of support has to deal with all of that, and that trauma is really overlooked. It's a trauma, a burden borne disproportionately by women, by female partners, by mothers, by sisters, by grandmothers, and it's made invisible. I think it's starting to be acknowledged a bit more now, but it's still totally under-recognized. Mass incarceration is not something that just happens to men. It happens to families and communities. It happens to networks of loved ones, and we have to appreciate the ways in which those people who aren't locked up are impacted and the ways they are a part of the struggle.

I'm a little uneasy with some of the rhetoric of "nothing about us without us," which is the idea that only formerly incarcerated people really have a right to speak about this. I think that formerly incarcerated people have a particular voice that needs to be recognized, but I think impacted family members and community members also have an important voice that needs more recognition. I think we run the risk of a narrow sectarianism if we simply say the only people that know about this are the people who are directly impacted. There's a danger in that. We have to be really careful about how we characterize who can speak on these issues. There are plenty of people who have done lots of time in prison who have very backward attitudes.

I think one of the most important parts of my experience was unconditional love. And that unconditional love came to me from several quarters. But probably most importantly, it came to me from my mother, from my partner, Terri, and from her mother.

My mother, Barbara Kilgore, she was a proper lady. She wasn't by any means an activist, probably wasn't even a Democrat. But she stood by me because I was her son; her only child. And she stood by me for twenty-seven years of me being a fugitive. She stood by me, despite the fact that she rarely knew where I was. I only visited her three times during those twenty-seven years: once in 1988, when I came to my parents' house, and stayed overnight on New Year's Eve. Once in 1987, when my mother came to visit me, in Sydney, Australia, and we spent about a week together, like tourists, staying in some Hilton hotel, went to the Sydney Opera House, rode a ferry, and just walked around the streets and visited. And then once in London in 1993, when I went to visit her, and we once again did touristy things and reconnected. Never throughout this whole period of time did she ever lambast me, criticize me, blame me for causing all the pain and anguish that I caused her and my father. And when I came home, when I was brought back to the United States from Cape Town, my mother was there every Sunday to visit me in Dublin. My mother had stopped driving by then, but she stayed about an hour and a quarter from the prison, and every Sunday her friend— her loyal, wonderful friend Susan—would drive her over to visit with me. And there we kind of rebuilt our relationship, learned how to communicate, shared our reflections on our past.

By that time, my father had passed away. He passed in the year 2000. I should say that he also stood strong when the FBI came around asking where I was, and he knew but didn't say anything. At one point, they were talking about forming a grand jury and dragging my parents into that courtroom and forcing them to testify about my whereabouts. But he didn't cave. At another point, he told my mother he didn't want to know where I was or what I was doing because he wanted to be able to answer honestly to the police who came around. But he knew my mother was in contact with me. He was very old school, a World War II vet who was totally traumatized by three years on a destroyer ship in the Pacific, but he never talked about it. A hardworking, honest Republican with a son whom he loved as best he could but a son who turned his world upside down and it never got right side up again.

But my mother was always there for me. She was only four foot ten, but she was a rock. She put money toward my lawyer. She was there in court. One of the great moments of my life was during my first court appearance in 2002. A reporter from the *San Francisco Chronicle* approached her after the judge had dismissed the hearing and asked her how it felt to have her son in court, charged with possession of an explosive device. And she, then at age eighty-nine, looked at this reporter and just said, "Drop dead." That was my mother.

When I got released, she moved from California—where she had lived for her entire life—to Illinois and stayed five minutes away from our family. And we managed to survive and build a relationship. My mother passed in 2017, but over those years, we had a wonderful time together where I got to see her almost every day and we got to share our lives. She was never someone who was particularly sympathetic to my general politics, but she was very respectful and loving toward my family. Unlike my father who kind of didn't want to know, my mother learned from this experience. She read about Zimbabwe. She thought a lot about race and gender. She had probably never dreamed she would have a Black daughter-in-law and Black grandchildren, but they became the world to her. She loved them so much, and they loved her. My partner and my mother-in-law were so supportive as my mother grew older and a bit more confused by it all. My grandsons also loved her a lot, and our oldest son named their daughter after her; they gave her my mother's first name as her middle name, Celia Barbara.

The other experience that I had of unconditional love came from the rest of my family: my partner, Terri, her mother, and my two sons, ages eight and twelve when I was arrested. I think it would be difficult to understand that sort of unconditional love without understanding the context in which I was arrested.

We had been living in South Africa for eleven years. My partner was a well-respected historian at the University of the Western Cape. She was producing important research on urban women in southern Africa and had been active in trying to organize the faculty union at the university. I had been an educator as well. First of all, I was an economics lecturer at a small community college called Khanya, which had a slogan of "education for liberation" and offered classes to people who had been involved in some way in the political struggle against apartheid, including Black activists who were barred historically from entering the best universities in South Africa. They had received what they call Bantu education, really an inferior curriculum. They lacked the basic academic skills to be able to enter these universities. So we provided them with support, taught them how to write essays and take exams, the kinds of things that students in well-resourced high schools learn.

But they never had the opportunity to learn. They were intellectually very advanced because of their life experiences and because of being involved in political organizations which had provided them with quite an interesting and complex intellectual life. But they weren't used to writing essays and doing the kinds of structured assignments that came with the university. I was a lecturer at that college for two years, and then I became the director of Khanya for four years. That was in Johannesburg. Then we moved to Cape Town, and I worked for a nonprofit organization called the International Labour and Research Information Group (ILRIG) that did popular education for trade unions and for community organizations. ILRIG and Khanya are both still fighting the class struggle. So, through my work I was fairly well known, particularly in trade union circles, in South Africa.

When I was arrested, the political movements that I had worked with and the academics that Terri had worked with were totally supportive. It was absolutely and utterly taken for granted that they would rise to support someone whom they considered to be a political fugitive, someone that they believed had made important contributions to the working-class movement in South Africa. I had everyone from Archbishop Desmond Tutu to the local heads of the trade unions writing letters in my support to the court. It was really Terri, with some close friends and comrades, who orchestrated all this. They were the equivalent of an informal defense committee, who managed to make sure that I had visitors, who managed to make sure that people brought me food (because in the South African prisons, people could bring in cooked food). I had a vast array of cooked food, from gourmet restaurants to some amazing dishes that people made in their own kitchens. I had a vast array of reading material. And this really stayed as a permanent condition of my incarceration.

My family, Terri and our sons, stayed in Cape Town for the entire time of my incarceration because they had support there. The unconditional love that Terri and the boys had for their partner and their father spilled over to the community. We made the decision that it was best for Terri and our boys to stay in Cape Town, even though I wouldn't get very many visits from them because they would have to trek all the way across the world to come visit me. Nonetheless, they did that from time to time, as holidays and finances allowed. I can't count the hundreds of letters that I got from people, especially from Terri, keeping me up-to-date with everything that was going on in their lives. I don't know how she managed to single-parent those two young boys, do her work, keep alive this communication with me, and keep that relationship alive. I never really experienced love like that, especially under those kinds of situations. I learned from all that that no matter what happened to her, or whatever happened to our sons, that I had to be ready to give that unconditional love back. Not that they saw it as a debt; but rather, for me, it was a lesson of how far that went. And that's an experience few people have.

When you talk about being incarcerated, everyone thinks about the horrors of it. And, yes, it's a horrible experience, under the control of horrible people. But there's a whole lot of other things that arise out of that, as people try to assert their humanity and show that they are still capable of love and solidarity in the face of the inhuman, punitive, hateful rulers of these gulags that have proliferated across the United States and around the world.

I couldn't really complete this without talking about Terri's mother, for whom, like her daughter and like my mother, it was never a question of whether or not she would support our family and me. There was never a doubt that was a part of her, what she saw as her duty, as her responsibility as a mother, as a grandmother, as a mother-in-law.

The act that for me was the most incredible—and this just kind of gives you an idea of the support that I really had—was that I wrote a novel called *We Are All Zimbabweans Now*. It was eventually published about the time I was released. But the rules of the prison made it difficult to orchestrate because I was handwriting this novel, but I was trying to get a typewritten version of it to a publisher. But I didn't have access [to a typewriter], so I couldn't type, and I couldn't produce a copy that was adequate for a publisher. So, some friends of mine, mostly people that I knew from Australia, organized a team of typists who logged my chicken scratch writing into a computer file. And they printed it out. Now the rules of the prison were that I could only receive ten pages in one envelope, that is if it was photocopies. Some of my comrades typed up the novel and sent the file to my mother-in-law. She printed out what she received and put ten pages in an envelope and sent it off to me. And that's how I got a two-hundred-page novel into the prison. I was able to read what people had typed, make some corrections and edits, and then send it back to them.

But what an amazing collective effort that was to produce that novel! I could talk about many other things that my mother-in-law did, particularly in terms of providing support for our two sons. But for me, that is a kind of a shining example of how she as a stalwart mother—and an academic and university administrator of some stature in her own right—managed to pull all that together. Probably not much sleep involved in all that exercise for her. But she was truly amazing. And her partner, my father-in-law, was—I don't want to say he was equally amazing, but he was in solidarity. They both came to visit me in prison. They sent me books and letters, they just kept a constant flow of information and expressions of love coming my way. That was an amazing part of this experience.

Of course, I need to round it off by talking about our two sons, of whom I am so proud. They managed to develop into caring, conscious people through all this. They kept doing their schoolwork, kept playing soccer and cricket and loyally bounced around the world with their mother to come and visit me. There was one way, though, I felt betrayed by them. When I left, they were boys—eight and twelve, small guys growing up. I could look down on them. But by the time I came home, they had grown to be taller than me—much taller—and, of course, much more handsome than I could have ever dreamed of being. They did so well in my absence. They were an inspiration for me, a future to look forward to. But I also think by [my] drowning them in bad poems, homemade crossword puzzles, short stories, et cetera, assembled in my prison cell, they recognized my love was still coming their way. With the support of Terri, her mother, and my mother, they were in the best possible hands. And unlike the vast majority of children of people in prison, they didn't have to worry about where their next meal was coming from or if the rent would be paid. That is not to say having a father in prison wasn't a huge, life-shaping trauma for them, but they didn't have to worry about basic necessities due to the class privilege they enjoyed.

So, ultimately, I think it's important that we don't only tell the tales of the oppression of prison, but we also tell the tales of how people on the outside fight back against a cruel and evil system. And how the tools that they fight with are love, solidarity, and determination. That's in such sharp contrast to the determination and hatred that rests at the heart of the prison-industrial complex, or whatever you want to call the monster that keeps locking up millions of people to the good of no one.

Mark Cook

Mark Cook was a member of the George Jackson Brigade (GJB) in the Pacific Northwest during the 1970s.[1] He spent four decades behind bars, more than half of which was for his political work. Mark joined the Black Panther Party while in prison and also worked tirelessly on behalf of prisoners' rights. He spent the majority of his imprisonment in federal facilities, namely Leavenworth, Lompoc, and Lewisburg, and also at the Walla Walla State Penitentiary in Washington. Now in his eighties, Mark is just as active and involved in movement work as ever.

Prison Life

I got support when I first came to the federal system. They were just waiting for me. They supplied me some of the little stuff and introduced me to other political prisoners at that time. I met the Puerto Rican prisoners, Adolfo Matos and Oscar López Rivera (I also met him when he got out of prison and came to Seattle), and Leonard Peltier.[2] Peltier and I were arrested about

---

1. The George Jackson Brigade was a guerrilla underground organization based in the Pacific Northwest in the mid- to-late 1970s. Members were racially and sexually diverse and carried out symbolic bombings in solidarity with national and international liberation struggles. The group was named after famed Black liberation politicized prisoner George Jackson.

2. Leonard Peltier is a Native American activist who has been wrongly imprisoned since 1977 for his involvement in a shootout with FBI agents on the Pine Ridge Reservation in South Dakota. He is a member of the American Indian Movement (AIM). See glossary. Peltier remains imprisoned as of 2023.

the same time in Seattle, and I did a lot of time with him in Leavenworth. I
met with a lot of the political prisoners, and we gave a lot of support to each
other. But I was accepted, and they were waiting for me no matter what
prison I went to.

They put me in Atlanta because the warden at Leavenworth refused to
take me. He said he wouldn't have me in his prison. But while in Atlanta, there
were a lot of murders, and they took everybody with first-degree assaults and
murder charges out of the prison and moved about three busloads, which
ran around ninety prisoners, and shipped us around the United States. They
finally put me in Leavenworth; the warden had to take me because nobody
else would take me. I was in and out of that prison lots of times.

I was lucky enough to end up in the law library, and I became a jailhouse
lawyer, so I did a lot for prisoners there. Like Ed [Mead], I had no real hope
of getting out; I had [been sentenced to] double lifes and long sentences.[3] I
figured I would never get out. Even after I got through the federal system, I
had to go to the state. But I helped prisoners with their reading and writing
and legal briefs, giving them encouragement to struggle because they *did*
have hope.

My early days as a political prisoner started in Walla Walla, where I got
excited about the Panthers and we formed the first prison Panther movement. We had a Panther movement there, and we formed one in Monroe. At
that time, most Black prisoners did not want to deal with the Panthers. They
thought it would hurt their parole chances. But in Monroe, we gave them
another name—the Black Prisoner Caucus. That thing still lasts to this day,
which surprises me. We wanted to start a Panther group up there, but they
just weren't ready for it. A lot of the work was done in Walla Walla; I worked
with the white prisoners, and we made some pretty good moves. I didn't stay
very long. I was doing a triple fifty-year sentence at that time. But they kicked
me out after I did about seven years and sent me to Seattle. When I got out,
I kept out of the Panther movement on the outside.

I had zero hope of ever getting out. I mean, they had to push me before
the parole boards to get me out. But while I was inside, I stayed in contact with some of the [George Jackson] Brigade members who were still

---

3. Ed Mead was a political prisoner for eighteen years due to his involvement in direct
actions carried out by the GJB. Ed's story is included here.

underground. When they were underground, they sent me letters. But when they got locked up in the women's prisons, we were able to communicate too—not legally, the administration didn't want us to communicate at all. So we just changed our names, and we were able to communicate in that inner circle. That's when bo, Therese, and Janine were still in prison. After they got busted, we still had contact.[4]

Those were the good old days when we got over on the prisons. We got them into doing some things they didn't want to do. At the state prison at Walla Walla, we ran an underground newspaper [*The Bomb*]. The administration was trying to find out who was printing the paper, threatening that they were going to lock the whole prison down trying to find this out, and they never did. But the way we organized the prison, we changed the concept that they had. It's kind of a historic situation, recorded by the media and everything. The administration ran half the prison, and the prisoners ran the other half. They ran the custody and security, and we ran education and entertainment, and those kinds of things. I kind of liked that. That's one of the reasons we left. They just didn't want us in there anymore.

My skill kind of derived from the Panther thing. I was always trying to work on the ten points of the Panther Program, so everything I did in prison dealt with that. We helped train prisoners in learning the skill of reupholstery, and we started a shop inside the prison and were even able to pay ourselves. When I got out of prison, I hooked up with some of the same guys I worked with in prison, and we started a business outside that employed ex-prisoners and people on parole and probation, both men and women. It was pretty successful, and it made me feel good knowing we learned something in prison, so we could organize prisoners and get things going to make a living at it.

Losing friends and family was terrible. I lost my wife while I was in prison and they wouldn't give me the telegram telling me she had died until after her funeral. They didn't want me to go to funerals. They did the same thing with my mother. Those were during my time in state prison. When I was in federal prison, it was different.

I missed my son the most. He was twelve years old when I went to prison. He would visit me, and in fact he had a son and would bring his son

---

4. bo brown, Therese Coupez, and Janine Bertram were members of the GJB who also served time in prison for their political commitments. bo brown died in 2021.

to visit me. That went on all the time I was in prison. There wasn't a month that went by that they didn't come and see me, even though they transferred me from prison to prison to prison. When he was really young, people outside would bring him in. And when he got older, he came with other adults. That's the only thing I regret about all of the stuff I've done. I don't regret my political actions inside or outside of prison, but I regret losing the years I could have had with my kids.

Every prison is different—remarkably different. Some are soft, some are hard. I've seen the hole, as they call it, get fancier names but become harsher than before. I've seen black-out cells, they call them boxcars, with no light, to places like Lompoc, where you have your own room and you have a key to your own room. But the worst things that happened didn't happen to me. It happened to others, and it was frustrating that we couldn't do too much about that. Luckily, that's one of the things that encouraged me to join the Brigade when they did something about it. The prison had some people in the hole and were abusing them. And it's hard to get their attention, real attention that it has to change. So the Brigade decided to bomb a department of corrections to get their attention. It got their attention and got some change at that point, but you can't do that every time a problem comes up. I wish we could, but it takes more than just a small group when so much work needs to be done.

Every day shocked me in prison, day to day. We had to play by their rules. Every prison was different. In one prison, we had to wear boxer shorts, in another we had to wear jockey shorts. You had to keep your hair cut or your face shaved depending on which prison you were at. It is totally irrational, dehumanizing you as much as they could. I wanted to go to school, but they didn't have any programs that I wanted to join. I'd been through high school and some college. I was really interested in education, and that's why I became minister of education for the Black Panther Party inside. That was my job. That was my division of labor, and I've stuck with it from that day to this day.

My proudest achievement was forming the Black Panther Party inside and being accepted by the administration. We were underground when we started, and we were told there would be no underground. So it became an aboveground Panther organization—the only one in the United States that I know of. That was a great achievement for me because the program that they set up against what was happening to the Black community outside was happening inside too. It was something that I could put my teeth into every day I was in prison. Of course, I was out of prison for a short time, maybe three years, then back in prison again fighting the same thing. The prisons were different, but they're still prisons at heart.

Yes, the local Panthers came down to the prison, and we communicated with them. They came down to bring the sickle-cell anemia program in there and tested all the prisoners in the prison. And this was accepted by the administration. Some of the Panthers that I met then I still know to this day. I was second in command. The captain fell in love with one of the Panthers from Seattle, and he supposedly committed suicide. Then I became captain. There are sad stories, very sad stories. I still work with the Panthers now and then. The last time I saw them was down in Oakland, when I went to the Panther gathering down there, me and the Seattle Panthers. They took me to see my comrade in the Brigades, bo. bo was getting old and had dementia. They dropped me off there, and I met with her. So, I have a close connection with the two different groups, even to this day. They're both dwindling. We're losing Panthers to old age and disease, and we're slowly losing ourselves, but we're going to hang on as long as we can.

Politics and Prison Dynamics

I've struggled the best I can against racism all of my life. As a kid, my mother used to do it too, and I didn't know what she was doing at the time. I didn't know she struggled against racism. She was the second generation after slavery, you know. In grade school, they had read these books that would make buffoons out of Blacks and humiliate them. *Little Black Sambo* was one of those books. It's programming other students, the white students, to look at us in that fashion. My mom didn't like that. When we got higher in grades, we read books like *Tom Sawyer*, and she'd go tell the principal that he had to excuse her children from listening to that garbage. He was an Italian principal, and he understood. He said, "I'll make sure that doesn't happen. They can leave the school or class any time without repercussions." One day, she was in Seattle and walking down in Pike Place Market, a famous place, with my sister, a little kid, maybe five or six years old, holding her hand, and a white woman told her to get off the sidewalk while she was walking by. My mom took an umbrella and beat that woman up and down through Pike Place Market, and she got a lot of cheers from the owners of the different shops. I didn't know at that time that she just couldn't stand being humiliated, with her own child, because of her race. She was a fighter, and I was a fighter.

When I was in prison, things came up, and I'd always get myself in trouble fighting crap like that. They had a movie called *100 Rifles* with Jim Brown and Raquel Welch in it, and a white prisoner said that's not going to be shown in this prison, so we locked the whole prison down. That changed the whole scene. We stayed in so long that the white prisoners ended up joining us. I was called before the warden with other prisoners, and I was speaking for Black prisoners, and I told them it was about racism. The warden said, "What do you mean, racism?" I told them about how they segregated the cells at that time, all Black cells and all white cells. And the warden said he didn't know anything about it, that he didn't know what was going on, which was a bunch of bullshit, of course. But it did change later on, and people were able to cell together if they wanted to cell together. That was one of my fights against racism, and, like I say, it changed the whole scene in the prison movement. We got control, and the Black Panthers were able to push other programs. With the underground newsletter, which I belonged to, we could speak to all prisoners and get everybody on the same page. Newsletters and journals are some of the best things that happen in prisons. Ed Mead is great at that and has been doing it both inside and out.

We'd never say who we were when we did our journal *Bomb* because that's the only way we could get all the prisoners on the same page. If we said we were a white group or a Black group or a Canadian group, it would have changed the whole thing. But as long as we remained silent and put in the common cause of all prisoners, they would do almost anything we said, and they would stop doing things that we told them to stop doing. They never knew who we were, but we gave good advice. The people that Ed dealt with for [*California*] *Prison Focus* and the *Rock*, and all the other newsletters that came after, it was the same way.[5] They listened to him, but they knew who Ed was and he got a lot of flak for being a strong Marxist-Leninist, gender-wise,

---

5. *California Prison Focus* is the newspaper of a grassroots organization with the same name that works to abolish the California prison system in its present condition, with a focus on ending long-term solitary confinement.

the whole thing. Sometimes he worked in fear, but he put out that paper without any fear at all. It had to be put out no matter what. I call that kicking ass for the working class. We were revolutionaries before our time, that's what my son says. He was twelve years old when he started seeing who I was, and he started saying then I was born before I should have been.

My whole thing was struggling in prison against racism. I had to fight, get up front and fight, you know? And you have to take some blows because people are going to resist it. In the early days when I was in prison—I call them the early days because there were maybe 17 to 20 percent Blacks in prison, now it's gone to over 50 percent people of color. But that same struggle exists now. And there's so many who have their own separate causes, and they fight against each other. When we Blacks were fighting against the KKK, we had the Native Americans and the Hispanics fighting with us.[6] But now they split up. Now the Hispanics have different groups within prisons. They're fighting against each other and fighting against everybody else. It's a new scene. I don't really understand it that much. It's not like it was when I was in.

Prisons are always different. It depends where you are. It's prison—they'll keep you locked up, and they'll abuse you. But there's an undercurrent within the prisoners and the prison staff that changes in every prison. Every administration has their cliques in there who run the prison. And wardens fight to try and get control of prisons every day.

I started in the state prisons, and I fought racism a lot, so I spent a lot of my time in the hole because of that. The prison boss wouldn't let Black prisoners work in certain areas, both Blacks and Native Americans. So I kind of attacked them as my only recourse. My best fight against racism was to never let them know who you are, just let them know that our causes are the same. They'll figure out who they are later on. But when the causes are the same, everybody will struggle together. The administration will pit one against the other any chance it gets so it can maintain control.

I met a lot of political prisoners on the inside, and the thing in common at that time was the Vietnam War. Everybody was against the Vietnam War. So, everybody who had a struggle, we could identify with that struggle because there was a bigger struggle that we all needed to identify against.

---

6. The Ku Klux Klan (KKK) is one of the oldest and most notorious white supremacist groups in the US. Members of the KKK are prominent in the prison system, among white prisoners and guards alike.

When we got through all this, when the war ended, a lot of that cohesion broke up. I became political with the Panthers to start off with. But when I got inside the federal system, I learned about the Native American struggle. Leonard [Peltier] told me, the thing that sticks with me the most, is that he had trouble with the progressive Native Americans and the conventional Native Americans. They fought themselves, and there was a constant fight. And while he is in prison, he has had to deal with this. He was considered a spiritual leader, but he said there were people who were against him, whom the government had stolen from the Native Americans, stolen their hearts. And he said that he found the same with the Blacks, some being very progressive and supporting things we support and others not so much. He said it's always a constant struggle. There's always that fifth column within you. There's people coming from the right, the left, the north, the south, and then there's somebody with you who is in the fifth column, fighting to help those who are trying to get in. That was important to me because I didn't believe that to start off. I thought once we got rolling, everybody would join us. But he said it's not that way. They've infiltrated every group that's out here. There is always somebody who will look for a favor to save themselves and sell you out.

I talked with a lot of political prisoners from different organizations, and I always got a little bit of wisdom, some things to keep in mind as you move along. Don't think everything's going to be perfect, or that everybody's going to join all at once. We got letters from prisoners in the California SHU [Secure Housing Unit], and a lot of them were very political. But you could read in those letters that they were looking for their own interests, political interests, their own struggle. They didn't think anybody was interested in their struggle but them, and everybody else was against them. And this deals with a lot of the white struggles inside, and the white struggles are varied. It's not just the white nationalists or white supremacists or Aryan Brotherhood or Nazis.[7] They're all separate, fighting for their own interests within the group, but they join together to fight against somebody else. It's a hell of a struggle inside. But among the political prisoners that I've met, whether it's the Puerto Ricans or Panthers or Black nationalists, everybody has their

---

7. The Aryan Brotherhood (AB) is a neo-Nazi prison gang known to be violent and white supremacist in their actions. The AB has members inside and outside of prisons across the US.

own cause, and they look to you to join their cause, not the one that's been established. The one that Huey Newton tried to establish was dealing with the community itself, not with the government, but dealing with things they needed in our community immediately.[8] That one struck me as a good struggle, but everybody didn't see it that way. They saw broader; they talked about international struggles when we haven't even dealt with the one we're dealing with internally. It was kind of good because every day we had free time, whether on the yard, or in our cells, if we had a good cellie, that's what we talked about. We thought the struggles were going to last forever, the struggles that we were dealing with, and they all started fading away. Not just with the Vietnam War, but with each struggle that fell separately, others soon followed. I'm lucky to this day that the Seattle Panthers and what's left of the Walla Walla Panthers are still working together, and we meet regularly.

Lockdowns? We just waited until it was over. Just like a strike or a riot, the energy runs down after a while; you just wait for it. It's going to lose its energy eventually, and the boss will get control again. They used to offer a bunch of ice cream or strawberry shortcake if guys would end a strike. It tempted a lot of people. But they will pay attention. When you lock down, that costs the government a lot of money, and they don't want to spend money on overtime and stuff like that. When you do lock down, the longer the lockdown, the more you're going to get because it is a bargaining point. Your labor is a bargaining point—you're running the prison, you're doing all the major work to keep that prison running. When you shut down and the guards have to pick up the slack, a lot of them don't know what they're doing.

Every time I attacked the guards, I ended up in the SHU. I don't argue with them and ask to be let out. When I do something like that, I feel good about it. They can keep me locked up as long as they want. There was one guard who was in the laundry who wouldn't let Black prisoners work up front, and, when I pushed him, they wanted to keep me locked up, in a sense, forever. But they couldn't do it because my cause was just; the cause was just, while the actions weren't.

But when in the hole, I just waited for them to figure things out. I

8. Huey P. Newton was a Black revolutionary and writer who cofounded the Black Panther Party in 1966. He spent time in and out of jail due to his politics, and he was a target of the FBI's COINTELPRO. Newton was murdered in Oakland in 1989 by a member of the Black Guerrilla Family (BGF). See glossary.

mean, they're running the prison, whether they do something in my favor or against me, they're running the prison. When I went before the parole board, I was doing three fifty-year sentences at that time, and I figured I'm never going to get out. When they give you those sentences, you think you're never going to get out. But they let me out within seven years, and that was with a fifteen-year minimum sentence. So just wait them out.

But when I do stuff like that, I don't expect to get out of it. I'm not bargaining for my freedom at any point when I go to prison. At that point, I'd lost it all. You lose your family, your wife, your children, and they're gone. Sometimes you regret it. I felt I was just in my political actions. I believe I was just. I know I was just, in everything I did, whether somebody got hurt or not.

Looking Forward

Individually, yes, I always felt supported. My supporters weren't trying to get me out or anything. They just gave me the support I needed. They communicated with my children or my friends outside. We managed to communicate with somebody else in another prison. I appreciated that, but I didn't think it was going to work. I hadn't even started on two life sentences. I felt in my heart that I wasn't going to get out, that I was there for the rest of my life. There were times when I was in the boxcars—no light in there, a hole in the floor, no clothes, guards would tease you with three square meals and three little squares of toilet paper—when it felt like hell. It was filthy in there. There's nothing you can do to get away from it. They had a grill on the floor that was your toilet.

The sentences are far too long. The more you stay in there, the farther you are removed from the economy and the culture outside. It's one of the main causes of all the crime and stuff that happens on the street. You work your life away in prison, and when you get out you have absolutely nothing. They may give you $40—or may have a little social program so you can go to the hospital with this ticket or you can ride the bus—but eventually ex-prisoners become the dispossessed. These people in these homeless camps aren't just ex-prisoners. These are people who are totally dispossessed. When prisoners get out, they have no other place to go and join the dispossessed. They wonder what's happening out there, why these camps are growing. I see it. When I first got out of prison it wasn't this way. When I stepped out of prison in 2000, it wasn't this way. This is growing, growing, growing. It's taken away everything they've got. They can't make enough money to live in the house so they have to live in a tent. And pretty soon they won't be able to live in that tent because every time they get arrested, the stuff they save gets taken away from them.

Prisoners have rights, and they have to realize that. They have the right to earn an income. They're running the prisons, so why can't they get paid for it? They need that money when they get out. It can't be pennies that they can spend in the commissary, and that's all they're getting. The first point of the Panther Ten Point Program is that we have the right to determine our own destiny. Whether by voting, labor, or whatever, we have the right to determine our own destiny. They do have that right, and they have to struggle and demand it inside. Prisoners need to make demands. If you're not going to give us the money when we get out, give us a job when we get out.

Rebecca Rubin

Rebecca Rubin received a five-year sentence for her involvement with actions committed in support of the Earth Liberation Front during the late 1990s and early 2000s. A shy animal lover from Vancouver, Canada, Rebecca found herself on the run for seven years before surrendering to face draconian charges in the midst of the Green Scare. She served four years and four months and spent several months in various holding facilities and Oregon jails before spending two years imprisoned at FCI Dublin in California, followed by time in a reentry center in Portland and then home confinement. She did not let this time impact her love for nature or her sense of humour.

Prison Life

To some degree, I was mentally and emotionally prepared for the experience of captivity. For seven years following my indictment, I'd felt it looming. I had run from it, but the fear of it followed me everywhere, menacing my thoughts, awake and asleep, and bearing heavily on nearly every aspect of my existence. I had no assurance at that time that prosecutors would be willing to negotiate a plea deal with a "fugitive terrorist," and I fully expected that, if caught, I would receive a mandatory minimum sentence of thirty-five years. For me, then, running from prison, and believing that I would of necessity be doing so for the rest of my life, was far harder than actually enduring a short time there. By the time I surrendered, I had been running, hiding, and

41

isolating for seven years and had spent half that time trying to negotiate a tolerable plea agreement; I was tired of living in fear and was resolved and ready to move forward and through whatever the system had in store. As it turned out, the prison hellscape I had conjured was far worse than anything my captors meted out (I realize I am extremely fortunate to be able to say this and that the "correctional" system, for the overwhelming majority of those it terrorizes, takes an incredible toll).

I feel fortunate for having had time to prepare for prison. I was indicted after many of my codefendants had been arrested, so I had the opportunity to run. I was able to process the shock and terror and betrayal stemming from the arrests from a place of relative freedom. I had the woods and the night as refuge and solace. I had time and space to think and feel and gather my wits about me. In the end, I chose to surrender and did so under terms that I could accept. I met so many incarcerated people who had been plucked unawares from their lives, suddenly snatched from their homes, their families, their dependent children. They were shocked and stressed and sick, overcome by grief and confusion, outraged and even surprised at the injustice and cruelty of the system. I was heartsick to see the cruelty up close, but I was not surprised. I had, for better or worse, been educated through the teachings of prisoners, former prisoners, and activists. I expected the worst, but knew too that there would always in darkness be beauty available to those on the lookout, so I knew to keep my eyes peeled for anything positive that might present itself.

I didn't prepare to go to prison, though, by reading about it or watching documentaries. What I did was attempt to load up on what I figured I'd need to endure. For seven years, nearly every day and night, in all seasons and conditions, I stood outside, eyes and heart open, and tried to absorb through all my senses, the big, wide, full, open feeling of freedom and wild nature so that, wherever I ended up, I would have that feeling with me. I was trying to absorb, really imprint on my being, how it felt to be on the land without anything binding my body or impeding my will to move in any direction I chose for any distance I chose at any time so I could take that memory with me.

When it came time to surrender, I entered the prison system with a rock-solid base of love and support from family and friends. I would not have had the resources or wherewithal to negotiate a surrender without them, and I wouldn't have had the courage to surrender without their promise of ongoing moral support. In fact, I had much more support immediately before and while imprisoned than I had while running. I could finally be myself, reclaim my name and history, and reconnect with all the people I had to steer clear of while in hiding. I could talk to loved ones on the phone, exchange letters, and visit with them. So, in a sense, I was at an advantage mentally when I went to prison because it felt to me like I was returning to the world rather than being taken away from it, which is how most of the people I met inside were feeling. Most of them had just recently lost everything, when I'd lost everything seven years prior, and the most important of those things—social connection—I was now regaining. I was also at an advantage for having the legal and moral support of two incredible lawyers. Most importantly, the people backing me respected my values and principles enough to support me even when they may have disagreed with the decisions I'd made in the past and those I was now making in the legal realm. While I did not go into prison with any direct support from the activist community, I did receive offers of support shortly after my surrender, which was much appreciated.

I imagine everyone finds it difficult to adapt to the routine and structure of prison unless perhaps they've spent significant periods institutionalized. The whole apparatus is constricting, choking, chafing. I found it very difficult to adapt to life under constant control and surveillance. I don't think I did adapt as much as I bore it with as much grace as I could muster, which sometimes wasn't much, and I suppressed the urge to scream and lash out, at least verbally but also physically, on a frequent basis. I often felt frustrated, angry, impatient, hateful. I hated the crowds and lineups. I hated having the timing and manner and geography of my every movement dictated by loudspeakers, taped lines, threatening signs, and razor wire. I hated creeps in uniform staring me up and down, suspicious and scornful, judging the fit of my uniform, my walk, my friends, the contents of my bag. I hated the pat-downs and strip searches. I hated my personal belongings, including photos of loved ones, being touched and tossed around. I hated cops scrutinizing and withholding my mail. I hated the barking guards, the self-important, lazy administrative staff who felt it their duty and pleasure to denigrate people and hold them back from any attempt to better their lives, and I loathed the medical staff who routinely and callously denied treatment to people in need of care. I hated the noise—the banging and slamming and clanging and constant loud human voices amplified by hard surfaces in every direction—and the utter lack of solitude and privacy.

When I was in the same location for more than a couple days, I tried to structure my days in county jail around exercise, writing, reading, cleaning my cell, and meditating—all of these activities, as long as I had books, paper, and a writing utensil, were activities I could do if and when I chose. I tried very hard not to count on things beyond my control and to keep my expectations low so as not to invite disappointment, frustration, or conflict with other inmates or guards. I tried to be present to my immediate basic circumstances, accept them, and not attach to what could be taken away— phone calls, recreation, classes, socializing with other inmates, particular TV programs, et cetera. I failed utterly, though, when it came to "outdoor rec"; despite myself, I'd be counting down the minutes to that rush of fresh air and disappointed to the point of near meltdown when it was denied, usually without apology or explanation, just a silent refusal of the doors to unlock and then a growing agitation among the women who had been looking forward to it. In the seventeen months I spent in jail, I don't think I gave up a single opportunity to be outdoors, even if the "outdoors" was actually indoors with a fresh air vent.

I love early mornings wherever I am, so in prison I took advantage of the dawn breakfasts (apples!) and the near-empty rec yard with its incredible sunrise skies and fresh earthy scents. On cool mornings, I often had the entire yard to myself. I chose to work in landscaping so I could spend my days watering and pruning plants, raking leaves, watching birds, and learning what I could of the local ecology. When not working, I spent the afternoons studying, reading, or playing guitar, usually in the rec yard but sometimes in the unit or the law library or even in my cell if the cellmates were out. Alone time in the cell was rare and precious, and I made sure to take advantage of it and to give the gift of solitude to cellmates when I could; nowhere else were we allowed any sense of freedom from watchful eyes.

Every evening after we were locked in the units, I read or wrote letters, caught up with my cellmates or other friends, and then meditated before sleep. I was very grateful to have roommates, for most of my time at Dublin, who were respectful, calm, motivated, mostly introverted, and also liked early mornings and quiet evenings. We socialized with our respective friends outside the cell, and, when in the cell together, we gave each other psychic space as needed. I was incredibly lucky to have been chosen as a roommate very soon after my arrival by a kind woman with a life sentence; my cellmate situation remained relatively stable as a result, and I was able to feel safe and to do my own thing even during lockdowns. While the third roommate did switch on occasion, counsellors were apparently more careful about who they assigned to the cells of "lifers," and the third cellie, therefore, was usually low-drama, a blessing in such tight quarters.

There was a lot to hate about prison. But there were certain aspects of prison culture I appreciated, respected, and even admired: the sharing of resources with those in need, despite it being forbidden, the trading of skills and knowledge, the strong bonds of friendship and solidarity that developed among women under a common oppressor, the incredible creativity that flourished in every jail and prison I passed through, and the incorrigible spirit of outlawry that existed inside the walls. Fucked up rules are made to be broken, and they were broken, no matter the risk or consequence. I also felt the prisoners were generally respectful of elders and mostly supportive of those in real physical or emotional distress. There was a lot of tenderness, caring, and love among the women with whom I served time, and on the whole I think there was a culture that tended toward kindness and compassion.

All the worst of human traits and tendencies also existed behind bars, and they overshadowed the good at times. To varying degrees, I felt a fairly constant underlying tension, suppressed pain and rage, I suppose, at nearly all times and in all places, a vibration in the air like one careless step would invoke an angry reaction from someone. I mostly felt safe among prisoners but never entirely. I treaded carefully and kept my guard up. Even if I personally tried to keep out of trouble and distance myself from danger, in the confines of a crowded prison, jail, holding tank, or transport truck it is impossible to do so all the time. And I was keenly aware that just being in close proximity to others engaged in illicit activity or prone to violence could land me in trouble, as well. A prisoner doesn't have to be party to an offense to get blamed for it or tossed in the SHU while the matter is investigated.

I certainly *never* trusted or felt safe with jail or prison overseers or with the prisoners that buddied up to them. For the most part, I conducted myself in prison much like I did on the run—walls up, head down, trying my best to fly below the radar. I cared about people without fully trusting them, and I didn't let people trust me with information unnecessarily. Better to see, hear, and know nothing about anything that might draw unwanted attention from other prisoners or guards. I chose, therefore, not to get wrapped up in the larger group social scenes or the black-market economy, two major aspects of prison culture.

My happiest moments inside were the times that contrasted most starkly with my expectations of jail and prison. So, "happy" for me was a measure of joy mixed with surprise, relief, and gratitude. My ultimate fear with regard to prison, and what I expected of it from having read about the experiences of a couple of my codefendants, was that I would be locked into a world of strictly human creation, stagnant and barren, severed from wild nature and from the elements. But my ultimate fear never came to pass; I was never disconnected from the wild world. There were times in county jail when the connection felt tenuous and fleeting—when the sun shone and the wind blew, I could watch shadow leaves dance against the painted window of my Portland cell, or, if I kept my head upturned while "outside" at SeaTac, I might catch a glimpse of a gull flying over the grate. But there were also times when nature made her presence known, undeniably, as when a fleet of baby spiders drifted down from the ceiling of my very first cell at the border, or when the rich aroma of slough seeped through the concrete of the jail outside Portland and the frogs bellowed beyond the walls. From the yard in Nevada, I saw roadrunners and coyotes! The wider world, the bigger, longer-lasting, infinitely more powerful world than prison was there for me to see and feel as long as I paid attention. From beginning to end I remained vigilant for signs of life; I looked and listened and felt for the more-than-human world wherever I was, and, to my immense relief, wherever I was, I was graced by some aspect of it.

There were many moments during my imprisonment that I consider a deeper, darker shade of happy, not joyful exactly but rich and life-affirming. There were far too many of these moments to recount, and in any case they are mostly indescribable. They are the moments I would find myself looking in admiration and awe at the human beings around me—jails and prisons are such a cauldron of courage, vulnerability, honesty, pain, suffering, perseverance, humour, madness, creativity, talent, beauty, brilliance, and resistance! And many times, in many circumstances, I felt honoured to bear witness to the goings-on, or to be included and trusted to listen or give feedback or even, in a few instances, to serve as peacekeeper.

One of the most gratifying moments of my time in jail was receiving a letter from a woman who had been released from my unit some weeks prior. She was a tough, hard-shelled, lifelong repeat offender and the unit bully. Our interactions had been amicable enough, but we had never spoken at length. What she knew is that I cared about animals, that I didn't eat them, and that I was facing time for defending them. In the letter, she explained that she could no longer kill insects "on the streets," something she'd thoughtlessly done all her life; now, when the impulse struck, she was stopped by the memory of my crestfallen face after she'd stepped on a bee in the rec yard. It may sound small, and in the scheme of things it is small, but it matters to me that my presence had some kind of impact for the better. My love for the little beings of this world got through her tough exterior and stayed with her when I hadn't even been trying (in actuality, I thought I'd hidden how upset I was about the bee!). There were other instances as well when fellow prisoners or even guards expressed support for my beliefs or let me know that the actions my codefendants and I had been charged with opened their minds or hearts to the ideas and motivations behind them.

At Dublin, I claimed Wicca as my religion and was, therefore, allowed access to a small garden space with a fire circle. Every single time I sat in a ceremony—the fire crackling, burrowing owls nearby, bare feet in sand, stars overhead, in a circle of brave, kind, strong women—I was struck so deeply with gratitude. Ignore the fences and it wasn't prison at all. Being in the company of that group of women, trying their best to live good lives in spite of circumstance, was medicinal. It may not always have been a positive space, depending on the inmates involved, but within a few months of my arrival, we managed to turn it into a welcoming, inclusive, safe space for anyone and everyone who came with openness and positive intentions. The circle was my happy place during a ceremony or relaxing with friends, but I also spent many contented hours there alone, tending the plants, meditating, playing guitar, and occasionally answering questions about paganism from curious women walking the track.

It was probably while walking the track with friends in prison that I experienced the most joy. We walked and talked, vented, commiserated, gossiped, laughed, shared memories, and made plans. We had pure, lighthearted fun. We made fun of ourselves and everyone and everything around us—dark humour at its best—and killed the tedium of endless circles inventing "silly walks" that had us laughing until we nearly peed our pants. I remember a time in jail too when a few of us broke into a spontaneous, hilarious game of amateur "interpretive dance" during outdoor rec. We were like giddy little kids, laughing hysterically, high on only fresh air and exercise after too long inside, but I half expected a shakedown of our cells afterward.

I learned a whole lot from the women in jail, about life, poverty, substance use and addiction and treatment, domestic violence, immigration, crime, and the state's failure to address, alleviate, or deal humanely with any of it. By virtue of just being there and having to cope and survive, my communication skills—listening, de-escalating, supporting—improved immensely. My time in jail was an intense, immersion education. It was painful but ultimately mind-expanding and heart-opening, and there is no other place I could have learned the lessons taught there. In prison, I learned from my roommate the value of forgiveness and of taking people for who they are in the present.

I lost my dear grandpa midway through my prison term. It was agonizing not to be with my mom and brother in the immediate aftermath of his death. But it was worse not to have been able to spend time with him in the several years before he died, especially since he never seemed to be able to grasp the reasons why. He suffered from dementia for years but he always remembered his family members. He knew me, remembered me, asked about me, and even exchanged letters with me while I was in prison, but he never seemed to understand or accept how his granddaughter could be in trouble with the police. It just didn't make any sense to him. So, I regret that our communications for the last years of his life were few and distant and lacking in real, mutual understanding. I coped with his death as I coped with our separation for all those years and like I cope with loss anywhere; I remembered and lamented and cried. Because I'd read and heard about the emotional suppression that men are forced to endure in prison, I felt fortunate to be a woman in prison among women; for the most part, we allowed each other emotional expression and supported one another through grief.

I also lost two very beloved canine friends while imprisoned. I had hoped with all my heart and believed that I would get to see them again. They would be old ladies when I got out, but they would remember me. The first dog died two years in and the second while I was at the halfway house with less than a year to go to release. I cried so long and hard over that dog, my roommate called psych support to the room. I cried for all the days she was dying and I couldn't go to her, and I stopped when I knew she was gone.

It is amazing how strong an impact seemingly small changes can have on prisoners' quality of life. When I arrived at Dublin, the windows in the cells had been sealed shut for a couple of years. But the new warden had them unsealed so that we could now choose whether or not to adjust the quality and temperature of the air in our cells. It was an enormous change for the better in most people's opinions, though a shocking number of women were too afraid of insects or dirt to open theirs. When, toward the end of my term, rumour spread that the windows were about to be sealed once again, the general mood began to plummet. If they would seal the windows, other negative change was on the horizon.

And, in fact, negative change had already begun. For several months before I left, the administration had been cutting down trees—big, old, beautiful pines and willows—all of which provided shade and comfort for the women and food and homes for wildlife. They had also started plotting out areas of grass to pave over. All under the auspices of security. However, many women had heard officers and administrators in recent times state that Dublin was "too pretty" and that it didn't "look enough like prison." It wasn't punishing enough, in other words. It breaks my heart to imagine how it must look now. It makes me sick to imagine the yard with no shade trees to read under, no nesting trees for the songbirds, no magnolia, no bottlebrush trees for the hummingbirds, and no women watching them with smiles on their faces. It was not just the "ecoterrorist" and her hippie friends who cared about the animals and plants and were affected by their destruction. When they chopped down the giant willow in front of my unit, officers had to cordon it off so women would stop walking out of bounds to pay their respects to the remaining stump. For a lot of women, a bit of beauty in the form of green grass and a sprinkling of flowers and trees provides a much-needed buffer from the barren, ugly reality of prison.

Our quality of life in the unit changed according to which officers were assigned to it that rotation. If we had the old guy about to retire who delivered our mail to the cell and said hello while doing it, turning a blind eye to anything amiss, we were a pretty relaxed bunch. But if we had the quiet sadist with the ball cap over his eyes, or the guys who got off on cell inspections and shakedowns, or the rager who celled us in for not wearing the right shoes in the lobby, or the guy who despised us and made us late for meals if we spoke over a whisper while waiting to go to the dining hall, or any one of a number of other power-trippers, then tensions rose and life sucked. Likewise, if the officer in the kitchen had any compassion or pride in their work, we looked forward to meals, and we spent a lot more on commissary when they didn't. The day-to-day quality of our existence rose and fell according to the quality of human beings in control at any given time. But the overall, longer-term quality of life for the compound seemed to be influenced by those at the top, and it was definitely on the decline when I walked out the gate.

I think I was shocked on a fairly frequent basis during my incarceration. The first shock came right away, when I saw from my SHU cell window all the general population prisoners doing each other's hair and makeup. I did not expect that. The second and most gut-wrenching shock came within a week of my time at SeaTac when a woman I had met in holding—the first prisoner I met after my surrender—was taken to hospital to give birth. She was returned to the unit less than twenty-four hours later, despite being promised seventy-two hours in hospital with her baby. She was on immigration hold and would be going to immigration detention and deported. The newborn would be staying with the father's family in America. Even more shocking were the many stories of medical neglect I heard in every jail and prison and the evidence of neglect, resulting in death, that I witnessed. Lastly, I was shocked in prison by what may have been the world's largest dildo, made entirely of melted Jolly Ranchers. Nothing really shocked me after that.

My proudest achievement was making new and meaningful friendships, despite the paranoia and distrust I carried with me from my time on the run. Some of the friendships last to this day. I am also proud to have been a source of emotional support for many of the people I met inside. I was a steady, grounded, calm presence in the county jail, where so many people were in the throes of panic, worry, agitation, anger, pain, confusion, withdrawal, and every possible manner of turmoil and being overwhelmed. I listened to people, sat with them while they cried or shook with fear. I talked people down from acting out, fighting, making decisions that would have been harmful for themselves or others. I told people to shut up and stop talking about their legal affairs. I told people to shut up when officers were listening and they were too spun out to pay attention. There were times, because I'd been in the Portland jail for so long, that the deputies let me sit with someone in distress until psych could get there, even when everyone else got celled in. I was also allowed to stand outside the doors of two women in severe distress in their cells, one bleeding and one at risk of self-harm. There was so much need in jail and so little in the way of help, but I am glad I had enough inner resources to be able to provide at least some of the women I met with a little kindness and compassionate company.

I am also proud of having inspired, purposefully and not, deeper thinking about animals and how we relate to them and to the earth, about consumerism, feminism, paganism, and the concepts of terrorism and "eco-terrorism." Most political or case-related conversations I had were begun by people other than myself, people curious to know what it was all about. I like to think I had at least a subtle influence in the direction of compassion and care for self and others, and I know I had a radicalizing influence on some.

Politics and Prison Dynamics

I felt conflicted a lot of the time I was imprisoned. I often wanted to express myself but held back to avoid conflict with others. It was a struggle for me to not side, loudly and honestly, with underdogs or people I felt were being treated unjustly. Mostly, I kept silent around cops, but with other prisoners I did at times attempt to de-escalate, distract, or redirect the attention of someone being aggressive or cruel. Even then, though, I wasn't really expressing an honest opinion so much as using different tactics to stop a behaviour I didn't agree with or like. I found myself, in the face of potential conflict, being very careful with my words, more diplomatic and strategic than I am in the outside world. I didn't call an asshole an asshole. Rather, I might try to appeal to an asshole's ego, self-interest, or sense of humour to get them to change course.

Being locked up—locked in with other people—is an ongoing, high-stakes test of one's social skills. I knew that unless I was willing to end up in an even more restrictive environment, like protective custody or the SHU, there was no escape from any situation or person. In order to avoid physical altercations or ongoing tension with others, I had to learn to get along, to be thoughtful and deliberate and considerate of an incredible spectrum of different people and personalities, while staying as true to myself as possible.

Every major conflict I experienced in prison had to do with my witnessing or hearing about cruelty to animals or degradation of the local environment. I had many tense interactions with staff—from guards to heads of departments to the captain and wardens—and other prisoners over their treatment of wild animals on the compound. The list of abuses is too long and painful to recount but includes guards throwing hot coffee in the faces of geese, prisoners kicking geese, guards harassing and separating goslings from their parents, staff letting birds slowly bleed out in razor wire in full view of helpless prisoners rather than have them euthanized, staff setting live traps for raccoons and not checking them or providing shade or water for days, guards crushing the active nests of swallows, and staff poisoning ground squirrels along with many, many "nontarget" animals. I argued and pleaded with guards and prisoners about most of the above. I wrote letters to two different wardens about the poisoning, spoke to guards and a captain about the entangled geese, and encouraged other women to speak up about their concerns. Some women did speak up as a result of my encouragement, and many more did so of their own accord. In some cases, we were assured that the issue had been addressed and, at least temporarily, the abuse would stop or become less frequent. In some cases, though, the guards just got sneakier, harassing geese at night, for example, once the warden and administrative staff had gone home and the women were locked down, watching from their windows.

There certainly was racism in every institution I passed through, but it didn't take anywhere near the extreme form it seems to among imprisoned men, and it wasn't as pervasive. Interracial friendships and interracial romantic/sexual relationships were commonplace at Dublin, and I don't recall anybody remarking on it, let alone making an issue of it. It was totally normal for people of different races, ethnicities, nationalities, genders, and religions to sit together, in pairs or in groups, at the dining hall or in the units, to walk the track or work out together, and to be cellmates. Staff at the halfway house in Portland tended to segregate both the women and men by race when it came to room assignments, and I suspected this was a carryover from the racial divide in men's prisons. But it was probably also due to the prevalence of white supremacist men and women in Portland.

Throughout my time in custody, I chose to try to keep a low profile among prisoners and outside activists. I said nothing and wrote nothing publicly, and I did no radical organizing. At the time of my surrender, I had been disengaged from aboveground radical activism for many years, having chosen covert action in my mid-twenties. I had also been disconnected from society as a whole while on the run, which is to say, I was used to lying low (and hiding my politics up my sleeve), and so I carried on that way while in custody.

I also knew how the BOP dealt with outspoken and influential activists in prison. I did not want to end up in a restricted housing unit for my own sake, but also because it would jeopardize my ability to communicate on a regular basis with my mom. She had already been through years of worry on my account, had done everything she could to facilitate my surrender and provide me the best possible legal counsel, had supported me despite my "stubborn" refusal to cooperate against others (though it cost me years and her many more thousands of dollars), and I felt immensely grateful and responsible to her. Selfishly speaking too, I had really missed having my mom in my life. So as long as it didn't require a compromise of my core values, I was going to take care of myself and try my best to maintain our connection throughout my term.

On the other hand, I did continue in prison, albeit quietly, with some of the work that is closest to my heart. At the pagan circle, for example, I facilitated meditations and deep ecology workshops. The concepts of ecocentrism and biophilia and animal/earth liberation were new to many of the women I met inside, even those drawn to the pagan circle. We discussed our relationships with animals and the earth, how our individual and societal actions affected them, and how we could all make changes for the better inside and outside prison. I was able to share with many of my fellow prisoners the books and other radical literature I received from outside supporters, and we would discuss a whole range of subjects inspired by those readings.

Despite my attempts to lie low when I got to prison, word of unusual charges travelled fast and very quickly, and other animal lovers and advocates found me. I was told every sad and sordid detail of how prison personnel treated the animals and land and water at Dublin. I tried to encourage people to speak up about things they witnessed, write cop-outs to the people in power, tell visitors, tell visitors to tell the media, and refuse to do whatever harmful deed their boss was demanding of them or switch jobs.[1] All moderate acts but acts that in prison required courage, some sense of personal empowerment, and at least a little hope that the system would actually respond in ways that were productive and not retaliatory or spiteful.

Amazingly, I was able to continue helping animals while imprisoned. I was recruited early on as backup "cat lady" to watch out for and feed the resident strays when needed and to replace their constantly confiscated water dishes. Once people learned I was a wildlife rehabilitator, I was consulted about every wildlife issue on the compound. I was called to catch and release birds from buildings, to disentangle birds from wire or string, to assess whether or not the condition of a goose or gosling required intervention, to tend to fallen nestlings, to get water to entrapped animals, and to help ensure that animals in need of medical care were kept hidden and safe from staff until we could get them out.

Among a sea of prison staff who either disregarded animals completely or actively detested them, there were two or three who were kind enough to help us help them. If we could get an animal in distress to them, they would take the animal out for professional care. Delivering the animals to them, however, was no small feat; it was risky for us and the animals and could be logistically complicated, requiring a network of allies with secret routes and safe spots. The animal might be at the farthest end of the compound from where they needed to go before the friendly staff member left for the day or several days; multiple prisoners, then, might need to relay the contraband animal across the compound, trading them off in view of guards, all within a ten-minute move. If we ran out of time (no running on the yard!) someone could be stuck out of bounds when the move ended or, worse, stuck with the animal still hidden in a bag or a shirt and trying to get back into a building that might suddenly have a guard doing pat-downs and searches. It sounds dramatic, and it was; I was terrified of what one of the crueler guards might do to an animal discovered during a search. The head of safety at the time believed that all animals were vermin and posed a deadly disease risk, so even having a helpless songbird nestling inside a building was considered a serious infraction. I once carried a dead jackrabbit into my boss's office as

---

1. A cop-out is the filing of an Inmate Request to Staff form.

proof that the prison was poisoning more than the targeted squirrels, and I was threatened with the SHU for my efforts.

Thankfully, imprisoned women on the whole are less casually violent than imprisoned men. The violence I witnessed or heard about in prison targeted usually a lover but sometimes ex-lover or an ex-lover's new lover or some such. All the twisted, selfish motivations and messed-up, abusive power dynamics that exist in unhealthy relationships on the outside can exist inside, and then some. Or the violence was between two people with competing, lucrative hustles. Or it was between cellmates getting on each other's nerves, but that was usually a milder violence.

I coped with the possibility of violence by minimizing my risk of being a target of it or a witness to it. I tried not to piss people off. I tried to stay out of drama and away from people who fed on drama. I steered clear of people I knew to be violent and people in tumultuous relationships. I used caution in off-camera locations or areas, like the outdoor weight room, where fights with weapons (weights) most often took place. I kept my senses turned up, especially on the rec yard when officers weren't present; a fight there could last a while before guards broke it up. I also watched out for people looking to join their girlfriend in the SHU because the quickest way to go there was to assault another prisoner. I also coped with the violence by talking with friends who were similarly disturbed when truly brutal events took place.

Looking Forward

Outside support was immensely important to me throughout my incarceration. My family and close friends were my main source of support, emotionally and financially. My lawyer as well felt like a true ally, solid in his support as legal counsel and human being, for the duration. I was also grateful for the experience of people engaged in prisoner support and their offers of assistance to my family in navigating the overwhelming jail/prison apparatus. At least half the heartache of being imprisoned came from knowing what it did to my loved ones outside. I think my mom and others were more afraid of my going to prison than even I was, so a large part of my work inside was making sure they knew I was okay. Supporters gave comfort to my mom as well, letting her know that they were following and keeping in touch with me. My mom was also offered the option of communicating with other mothers who had been through similar circumstances, which was lovely and very much appreciated.

Prisons and jails are such encapsulated worlds. Supporters, both those I knew and didn't, sent photos of beautiful places and people and plants and animals, reminding me of life beyond the walls. They sent photos and news of actions and action camps. They sent drawings and other artwork and incredible, colourful cards. And in turn I was able to share all of it with other women, many of whom had little or no outside support. I found that even tiny gifts were received with such joy and gratitude inside. A little beauty in an otherwise barren cell could go a long way in helping people feel loved and less alone.

The one thing I would suggest supporters do more for prisoners is send news of positive goings-on in the world. Whatever the issue(s) of concern for political prisoners, there has got to be good news resulting from the struggle. We may have to sift through reams of negative news to find it, but I believe it's there. It may be small, tucked away, and temporary, but when we find it, it feeds the spirit and makes us hungry and hopeful and determined for more of the same.

It seemed to me that women in prison were unified when it came to sub-verting the rules in prison. It was generally agreed or accepted that we broke rules when they were harmful to self or others, when they seemed invalid or unnecessary, when they interfered with commerce or relationships or fun. The underlying motivation for rule breaking, though, more often than not, was self-interest rather than the betterment of the population generally. It was resistance of a sort, but it didn't really challenge the operation of the institution or the values of society generally. Capitalism was in full swing, as was the pursuit of instant gratification. And the cops ignored a lot of it, in part because it wasn't truly threatening.

I do have one memory of unified defiance that stands out starkly in my mind like a snapshot. It is a blazing hot day and I am on my knees in the rec yard picking tiny green poison-coated grains out of the desiccated ground with my bare fingers. The grains are everywhere, in the thousands, scattered throughout the crispy grass and inside the dry fissures and holes and under-ground homes of squirrels and burrowing owls, and I am desperate to find and gather as many as I can before the wild animals do. These poisoned grains have been spread via grass seeder over the entire prison grounds by inmates under the direction of the "safety" and landscaping departments. The purported intention is to kill ground squirrels for "security reasons," but in actuality they are killing squirrels, blackbirds, jackrabbits, scrub jays, and many other foraging species dependent on this plot of land for food. Women have been crying over slowly dying squirrels outside the commissary, tallying songbird bodies outside their unit windows, staring with horror at the hawks and vultures feeding on poisoned bodies where they aren't being collected behind the units. Traumatized women being retraumatized.

I've already been warned that I could be charged with interfering with the operation of the institution or some such nonsense if I collect any of the grains, and my friends are also aware of the risk. The perimeter truck is honking persistently, and my boss is walking toward the truck, having told me quietly in passing that he can't see what the hell I'm doing but I'd better stop. When I raise my head, swiveling to look everywhere but at the truck as though terribly confused about why it's making such a ruckus, I see that at least eight other women have joined me, gathering grains with brooms and dustpans and pails and pockets as quickly as I am. All of them are ignoring the truck and its now bellowing guard. In the end we did disperse when we were told the lieutenant was on his way and that he would order another poisoning if we continued, but we and many others continued surreptitiously collecting and disposing of grains until they were gone. Sadly, I am certain that way more of the grains were consumed by animals than collected by us. And, I have heard that the poisoning continues. But the outpouring of cop-outs and distressed pleas to the warden and other staff that occurred after the poisoning I witnessed seemed to win at least a few years' reprieve for the animals.

I can say that my time inside was tolerable because I could stand by the decisions I'd made, before my indictment and after. With the wisdom of hindsight, I may have realized I would do some things differently, but I had acted in accordance with my conscience in the moment, and that's probably the best I can ever ask of myself. I also entered the system with a simple, but very valuable, statement from a Buddhist teacher in my head: *no one can humiliate you but yourself*. In an environment that is forever attempting to denigrate and dehumanize, it is worth remembering. The officer telling women on their period to cough hard enough to "drop a clot" while being strip-searched is only an embarrassment to herself. Nothing prisoners are forced to endure is a reflection of their quality as human beings, but a reflection of the perpetrators, individually and collectively.

If I could tell my younger self about prison when she was alone, sobbing, terrified, and considering suicide as an alternative, I'd have a few things to say. Prison will be hard but survivable. Erase the prison horror movies from your head; in important ways, women's prisons are not like men's. You will come out of it with your heart and soul intact. You'll meet some incredible people with colourful pasts, become friends with them, and laugh together. Even cops and guards can be human, think critically, and see through the "terrorist" hype. You will never be severed from the wild earth but instead held in its web at all times and in all places; there will be flowers and endangered species! Think of prison, and life, as a school of hard knocks, learn from it, and share what you've learned; there might be value in it. Your time won't be lost, but lived differently than you would choose. Prison will cost you less in the long run than if you had lived your life at all costs avoiding it.

Hanif Shabazz Bey

Hanif Shabazz Bey (Beaumont Gereau) is one of three political prisoners known as the Virgin Island 3. Hanif Shabazz Bey, Abdul Aziz (Warren Ballantine), and Malik Smith (Meral Smith) were wrongly convicted of murdering eight people in the US Virgin Islands in 1972 at the Fountain Valley Resort. During the 1970s, as with much of the world, a movement to resist US colonial rule began to grow in the Virgin Islands, growing into a small-scale Mau Mau rebellion on the islands.[1] Hanif has served time in over ten different federal facilities, both in the continental US and in the Virgin Islands, during his over forty-eight years of incarceration. At the time of this writing, all three of the Virgin Island 3 are imprisoned at the Citrus County Detention Facility in Lecanto, Florida.

Prison Life

The first three years of any lengthy prison sentence are usually the hardest in trying to adjust to having your freedom taken away. During my first years of adjustment, I had the support of my family and comrades. Adapting to prison culture was made easier for me by being part of a prison collective. A prison collective is a group of comrades who look out for each other, share with each other, study together, and exercise together.

---

1. The Mau Mau rebellion was a war between Kenyan freedom fighters and British colonialists in the 1950s. The resilience and audacity of the African freedom fighters inspired later liberation movements of the 1960s and 1970s.

I would say that my one year, 1979–1980, at Lompoc, California, was the best time I did, due to the comrades I was surrounded with and the unity inside the prison. The unity was much stronger in 1979–1980 because much of the rebellious spirit that was prevalent in prisons during the Civil Rights Movement still lingered in the prisons. Today the generation of prisoners is more about "what can you do for me?"

I have never lost hope. There are days when the future looks dim, but those are the times when I tell myself, "This too shall pass."

My happiest times in prison have always been when I and other prisoners are locked arm-in-arm in some form of protest or making demands against the prisoncrats. The protests and group demonstrations that stick out to me are the ones we waged to make them stop feeding us pork.

I lost both parents, two siblings, and my grandson since being incarcerated. I have dealt with these losses by telling myself that death is no enemy to human beings. It is a friend, who when the work of life is done, just cuts the human cord that binds us to Earth, that one may sail on smoother seas.

My proudest achievement [so far] was spearheading a hunger strike at Atlanta Federal Prison in 1996 where three floors of a housing unit supported the food strike for one week.

Politics and Prison Dynamics

In the federal prison system, I met dozens of political prisoners and developed working and support systems to help each other. Veronza (Daoud) Bowers, Michael (Ashanti) Alston, and Richard Picariello were all part of our collective in Lompoc. Other comrades that I have interacted with are Rafael Cancel Miranda, Mutulu Shakur, Sekou Odinga, Jihad [Abdul]mumit, Grailing (Kojo) Brown, Bill Dunne, Joseph (Joe-Joe) Bowen, Tim Blunk, Herman Bell, Gabriel Torres, and Kevin (Rashid) Johnson.[2]

---

2. Veronza Bowers Jr., Kojo Bomani Sababu, and Joe-Joe Bowen are current Black liberation political prisoners as of 2023. Ashanti Alston is a former BPP and BLA political prisoner, an anarchist, and a lifelong Black liberation advocate. Herman Bell was a political prisoner due to his involvement in the Black Liberation Army (BLA). Herman's story is included here. Dr. Mutulu Shakur was active in the struggle for Black liberation his entire adult life and was imprisoned from 1986 to 2023. Denied parole ten times, Shakur was finally released in 2022 after being given just months to live due to late-stage cancer. Sekou Odinga was formerly a member

Lockdowns are actually advantageous to prisoners, as you have more time for constructive work and study, and you are free from the everyday prison routine.

[If I could change anything about the time I've served so far,] I would try to give or make a balance of what I was sacrificing to the struggle to what I give to my family.

Looking Forward

I am satisfied with the support I have received throughout the years from outside supporters. To do a lengthy sentence, you need two things: 1) outside supporters and 2) to be committed to something.

If you are facing a long prison stretch, do one of two things: 1) get into the law books to have your sentence overturned or 2) start writing and tell your story.

---

of Malcolm X's Organization of Afro-American Unity (OAAU), the Black Panther Party, and the Black Liberation Army and spent thirty-three years as a political prisoner. Jihad Abdulmumit spent twenty-three years in prison as a political prisoner for his involvement with the BLA. Since his release from prison, Abdulmumit has served as chairperson of the National Jericho Movement. Rafael Cancel Miranda was a member of the Puerto Rican Nationalist Party and was imprisoned along with Lolita Lebrón, Andrés Figueroa Cordero, and Irvin Flores Rodríguez for attacking the US House of Representatives in 1954 (his sentence was commuted in 1979). Bill Dunne is an anti-imperialist political prisoner still imprisoned as of 2023. Bill's story is included here. Tim Blunk was imprisoned for his anti-imperialist actions in connection with the Resistance Conspiracy Case. Gabriel Torres was a codefendant of Herman Bell and Jalil Muntaqim. Bell served forty-five years in prison, and Muntaqim served forty-nine years, as political prisoners before being released. Richard Picariello was imprisoned for bombings and expropriations. And Kevin Rashid Johnson is an imprisoned revolutionary and writer, as well as a founding member of the New Afrikan Black Panther Party. See glossary.

Chelsea Manning

Chelsea Manning served seven years in federal prison for the 2010 release of 700,000 classified military and diplomatic documents to WikiLeaks while an intelligence analyst in the US Army. This was and still is the largest intelligence leak in US history. Chelsea was sentenced to thirty-five years in prison, but their sentence was commuted in 2017 by outgoing president Barack Obama. The day after their conviction, Chelsea declared their gender identity as a woman and began their transition while in the federal prison system. In 2019, Chelsea was imprisoned again for nearly a year when they refused to cooperate with a grand jury investigating WikiLeaks founder Julian Assange.[1] Chelsea continues to speak out against the inhuman treatment that prisoners face in the US and published the book *README. txt: A Memoir* (Farrar, Straus and Giroux, 2022).

Prison Life

I was arrested for the leaks in May of 2010. They say "arrested," but you're really ordered into confinement in the military because you're already in military custody. An officer comes along and signs a piece of paper saying "I

---

1. WikiLeaks is an organization that publishes news leaks and classified information provided by anonymous sources. It was founded by Julian Assange in 2006, and he was indicted on espionage charges by the US government in 2018 based on the release of information by WikiLeaks that was provided by Chelsea Manning in 2010.

order you to jail." It's a formal process of sitting before my commanding officer being read my rights and being carted off to jail. That's a slightly different
process than in the civilian system.

I was taken to Kuwait, where I was put into an eight-by-eight-by-eight
cubic cage inside of a tent with little air-conditioning. It was extremely dusty.
This was Kuwait in the middle of summer, so it was very hot. I was in a cage
with no contact to the outside world. With the way the tent was set up, I
couldn't even tell if it was day or night. My brain melted. My sense of who I
was, my sense of anything, began to evaporate.

Eventually, after fifty-nine days, I was taken by navy staff—because I was
in US Navy custody in Kuwait—and they gave me a lot of misinformation.
They told me, "You're going to Guantánamo. You're going to a cruiser off the
coast of Djibouti. You're going on a ship off the coast of Africa." They were
telling me all these things that I was going to have done to me, so I didn't
really know where I was going or what was going on.

I eventually landed stateside and was carted off to Marine Corps Brig,
which is at the Marine Corps base in Quantico, Virginia, about twenty to
twenty-five miles south of Washington, DC. While they said that I could
communicate and interact with other prisoners, there were no other prisoners [to communicate with]. I was the only person held at this jail, so the
circumstances were similar to my cage in Kuwait. It was sort of a moot point
there from a regulatory framework perspective.

I spent the next nine months in a constantly lit cell. I had running water
and air-conditioning, which was a massive improvement from Kuwait. The
only food that they had at the Marine Corps base was from the officer dining
facility, so I actually got fantastic food. Ironically, despite being in solitary
confinement and not having a sense of who I was or what was going on at all
times, I had officer-level food. I actually started to gain quite a bit of weight
from lack of exercise in this jail.

I finally started to speak with lawyers, therapists, and experts. My restrictions were higher than typical solitary confinement conditions. They cited
my own "health and safety" and used my trans identity against me, claiming,
"Oh, you can't have [certain] things in your cell." I had very limited clothing,
only very padded items of the suicide-restriction type. I was not on suicide
watch per se—but they were highly restricted items and objects. Any item
that I could have used to harm myself or anything that could be made into

a "weapon" was taken away, including underwear. I was not allowed glasses, even though I couldn't see. I am fairly nearsighted. While I was allowed to read books, I had to actively be reading the book to be using glasses. Even if I wanted to flush things in the toilet, or use the restroom, or brush my teeth, or engage in any other hygienic practices, I had to ask the Marine Corps guards who were planted outside of my cell at all times watching my every move and annotating them from behind a one-way mirror. They saw me, and I saw my reflection. That's all I saw: a fluorescent light reflection, and I had to ask for toilet paper to use the bathroom and then return the item. I had to ask for a toothbrush and toothpaste.

I was not allowed to lie down or rest or be in any kind of comfortable position from 7:00 a.m. to 7:00 p.m. For twelve hours a day, I was sitting upright with nothing to do in my cell. These were my days for nine months continuously.

Eventually, I guess due to public outcry and pressure, the Obama administration finally relented, and I was moved to the general population at a US Army base at Fort Leavenworth in Kansas. I was held there for the remainder of my pretrial confinement.

I needed a period to cool down. It took me about a year to really reset my schema, my paradigm, my understanding of the world again after being in solitary confinement for this extended amount of time. I was resetting my brain by interacting with other prisoners, and I had to lean on them. My first interaction with other people for the first time in a very long time was with other inmates.

Then I started going to the law library, learning about my case, about the legal structure, about how criminal cases work, and how civil cases work. Eventually, I had a very lengthy court-martial process, so I frequently flew between Howard County Jail in Maryland and Leavenworth, Kansas. I had limited access to the civilians, but I was communicating with and interacting with the mostly civilian jail staff and civilian inmates, which are basically the same thing. There isn't really a distinction between the military jail apart from the uniforms. That was the extent of interactions with people in general population.

I eventually had a trial, was convicted, and went through a lengthy sentencing phase. I was given a thirty-five-year sentence, which I used as an opportunity to come out as trans to the world. I came out through the *Today* show through my lawyer and told the world, "Hey, I'm Chelsea Manning, I use she/her pronouns" (now she/they pronouns), and I came out to the world, which I guess was its own controversy.

I didn't know anything about the controversy because I was immediately flown to Kansas and held in a reception phase where I was integrated and introduced to the general population. I had to learn how to live and be and interact in this environment. I spent the next year or so integrating myself into the general population and then building ties. I didn't use my privileged position or my fame in any way. I didn't do any of that. I just sort of hung back, interacted with people normally, and tried to live a normal life.

As I worked my way through the "ranks," I decided I wasn't going to engage in prison drama, prison politics, or anything like that, which did exist. I just became somebody who wanted everybody to get along, to be chill, to have fun, and to have as normal an experience as possible. So I took on the diplomat role. I was somebody to come to whenever there was a dispute that needed to be resolved, especially between different groups within the prison and between the facility staff, who were always causing problems.

I found my place in this environment where I had to really depend on the inmate population and be a leader while not being in charge. I wasn't somebody who could say, "Hey, you go do this and you go do that." I wasn't managing anybody or trying to control anybody. I was just like, "Hey, this is how we should deal with this. This is a fight that's worth fighting, or this is a fight that's not worth fighting." Doing what I would call union organizing.

I believe very strongly in prison unions. I was familiar with the concept of prison labor, prison unions, prisoners' organizations, et cetera. I played an active role in organizing and working with prisoners to ensure that our rights were not being exploited too much because, obviously, doing prison labor, everyone is essentially being exploited anyway. It's a matter of how much give-and-take you get with that. I really fit within this role and lived my life as a prison labor organizer.

At some point it started to become more and more real that I might have my sentence commuted by the Obama administration. The military would not consider me for clemency, and they rejected our requests. Our requests for clemency to the White House for consideration were denied, so we actually had lawyers that went directly to the White House to ask for a commutation down to ten years, which was what we asked for at trial during sentencing.

Obama commuted my sentence to time served plus 120 days, which allowed me to be released on May 17, 2017. However, this meant that I essentially spent the next 117 days under the new Trump administration, which was unlike any other administration that we had seen previously in that it did not seem to play within the standard role of government. It was very interventionist, had very different policy proposals, and was very aggressive. Every bad policy that you could think of was actively being implemented and being made profitable through the privatization of prisons. Dependence on the liberal establishment and on the "rule of law" were being circumvented. Every single loophole and vulnerability within the system was being exploited, so I had a lot of concern.

However, I was released from prison on May 17, 2017, without a hitch, and was back in public again without a playbook. I had never been a public figure before. I went from working in the military in a very, very secretive role to being a public figure that everybody knew. Even if I'm not in the foreground of people's minds, they generally tend to know who I am, which is quite overwhelming for me. I've been learning how to adapt to this process ever since.

The Trump administration did eventually decide they wanted to come after me, and in January 2019 I was given a grand jury subpoena. It was unclear what they actually wanted. The prosecutor informed my attorneys that they wanted me to recount what had happened in 2010, which I'd done previously before a court-martial. We were very suspicious about this whole process being used as a tool to come up with additional charges. We were under the impression that the Trump administration was finally trying to undo the commutation in some way. I decided that I was not going to participate in that process, and so I was held for almost a year in confinement, all the way up until the COVID-19 pandemic began.

When I was released from that, it was a much quieter release. I went into a dark time in the history of the world with lockdowns and everybody was very much in shock. Subsequently, over the last two years, we've been dealing with the aftermath of the capitalist infrastructure being like, "Oh, shoot, we can't run this machine as well as we used to," and the sort of disaster capitalism that we've seen over the last two years, controversies and culture wars ramping up, and everybody moving online. It was a good time for me to be released from the grand jury process but a bad time to be released in the sense of not really being able to go back to living what little life I had before the eighteen-month grand jury sentence.

While I was in confinement, I found that my mindset shifted to a day-to-day-to-day approach toward things. I subsequently adopted this policy in my personal life today. I don't have control over everything, and I shouldn't worry about things that I don't have control over. But what I have control over is how I respond to things and how I interact with what things are in front of me, so I focus on a little bit of meditation and on eating well. In the military, we say "chow," so I would go from chow-to-chow-to-chow-to-sleep, and focus on these chunks of time that were much easier to work through and much more survivable compared to thinking, "Oh, there's so many years in front of me. Oh, there's so much hardship that I have to deal with." But if I could focus on things that were in my control, then I could slowly start to regain some semblance of self, some sense of identity, some sense of what I want. That became a foundation upon which I have been able to survive, not just jail or solitary confinement but all kinds of circumstances. This applies to quarantines, crackdowns, a lot of uncertain situations; just focus on health, safety, and well-being first and foremost. I can't think about all this other stuff unless I have the things that I have specific control over taken into account.

You can segment the places I've been confined into three groups: First, there was the extreme but temporary stuff that the military and the national security apparatus imposed on me in my first eleven months. Second, there was prison itself—about half of my time in confinement was in prison, which had programs and stability and many inmates. Sometimes, dare I say, I would forget I was in prison because I had so little contact or interaction with anyone other than inmates. Really, sometimes the staff sort of ran on autopilot. You wouldn't really encounter them. Like doors would open for you, but they would open for you from a distance, without guards being around all the time. It was a lot more transparent of an environment and much more transparently normal-seeming than the middle ground, which was the third group—jail.

In jail, you're interacting with guards constantly. You're not going to have a dining facility all the time; sometimes you'll have trays delivered to you. You spend a lot of time watching TV because you don't have a work program or education programs to attend or chapels to go to. Instead, you're mostly in the housing unit dealing with inmate drama more and more aggressively because you're interacting with guards all the time and the correctional staff fucking with you, being a pain in the ass, and really making your life miserable. They like playing inmates off of each other, playing favorites, and creating drama just because they're bored.

I would say that the US disciplinary barracks was the most normalized environment simply because it was an environment that was most inmate-focused and inmate-run. If you weren't in the Maximum Housing Unit, the SHU—the Special Housing Unit where you were with the people who are in solitary confinement—and you were actually in general population, you could at least get some semblance of normality that would be punctuated by the intervention of the prison staff. I always find it remarkable how the amount of interaction you had with the staff directly affected the amount of frustration and discomfort you experienced. Generally, if it was inmate-run, you didn't have problems, but if it was staff-run, then you had problems.

After the Pulse shooting in Orlando in 2016, I got very depressed about the state of things within the US, homophobia, transphobia, et cetera.[2] It was very demoralizing for me personally and started my path toward depression.

But I saw a lot of inspiring things also. I saw people who changed while they were in prison and grew and matured as good people. One of the rules we had was that we tried not to learn about each other's past. It was like, as long as you didn't fuck with me in the housing unit, then we're good, but we didn't allow that to really color our housing unit interactions as much as possible.

People band together. I saw these two people who were the worst of enemies, but whenever the prison staff would come and try to screw them over, everybody would band together, and these two enemies would all of a sudden be allies. It was camaraderie. It operated as a mutual aid support network that was vital to our survival and well-being. Seeing that working and pushing back against the prison staff was quite inspiring and has colored my whole relationship with organizing and politics in the outside world.

---

2. The mass killing of forty-nine people and wounding of fifty-three more at Pulse, a gay nightclub in Orlando, Florida, on June 12, 2016.

I appreciated seeing art and listening to music that was produced in prison in the music halls. The limited bits of freedom that we were given in which to show creativity and humanity would just shine through so much. It was so incredible and such a deep and powerful thing to witness firsthand. It's so fleeting because there's no record of it. It doesn't go anywhere. It's kind of sad that there are these moments of incredible inspiration that only exist as memories now.

I've said this many, many times over the years, but I can't stress this enough. I've been in maximum security environments with people who are in there for murder, rape, all kinds of very long sentences—by society considered very heinous offenses and things—and time and time and time again, the most awful and violent and dangerous interactions I've ever seen have come, with impunity, from prison staff. The only common denominator in every single jail, every single civilian and military prison, at every security level, was just the awful brutality of prison staff toward inmates. The worst people in jail or prison are staff, time and time again, and this was true across the board no matter where I went.

Politics and Prison Dynamics

I was held in men's prisons. I forgot about this, because the distinction is moot, in my opinion. Yes, I was held in a male facility for all of the time in the military prison system. Then for the grand jury process, I was held in the women's wing of the jail, in general population, so I got to interact with people there.

There was not a whole lot of racism that I saw, per se. Certainly the prisons and jails tended to try to stoke racial tensions in the jail. They put all of the white people in one corner, all the Black people in another corner, and then all of the mixed-race people, Hispanic people, in another corner, and tried to stoke that. However, I never got the sense, especially in the military, that it really ever worked, so I did not really see a lot of this.

The jails would try to encourage segregation through their own policies, but inmates tended to not abide by that. The county jail that I was in—both in Howard County [Maryland] and in Alexandria, Virginia, for the grand jury sentence, the two typical civilian jails that I was in—the inmate population was 90 percent Black, so it was not really an environment where you would see a lot of racism. Even the staff was very Black and mixed-race, so I didn't really see racism directly.

As for sexism, definitely. The constant denominator was sexism by staff. Even among staff, the women guards were treated like shit by the male staff. Male inmates tended to be quite sexist in general towards women. I didn't really face that directly in either sense, but I definitely witnessed it.

I think prison has had the most impact on my politics. A lot of people these days would say that they are liberal, centrist, or whatever. I just had a very policy mindset. I viewed myself as not identifying with a political party. Rather, I have a vision of how things should be, and that vision of how things should be has shifted over time. While my politics are very left-leaning, I don't identify as a specific thing. I don't view myself as liberal. I don't view myself as socialist, per se, or communist or anarchist or any of these different labels. There's a certain skepticism of certain institutions that I have, and certain practices that I think should be implemented throughout society, and approaches to things—whether that's in respect to privacy, surveillance, criminal justice, prisons, healthcare, government programs or assistance, or just having a decent "let's take care of each other" kind of society.

This causes me a little bit of friction, I think, with younger people because I still have that policy perspective. I don't care who does the thing—I mean, obviously, I don't want fascists to do the thing. But I don't care so much about labels, and I'm willing to work with a more general group of people, as opposed to I need to stick to this very niche set of people with this very niche mode of ideas. I learned that mostly through prison. I didn't agree with 90 percent of the people I worked with in prison about anything. You can't do diplomacy in prison without taking into account the needs and the demands and the wants of everyone there. It's the same thing as out here: you don't cater to what this racist neo-Nazi wants, which is not that common, but if it does exist and there is a strain of that, you're not going to deal with that. People obviously have differing visions and interests and things, so you have to be a bit more compromising. If in the eyes of some younger folks that makes me "lib," I'm okay with that.

[When dealing with extended lockdowns,] there is no magic bullet; you either learn to survive in there or you perish. There isn't a tool or a handbook or anything that I can provide for people, but I got through it, and all I can say is that it is survivable. This is not a justification of it. I'm not saying that. I don't want that to be taken the wrong way. It's a horrific institution that we should abolish. That said, if you are inside of it, just remember that people have made it out the other side before.

You never know what's going to happen. I had no idea when all this started that I was going to end up getting a thirty-five-year sentence or be held in solitary confinement for almost a year continuously. But I also did not know that I was going to be released and come home to a welcoming community and family and be given access to opportunities in life again. So you never know. Don't lose hope, because things can actually happen. I doubted that, to be honest. While I was in that process, I was like, "Oh yeah, I'm never getting out. This is never, never going to happen." I was very much in denial for a chunk of time, and I totally understand that and relate to that concern that a lot of folks might have while being incarcerated.

I was in a restricted communications environment that was specific to me for several months. Being disconnected from the outside world was very harmful to my emotional state. I assumed over time that I was forgotten about, despite the fact that I had many people thinking about me. This is the purpose of this kind of control—to psych you out into thinking you're forgotten about and have no hope.

Looking Forward

Pay attention to who's providing food to jails, where jails and prisons are getting their food, how they're getting their food, just as much as what food is provided. The back-end infrastructure for most prisons in society is the same couple of companies and vendors. It's the same with commissary—pay attention to that stuff. They have a monopoly on the stuff. They're price-hiking a lot. The cheapest and least healthy food is provided to inmates at minimum. Commissary has the good stuff, but the price is hiked to an astronomical degree. I'm not going to name these companies and give them any credit, but they do exist and people should learn about them because they are deeply a part of this institution. I think they are an unlocked pressure point in the privatization of prisons. Everybody is focused on private prisons, but don't forget about the privatization of the phone systems, the communication, visitation, commissary, where prisons are getting their food, how uniforms are being made, how they're getting access to all these different things. They are just as much a part of the prison-industrial complex as the prisons and jails themselves. They are an exploitative industry as much as everything else, and that is a major pressure point.

There's a lot of solidarity work that can be done because the USPS is the only protected means of privileged and free communication that inmates have. If the Postal Service goes, then the only protection that inmates have for communication with the outside world is lost, so I think that there's a lot of solidarity work and advocacy that can be done in that area, as well, especially with the massive lockdowns that have happened with the COVID-19 pandemic in jails. I think that those are key areas that I'd be looking at. Looking at the rest of the privatization of the jail system, not just the privatization of the prisons themselves, and the mail system ensuring that people have access and communications to the outside world. I'm a prison and jail abolitionist, but if we can do harm reduction or harm mitigation in any way that we can, we should.

My advice to people in prison today is don't give up hope. You have people on the outside who care about you and who haven't forgotten about you. Also, I think the tide is turning. I think people are turning on the prison industrial complex. Even the news that people watch on television and social media are two totally different areas. I think that the public sentiment is much more to the left now when it comes to prisons than they can see on their jail TVs. The only people who are really watching TV are older people, and you can tell it by the medication ads that you see on TV for this demographic. Whenever you're watching the news and you're watching how things are being portrayed in all of these older, traditional media outlets, they lean more conservative in their audience. This is not the sentiment of the typical person out on the street today. I think people are much more skeptical of these institutions. There's a lot of growth, and there's a lot of interest, and I haven't seen this much prison advocacy or activism before, and it's only getting bigger and bigger.

It's easy for inmates to forget that because the mainstream media—the "mainstream" media outlets, which are not really mainstream anymore, like your local news, the stuff that you get access to while you're in prison—that is already limited and is just so disconnected from the average person.

The way pop culture portrays the criminal justice system is that the story ends with the "bad guys" going to jail. For many, years of change and transformation and growth are forgotten about or ignored. This is often the beginning of a story rather than the end.

Oso Blanco

Oso Blanco (Byron Shane Chubbuck) is an Indigenous rights activist and anarchist who is currently serving fifty-five years in federal prison for bank robbery (expropriations), aggravated assault on the FBI, escape, and firearms charges. Oso Blanco is a Wolf Clan Cherokee/Choctaw raised in New Mexico whose Cherokee name is Yona Unega. He was known by the authorities as "Robin the Hood" after the FBI and local gang unit officers learned from a confidential informant that he was robbing banks in order to acquire funds to support the Zapatista rebellion in Chiapas, Mexico, throughout 1998–1999.[1] While in prison, Oso Blanco founded the Children's Art Project (CAP), which creates greeting cards with Indigenous prisoners' artwork with all proceeds benefiting the Zapatistas. Oso Blanco has served time in over a dozen federal penitentiaries and supermax facilities across the US. He has published two books, *Love Me Rebel Love Me* (Xlibris, 2011), and *The Blue Agave Revolution: Poetry of the Blind Rebel* with Michael Novick (BookBaby, 2022).

Prison Life

Routine: 4:30 a.m. to 6:00 a.m. prayer in Cherokee. Six a.m. go to breakfast and work. Then eight hours at work. Then to the yard to work out for three

---

1. The Zapatista Army of National Liberation (EZLN) is an Indigenous paramilitary organization based in Chiapas, Mexico, that opposes globalization, capitalism, and neoliberalism. See glossary.

hours. Sweat lodge one day per week. Drum and singing meeting for Natives one day per week, including pipe ceremony. Make calls, check emails. I hate technology; it's all just spy tools for this evil government. At 5:00 p.m. I pray with my eagle feathers and medicine. Then I also pick up the Sacred Pipe to pray for sundown. I must pray with the pipe at sunup and sundown.

I work cleaning up the compound. Blood, bird poop, all types of things. But mostly I go all over looking for birds to help, and other animals. I run an animal hospital in my cell, no joke. Many call me Bird Doc.

I know the Creator, and my ancestors' blood is all warrior blood, so I was happy to be back in prison so I could start working on recovering from being shot in the back by an FBI Gang Unit on February 7, 2001, in Albuquerque, New Mexico.[2] But I've been in prison before, in the 1980s, when it was really dangerous. In the 1980s, it was easy to get killed over any little thing in prison. I've been in the fire. So, yes, I was really mentally prepared. I had family and homeboy support. I still do. But I reject money from various people.

I've never been able to adapt to prison. It's unnatural and foreign to Native/Cherokee people. I'm in a living hell living in this cement coffin. I'm not a lab mouse so I can't ever adapt to this abuse. I'd really be okay if they would give me the death penalty, which would be better than to do thirty more years I have left on this sentence. Prison culture is for foreign people. Natives never master this modern slavery. I hate being in prison, anywhere, at any time. That's why I fight on a life-and-death scale whenever a pig tries to take me to jail.

I lost a lot of people. So, I made a promise to get revenge on the oppressor of my people and destroyer of my land. I'm Cherokee; we have a culture of eye for an eye, tooth for a tooth. "Balance" is our real law and part of our Shaman way. Clan law or the Blood law. We have to pay back those who rob us of our lost people, and I was not there because of the feds and snitches who helped them. So, I live to return the balance to those who robbed me of my life and loved ones' last days.

The quality of life [in prison] has gone down. Yes, way, way down. The feds are worse than ever. Bad, low-grade food, old socks, old boxer shorts,

2. The FBI Gang Unit, also known as the Violent Gang Task Force, pursues "violent gangs through sustained, proactive, coordinated investigations to obtain prosecutions on violations such as racketeering, drug conspiracy, and firearms violations," according to the FBI website. They are known to engage in extreme violence, both inside and outside of prisons.

old T-shirts. I have to buy government-issue cleaning supplies. You can't get medical help unless you're bleeding. These places are like big county jails with no money to run them. The Bureau of Prisons' Central Office in DC is extremely corrupt. It's all a sham and a scam.

What shocked me the most was how many guards seriously assault prisoners and get away with it. And now many break the laws and do illegal things like selling dope, doing dope, robbing our property from our cells, and destroying mail.

My greatest achievement so far has been keeping clean off drugs for twenty-one and a half years and keeping a workout routine that improves my health and mental strength. Without being clean and working out, I'd most likely be dead or in ADX for a killing, since I'm surrounded by negative jackasses galore.[3]

Politics & Prison Dynamics

I've been in about thirty fights, beating up rapists and baby killers, and fights with gangs in Native culture. I won every time except once. The man who won the straight fight was a communist from New York. He was also into using martial arts. He was my cellie, and he was radicalized in prison. But he had a habit of insulting me and Leonard Peltier and our faith in Creator, the sweat lodge, and the Sacred Pipe. So, one day I took it to him and crushed him.

There are gangs in Native culture. They wanted a beef with me in Leavenworth USP. So, it set off years of them getting crushed until they wanted peace in 2009. It was over chomos [child molesters], rapists, or sex offenders. I crush them whenever I catch one (meaning, get around one the COs are not protecting). They slip up, and we get at them sometimes. So, I give the victims justice, if I can get them. What do you think? I'm a warrior above all else.

I've spent a lot of money writing letters over the last twenty-one years. Preaching revolution and being prepared for the fall of this evil empire.

---

3. ADX refers to administrative maximum, or supermax, ADX Florence in Colorado, a secure "control unit" federal prison.

Children's Art Project (CAP) has been a project I've been trying to make happen for many years. Since 2012. Many people told me we would do it but did not come through for many more years. Now it has started, thanks to Josh and Jo and Illy and Sam [founding members of the Children's Art Project along with Oso Blanco] I've collected tribal members' art to enlarge CAP, as they are much better artists than I am, and all are [tribally] enrolled. CAP is a good project, and we are going to help a lot of native kids in Mexico and on reservations up here, in what is called USA, but is truly Turtle Island and Aztlán.

I started writing when I was in second grade. *Shane the Crain Lost His Feather* was my first book, in the 1970s. It's at my mom's house, hidden someplace. I started to read better when I was nineteen and in state prison in 1986. In Colorado, I started to write poetry. For sixteen years I collected works with my grandma, Vinny Stance. This is now my book, *Love Me Rebel Love Me*. But I was unable to read and write very well at all until I was nineteen, in prison. Raising horses and hustling money off the streets was all I knew. I grew up on a horse farm in northern New Mexico, a place called Bloomfield. My mom is from Albuquerque, New Mexico. So that's how I got into the street hustle life.

During lockdowns, I work out, write, create art, use other art to make my own art, and I fight the best I'm able. I did nine years for fighting for my life in self-defense and got sent to the SMU [Special Management Unit]. It was a living hell at Talladega, USP Lewisburg, and USP Florence. Two times I was sent back for 100 percent false charges or set up by the administration and sent back to SMU. Hell on Earth. Most [people] can't understand how bad it really, really was. The COs brutalize you and set you up to fight bad people or your enemies. They torture you with cuff chains and shackles. You are a fish in a bucket, and they love to shoot you in that bucket hundreds of times.

Looking Forward

I made many good relationships with people. Good activists, good Earth defenders, good Native and land rights defenders. A tiny handful stay with me, mostly because I'm not a very nice person to people if I think they're fake, or just posers trying to be cool for the pretty anarchist girls. There are a lot of drive-by anarchists these days. They are mostly out of school now trying to make money to buy a big house and serve the evil bankers and [live] the American Dream. Feel me? They look back now at us rad people and roll their eyes. I'm sure of it. They wrote me from a class setting fifteen years ago, or nineteen years ago, or six years ago; now they have kids, a wife, and don't give a fuck about helping the Earth or Natives.

People can't really understand who have not been in prison. With more than a seventy-year sentence, a whole new reality manifests. People must realize support by *real* folks is a lifeline. Positive, loyal people can mean everything. Yes, there are more powerful works by supporters that can be done. Addiction is destroying all our strength. No unity in poison! Ninety-nine percent are afraid to unite. Racist and old views of segregation of races hurts us.

Don't get high. Don't be foolish, like a child. Don't borrow money or gamble. Don't be a tough guy if you're not sure you're a real badass! Nobody is your friend. Live a spiritual life, not a secular life in here.

I want out! I want to be "free" no matter what so I can continue my work. The answers I gave so far, that's good enough, bro. The details are that I'm in a living hell. If someone gets me out, I'll answer all they want.

Love, OB

Ann Hansen

Ann Hansen stood trial as one of the Squamish Five, members of a radical Canadian anarchist group known as Direct Action who sabotaged government and corporate property in the 1980s.[1] Ann was handed a life sentence but was released from Canada's infamous Prison for Women (P4W) after nearly eight years. She spent over thirty years in prison and on parole and has returned to prison twice for parole violations. Now on the outside, Ann tirelessly continues her abolitionist efforts and continues to inspire younger generations. She has published two books, *Direct Action: Memoirs of an Urban Guerrilla* (AK Press, 2002) and *Taking the Rap: Women Doing Time for Society's Crimes* (Between the Lines, 2018).

Prison Life

My name is Ann Hansen, and back in the 1980s, I was part of a group called Direct Action, and we identified as anarchists. We were preparing for our urban guerrilla campaign for several years, and we were very influenced politically and philosophically by the Indigenous community. At that time, the American Indian Movement was still very much active and part of the

---

1. Direct Action was an underground group of five anarchists in Canada during the early 1980s. Once arrested for their bombings and other actions, the Squamish Five served various prison sentences.

local communities.[2] We were very influenced by Indigenous thinking or philosophy and by anarchists in general. At that time, the prison abolition movement was very strong, and then there was the punk rock movement, and of course, feminism. So, we were influenced by all those people in Vancouver and wherever we'd been.

I had gone to Europe through an independent studies program at the University of Waterloo. I went to study anarchism in Europe and ended up living in a Red Army Faction support apartment in Paris, just through a series of coincidences.[3] I was super-impressed by these people, just the dedication and everything. As time went on, I had a little critique of some of their actions and some of their political philosophy. But even in high school I wrote a paper in support of the FLQ in 1970; I think I was like in grade twelve.[4] I really knew nothing, but I seemed to have this knowledge, even when I was relatively young, that it would be very difficult to make systemic change through reform. I was not a violent person or someone who was fascinated by assassinations and bombings.

So, long story short, Direct Action engaged in a political campaign for several years, and then we were busted. I ended up with a life sentence, but I got out on parole after seven years, which is pretty good. I wasn't a model prisoner. Since then, I've been living in the Kingston area and have done different things, but I am now retired. I've actually rarely had a real job to begin with, but I'm living on a self-sufficient farm.

At the time, there was only one prison for federally sentenced women in all of Canada. People were shipped from up in the Yukon all the way here to Kingston to do their time. It was really difficult for a lot of women.

I spent just under eight years in the actual penitentiary itself, and then my parole was suspended a couple of times. I was sort of making lemonade out of lemons. My parole was suspended, so I had to go back into the federal system. But I got to go to Grand Valley Institution (GVI), which here

---

2. The American Indian Movement (AIM) was founded in Minnesota in 1968 to address police brutality, poverty, and violence and discrimination in Native communities. They organized for treaty rights, self-determination, and the reclamation of tribal land. See glossary.

3. The Red Army Faction (RAF) was a West German underground anti-imperialist organization active from the early 1970s through the late 1990s. The majority of the founding members died tragic deaths while in police custody.

4. The Front de libération du Québec (FLQ) was a militant Québec independence group that carried out several actions in the 1960s and into 1970. See glossary.

in Canada was one of the new federal prisons for women that they built after they closed the Prison for Women (P4W). So, I got to see what these so-called reformed new prisons were really like, twice. Once when they first opened and then another six years later, after they were well underway.

I was a lifer, so according to their regulations they're not allowed to hold you for more than three months. You have to see the parole board within three months. In other words, you're going to serve three months, no matter what. In that particular case, I know it sounds unbelievable, but I'd shown a film on Prisoners' Justice Day [August 10] in the public library.[5] But, it was in conjunction with a lawyer doing a talk on what are your rights in a civil disobedience action. So, for that my parole got suspended and I did three months. Luckily, I had people living with me who could take care of the animals, but it also cost like $4,000, and that was with a pro bono lawyer. It's because I owned a house; we'd bought this house. That's routine procedure. But most people do not get out. Once you get your parole revoked, usually that's it. I have often said that I am privileged in a sense. Because of my history of being with Direct Action, I've always had radical lawyers who've been willing to help me, whereas a lot of social prisoners don't have that privilege. You don't get all kinds of lawyers lining up to do pro bono work. For the average prisoner, if you don't have a lawyer, the odds of getting out are much, much lower than if you have one.

In the Prison for Women, they hadn't developed the kind of technology in the 1980s that they have today, even in the early 1990s. We didn't have any audiovisual surveillance. For a prisoner, that makes a *huge* difference. The Prison for Women could be used as a set for any Hollywood movie that wants to portray a stereotypical prison scene. There were two tiers, the bottom tier with just the bars and then the top tier with a little walkway and the barred cells. At the same time, I was in the same cell for seven years. The women around me were, by and large, there for many years as well. You're living in this little community on these ranges. They have this giant metal door, electronically controlled, that slides open and shut, but it makes a huge amount of noise. So, we knew whenever the guards were coming on the range. We could sort of do whatever we wanted for much of the day

5. Prisoners' Justice Day began in Canada in 1974 as an act of solidarity and is now celebrated internationally on August 10 to support prisoners' rights and to honor those who died while behind bars.

because there were no cameras. There wasn't even any intercom system. It wasn't great, it wasn't like some idyllic place to live, but in retrospect we had privacy.

The Prison for Women also had a woodshop, like a high school woodshop. There was so much corruption. Every spring the CSC, the Correctional Services of Canada, would bring in piles of wood, and it would be gone in a week. It was so blatant. The guards and different people would arrive and carry out all the wood and leave us just enough to make jewelry boxes and typical stuff. We had an upholstery shop within the woodshop, and it was the same thing. All the guards would openly bring in their sofas and chairs to be reupholstered for free by the prisoners. This is how it was.

The Prison for Women was closed in 2000. The prisoners in segregation were acting up, throwing things, and yelling and screaming mainly because the guards had done something. They didn't just keep this up for no reason. They called in the goon squad from the men's penitentiary, which was right across the road from the Prison for Women. It was built in 1835, and the Prison for Women was built in 1934. When they built the Prison for Women, they built a tunnel that went under the road that separates them. So, whenever the goon squad came over—and they came over routinely to quell any kind of disturbance—they would walk through that tunnel. They'd have their batons and their shields, beating on those shields rhythmically as they marched through this round, cement tunnel. The sound would reverberate and increase. For the people in segregation, and even those on the ranges, it's nerve-racking. They could be bringing the dogs over. So, they went into segregation, and they stripped the women with scissors, and they filmed it, which they always do. All of this was routine procedure. They left the women with their clothes cut off lying in their cells hogtied. The windows were smashed, possibly by the women, but it was cold.

In this particular case, the footage which the guards took—they're supposed to keep a record of what was going on—but somehow, someone (and we don't know who, but obviously a sympathetic guard or someone like that) got it out to the TV station, to the CBC, which is like PBS. They aired it, and the public was absolutely outraged. It was like a grainy black-and-white porno film, with these guards dressed up in their black leathers and their helmets, forcibly cutting off these women's clothing, [women] who are screaming and crying in the dark, leaving them hog-tied, and all this. There was a big uproar. The government, of course, had a commission, which they always do to sort of let the pressure off the situation.

As it turns out, they forced the government to say that they would close the Prison for Women and build six new federal prisons across the country, one in each region of Canada. They were really billing it as being six new reformed prisons that would incorporate all these reforms, women-centred, Indigenous-centred, sexual abuse counsellors, and all this stuff. I went there in 2006 when my parole was suspended, and I spent a month or so in a local remand centre. I'm sure it's the same in the States. These remand centres are the worst, where you get stashed until they ship you to a prison. We had three women in a one-person cell, so it'd be like putting three people in a small bathroom. Everybody's coming down off crack in those days, so you're in a cell with at least two other women coming down off crack. It was so overcrowded, even though there were only twenty-four women in the entire women's unit, we had to take turns being locked up—one hour locked in and one hour out.

So, when I got to this new prison, called Grand Valley Institution for Women, I was like, "Wow, this is great." I didn't want to think that, but I couldn't help it. At the time, there were these bungalows, basically houses, and there were ten of them. Then there was the administrative building. There were no guards in the houses. There were ten women in each house, and you could just walk around outside from 8:00 a.m. until 10:00 p.m. You had to go in for count, which was three times a day. I thought, this is really working. All my critiques of reform are just going to go down the drain. It felt like a women's sort of communal collective place, but it didn't take too long to see that this was just a real illusion, although it was not bad in the beginning. To give one example: There's ten women in a house and one of them is designated the cook. But because people are inevitably going to use anything they can as a means of getting drugs, money, or contraband, pretty soon food was a very desirable item. Not to eat, but to trade in. So, the cooks were usually the strongest, toughest women in the prison. You'd be very hard-pressed to find anybody eating roast beef, pork, or steak because they were being traded for cigarettes, which were contraband as well.

I got out in a short period of time because I was just suspended. But then I went back in 2012, and that was a real wake-up call. I was put into the maximum security unit right from the street, for nothing. The parole board even let me out after three months because they had no charges against me. But in every one of these federal prisons, six of them, they had a maximum security unit, which really is another word for Special Handling Unit (SHU). They were small, separate buildings that held roughly twenty women. In the entire building, it would be twenty prisoners, but they'd be separated into what they call pods, which is a typical word now in prison lingo. A pod was just a small unit within the maximum security unit that held five women. Although, as time went on, even when I was in there, they had double-bunking in the pods. You'd have five women in this little, tiny pod and they would have audiovisual cameras, 360-degree video cameras, that were always on, on each end of this range that only held five women. We're talking about intense surveillance. And they have a guard or two sitting down on the main floor, in what they call a bubble. It's just a glass-enclosed room, and all they do all day is sit and watch all these video screens of the three different pods. There were three pods in each maximum security unit. They'd sit and watch what's going on, and you weren't allowed any physical contact whatsoever.

Once you start talking about prison, there's just no end to what you can say. It's just so much bullshit that you can go on for the rest of your life about one story after another. Here's another example. So, this poor woman had basically been in segregation for fifteen years, but they would let her out every now and again, so that it wouldn't look so bad if the media ever got ahold of it. They'd let her into our pod at the time while I was in there. She was so disturbed from having been in segregation most of the time for fifteen years that she was very paranoid. People didn't like her because she would misinterpret everything, and she was a very large, strong woman and was prone to act out. One day, she asked me if I could put on her nail polish because she had a hard time reaching her toes. So, I just sat there and started putting nail polish on, and a loud voice booms out, "No physical contact!" They're threatening to take us to segregation just because I'm putting nail polish on her feet. She has her foot on my lap so I could put nail polish on. Or if you were to hug somebody because they were crying [you could be threatened with segregation].

Obviously, sexual relationships do occur, but you have to know the ropes to figure out how to do that quickly, very quickly. They have the intercom, and the guards are constantly reprimanding people for ridiculous stuff. You could try to lend somebody something surreptitiously. You could open your cell door, which might block their view of you from one camera, so you're hoping they can only watch one while you're trying to give some woman something she may really need. Then, if they see you, you're charged. This is the sort of thing that's going on in the new prisons, having maximum security units which are for anybody, really. If you get convicted of murder, and most women—over half the women—who are in there for murder have murdered someone who they've already reported to the authorities [as] having abused them. In other words, the women have been abused by their husbands or their boyfriends or whomever are the most likely people to be in prison for murder. And they automatically have to spend two years in these Special Handling Units. You don't get off these pods, there's no job, so you're in there all day, except for one hour in a little yard the size of a doubles tennis court. It was a big step down from P4W, where maximum-, medium-, and minimum-security women were all in the same prison, with no audiovisual surveillance, and we all had the same sort of programs and rights and privileges.

I used to say I was lucky. In the second book that I wrote about prison [*Taking the Rap*], I frequently use the word "lucky." I had an editor who is Indigenous, and she pointed out right away that it wasn't luck that I had radical lawyers and a lot of community support in general. It's because I'm a white person and I come off as middle class to people, like parole officers. If you're Indigenous, you don't get the same outcomes, and it's basically just because you're Indigenous and everything that comes with it. Also, I had worked with people in *Bulldozer* [a collective that published prison-related newsletters, including *Prison Legal News*], and I was very involved in the prison abolition movement when I was young.[6]

It wasn't really hard for me to adapt to prison culture. It's sort of funny when I look back on it. There had been a film that had just come out a few years before we got arrested about the Prison for Women by a couple of feminist filmmakers. I don't think they intended to glamorize prison, but they did sort of track these two women, a couple, who were in the Prison

---

6. *Prison Legal News* is a monthly periodical that has been reporting on criminal justice issues and prison litigation since its founding in 1990. *Prison News Service: A Bulldozer Publication/The Marionette* was a prominent prisoner-led abolitionist paper during the 1980s and 1990s.

for Women who just so happened to be attractive young women. It wasn't that they were intending to glamorize the situation; it just sort of happened that way. They weren't given access to the women who were in segregation. So, a lot of the film revolved around their life. I remember myself and other women thinking, "Wow, it's not that bad." Here's this prison, it's all women, and we saw them in the film playing baseball. The gay culture was the dominant culture in prison, and still is, so that appealed to us too. But once I got there, I realized that the dark side had not been shown in that film. I wouldn't blame the filmmakers because I've met them since, and they're progressive feminists. But they weren't given access to segregation. They just didn't get to see the underside of the belly of the beast.

I didn't come out of the juvenile detention centre or have foster home syndrome, but so many prisoners have been in institutions since they were children and have been sexually abused. The history of most prisoners is not a happy one, from childhood on. That's a lot of the reasons why they're in there. Or they're Indigenous and nonwhite populations that have been surviving colonialism and racism. I hadn't gone through all that.

I was shocked by the complete lack of rights. The complete power of the guards and how the whole thing operated. For example, in the remand prison where I first went, they have a very small visiting room; if you had a visit, there might be room for one other person in there. I had noticed that there was this one woman who basically always got heroin at her visits. This is a long time ago, so they're all dead, but I certainly wouldn't name names. But you didn't have to be a rocket scientist to figure out that this woman was getting drugs on her visits, pretty openly. Then, after her visit, her best friends and people that went along with her were all super-high. This was all going on underneath the nose of the warden. That's how the prison was run. That's how a lot of prisons are run.

The wardens and the guards figure out pretty soon which prisoners are not radical by nature but are very powerful figures. It's a bit of a stereotype, but there are times when there's a lot of truth to the stereotype. It doesn't always happen this way, but it's not that uncommon. These people will somehow end up being able to get drugs, whether it's through the guards, because there's always corruption within the guards or just by being a little slack in their visits. They will be used by the administration to crack down on prisoners who could be setting up for some kind of resistance, like a lockdown.

The prisoners who are running the show say stuff like, "What the fuck, you're going to ruin our visits. How are we going to get to see our kids? What the fuck, I haven't seen my kid in months." And that, of course, rings true. That's the sort of thing that'll happen.

I'm not saying this is routine procedure, but I'm saying it does happen in prisons. That's how the administration can run the show, by finding prisoners who will do their bidding without even hardly saying a word. Just the threat of losing their open visits is enough to have that prisoner go back and use family disruption to keep people from resisting. There are all kinds of sneaky ways of keeping resistance from being rampant in prison.

I never really lost hope of getting out. In the beginning, I actually never believed I'd ever get out. I totally adjusted to the prison subculture. I was living with a woman in there, in P4W. Like I said, homosexuality was the norm, and most women who were in there for more than two years would become involved with another woman. There were a significant number of guards who were gay, as well. I just resigned myself to the fact that this was going to be my life. But as time went on, I realized that I was going to get out. I never actually felt as though I did anything special to get out, like I never joined groups, never renounced my political views or anything like that. But as time went on, I had a parole hearing, and I was sent to the minimum [security prison], and eventually I was released.

It was very heartening, the resistance that we had. I found that, as a rule, when you're in prison, people are just like people outside. They're not these people with sophisticated political analyses. So, you don't go in there and expect to be able to just sort of run the show because you're a politicized person. People always seem to think they can go to jail and teach people things and organize this big resistance movement, but it's not that simple. Because most of the people that are in prison have been in some form of prison or another since they were children. Most of the prisoners have been in foster homes, training schools, juvenile [facilities]. If you go in there with this attitude of trying to organize these people and having lockdowns to force them to stop keeping people in segregation for years, the other prisoners are going to very quickly put you in your place. The one thing they've experienced is having people look down upon them and not recognizing their intelligence just because they haven't been to school or they don't have any formal education. They are very sensitive to being treated in a condescending or even patronizing way. Even if you tried to go about it in a way that was humble, I'd say most people who've spent many years institutionalized are *highly* sensitive to that kind of behavior. It's the kind of behavior social workers and parole officers exhibit. Phony politeness.

I can't say that I ever tried to organize a big resistance movement or anything. I remember one year, the guards tried to lock us up early on New Year's Eve at 11:00 p.m. That's the sort of thing that doesn't go over well. So, there was this decision by everybody that we weren't going to go in ourselves until midnight. This just shows how overactive they are to something that is so insignificant. Everybody just said we're not going in until midnight. Nothing bad was happening; everyone was in the common rooms playing their big boomboxes, blasting them and having fun. But all of a sudden, just before midnight, they warn us that if we don't go back in ourselves, they're calling the goon squad. But within seconds of saying that, we could hear them coming through the tunnel; we could hear the dogs and everything. And this is just because we had refused to be locked at 11:00 p.m. But it was a happy moment because everybody stuck together, and nobody went to their cells. Everybody blockaded ourselves in the common room and we had all this furniture up all over the doors and it was pretty cool. Eventually they came in and they filled up segregation, like tripled the people in each cell. But everybody stuck together. There were actually quite a few moments of solidarity like that. That always made me happy. It wasn't because I was political; just whenever there's unity like that—and *any* kind of resistance against that kind of authority—you get a real buzz from it.

Because there were so many Indigenous women, and my girlfriend was Indigenous, I did learn how to make moccasins and stuff, which is enjoyable to do. I worked in the woodshop for many, many years. I really enjoyed that. That's why the Prison for Women was a lot better than the newer ones. The newer ones don't really have much for a person to do all day. We worked out. I did a lot of jogging and stuff and played baseball with outside teams that were brought in. That was always hilarious.

I just want to say, it's hard to talk about prison. On the one hand, our relationships with each other were really great. Of course there were problems, but compared to any other relationships I've ever had—and I'm not the only one that will say this—we have an unusually close-knit group of women. We just had Prisoners' Justice Day here in Kingston, and ten women, we're all old, we came from all over Canada to Kingston to the old Prison for Women site. The Indigenous women organized a healing circle. I have to admit, I am still to this day closer to my best friends who are women I was in prison with at P4W who live here in Kingston. We still hang together all the time and do stuff together. Often when I hear war vets talking, hanging together at the legion, I think it's similar. Because you've been through an experience that's so unique that other people don't understand it. The bonds are so strong because you actually risk losing *everything* to be supportive of a comrade.

Let's say you're going up the stairs and someone's got a bag of sugar that they want to sneak through because they want to be able to put sugar in their coffee—which seems like nothing—but then they can see that they might be searched. So, you say I'll take it through, because you know that woman has a child who they're going to have a visit with, and if they get caught, they lose their visits. So now you may get caught and then you're losing something because of it. Your relationships have much more at stake than you have here in the outside world. On the one hand, there's a danger of making it sound like prison's so great—because the relationships can be so powerful and intense—but the actual conditions in prison are really inexcusably bad, for sure.

It was very, very hard for the woman I was involved with when I got out. I was in the minimum security house, which was right across the road from the prison. I went over to the prison one time to have a new ID photo taken, and she was behind the bars in a part of the prison. She must have known when I was going to be there, and she was all white and very pale. She said she was very depressed. Then she hung herself not long after. I was told it was very traumatic. And she survived, but she had severe brain damage. So, I was on my way out of the system, and I used to visit her at the hospital regularly. She was very brain-damaged. And the worst part of it was that her adopted parents, not her real parents, had told the hospital after a short period of time that they didn't want *anyone* visiting her other than her immediate family. Including the Indigenous elder who went to the prison, or me, or any of us. She was completely alone in the hospital, except for the nurses. It was just terrible what happened to her, that she hung herself and then did not die. She spent a couple of years in Kingston General Hospital, strapped to a chair and unable to communicate. Nobody knew if she could understand anything we were saying. And then they flew her to Saskatchewan where her parents wanted her to be buried. Meanwhile, her family never visited her, the adopted family never visited her. Her brother, who was adopted, visited her once. That's it, in two years. And yet they were very religious people. She died in the plane over Saskatchewan. Everybody always believed that it was some sort of a mystical thing. She had written in her suicide note that she wanted to be buried in a certain place in Saskatchewan by one of the Indigenous women that she was very close to in prison. Maybe all along she knew what was going on but couldn't speak.

The quality of life in prison has gotten worse. It's funny, I wrote an article once for this little feminist paper here in Canada, back in the 1990s, and I was talking about how reform seemed impossible. Yet I found myself over time sort of justifying it with the harm reduction analysis. I have been addicted to opiates for a long time. I've been on methadone for twenty years or something like that. So, I really believe in methadone because when I was an opiate addict, I tried everything: treatment centres, just going to my mom's, the typical cold turkey thing. I could not quit. And I was never abused as a child. I have none of those factors that people usually use to describe why somebody becomes an addict. I had a *Leave it to Beaver* childhood. I could have been in *Leave it to Beaver*. I always consider myself a very lucky person. It's really white privilege. And yet I still immediately loved opiates. In my case, I think it's brain chemistry. And I think the only reason I'm alive today is because in 1998 in Canada, they began opening up methadone clinics, harm reduction clinics. And methadone worked great for me, and it does for a lot of people.

I didn't invent this harm reduction analysis to justify reform. But I thought I did, at first. I was writing about it in the early drafts of that book that I wrote on prison [*Taking the Rap*]. I think many people in the addiction community started making the connections between harm reduction strategies and political strategies. It is difficult to say to people, especially people who really are suffering, that we have to have revolutionary change. We don't even want to talk about improving conditions because that's reform. It's a waste of time. Right? Especially if you're not suffering yourself as a political activist; you're not living with ten people in a two-bedroom apartment and you're not an immigrant from Nigeria. It's a different ballgame for them. They may go, "Are you fucking kidding? My children will be dead before there's a revolution." They'll say that sounds a bit like heaven to me. And

I can relate. It sounds a bit like a religious thing almost. If you believe in God, then you believe there's going to be heaven and we're going to sacrifice everything because we know we're going to go to heaven someday, right?

It's a classic example of reform. They close the Prison for Women because it had been condemned over and over. When they were planning these new prisons, they included the Native Women's Association and the Elizabeth Fry Society, which is reform, but a lot of feminists are involved in it.[7] My first experience of that was positive. When I first went there, I thought, Wow, this could be a feminist commune here. But by 2012, it was just horrible, way worse than before. I didn't even cover how bad it was earlier in this interview. My actual experience of attempts to make reform within the system do not justify it.

Now when I think about it, it's so difficult. Because you don't want to just say to people, "Too bad if you have no food, or too bad if you've been in segregation for two years. We are only going to fight for the abolition of prisons. We're not going to just focus on getting rid of segregation (which they just did here)." The government spent considerable time going over all the rules and regulations involved in segregation in Canada, because notoriously—and I'm sure it's true in the States—there are people who [have] spent years in segregation for nothing. Or for yelling at a guard. And once they're in, they may tell a guard to fuck off and they get another six months. But, no, they do not eliminate segregation; they just made some little tweaks to the system so that they have to review your sentence every thirty days. Or you have to be able to get out more every two days or something. But they didn't eliminate it. It's just the same old thing.

You don't like to say that nothing is worth doing unless it's directly related to revolution. And yet, in fact, that does seem to be the case. I could say that the problem with methadone, the reason I've been on methadone for twenty years, is because when you're on methadone, you don't learn how to cope with your cravings because it takes them all away. So, you end up staying on methadone for a long time because it's very addictive too. I could argue that, yes, I'm still alive and I'm happy because I'm on methadone. But

---

7. The Native Women's Association of Canada (NWAC) is an organization that advocates for the rights of Indigenous and First Nations women and gender-diverse people. The Elizabeth Fry Society is a nonprofit social service agency that provides support for women and girls involved in the Canadian "justice" system.

I never actually conquered my drug addiction. So maybe my original reason for using harm reduction philosophies as a way of justifying reform is based on a false premise. Because even though methadone saves people's lives, for sure, and you feel normal, you don't actually overcome your addiction. You just have a legal drug that you can take every day that allows you to be very functional. And it's free. It's a substitute, but it's not the solution.

I think what shocked me the most was the situation in segregation. It really is shocking. Even in the Prison for Women, the segregation unit was right behind our range. There were two ranges back to back. All that separated us was a plumbing and electrical corridor that ran between our cells. So, we could literally hear everything. One woman, who was mentally challenged, was always in segregation because she would do things like swear at the guards, which she just couldn't not do. She'd say "fuck you," and she had a hard time controlling herself if they were being abusive. And they *were* abusive. She'd start tearing apart her cell, and, as she's doing all this, they're just writing up one charge after another. By the time she's acted out and been really mad, she's in for another year. And these are people who are mentally challenged. This was routine procedure. The people in seg who are there for years are almost always people with emotional issues. It's usually the people who have the least support and people with the biggest trauma issues because they're the least capable of not responding when the guards provoke them. And they just get worse, and it's still going on.

Here in Canada, Ashley Smith was a very young Indigenous woman who was moved around like fourteen times within a two-year period. She deteriorated to the point where she was constantly trying to kill herself. She was under permanent, twenty-four-hours-a-day surveillance because she was constantly trying to kill herself. Eventually, the CSC here in Canada— Correctional Services of Canada—ordered the guards to not go into her cell. She was putting ligatures around her neck, anything, shredding up part of her sheet, just desperate to die. And she did it constantly, so that eventually they sent orders down that they were not to act, not to go into her cell and take off the ligatures unless they really thought she was going to die. One time they waited too long, and she died. They had inquests about it and everything. She was young, only nineteen. It just blows my mind that we live in this kind of a world. If you're going to judge people by how people treat their poor, it's a condemnation. It's just brutal.

Prison changes all the time, [as does] the prison subculture, in any prison. Let's say the person who's running the show is a real asshole and picks on people with intellectual disabilities—a bullying subculture. But we were very fortunate that somehow within this group of women there was this subculture that was against bullying, picking on people who were older, or [people who] had some kind of disability. That wasn't my achievement, but I contributed to it. Lately I've been thinking this is very unusual and great because most of these women are also tending to be activists now too. Even doing interviews is a big deal for women on parole or who have done time. So, I'm very proud of having been part of that period of time in Canadian prison history where a group of women who were all in there together still maintain ties and are actually very progressive.

Politics and Prison Dynamics

You always have a few problems with another prisoner or with the guards, for sure. I mean, I had a few. It's especially the case where you don't know anybody. When I went to the remand centre where there were three people per cell, I remember, I was keeping a little journal, but not using people's real names, or anything really about prison. It was just sort of about my head-space. I knew enough, even at that point, not to write about what's going on. But they searched our cells and took everything out. And one time, one of the guards complained about how many letters I was writing because I'd given them to my lawyer so I wouldn't have to go through censorship, and for him to keep so when I got out, I'd have my memoir stuff. So, I had a lot of trouble with the guard over this. And that guard also happened to be some-body who was giving cigarettes to the prisoners. And there were only about twenty-four women in the unit itself. This guard had manipulated some of the women who were running the show, so to speak. The guard was bringing them cigarettes, or pot joints, or even little letters and stuff. This guard was trying to get them to not like me because she thought I was writing about what she was doing. That really would never be my goal, to eliminate a con-traband source for the prisoners. So, I didn't end up having to fight. But I had to make it clear that if this woman didn't lay off, I was going to beat her up, like I had a fight with her. And she did lay off.

But it's very difficult to go through time in prison without ever being in a situation where you may have to fight with somebody. It's just the way, because there's no cops. Here on the outside, it's very rare that you'd be in a situation where you'd physically fight with somebody, but in prison, you're all over each other. You always have to be ready to defend yourself or align yourself with people who will protect you. It's just reality.

When I first went to P4W in the 1980s, there might have been one Black woman prisoner at any given time, but over the years, the percentage of Black people in prison, relative to their percentage of the overall general population in Canada, has really increased. To put it succinctly, there is a disproportionate number of Black people in prison, as there are Indigenous people. I must say, it's really unbelievable how tough the prison regime is on Indigenous and Black and nonwhite people. I'm a perfect example of that: I'm still classified as one of a very few, classified as a terrorist in Canada. I have parole conditions that oblige me to report anything I say or do that is political in the public domain. Yet, despite being classified as one of a few "terrorists" in Canada, I was released on day parole on my full parole date, which is common for lifers. I was essentially treated as any other lifer would, as opposed to being treated more harshly by the parole board due to my label as "a terrorist." However, I know an Indigenous woman who spent more than thirty-five uninterrupted years in federal prison for allegedly committing two crimes that she did not do.

In order to make my point, I am going to tell you this story without using the real peoples' names and even changing some facts surrounding this case because I don't want to talk about other peoples' real experiences. Let's say there was an Indigenous person who took the rap and pled guilty to a charge that their brother actually committed. Maybe this young woman decided that she would do the right thing and plead guilty to this crime to spare her brother a very long sentence. As a result, she ends up in a federal prison. One thing leads to another, and before you know it, she's in there for twenty years. It is not uncommon for Indigenous people to end up in prison for things they did not do, or they end up doing an inordinate amount of time due to the many aggravating factors that come along with being Indigenous.

It's quite mind-boggling that I, who had a very serious set of charges, and was never a model prisoner, got released on day parole at the usual time any other lifer would. I was not a prison tough, but neither was I a model prisoner. But on the other hand, I was always surprised that I got parole when I did. I attribute my good fortune to the fact that to my parole officers and the parole board, I look like their aunt or their sister or someone else in their circle of friends. I speak like them. I look like them. We share similar life experiences. They're all white people, so they're not going to identify with Indigenous or Black people. Back in the 1980s, the percentage of Black people in the Canadian population was very small. It started to rise in the 1990s with the increased immigration of Black people from South America and the Caribbean. So, there were very few Black people in the Prison for Women. However, roughly 30 percent of the prison population were Indigenous. When you take into account that about 2 percent of the general population was Indigenous, racism was just standing there right in front of you. Like, wow, these people aren't genetically predisposed to be criminals. Very few people are going to use that argument. So how the hell can you justify such a disproportionate number of Indigenous people in prison?

Using transfers as a social control mechanism is a concept that's worth mentioning. It was very important for us that in the Prison for Women—we didn't even realize how important it was at the time—I was in the same cell for seven years, and my neighbours on the range were there for years as well. So, we were able to develop these incredibly powerful relationships and solidarity with one another. In fact, I think in a lot of ways, we influenced what the administration did without even knowing it because there's a lot of things they just wouldn't even attempt to do because they knew that we just wouldn't obey, that we were very tight. Whereas, when I went to GVI, I noticed that people were moved often. In the maximum security unit, the last time I was there, I couldn't believe it. I was transferred twice, and there were only three pods. I noticed that even before I was transferred. One day, one of the five women on our pod was moved to another pod. I thought, "Why the fuck did they move that woman? She was getting along with everybody. Wouldn't it be more disruptive to the guards too, if people don't feel comfortable?" But it was definitely happening a lot.

The whole concept of transferring is true even within prison populations. In my experience in Canada here, it didn't used to be the case that they would move people around constantly, whereas now they do. This guy on the phone, he said that he had been in the cadets in the army when he was young, and they did the same thing. They move them from one hut to the next in order to prevent the guys from developing more unity within their own squad than they had loyalty to their commander. He said it was a conscious thing that was going on in the army to prevent that kind of solidarity amongst the young cadets. And I believe that throughout history, there never used to be so many university departments with criminology, psychology, et cetera. The study of crime and prisons is now rampant. Here in Kingston at Queen's University, they have a whole department that studies prison; they call it Prison Critical Theory. There are a lot of academics, and they're involved as well in prison support work.

Looking Forward

I think support is very important. The people who are in segregation for years are people who don't have a lot of support as a rule. I mean, there are exceptions to that. I think Leonard Peltier, I don't even know where he is now, but I'm pretty sure he was in Marion or one of the really high security prisons for many years, and he had *tons* of support, even from celebrities.[8] That didn't get him out, did it? No. But having support is one of the main reasons that people don't get abused. If they have outside support and a lawyer, it helps. It's extremely important.

It is important to try to develop direct communication with prisoners. I don't know about the States, but it's really become difficult in Canada to even write prisoners. I've tried to write many times to the Inmate Committees even, and my letters haven't gotten through. They've really increased the criteria for writing or any kind of communication. There was a group here in Canada that was operational for many, many years called Joint Effort. It was a women's group in BC, and they would go in every week and visit with the prisoners as a group. They'd do whatever the prisoners wanted. So, if they wanted to do hobby craft, they'd do hobby craft. If they wanted to write letters, they'd write letters. They were very receptive to what the prisoners wanted, which I thought was great. But then all of a sudden, new regulations

---

8. Marion refers to United States Penitentiary, Marion, a former supermax prison in Illinois, the other supermax being ADX Florence. See glossary.

came into effect where in order to be a volunteer group, like Joint Effort, you have to put in an application. People say it's on the same level as applying for a job with the CSC. You have to agree to let them look at your bank history to make sure you don't have any bankruptcies. You cannot have a criminal record. Joint Effort has refused to fill out those forms, so they are no longer going in. Instead, there's this group called Walls to Bridges, which is mainly academics and university students who go in and teach classes. They've had to go through the same procedure, but they're more likely to get in. The women I knew from Joint Effort were real anarchists; they hadn't been to university and were just grassroots people. I'm not trying to be critical here of people who are involved in Walls to Bridges, because I know some of them and they're very good people, especially the women. But let's face it, they're still people involved in university, and it's just a little different.

I know some people here who visit David Gilbert, so he seems to have access, or people have access to him.[9] But it could be that they'd still allow people who are high-profile to have some access, I'm just guessing here, because they know that there would be a lot of pushback since he has a lot of supporters. If he's released on parole, that'd be so fantastic because he's such a great example of someone who's never lost their integrity. I've always admired him; I've read all his books, and he is great [editor's note: David received clemency and was released from prison in November 2021].

I think I also was affected by stereotypes. You don't realize when you go in there how intelligent the women are, or the men. It's very easy to think otherwise because people have not been to school and the way people talk or whatever. But I think when you go into a prison, you really have to see yourself as someone who's got a lot to learn. No matter how educated, no matter how in-depth your political analysis is, no matter how much you believe you know about radical politics, revolution—even if you've got a PhD in anarchism or whatever—when you go to prison, you're dealing with the experts there. It's something you can't read and learn. You have to be there to learn, to know what it's really like.

I think it's very important for people going to prison—and I've said this so many times before—to just shut up, listen, and just observe at first.

9. David Gilbert is a lifelong activist and was a political prisoner for forty years due to his involvement in an expropriation gone horribly wrong. David's story is included here.

Because if you go in there and right away start talking—and I've done this before, because I tend to talk—people don't like that. They see that as arrogant—you obviously think you know everything, and who are you to be sitting there blabbing away while other people are quiet? It is a good idea when you first arrive in prison or are transferred to another prison or part of one, to just shut up, learn and listen, because the people who are in prison are the PhDs of that world and you'd be surprised how much they know. Of course, there's complete assholes in there too. It's just like the outside. But still, it's a totally different world, and you can't just go in there and think you know it. I did think I knew a lot from having visited people and having read so much, but I really didn't know anything.

Sometimes the people who are the least educated are the people who know the most about prison. People can be very compassionate who may not look like they are. You've got to learn a lot before you can go out in a prison environment and try to organize things. You'd be amazed at how many people think they can do that. And you'd be surprised at the shit that they get thrown at them from people. Within hours the people can smell it; they can just smell somebody who thinks they're smarter than them. And there's nobody to hate more than people who think they're better than them because that's who they've dealt with their whole life. Social workers and cops, and that's the category they put you in if you act like that when you come in. So, lesson one is just shut up, learn, and listen.

Sean Swain

Sean Swain has been held without legal conviction or sentence since 1991 for the self-defense killing of a court official's relative who broke into Sean's home and threatened his life. In 2012, prisoners calling themselves the Army of the 12 Monkeys (A12M) rebelled at Mansfield Correctional Facility. The prison authorities assumed that anarchist Sean Swain must have been behind it (an assumption Sean denies) and threw him in supermax isolation. While in prison, Sean became a jailhouse lawyer and in recent years converted to Islam. Sean has served over thirty years in prison, mainly in Ohio state prisons, though he has also been shipped to Virginia state prisons. He is a member of the Fire Ant Collective.[1] Sean has self-published numerous zines and has written three books—*Last Act of the Circus Animals* (with Travis Washington, Little Black Cart Books, 2017), *Ohio: The Truth behind Bob's Lanes* (Little Black Cart Books, 2021), and *Opposing Torture* (Little Black Cart Books, 2022).

Prison Life

I was *not* mentally prepared for prison. In fact, no one was ever less mentally prepared. I was twenty-one years old and a noncriminal and had spent only a

---

1. *Fire Ant* is a publication focused on spreading the words of anarchist prisoners, generating material solidarity for them, and fostering communication between anarchists on both sides of the walls.

total of thirty days in the county jail. I arrived at the prison in complete shock and didn't identify with the criminals and degenerates surrounding me.

I didn't have a hard time adapting to the prison routine because I refused to adapt. I was in denial. I wasn't guilty, so I knew I was just passing through. I attempted to stay invisible as the prison complex functioned around me. I saw the system as legitimate and saw criminals as deserving of punishment, and I thought of my conviction and imprisonment as an anomaly that would be corrected; this view was reinforced when my conviction was reversed and I was remanded for a retrial.

What opened my eyes to the true nature of the system was the conduct of the court when I returned for trial—and the court did everything possible to tilt the scales and guarantee my conviction. When I was found guilty again—a foregone conclusion, given the court's conduct of the case—the prosecutor said, loud enough for me to hear, "It takes a good prosecutor to convict a guilty man; it takes a great prosecutor to convict an innocent one. I got this guy twice; what's that make me?"

So, this became a critical disjuncture where I finally awakened to the reality that this larger system was not mine, that I was disposable to it, that my allegiance and loyalty had been misplaced, and that I had far more in common with the rabble I had so long believed to be beneath me. I accepted the possibility that those with distrust for this system, who rejected its authority with their actions, might know something that I did not, rather than believing I knew something that they did not.

A transformation occurred for me as I began recognizing some fundamental truths about why the world operated as it did, and I began sensing that I had been duped, tricked, manipulated by a false narrative I had accepted without question, and I allowed myself to be open to the humanity around me. It was, in that sense, my own humanization. I no longer assumed my experience to be the only valid one and sought to understand the truths of those whose experience was greatly different than my own.

I am always hesitant to reminisce about the good old days of prison. But there are two eras. In the 1990s at Mansfield, there was a really progressive administration. Wardens had power, and central office hadn't yet created cookie-cutter standards. Wardens could run their own prisons.

At Mansfield, we had an inmate liaison committee we elected who acted like the warden's cabinet, proposing rule changes. We had food and clothes boxes, where family could shop and send in the boxes from home. Visits were very lax. Security staff didn't hassle anyone getting a tattoo or being in others' cells playing guitar or even smoking pot or drinking hooch. I remember an officer who paid a prisoner for tattoo work, and we had to watch out for supervisors so they wouldn't get caught. We had a program during the holidays where we could order food from Kroger [a supermarket in the US] off of an order list that was dozens of pages long. We had a celebratory yard day and fair day with all-you-can-eat burgers and hotdogs, bags of chips and sodas, with live bands and boxing matches. One time, they let in bikers with motorcycles lined up on the recreation yard for us to check out. Men and women, and some of the women were not exactly dressed to meet visitation standards of proper attire. All of that is different now. It's an era of centralized control.

It's easy to remember the good from that previous era. But, if we're being honest, I also have to tell you about going into the gym bathroom to take a piss and hearing the sounds of a rape occurring in the toilet stall. Or watching a guy get his throat cut in the commissary line and stepping outside long enough for the porter to mop up the blood before we got back in line, blood dripping from the ceiling. Or the big kid with a learning disability getting wheeled out on a gurney, lying on his stomach, a paintbrush broken off in his rectum. It was an era when I learned not to run when a stabbing happened in the chow hall, because you just had to turn your back to it and lean over your tray to keep blood from getting in your food. No sense running as the victim was already selected—and it wasn't you. That's no longer the norm. Greater control also equates with far less serious violence and predation.

So when anyone waxes reminiscent about any era of captivity, I always like to challenge them to remember the whole picture. Even me.

I have many times been ten thousand miles in the mouth of the graveyard. All hope is lost. I experienced a year of torture, slowly starving to death in freezing cold, denied soap and contact with the outside world, subjected to months of sleep deprivation and really creative torments—including days of dirty toilet water raining down on everything in the cell.

There are a few things I did to try getting through all of it as whole and functional as possible. First, when it feels overwhelming, remember: it's supposed to. That's the point. It's why your enemy does it. They employ all of the torments upon you that they know would break them if they were subjected to the same torments. So, each torture employed reveals a little about the weaknesses and vulnerabilities of your enemy. Second, it's all temporary. It feels like it will go on forever. It won't. And so, you don't have to endure a year of whatever condition . . . or a month . . . or a week. You just have to survive through today. Just today. And you know you can do that because you survived yesterday. In that sense, I didn't survive a year of torture; I survived one hour of it . . . twenty-four times in the course of a day . . . and I survived a day of it . . . 365 times.

Third, I reminded myself that I didn't have a choice. I could either survive or else surrender and sit down on the curb and, sooner or later, the dogs and birds would eat me. I couldn't surrender and sit down on the curb and let the dogs and birds eat me because I didn't own me; too many others did. They were invested in me with love and blood and sweat and tears, and I owed it to them to get through everything by whatever means. Which leads to the fourth principle—I wasn't alone. I reminded myself of everyone who was with me, at least in spirit.

None of us are ever alone. Others are with us. We're together in the same space—just kinda far apart. Sometimes miles. But together, just the same, because my struggle is our struggle; your struggle is our struggle; her struggle and his struggle are our struggle. I imagined their faces, I spoke their names, I included them in my daily routine. Our enemy doesn't confront a solitary individual. The enemy confronts an army. And again, when it feels hopeless and endless, it's supposed to. That's how the enemy designed it. But it's not. It's not.

Exercise personal power to whatever degree you can. Determine the purpose of what you endure and how you can use this experience. Determine to continue resisting in creative forms. Give the experience meaning. How can you use this to help others? Never sink into, "Why me?" Always remind yourself, "Why *not* you?" Better you than someone else, someone who would break, would surrender, would submit to the forces of self-murder and oblivion.

I've been ten thousand miles in the mouth of the graveyard. I crawled out, foot by foot. I'm not exceptional; what I can do, you can do. You'd be surprised at the shit you can crawl through and make it out alive.

There are millions of little victories. When Anthony Rayson first published my writings, I actually cried. When friends developed *seanswain.org*; when LBC [Little Black Cart] published *Last Act* and then *Ohio*; when the

Final Straw radio show interviewed me and then invited me to contribute regularly; when friends and supporters rallied to raise funds for counsel to protect me from the evils of the oppressor. All of these had meaning to me and brought me a sense of gratitude because each instance was a situation where others truly valued me and gave me the chance to make a difference in their lives and in others' lives.

My dad died last March [2020]. He had been diagnosed with serious heart trouble the previous October, but no doctors were in a rush to get him to surgery. By the time he had a bypass, his heart muscle had sustained too much damage. The elderly get ignored. If I had been home, they wouldn't have done that to him. I wouldn't have allowed it. He might still be alive. I think of the years my communications were silenced while he was alive, years I missed him. I think of all the denials of parole that kept me from being home for him. My dad was a really incredible guy. I miss him every day. I found out [he died] in a call from my mom. We spoke and cried. Then I went on with my regular routine, sitting in the day room and writing, conversing. My dad would want me to continue doing what I do. If it was important enough to do it when he was alive, it means even more to do it when he's gone. I loved him. He knew that. I still do, and I honor him with everything I do. Those we lose only live on through us. We manifest them with our actions, our memory.

I also lost someone I cared for very deeply. My friend Ihsan suffered great injustice and trauma and had lasting struggles with brain injuries. It became more and more difficult for her to manage her life, and others had her hospitalized . . . and we lost contact. She died four months later of an overdose. Again, I have to wonder if I had not been in prison but had been out there in the world, perhaps I could have been an advocate she needed, and maybe she would still be alive. I don't know.

Everything is relative with quality of life. We have phone tablets and email, movies on disc played over the institution movie channel. The medium prison in Virginia I just left had great pizza on Wednesday. But there's also a danger in comfort. Comfort is not freedom, and too often we confuse them. I see prisoners routinely who have forgotten this is prison, who have given up struggling for freedom and have accepted relative comfort. When that happens, when enough prisoners surrender to comfort, collective freedom becomes impossible.

Maybe the most shocking thing is how un-shocking all of it is. The mundanity of human captivity, how it grinds along. After this experience, having strangers look up my asshole, having my head open steel doors while I'm cuffed and helpless, watching someone dive off the second floor railing onto linoleum and seeing everyone stare at the growing blood puddle, hearing guards talk about sports while kicking a food tray under a rusty cell door, with metal and bug corpses falling into the food, seeing guards unleash a billy club attack and snap someone's arm, the routine commonness of all of it. I can imagine passengers stepping off cattle cars between rows of Nazis, stripping naked, accepting bars of soap and stepping into the linoleum-tiled room. I can imagine those Nazis discussing the soccer game or their wives' cooking, can imagine them going home to laugh and play with their kids after dropping the Zyklon B canister into that linoleum-tiled room, after dragging out the bodies while complaining about the cost of auto repairs. I can see the bored looks on their faces as they inspect the bars of soap they pick up off the floor and put back into the box, waiting on the next train and exchanging humorous tales of binge-drinking excursions, looking at the sky and pondering whether it might rain while kicking a corpse into the mass grave. The shocking thing, maybe, is how routine, how uneventful atrocities can be.

I hope there are small things I've done—stuff I wrote or said—that made some kind of difference in someone else's life. I don't necessarily know what those were. But those people do. A famous dead guy, Gabriel García Márquez, once wrote that being a revolutionary is like "plowing the ocean." Hard to see the results of your work. I'm not a home run hitter. I'm more of an on-base percentage kind of guy. Hopefully my singles add up to something.

Politics and Prison Dynamics

Prison or not, we all have to ask ourselves, "Is this something I can live with?" And I find the folks I emulate generally had longer lists of shit they would not do than the profiteers and opportunists I despise. A question for us all: can I keep contributing to this swivelization program murdering our planet and our future? If the answer is no, then you have character—and probably a lengthy FBI file. So do I.

It used to be that when you arrived at a new prison, someone would try you—demand protection payment or pick a fight over nothing or call you a bitch to provoke you. How you respond proves if you are solid or not. But now, for me, it's not prisoners trying me, it's a warden or prison investigator who looks at my file and thinks he or she can break me when everyone else failed.

Then I make that idiot famous, draw a cartoon of him fucking a dog, give her a nickname that sticks with her coworkers, talk about them on the radio or online, and their phones go nuts, and the fax machines fling out death threats, and someone posts a home address and then smashes a windshield. You can't stop the first idiot from trying me. But you can stop the second and the third and the fourth, when they see what you did to the first one. That goes for wardens and directors as much as for gang bangers running the cell block.

I made a conscious decision early on to be who I am. I won't be anything else, won't pretend to be. I associate with people I respect, and I value opinions of people I respect. Everyone else can fuck off. I don't need their approval. I'm not adhering to anyone else's sense of what I ought to be or who I should avoid. No one is entitled to an opinion, particularly a racist.

There's no such thing as an apolitical prisoner. The state is a political construct; judges hold political office; prosecutors make political choices; criminal laws are passed by politicians. The act of caging a human being is a political one. To violate law, to say, "I am above the state rather than the state being above me," is a political act. All prisoners are political. Some are more consciously so.

I have been accused of political work. Prison officials have, since 2008, accused me of encouraging a work stoppage, leading three riots, threatening the entire work force of the prison system—twice extorting prison officials—twice promoting "terrorist-type activities," arranging for all prison employees' home addresses to be posted online, conspiring to use drones to drop guns into the prisons, plotting to blow up the Ohio statehouse, and committing incalculable numbers of unauthorized group activities.

I have challenged Ohio statehood in international court as a way to expose the invasion and colonization that passes as settlement and legitimate authority, *Swain v. United States*, in the Inter-American Commission on Human Rights (IACHR), Case No. 14.146. I have two books in print and a third on the way (exposing the domestic torture program employed in the US) and years of radio segments. The FBI monitors my segments and publishing, and I have over four thousand pages of FBI files, only a few hundred of which are not related to ongoing investigations. It seems that those in power think I'm involved in political activity. I will, in this one instance, uncharacteristically defer to them.

As for the violence, I find that prison violence is rarely random. It's virtually always foreseeable if you're aware of what others are doing and to whom. In fact, random violence is more prevalent out there. School shootings, folks driving down parade routes, road rage, drive-bys, random attacks, cops and vigilantes gunning down protesters.

If I had things to do over, and if I could change anything, I suspect I wouldn't give prison officials so much credit. What I mean is, I know my rights. I know what the courts say. But prisons are run by bullies in suits who don't read and who solve all problems by pounding them with a hammer. Don't ever expect them to apply reason. They can't. Don't appeal to their sense of justice. They don't have one.

The same generally applies to the entire apparatus of the state. If you want to protect and insulate yourself from harm, in all of your dealings with the state, from the clerk at the Department of Motor Vehicles to an audience with the president, don't suppose yourself to be interacting with a human being but, instead, imagine that State representative to be an armed concentration camp guard holding pliers they just used to yank a gold tooth out of a corpse's head while holding a coffee can full of teeth as they look into your eyes to ask you what you want. Attribute to that State representative all of the moral and intellectual characteristics you would think that concentration camp guard to have. It helps you maintain healthier expectations.

Looking Forward

Outside support has saved my life, quite literally. My captors would have killed me—and in fact plotted to kill me—if not for responsive supporters outside exposing the plot publicly. Even now, my path home winds through outside support who magnify my voice and gather funds for counsel and coordinate on my behalf. On at least some small level, officials know the eyes of the world are watching, and I imagine that tempers their abuses and repressions to some degree.

Advice for anyone involved in support work: the worst thing you can possibly do is to say "yes" and to do "no." That's important to remember before you say yes. For me, I would rather hear you say, "No, I can't do it," and then give me the chance to find someone who can and will get it done, rather than you tell me "Yes, I've got that" and then not do it, or else get it done too late to be of benefit. "No" doesn't hurt my feelings. Unfulfilled "yes" hurts my chances.

So, it is important in support work, I think, to distinguish between all the important work you want to get done if you could click your heels and make a wish, and the projects you can reasonably and realistically get done in the midst of real-life demands. And if ever you say yes to a project and discover you can't get it done right and on time, speak up as soon as you figure out you can't do it and maybe help find an alternative. Will anyone be mad? Maybe. But it's better than letting the project not get done or slapping something together. There are, of course, realistic limits.

If the goal is to get prisoners out, that's a simple process. There's a SEAL team composed of otherwise ordinary Americans who went to Pakistan, infiltrated an armed compound, got Osama bin Laden, and left. They're not superhuman. They're not ten feet tall or bulletproof. In fact, anywhere in the world, institutions of captivity are constructed to keep people in, not to keep people out. If there's a dedicated cadre of outside support who really want to get a captive out, there is no security system that can account for all of the various strategies that that cadre can employ. Period. That's just the reality.

But when we talk about getting captives out, we don't mean using drones or helicopters, guns or explosives. We mean appeals to the captors' courts or arranging presentations to their parole boards, and those are processes that are more complex and necessarily involve recognition of State legitimacy and authority, and probably involve a requisite "snivel-fest"—some kind of admission of guilt and implicit rightness of the State response to crime, and so on. This involves groveling to the armed concentration camp guard—with the bloody pliers and the coffee can full of molars—to do the right thing. He's holding a coffee can full of the results of prior such appeals. I know. I've had too many encounters with him myself. Some of my teeth are rattling around in there.

And, again, realistic limits. There's a difference between direct action and its predictable results and reformist appeals with their unfortunately predictable results.

I don't think the process [of abolishing prisons] has started. I say this not as a critique but as an observation. If you want to tear something down, you get a sledgehammer, you get the tools for tearing it down; you don't show up with a picket sign or a petition or a bullhorn. Nobody ever tore anything down with a bullhorn. That's not to say those aren't useful tools for what they do. They are. So if you want to raise consciousness and gain popular support and so on, those are useful. But that's not tearing anything down. I think if you want to tear something down, if that is your goal, then you have to focus on the question of how to tear it down—not the question of how to get others to agree with you. Tearing it down is a simple process.

An analogy. I don't know how a computer works. But I know how it doesn't work. If I want it to not work, I don't need computer science classes. I need a screwdriver to leverage the panel off so I can rip out the wires. I don't know what the red wire does or the green wire. I don't give a fuck. I'm yanking. And then the computer doesn't work. It's not brain science or rocket surgery. This goes for any complex system. See how it works. Interrupt its process. Very simple. But to achieve it, we must first think about it as a goal and talk about it and work toward it.

If enemy terrorists had an armed base I wanted to shut down, I could directly assault it and take losses. That's one approach. Or I could locate its external warehouse where it stores its instant potatoes and toilet paper, and I could burn it to the ground. The enemy won't last long without potatoes, without toilet paper. That's just one vulnerability. We could identify a dozen in seconds and develop a strategy for attack. But, again, there are realistic limits. There are powerful deterrents. If only we transcend those, we could easily succeed.

Change never happens as a consequence of unity or by majorities taking action. It's always the minority, the small number of dedicated radicals who create change and do so through radical means.

If coming to prison, be genuine. Be yourself. Don't try to be someone you're not. Other prisoners will sniff you out in no time. Be cautious. Don't loan or borrow. Be aware of your surroundings, but don't let on that you know anything. Set clear boundaries with others and enforce them.

Imprisonment is a question of geography. Your carcass is on one side of a fence instead of the other. But there's no magical barrier between the world and you. You didn't get blasted to Mars. You're the same person you were on the outside of the fence, and it's not impossible to continue social and political engagement, to continue impacting the world from wherever you are.

The world is burning. You have a responsibility to stop it, and prison doesn't give you a free pass to opt out. You know how capitalism creates disparity and victimizes the poor? Yeah. Well, here they are. Say hi. You know how structural racism hurts real people? Yeah. Well, here they are. Say hi. You know how the educational system lets too many fall between the cracks? Yeah. Well, here they are. Say hi.

Henry David Thoreau, a famous dead guy, said that in an unjust society, the only place for a just person is in prison. Congratulations. You finally arrived. Get to work.

Martha Hennessy

Martha Hennessy is a peace activist and member of the Catholic Worker Movement, which was started by her grandmother, Dorothy Day.[1] Martha has been imprisoned multiple times for her protests against nuclear weapons, drone strikes, and the torture being carried out at Guantánamo Bay by the US government. Most recently, Martha was imprisoned for taking direct, nonviolent, faith-based action for nuclear abolition at the Kings Bay Naval Base in southern Georgia on the fiftieth anniversary of the killing of Dr. Martin Luther King Jr. on April 4, 2018. Martha spent five months at the women's camp at Danbury Prison in Connecticut and then two months in a halfway house in Manchester, New Hampshire, for her involvement in the Kings Bay action. In the 1980s, she spent three months imprisoned at the Brentwood Women's House of Correction for her protests against the Seabrook Nuclear Power Plant in New Hampshire. She also spent a week in prison at the Onondaga Justice Center on two different occasions for her protests against the drone program at Hancock Airbase in Syracuse, New York. Martha has also spent time in the DC central jail for her protests of the torture at Guantánamo.

---

1. Started by Dorothy Day and Peter Maurin in 1933, the Catholic Worker Movement has autonomous groups of nonviolent adherents around the world who live in accordance with the teachings of Jesus Christ and who participate in civil disobedience to bear witness to state violence. See glossary.

Prison Life

In prison, everything is dictated to you: what you eat, what you wear, what you do each day. It's very regimented and yet very dead of things to do and a lot of downtime. But I worked in the library. I refused to do any kind of paid work because I refuse to pay restitution for the nuclear weapons. I took up knitting. They had a guitar there, so I was able to keep up a little bit with my guitar skills. I had a very large mail correspondence.

I tried to help other women as much as I could. That included talking to people on the outside, getting phone numbers, getting names, getting information. Danbury does hold the Vermont federal women prisoners, so there were a couple of women there trying to work with Bernie Sanders's office, just trying to get information and justice.

With Seabrook I would say no, I wasn't prepared. But for Danbury, I definitely was. I had never served jail time with Seabrook, and it was a county jail right next to the nursing home (two industries). But I was with two other women, and I don't remember it being a terribly traumatic transition, other than being separated from my two-year-old son. That was very hard. But with Danbury, I knew what I was in for. But just the same, all those bars and all that razor wire still is very shocking.

At Danbury, because of COVID, there were no family visits. They were starting to do that just as I was leaving there. My support team was absolutely wonderful; the King's Bay Plowshares support team has been amazing.[2] With most Plowshares actions, it is an amazing community that comes together. Even in Manchester, New Hampshire, at the halfway house, I ended up with a local support group there. It's just fabulous.

I think the hardest thing for me was all the swearing. The cursing on the part of the prisoners and the staff, it's horrible. And the food, the food was very hard to adjust to. But I'm a very well self-regulated, organized person, and I just sort of went right into the routine. I was in quarantine, and I was being held in a cell that had no toilet. I was being held in the place where they bring people in and discharge people from. It was not at all intended

---

2. The Plowshares movement consists of Christian pacifists who protest against nuclear weapons and war. The name refers to the prophet Isaiah who said that swords shall be beaten into plowshares. Many Plowshares activists are jailed for their civil disobedience. See glossary.

for long-term, and I was there nine days. That was pretty miserable. But the human being adapts to amazingly awful things.

She [Dorothy Day] was still alive when I did my three-month stint for Seabrook. A lot of the folks from the Catholic Worker Movement in New York were actually doing prison time too, for the same reason, so she was very much aware, very supportive. I wrote her letters. That was toward the last year of her life, so it was not easy for her to stay in touch with me. But I don't remember ever asking her explicit questions about her experience in DC with the suffragists. I think that was the worst, where she was physically brutalized, like many of the women during that time.

I think a really important skill that I learned was listening, just listening to other people's stories. Those stories gave me moments of great sorrow and also moments of joy as well. One woman, her father was very much into the labor movement and workers' rights, and sitting and hearing her stories was fabulous.

Prisons keep getting worse; everything deteriorates. Back in 1980, this is before I had my training as an occupational therapist, I knew the women that I was with had these special needs that were not being met. And then that became even more apparent with my week-long experiences at Onondaga Justice Center. The women of color, the Indigenous women, the racism, that's why they were there, because of who they were. I do remember in New Hampshire in 1980, there was a woman that they brought to us from Concord State Mental Facility; she was actively psychotic and that was just a real eye-opener for me to see what was not done for her. Most recently, at Danbury, the pill line is really long; everybody's getting their psychotropic meds. People definitely deteriorate. One woman had a heart attack. Luckily, the CO who happened to be on—corrections officer, not conscientious objector—the CO just happened to be a person who was intact and paid attention. At the halfway house in Manchester, it was damaged people, both residents and staff. As far as deterioration goes, there were guys at the halfway house who didn't have their ID papers in place, and so they couldn't work, and they were simply sitting there. It was so unnecessary, so unnecessary. The basics were not being provided for people. The mental deterioration is very clear. I was able to see it and understand it better because of my training as an occupational therapist.

I think that my choice of vocation [as an occupational therapist] was certainly influenced by my mother and my grandmother. You don't push papers, you don't sit at a machine, you work with people. Reading the curriculum really resonated with me, and I thought, "Oh, I love that combination of psychology and manual arts and independence, trying to gain independence after injury." All of those appealed to me, so, yeah, I think I chose the vocation based on the examples that my mother and grandmother set for me.

I think the lack of recognizing us as humans is the most shocking thing. This whole creation of a system where the sole, single goal is to punish and to criminalize. People are more than just what their charges were. My situation was different. I mean, I was kind of like a "volunteer" walking into that. The dehumanizing I found to be just so, so shocking. One woman tripping and falling and fracturing her elbow, and the way they treated her. They didn't give her care, and that was incredibly painful to watch.

For those incarcerated, we end up policing each other in really bizarre ways because of the use of collective punishment. You don't want to put yourself at risk, and so community is deliberately broken down. I mean, the women are very strong and do support each other in many ways, I found at Danbury. But that can go only so far, where people just start policing each other, and there are snitches and all of that.

Politics and Prison Dynamics

Prison conflicted with my personal ethics constantly. To give you concrete examples, let's take smoking. I hate cigarette smoke. I hate this corporate ripping out of people's lungs for profit and people doing it to themselves, and it just infuriates me, and I get militant about it. No, I don't want to breathe cigarette smoke. But there were women who were keeping themselves together with at least feeding that one addiction. I would complain when I stepped out the door, and it was all illicit, of course. I felt like I couldn't defend myself. And it was much more acute at the halfway house, where they were smoking in the bathroom because we were not allowed outdoors at all. I wanted to complain, and I didn't want to breathe the smoke, and I was putting them at risk. So that was a real issue.

At one point at two o'clock in the morning, we were all lined up against the wall because someone had dropped contraband off at the assistant warden's house. They got the wrong place! And he woke up infuriated, and he came, and he punished us and took it out on us, and he was awful. One of us actually fell to the floor and fainted because she was woken up really quickly. She was on these particular meds, so she just passed out. Then after a while, I started feeling sick. And I didn't know what to do because I thought, if I tried to defend myself, it's just going to make it worse for everybody else up against the wall. So, there are dilemmas constantly.

And also talking about nuclear weapons to some of the other prisoners and guards and talking about Catholicism. For the most part, people understood immediately who I was and why I was there. But there were other people who were just defending the status quo, and that really challenged me in terms of, "Okay, Martha, are you going to evangelize in a way that people can hear you, or are you just going to piss people off?" So that was a real challenge. I tried to evangelize more than piss people off. They all understand systemic oppression.

I experienced ageism more than racism for some funny reason. But, yes, once we started eating in the cafeteria together, everybody self-segregated. I ended up at the table with all the white blondes, bleach blondes, and I thought, "I'm not doing this." They actually invited me to it. I ended up just rotating tables with different meals to try and break it up, to make the point that I wasn't sitting at the whites-only table every single time. The women knew me; I was so mouthy, they tolerated me in many ways. I was like one of the oldest there. People were good about not giving me a hard time. It could have been much worse. As far as ageism, the young people wouldn't take the time to listen to you. They interrupt you. That happens a lot anyhow, but they just couldn't and wouldn't relate to me. Also, with this ear tumor, I wear a hearing aid, and the hearing is always a difficulty. One woman—whom I actually got very close to because she had never been in prison and she was just barely holding on to her emotional stability during quarantine—she was from Bangladesh, and at one point she was ridiculing me because I wasn't hearing things properly. But she had great respect for me. But there are other US women for whom the culture does not respect the elderly. And so, I did experience some of that.

I was imprisoned with Liz McAlister for two months down in Georgia.[3]

---

3. Elizabeth McAlister was Martha's codefendant in the Kings Bay Plowshares action. Her story is included here. Clare Grady, mentioned in the next sentence, was also a codefendant in

At Camden County Jail, Clare Grady and Liz and I were in the same cell. Clare [slept] on the floor. Then in Glenn County, I was with Liz briefly, and then they moved her to another pod. They intentionally separate codefendants, but at Camden County they couldn't.

I worked in the library, and my case manager's little office was right next to the library, and I found this picture of Abu Ghraib, where the prisoner was standing on the box with the hood over his head—a classic CIA torture scenario—and I took the book next door and put it right in the face of my counselor, my case manager. He said, "I don't remember that. I was in high school." And I said, "Yeah, that's why I'm showing it to you. This is our history." So, every chance you get you try to make these points. Anytime I saw a head honcho coming through—once they came right into the library, and I just immediately started proselytizing about the books that I was bringing into the library and how this prison complex industry needs to be talked about. People got tired of listening to me, that's for sure.

At the halfway house, I kept announcing Daniel Hale getting four years in prison.[4] I don't know if I converted anybody. I think they understood where I was coming from; they appreciated the fact that I felt freed up to speak my mind, but, as far as converting anyone, I don't know. Then there is this whole question of Christianity. There was this book on the shelf by General McRaven called *Make Your Bed*, and he's an extreme right-wing warmonger. I put together prayer groups in the morning to do the daily readings, and I had a discussion with one of the people I was with about that particular book and what he was saying. It was rough. When she first heard that I was the granddaughter of Dorothy Day, she got all excited, and her husband was a cradle Catholic. She asked him to send the two books, *The Long Loneliness* and *The World Will Be Saved by Beauty*, one by Dorothy and one by Kate Hennessy, my sister. The moment she started reading these books, she realized what she was in for and couldn't talk about it anymore. Similar to my experience at the induction of Dorothy Day at the Women's Hall of Fame: my hosts were all excited, but the moment they heard her words, it was like,

the Kings Bay Plowshares action, and she has done numerous stints in jails and prisons for her actions against military and nuclear targets.

4. Daniel Hale is a former National Security Agency analyst who leaked drone warfare intelligence information to the press and was sentenced to forty-five months in prison in July 2021 for violating the Espionage Act.

"Oh my God, that's what this is about?" And they couldn't go there. They jump on the bandwagon when they think they're onto somebody who people love or like, and then they realize it's not their politics.

Without my faith, I would have been more bitter, I would have been more angry, I would have been cursing a lot more. We have the example of Jesus trying to heal people, hanging out with the lowest, the supposed lowest of society. There you are, with drug addicts, with mothers who have abandoned their kids, mothers who were separated from their kids and they want to take care of their kids, just terrible situations. The faith component of it, that's the tradition that I come from, conscientious objector, Catholics in action. No, I would not have had the presence of mind or stamina without that kind of background.

Looking Forward

When you're on the phone, let the prisoner talk. That's pretty important. Outside support is critical, crucial. I just learned so much about how corrupt prosecutors and lawyers are, my God. My support people were wonderful, just absolutely wonderful. Not everyone in my family fully understands my faith journey, never mind this nuclear resistance journey. But it's really, really important to give the prisoner room to express themselves. Make sure they have enough stamps and envelopes. Make sure that you know somebody is staying in touch with them, so they feel like they're not totally, completely abandoned. Support is so critical. The BOP has billions of dollars to work with to keep this horrible system in place. We need to seize those dollars from the BOP and use them to get these women back to their families, to get them housing, jobs training, and childcare. It's just outrageous the way the money is being used to punish and to kill and torture, instead of taking care of people.

All of this is very preventable. All of the huge prison population is an absolute result of capitalism. Capitalism makes sure that we have illness, that we have sickness, mental and physical. Capitalism is feeding all of this, and that just so desperately needs to be changed. But I really indict the media; they're just not doing their jobs. Even if it's one tiny, little voice saying no to the insanity, it's worth it. The mainstream media is bought off.

There is solidarity, but everybody is so fragmented, and they're just trying to survive their day-to-day lives. Prisoners desperately need a Dan Berrigan to walk amongst them, to organize them, even just to start with a prayer group.[5] I wasn't good enough at that. Even some of the prisoners who really were in solidarity with each other were willing to work with the staff in ways that didn't help prisoners. That's a really, really tough thing, really tough thing. I don't know if we could do some kind of infiltration project to get political prisoners in to help organize on the inside. That's really, really needed, but it's so risky, it's so brutal. We have people who were definitely designated as snitches and were treated as such.

Hold on to your humanity and realize that you don't have to scapegoat each other. At a certain level, that is innate and that does happen. It's incredible how some people go through that system and come out okay and don't ever come back. There are stories of that level of so-called success. But in terms of advice, just greet new prisoners and introduce yourself. I did this at the halfway house. People would be coming through all the time, and people would be leaving without a word, and I would try and encourage—and other prisoners did this too—people to say goodbye to the folks leaving and introduce yourself to the new ones coming. Just maintain that basic humanity and social skills, if you can. And nonviolent commitment, that's huge.

We've got to change it, we've got to change it. We've got to care, we've got to pay attention, and we've got to act.

---

5. Daniel Berrigan was a Jesuit priest and a lifelong radical activist who protested the Vietnam War as a member of the Catonsville Nine along with his brother Philip, and who spent many years in and out of jails and prisons due to his activism.

Jalil Muntaqim

Jalil Muntaqim served just under fifty years in prison for his involvement with the Black Liberation Army. Jalil became affiliated with the
Black Panther Party at age eighteen. Less than two months before his
twentieth birthday, he was captured with Albert Nuh Washington in a
midnight shootout with San Francisco police.[1] He was subsequently
charged with a host of revolutionary activities, including the assassination of two New York City police officers. Jalil was also implicated in
the San Francisco 8 case and pleaded guilty to a lesser offense.[2] He
was imprisoned for forty-nine years in numerous maximum security
facilities in both California and New York and was released in October
2020. Jalil has published two zines—*On the Black Liberation Army*
(Abraham Guillen Press, 2002) and *Letters From Jalil Muntaqim:
Reflections From Inside Prison Walls on Resistance to Police Terror*
(P & L Printing, Sacramento Prisoner Support, 2015)—and two
books—*We are Our Own Liberators: Selected Prison Writings* (Arissa
Media Group, 2010) and *Escaping the Prism... Fade to Black: Poetry
and Essays* (Kersplebedeb, 2015).

---

1. Albert Nuh Washington was a soldier in the BLA who spent nearly thirty years in prison
before dying of cancer behind bars in 2000. There is a collection of his writings called *All Power
to the People* (Abraham Guillen Press/Arm the Spirit, 2002).

2. The San Francisco 8 were former members of the BPP who were arrested in 2007 in
connection with the 1971 murder of a San Francisco police officer. Herman Bell pled guilty to
involuntary manslaughter and Jalil Muntaqim pled no contest to conspiracy to commit voluntary manslaughter, though all eight of the defendants suffered tortuous conditions during their
confinement.

Prison Life

I'm Jalil Muntaqim, and I'm a former member of the Black Panther Party and the Black Liberation Army. I was arrested on August 28, 1971, in San Francisco. It was basically a shootout with cops, and they captured me and my comrade Nuh [Albert Washington], who passed in 2002 of cancer in prison. We were charged with a host of cases as a result of our activities within the BPP and the BLA. As a result, I was sent to prison from the age of nineteen, and I was released in October of 2020. That's about forty-nine years and a few months in prison.

I have always had family support. My family was always there. But there were times when I didn't have community support or outside support from organizations and so forth. I remember one time—I'm not ashamed to say it—I had to collect bottles in the prison in order to have sufficient funds to go to the commissary. Not long after that, a new organization in the community began to organize fundraisers for political prisoners.

One organization in particular was the ABCF, the Anarchist Black Cross Federation.[3] That organization was very generous. They used their war chest very diligently, with certain individuals receiving a stipend, either monthly or every two or three months. That was helpful to me. And soon after, other organizations began to consider that political prisoners needed some kind of assistance.

Because you have to remember that at the very beginning, especially after the more militant development of the struggle had diminished, there was no more "Free Huey!" or "Free Angela." No more "Free the Chicago 7" or the New York Panther 21.[4] As soon as those cases died down, then the idea of political prisoners, for the most part in public narrative, became

---

3. The Anarchist Black Cross Federation (ABCF), or Anarchist Black Cross (ABC), is an anarchist political-prisoner support organization dating back to Russia in the early twentieth century and popularized in Europe in the late 1960s. ABCF chapters began to appear in the US in the mid-1980s, providing support to political prisoners from the liberation movements of the 1960s and 1970s.

4. "Free Huey" refers to the 1967 campaign to free Black Panther Party cofounder Huey P. Newton from jail, and "Free Angela" refers to the campaign to free Angela Davis in the early 1970s. The Chicago 7 refers to defendants charged with conspiracy for their involvement in the 1968 Democratic Convention, and the New York Panther 21 were arrested and accused of planning bombings and attacks on police stations in 1969 but were all acquitted by a jury in 1971.

extinct. There was no discussion or talk about political prisoners to any large degree.

Of course there were certain militant organizations that continued to support one another, like the National Committee for the Defense of Political Prisoners (NCDPP), with Yuri Kochiyama and Safiya Bukhari, which evolved out of support for the Panther 21 and did a ton of good work.[5] In San Francisco, there was an organization called the United Prisoners Union (UPU) that was very supportive when I returned to San Quentin.[6] Also, the Prairie Fire Organizing Committee (PFOC) came into existence and began to help people inside prisons.[7] But for the most part, a lot of us in the early years, in the 1970s and 1980s, we had to fend for ourselves in terms of our own subsistence.

Then, imagine, when I began to organize the Jericho Movement in 1998, we started to get a real, serious federation of friends and supporters who began to give recognition to the resistance of political prisoners. Prior to that, the question of political prisoners was a nuance in the movement and not an actual thing or entity, or an issue that really needed to be considered for care and support.

You survive; you do what you have to do to survive. You adapt. As human beings, in and of ourselves, we are adaptive to certain circumstances and situations, and so we adapt. I adapt. By adapting, I continued to study and continued to organize. That's how I survived in the prison system.

I do not relent in terms of my own identity or who I am as an organizer and as a revolutionary. And so, me knowing myself and my own identity and

---

5. The National Committee for the Defense of Political Prisoners (NCDPP) was founded in the early 1930s by the Communist Party USA in defense of the Scottsboro Boys and others facing white supremacist terror. Yuri Kochiyama was a civil rights activist and lifelong political prisoner supporter. Safiya Bukhari was a former political prisoner and former member of both the BPP and the BLA. Both Bukhari and Kochiyama worked to free the New York Panther 21 and were integral in kick-starting the Free Mumia Abu-Jamal campaign.

6. The United Prisoners Union (UPU), formerly called the California Prisoners Union, began in 1970 and worked to unionize prisoners and former prisoners in order to realize their rights and improve their conditions.

7. The Prairie Fire Organizing Committee (PFOC) was a revolutionary anti-imperialist organization active from the mid-1970s to the mid-1990s They were an aboveground affiliate of the Weather Underground Organization (WUO), and their name comes from the 1974 WUO manifesto *Prairie Fire*. The PFOC focused primarily on international solidarity with people's movements in Nicaragua and El Salvador and support of the Puerto Rican militant organization Fuerzas Armadas de Liberación Nacional Puertorriqueña.

understanding that I wasn't as sharp as I am today, but as a young guy, I knew there was something wrong with the system that must be changed. So, it was up to me to continue to study.

As a matter of fact, my mom gave me instructions. She said, "Listen, if you're going to be in there talking all that stuff, you better read, and you better go to school. You better learn how to speak and how to write." She's the one who really told me to get into books. She said, "Go get a dictionary and read it." And that's what I did. I took a dictionary and read it from cover to cover. Then I started using words in their proper context.

So, it took some time for me to really understand the nature of prison. That this is an opportunity for me, for my own growth and development, and how I will be able to continue to contribute to the overall struggle.

I never lost hope, but there are days when you become depressed. Prison is a depressing situation, period. You don't go to prison to find joy. In prison, you're in the company of miserable people being guarded by miserable people. You're in a cesspool of misery, and people are coping within that. So, naturally there are times where you feel depressed as a result of, for instance, going to the parole board fourteen times, as I did. I was eligible for parole in 2002, and I didn't get released until 2020, and I've had a couple of reversals and returns to the parole board, and I was still denied. Those kinds of things are not only depressing for me but also for my family.

I'm a hopeless optimist. I always believe we're going to come out on the other end and be good. My strategy is to achieve that. Therefore, every time I get knocked down, I find a way to get back up. There have been times when I've had bouts of depression. I even wrote a poem about that in one of my books. You find a lot of that—people trying to cope with depression in prison—particularly in the isolation wards.

My happiest moments inside were when my children came to visit. The first time I had a conjugal visit with my family and was able to go into a trailer for a couple of days with my family, which was extremely, extremely important to maintain some semblance of normalcy. Because prison is not normal. Prison is an aberration to human social order. For me, having those opportunities to be with family for an extended period of time during those trailer visits was very comforting and brought me a lot of joy. Of course, at the end of the visit, when they got to leave and you go back to your routine, that's sad. But for those two days that you're with your family—able to cook and really enjoy time with them—that's the best.

Prison is a reflection of what's going on in the streets. Keep that in mind. So, when there's a high in political organizing and militancy in the streets, there's a high in political organizing and militancy in prison. When things are low in the streets, then the prison system becomes a cesspool of misery.

When I first came to prison in 1972, it was right after the assassination of George Jackson and the brutal assault and murders of prisoners and guards at Attica.[8] There was an organized prison movement at that time, in the late 1970s and early 1980s. This was the result of the incarceration of many people who had been part of the movement during the 1960s and the 1970s—people who are now in prison and continuing to raise the issues of white supremacy, anticapitalism, and anti-imperialism inside of prisons.

But because the movement on the outside had diminished, there was no real support base for those on the inside who tried to continue to build and organize. So, there came a period of time where there was no actual, real movement going on inside prison. Because there was no real movement going on in the streets. There was no synchronicity, no linkage, between the two.

This was mainly in the 1980s and leading into the 1990s until we began to rebuild a movement in support of political prisoners and the idea of a prison movement. I watched the diminishing of—the degrading of—the consciousness inside prison as the individuals coming inside prison were more "social criminals." Drug dealers, gangsters, and gangs came into the prison system in droves. As a result of that, it basically disturbed the prison system the way it was operating before, prior to this inundation of gangs. If you find gang violence in the streets, you'll find gang violence in the prisons.

Politics and Prison Dynamics

I have had problems with other prisoners but none that led to any violence.

---

8. Jackson's murder during a supposed escape attempt was in August 1971, and the uprising and subsequent massacre at Attica Prison was the following month.

There are always contradictions because you have totally different personalities and characters that you have to deal with on a daily basis, but nothing that resulted in any form of violence or anything of that nature. In regard to prison guards, I definitely had conflicts with them. There are about three physical confrontations that I can recall having with guards over the years that landed me in solitary confinement. But nothing that resulted in any serious injury to me.

Of course, there are individuals who are in prison who are politically conscious, so I always had relationships with them, Black, white, and Brown. These people tend to be motivated by the same principles and ideas as I [have]. Those people do exist. And then there's also those who are contrary to that—white supremacists, the Aryan Brotherhood, and stuff of that nature whom I have conflict with. No physical conflict but an understanding that we have to stay away from each other. Otherwise, there will be a problem.

There is one Aryan Brotherhood guy whom I befriended at Southport, and I saw him a year and a half later, when we were both at Auburn. He told me then that he was no longer engaged in any of that. He attributed his leaving to the friendship we had built up while together at Southport. He came up and told me that, and that made me feel good.

I don't know what it's like today, but New York used to be notorious. Especially at Elmira, Comstock, Clinton, and Attica. You couldn't get away from the idea that you may be dealing with a KKK member or a Nazi adherent in the prison system. They run in droves in the prison system.

That's one of the reasons why, in 2016, the *New York Times* did an exposé on racism in the New York state prison system. It was a pretty big, pretty significant exposé, and guards, institutions, and organizations were being called out. That turned the lights on, because they got away with a lot in the darkness. When you turn the lights on, the mice and rats scatter. That exposé by the *New York Times* in December 2016 shed light on the extent of white supremacy and racism in the New York state prison system.

I did time with a lot of other political prisoners. They kept me and my codefendants separate from each other. We've never been in the same prison together unless we were traveling to go to trial or coming back from trial. Besides that, Herman [Bell], Nuh, and myself have never been in the same prison together. I was with Nuh at Clinton, before he passed, very briefly before they recognized we were codefendants, and then they separated us. They decided to send one of us to another institution. But then again, there were other BLA members and BPP members whom I got to spend time with while in New York state prisons. One person was Teddy "Jah" Heath, who passed away in prison in 2004, I think.[9] Also, Robert Seth Hayes and I spent time together in different institutions during different periods of time, and we got to spend a lot of time together.[10] I am so glad that he was able to make his transition outside of prison.

When I was in San Quentin in 1975 until 1977, I began to organize a petition to the United Nations. The first petition to the United Nations was in 1977. It was the US Prisoners' Petition to the United Nations.

While I was there in San Quentin in 1977, I also organized the first national revolutionary prisoners' newspaper, which was called *Arm the Spirit*. *Arm the Spirit* evolved out of a newsletter that was no more than four or five pages, originally called the *Voices of San Quentin*. Both of us who were at the Adjustment Center at San Quentin, which is the maximum security part of San Quentin, were writing our thoughts and political essays, and sending those to organizations in the streets who would type them up, staple them together, and distribute them to various progressive organizations and groups in the Bay Area. People really wanted to see these, the *Voices of San Quentin*, so I decided perhaps we needed to do something bigger and devise a paper. With the help of the United Prisoners Union and the Prairie Fire Organizing Committee, we began to organize those newsletters into a single newspaper, and we titled it *Arm the Spirit*. This became the first revolutionary newspaper created by prisoners in the whole nation. Claude Marks and Diana Block were involved with Prairie Fire at the time, and I think they may have assisted in the printing and distribution.[11] But the writ-

---

9. Teddy "Jah" Heath was a political prisoner affiliated with the BLA who spent nearly thirty years in prison before dying of cancer in 2001.

10. Robert Seth Hayes was a political prisoner affiliated with the BLA who spent forty-five years in prison before being released in 2018. He was a founding member of the Certain Days: Freedom for Political Prisoners calendar collective, and he died in 2019.

11. Claude Marks and Diana Block worked in the anti-imperialist underground for several decades, primarily in support of Puerto Rican political prisoners and with the Prairie Fire Organizing Committee. Marks spent time as a political prisoner and has since founded the Freedom Archive, which compiles information about the Civil Rights and Black Liberation Movements. Block has written several informative books and newsletters and was a founding member of the California Coalition for Women Prisoners.

ing and the editing was a brother named Kalima Aswad, who was one of the major editors.[12] After I was paroled, he took over the editorship of *Arm the Spirit*.

Then I was involved in a lot of lawsuits against the Thirteenth Amendment, lawsuits for a prisoners' right to vote, and campaigns around that. Then, in 1998, I called for the March on Jericho, which evolved into the National Jericho Movement. I'm the last living cofounder of the National Jericho Movement, which has been going for over twenty-one years now. The Republic of New Afrika (RNA) had these marches in Washington, calling for the release of political prisoners, what they called Jericho marches.[13] By 1997, they had stopped doing them, and I didn't understand why. I felt it was needed, so I made a proposal for a reinstituting of the Jericho march. Comrade Baba Herman Ferguson and Sister Safiya Bukhari came to visit me at Eastern Correctional Facility, listened to what I had to say, and agreed to help resurrect the Jericho marches.[14] They began to organize and build a campaign in support of this. Then we had the national march in Washington, DC, in 1998, and about six thousand people came. As a result of that enthusiasm and support, we began to feel that this had to continue and we organized the National Jericho Movement.

I've written books, one of which was called *We Are Our Own Liberators*. In part of that book, I called for the building of a national liberation front. As a result of that, a group of revolutionary nationalists came together and began to organize the New Afrikan Liberation Front. Unfortunately, we did not maintain the organization for various reasons, but it set in motion the idea of the need for a national liberation front. Then I wrote another book called *Escape the Prism: Fade to Black*, which is a compilation of essays and poetry.

---

12. Kalima Aswad spent forty-six years in California state prisons and was a leader in the Black Liberation Struggle while there. He edited *Arm the Spirit* for years before finally being released in 2015.

13. The Republic of New Afrika (RNA) was a Black nationalist organization founded in 1968 in part based on the teachings of Malcolm X. The RNA has had many prominent members and seeks to establish a Black-majority country in what are now the five southern states of Louisiana, Mississippi, Alabama, Georgia, and South Carolina.

14. Baba Herman Ferguson was a progressive Black nationalist educator in the New York City schools system and an associate of Malcolm X in both the Muslim Mosque, Inc., and the Organization of Afro-American Unity (OAAU). Ferguson was also a member of the RNA.

Organizing petitions, organizing strikes, organizing demonstrations, all those things were part of my own sanity and trying to make sense of this madness. I had the attitude that we have to fight back.

In 2018, I was in solitary confinement at Southport Correctional Facility for four months for a disciplinary charge that was ultimately reversed and expunged from my record. They charged me for teaching a class at Attica, teaching a Black history class that I was approved to teach. But they didn't like the curriculum. I started the class from 1861 and brought it all the way up to October of 1966, when we talked about the Black Panther Party. They took umbrage with the fact that I was teaching the principles, policies, and history of the Black Panther Party. I compared and contrasted the principles and ethics of the young people who joined the Black Panther Party to the attitudes and behaviors of the three gangs that we have on the streets today, particularly the Bloods and the Crips.[15] For some reason the administration felt that I was trying to persuade these street organizations to become revolutionaries, and so, by virtue of my teaching, they put me in solitary confinement for four months.

Looking Forward

We need to increase our capacity to highlight the existence of political prisoners inside prison. Use all of our print, digital, and social media platforms to raise the idea that political prisoners exist in the US and that they should be supported. Also, in doing so, we have to raise the question of why there are political prisoners. This supports the overall struggle itself, which political prisoners evolve from and respond to.

We need to build and strengthen a prison abolitionist movement. We need to build a campaign like BDS [Boycott, Divest, and Sanction] in terms of a fight against mass incarceration.[16] Any corporation or business that

---

15. The Bloods (Brotherly Love Overcomes Overrides and Destruction) and the Crips (Community Revolution in Progress) were formed in Los Angeles, California, in the late 1960s and early 1970s as youth community organizations turned street gangs. Members of both continue to be targeted for imprisonment.

16. The Boycott, Divestment, Sanctions (BDS) movement works to end international support for Israel's oppression of the Palestinian people with the intention of pressuring Israel to comply with international law.

does business with the prison industrial complex should be boycotted and sanctioned. BDS is important in that regard, so we need to build a BDS movement and take the money out of prisons. Fight the corporations that are exceedingly exploiting prison labor. Challenge them and raise these questions in the name of political prisoners. If you do so, that'll be a tremendous help in regard to the issues of building a campaign that is opposing mass incarceration. Keep in mind that the idea of the abolitionist movement is to correspond with our history of the abolition of slavery. Why? Because slavery was never abolished in the US. The continuum of that needs to be brought into focus, this narrative of why we are against mass incarceration. There were abolitionists against slavery back in 1619, when they were first bringing African people to the US. We have to look at the exception clause in the Thirteenth Amendment, which indicates that slavery has never been abolished for those convicted of a crime. So, the penal systems in the US are basically slave institutions. Thus, involuntary servitude and slavery does exist in the US in the prison system. Therefore, if you create that narrative of abolishing slavery, then you actually have a BDS movement as part of that process, taking the money out of the prison industrial complex. Then you would really be building something substantial in this fight against prison slavery and in support of decarceration.

Anyone who is concerned about mass incarceration, who is opposed to prison slavery, needs to bring these issues to every struggle. There should not be an issue in the community that is not attached to prison slavery, whether it's housing, working, or minimum wage. If you're fighting for a better minimum wage outside of prison, imagine what the minimum wage is inside of prisons. That kind of interlinking [of struggles] is very important. If we can do that, then essentially you have made that movement whole. You cannot have the organizing of the prison movement, or organizing the workers' movement, because they go hand in hand.

There are efforts made by those individuals who are in my opinion "apolitical prisoners," as a result of them having changed their relationship with the state. They went from socially conscious prisoners to political and revolutionary conscious prisoners. As a result of that, they're changing their study, and their relationship to the state is evolving. They are then treated more harshly than regular, common prisoners because they are fighters. They resist the forms of oppression and white supremacy that go on inside prisons, either illegally or by organizing or by speaking out against it. Therefore, as a result of the change in their relationship to the state, they qualify as political prisoners. So, those individuals inside prison, like Rashid Johnson or Kwame Shakur, and many others across the state, are organizing a resurgence.[17] There have been some strikes in Alabama, in Florida, and there's a major hunger strike in California. Please do not forget those brothers in Pelican Bay who have been on a serious hunger strike. I think one or two have died as a result of that hunger strike. They have resurrected, in many instances, a movement or an idea that there needs to be resistance inside the prison system.

At the same time that Jericho came into existence in 1998, so did Critical Resistance. They weren't competing, but there were contrasting viewpoints in regard to organizing the support of political prisoners, organizing support inside prisons, and opposing mass incarceration. This helped to raise the profile of prisoners who are conscious and are fighting back inside prison. And it gives them a venue by which they could speak, and by virtue of that to organize inside prisons.

Kwame Shakur has now organized Prison Lives Matter, and there are individuals and organizations across the prison system who are joining in Prison Lives Matter. I encourage that in order to build something substantial in alliance with the new resurgence of a movement that's going on in the streets today.

Study. Recognize you don't know what you don't know and find the means to find out. Do the research, study, and take advantage of any college programs. Most people coming to prison have no GED, have no education. Some are functional illiterates. The first thing I would suggest, and I always said while I was in prison, is go get your GED. That's the first thing. Second thing, if there's a college program, get into that college program.

When I first came to prison, the old guys in the system would go out in the yard and tell the younger ones to go get a GED. That you can't hang out with us, walk the yard with us, until you get your GED. That was the principle of the older guys coming into the system in the 1970s and 1980s. Also, the guys who were in the college program were going into the yards and trying to persuade some of the young guys to go to school and get their GED as

17. Kwame Shakur is the cofounder and chairman of the New Afrikan Liberation Collective and the national director for the Prison Lives Matter movement.

a way to keep the college program going. So, the more people you had out there encouraging others to get their GED and take the college program, the better.

That's one reason why, in 1994, they wanted to take college programs [the Pell Grant] out of prison. I think it was under the Clinton administration. As a result of that, there was a dumbing down in the prison system. You now had guys coming into prison who had no way of getting a proper education. At one point in prison, they were telling guys that an eighth-grade education was all the knowledge you need, that it was sufficient. This idea stretches back through the history of slavery in the US, where they didn't want to teach African people how to read.

There has been a dumbing down of the prison system across the country. That's one of the reasons why it's so important to support our political prisoners, because they are the stalwarts who speak truth to power inside prisons. That's one of the reasons why they need to be supported by the movement, in whole and in part.

That is what I would tell young people coming in. It's what I was telling people on the inside when I was there. You can't hang out with me if you don't have your GED. You can't walk the yard with me if you're not trying to improve yourself, if you don't get your GED or go to a vocational training program. Do something so that when you come out of prison, you have become an asset to the community rather than a liability.

When it comes to prison, you have to have an end product. As far as the community and its relationship to the prison, there's no community scrutiny of that end product. There's no community watchdog of the end product. If an individual spends ten or fifteen years in prison and they come out, they're going to be aged. This is not good for the community; it does not serve the community well. The end product of a person coming into prison in terms of rehabilitation and redemption is to be a better person. The prison system won't do that, and it won't do that because that would end recidivism. It would stop people from returning to prison. Recidivism keeps the system going. It is important that the community at large challenge the prison system and ensure that the individual coming to prison, for the most part, will get a good education and/or a vocational skill. That will transfer the funding of prisons into the areas that better serve prisoners. Of course, this must support the abolitionist movement. I'm not advocating that we've got to keep prisons open in order to improve people's lives. No, that's not what I'm saying here. Certainly, we must ensure that when people come out of prison, they are an asset to the community and not a continuing liability. We have to have a symbiotic relationship between the prison system and the community.

Keep in mind that the majority of prisoners, particularly in New York State, come out of five different boroughs. And those are the boroughs they are coming back to. My argument is that if the community is not organized, if the community is diseased, and you take a person out of that community and put them in prison, and that person is then brought back to the community without challenging conditions in that community, then we are just putting that person right back into a diseased community. They have this symbiotic relationship. We have to improve the conditions outside of prison, in the community at large, and we have to make sure that those individuals inside prisons, when they come back to their communities, that they are an asset.

The struggle continues, *a luta continua*. There is no break. You're not going on vacation if you're going to prison. You're going into another battle-field. It's important that you understand that the movement continues, from the streets into the prisons. And that's what I did. I was organizing before I was in prison, I was organizing in prison, and when I came out here in the streets, I'm organizing again. That's what I do.

Second of all, education is important inside prison. Get as much education as you can, and study all that you can. At one point, I had five hundred books in one of my cells. They hated searching my cell! I had so many books, bags of books, that I was studying in the cell.

Let me make one last point, and that is the issue of white supremacy. The idea and the thinking of white supremacy is a human aberration. It is a scourge on the planet. I think it is a neurosis. For any people, any person, to believe they are superior to any other people on the planet, they are the problem. It is either extreme narcissism or some kind of maniacal thinking in terms of who they believe they are.

I'm going to take a lesson from El Hajj Malik Shabazz, Malcolm X.[18] Reading his book, he once said that after he gave a presentation, I forget where, a young white woman came up to him and asked him what she could

---

18. El Hajj Malik Shabazz, also known as Malcolm X, was a Black nationalist leader, a minister with the Nation of Islam (NOI), and an inspiration for millions before and after his assassination in 1965. He was politicized while in prison.

do to help. And he told her nothing. That this is a Black problem, and we need to resolve it ourselves. And so, this young white girl was discouraged, and she walked away. After his own evolution, El Hajj Malik Shabazz regretted having told her that. He stated that he should have told her to go back into her community and deal with the issues of white supremacy, the issues of white racism. That is the lesson that we need to address, continuously, regarding the issue of white supremacy. White supremacy should not be a Black or Brown or Yellow person's problem. It's white people's problem. So, it's important that white people go back to Aunt Jenny and Uncle Buck and Sister Sue and tell them to put down that Confederate flag, and tell them what they're thinking, how they're thinking, is an aberration to our common humanity. If you do that, then it lessens our problems in terms of our own quest for freedom and liberation and emancipation. White supremacy is only my problem when you try to impose it upon me. When you try to systematically, or systemically, or physically impose your idea that you are superior to me just because of the color of your skin, then you essentially violate my human rights. This is a narrative that needs to be expressed all across the country; that white supremacy is white people's problem, and they need to address it.

This has happened before, in part, as a result of the Civil War, the North against the South. This was white people fighting against white people to maintain the idea of slavery. We are saying that similarly, we have to engage in that kind of struggle today to end the scourge of white supremacy. We need to free people of color from the scourge of white supremacy. That means white people will have to go against white people in order to make it happen. I'm going to end with that.

Once we can get people to really understand that dynamic of the prison industrial complex, that is not in fact divorced from the history of slavery in the US, they get it. That light bulb turns on. Then we can make the charge that we are abolitionists, and we come from a long history of abolitionists and abolishing slavery. Let's abolish slavery. If we abolish slavery, we'll end the prison system or at least knock it down a bit.

Jeremy Hammond

Jeremy Hammond is an activist from Chicago, founder of the computer security training website HackThisSite, and former political prisoner connected to Anonymous.[1] Arrested numerous times for his civil disobedience, Jeremy has served two prison sentences for his activism: one in connection with a hack of the pro-war Protest Warrior website in 2005 (for which he served almost two years), and again in 2013, for hacking the private intelligence firm Stratfor and releasing data to WikiLeaks (he spent over nine years imprisoned on this second case). In 2019, while still in prison, Jeremy refused to cooperate with a federal grand jury investigating WikiLeaks and its founder Julian Assange, and he was held in civil contempt of court. Jeremy served most of his time in county jails (Cook County and Grady County), various federal prisons, and the Alexandria Detention Center in northern Virginia. He was released from prison in November 2020. Jeremy is the co-host, along with his twin brother Jason, of the podcast *Twin Trouble*. His sentencing statement is included in the book *Defiance: Anarchist Statements Before Judge and Jury* (Detritus Books, 2019).

Prison Life

Obviously there's a very big difference between jail and prison. Also, in solitary you're kind of in your own world, and you develop your own routine.

---

1. Anonymous is a decentralized hacktivist collective that started in the early 2000s and has targeted corporations, governments, institutions, and individuals for their lack of transparency and their criminal and immoral conduct.

Prisons are very structured and regimented and political, where people are doing longer stretches of time and stakes are higher. Every move is calculated and unpredictable.

I'd been arrested, I think, two or three times before I actually did any kind of time. A night or two in jail is not at all preparation because you're by yourself mostly. And so, doing prison, I was really young, like nineteen or twenty when I actually went into a medium security federal prison. And there you're dealing with people who are doing ten, twenty, thirty years, sometimes life, who have already done so many years. I was of a completely different mindset at the time. Even though you do the best you can to think about it and prepare yourself for it, I wasn't prepared. It was all very shocking. But I was supported by my friends and family, obviously much more the second time around. I wasn't alone; I was never alone through the whole thing, actually.

First of all, you have to adapt. It really is a sink-or-swim type of situation. There's a lot of fucked up things about these rules and these systems. The most shocking, obvious thing I think is the outright segregation and racism. There's just no way around that. It just permeates every part of prison culture. I've never had to experience such clear-cut racism. Also, being a white person going to prison, the expectation is that you're supposed to fall in line with your race and you're supposed to keep your head down and play along. I wasn't like that, and it's a tough balance.

For one, that's just how the rule is in prison, so they say. There's pressures and expectations and risks you take going against the grain, certainly. But ultimately, we're not here to keep our heads down. Wherever you're at, that's where the battle lines are. I was never the person to just play along and compromise my principles. Just me being who I am, interacting with people and going against the grain, definitely got me in problems, especially the first time. Fortunately, there were people who respected that too. I was kind of taken in as well by other people.

Developing a routine is a very easy way to regiment your time in a way that's structured and productive. People recognize that too. As a matter of fact, at most places if you aren't following the program, people are going to look at that and be like, "Man, you better get with the program." I think it's a configuration where the whole thing is just to make sure that everybody has the ability and freedom to do their own time and do the easiest time possible.

Of course, it's so full of contradictions because everybody can't do what they want because nobody wants to be there, obviously. It results in a lot of risks and desperate moves and conflicts all the time because not everybody is going to be able to get what they want. Then, of course, there's the politics and the racism; that is a whole other dimension to prison life.

But I worked out and read a lot. Basically life revolves around the movement of the clock, on count times, and what type of job you're working or who you're hanging with. You make your own schedule, but a lot of it just revolves around the prison schedule. So, I was able to adapt to it. Once you get into a groove, it's better. Honestly, people want to get into a groove because time flies that way. When things are unpredictable and uncertain and things are being changed, this stuff is actually kind of irritating. You might be used to a workout schedule that's every day at six, and now it's not. It's just a workout schedule, but if something were to happen, some prison security situation where all the moves are canceled for the night, then your whole night's messed up, your whole day's messed up.

All these rules are set up, and you're forced to play along. You don't just bump into somebody without saying, "Hey, I apologize, brother," because anything like that could trigger some type of action. There are rules to prevent these types of things from happening in the cars and stuff too.[2] But there's also an unpredictable element. You're dealing with people who are broken people, who could at any time just . . . You're not supposed to get in conflict with somebody; you're supposed to ask permission, you can't just fight somebody. But sometimes shit happens, so it's just unpredictable.

One of the earliest lessons I learned was to mind my own business. Be careful what you say to people; don't repeat stuff. But even in that case, it wasn't anything that I was revealing other than what a lot of people already knew, but nevertheless, sometimes you say things that can start stuff. So anyways, it's just the pressures of being a white person who isn't like that. Throughout my bid, I had all kinds of cellies of different races. I never respected that rule. Over time, you gain the trust, and people recognize your character. Really, if you're down with the convict code, even some of the white boys who saw me as a race traitor, they kind of recognize my character,

---

2. In prison, a car is the group or clique that one "rolls" with and allies oneself with. This is generally based on race, geography, or political affiliation.

even though I didn't respect anything that they were doing. Nevertheless, they see that and they kind of just let it ride.

The other thing about it, because I was kind of accounted for by a different group of people, they couldn't even do anything to me. Prisons are set up that way. They could have whatever opinions they wanted about me, but I don't answer to them. The thing that sucks is everywhere you just start over. When you get transferred somewhere, you start with nothing, and you've got to do the whole thing over again, which sucks.

Also in prison, spending years in the feds, it's kind of a small world. Eventually, everywhere I've been, I've always known people that I've seen at other prisons. So people would speak for me. And, of course, people do background checks too and then realize that you are who you are. So, I was often in some places the only person in the prison who could go sit with the white boys and also go sit with the Chicago dudes. So people respected that about me, and I was one of the only people who could do that because it is kind of bold. But people knew that I was just the type of dude who could do that. And people have their own opinions about that, even the white boys, but they couldn't do that either. There's a lot of different ways to think about it.

There's something to be said about being a white antiracist: you should be organizing other whites to become antiracist. Absolutely. Also, I didn't completely just say "Fuck all white people" either. In prison, you get actual white supremacist gangs, Aryans, then there's also the independent white boys, who are supposedly not racist. They were kind of formed in opposition to white supremacist gangs, saying you can still be a solid white boy, and we will keep everybody accounted for and protect each other. It's stupid as hell; it's still self-organizing white people just because of resentment and fear.

But nevertheless, because I was also not a rat and not a child molester—which is basically the two criteria to where you could become vouched for—even just based on the strength of that, everywhere I always went, I always went to the independent white boys and the shot callers and said, "Look, here's who I am, I'm a solid convict, I'm not a rat, and here's my paperwork. This is so you all know who I am." Because a lot of times people go to other cars because they're hiding stuff. They might have burnt the white boy somewhere down the line because of something stupid, like they owed a bunch of money, and then they turned and told on everybody and then went to another prison. They don't want to roll with white boys in case they check who they are, so they go and answer to somebody else. So, a lot of times a lot of white boys will also look at other people who don't hang with them out of suspicion and skepticism, like there's something wrong with them.

I never met a jail I liked. I mean, there definitely are degrees. Jails are often designed to break somebody. They basically provide the minimum possible conditions, and they're not at all concerned about programming or yard time or anything like that. It's basically a tactic to get people to plead out. You just want to go home at that point or do something to get out of there. You'll even accept some terms just because the time is easier at prison.

What makes it more tolerable, to be honest, is just when the guards leave you alone, when you're in a groove where you never have to have any type of interaction with them. If you could go a whole day without ever having to talk to a cop, that is ideal. The things that made it intolerable was when they're around walking in your face, stopping you, getting in the way of doing what you want to do.

What made it more tolerable was just having the most amount of freedom. To be able to move to the yard, to be able to go to the library if you want to that day, or to be able to have the day room open so you can play cards with your friends. When things are a little bit more opened up, when there's less security and restrictions and less cops and less work. If you're not working, you have more freedom to be able to decide your own schedule. It's just all about autonomy and personal freedom.

I never really lost hope, being in and out of jail so much. I also had it a little bit easier, the first time at least, when I got a chance to self-surrender and I could psych myself up a little bit. So I had that little bit of freedom there, which is a privilege that most people aren't afforded. As far as the uncertainty when first getting locked up, you just don't know what you're looking at when you first go in. It took me a day or two before I even knew what I was charged with by the feds because I was arrested and they wanted to talk to me, and I refused to talk. So, basically you don't know anything. What did they get me for? Is it this, is it this, or is it this other thing? What am I being charged with? And then when you do find out, you're told the worst you're facing is maybe thirty years, but if you cooperate it could be less. The uncertainty of not knowing is certainly a huge stressor. Also, when you are pretrial, the outcome of it is based on your decisions. There's a lot of stuff that, of course, is above and beyond your hands, and that's another characteristic of prison. As much as we talk about serving time, we are just passive spectators for the most part. You could buck and rebel, no doubt. And we have to. But there are some big systems in place here, so sometimes we're just a number being fed along a conveyor belt.

When you accept the worst, you're never disappointed. They could take everything from you—literally everything—but your body and your mind. That's all you have. So, when you just accept that that can happen, then it's harder to be disappointed.

It's also easy to lose hope when things are happening in the world that you're completely unable to be there for, things having to do with your family specifically. I don't have kids, so that's another thing I didn't have to worry about or stress over, which is the hugest thing for a lot of people. The hugest thing, of course. My grandparents passed away while I was in prison, and not being able to be there for them was a major thing. When my brother and father were both locked up at the same time, it was really hard. You're viewing things from afar, almost like you're watching reality from a TV screen, and you can't interact with them or do anything about it. So there's a little bit of hopelessness there. Although people do find ways to be involved. But just not being able to be there is hard, and, sadly, sometimes people move on with their lives. Even friends and family members.

As far as how to manage that, like I said, they can take everything, but they can't take that last thing. And if that's all we've got, we've got to live with it. You have two hands and you could always do things with your hands, you can always do things with your body, so you just practice autonomy where you can. I don't have any hope in a cosmic sense that things will naturally arc toward one way or the other. I think things just happen when people make it happen. So, even if they took everything, you still have to do your best to make it happen, even if it takes a long way to chisel away at the brick. Even if it sometimes seems futile, it's like sand and little drops of water eating away at concrete, even if it takes a long time. I never lost hope. But it is probably very different for me because I was never alone. I always felt basically every step of the process that people had my back, so maybe it was easier for me to keep going in that sense.

Knowing that what you do makes a difference is important. It's easier to see that in my case, where there was attention on what I was doing. But in a lot of places, people who don't have that level of support, maybe they don't realize that what you're seeing does make a difference, but what you do does make a difference.

Whatever skills, hobbies, and accomplishments people make in prison are always because of stuff on their own, almost always, and not because of prison. It's almost always in spite of prison, actually. They basically erect a lot of barricades and hurdles to prevent people from being able to do that. Even though, of course, ostensibly the whole thing is about programming and rehabilitation, but that's just a big lie. I learned how to play guitar during my first bid, which was kind of cool. Also, it took me years, but I can finally read Spanish pretty well. I was in a prison [Manchester] one time that did have vocational training, so I managed to weasel my way into that, and they had a carpentry program and an electrical program, and I took those for a while. That was the only prison I was ever in that had that type of programming.

As a general rule, prisons always get worse. They always take and take and never give, man. For one, the COVID lockdown has changed everything, of course. At most places you can't go to the yard, or you can go to the yard but you're only going to the yard with your group of people. It used to be that you'd be able to go to the yard with everybody. Now, you might not ever see somebody on the other side of the prison. You might not even know that they're there. You definitely can't share anything with them, be it a book or a story of something in the world. You're not going to be able to see them. Whatever individual study programs you might have had with somebody, those are all gone. Most places don't have libraries anymore or programming. Everywhere is different, and maybe it's changing back a little bit.

Everybody had to go through a lot because of the pandemic, but they really don't give a damn about protecting people. I mean, they're completely unable to stop people from getting sick. I caught COVID twice in the BOP. Memphis, at the time when I got back there, it was kind of a flagship for COVID. I was only there for like another five or six months, but in that time it became an epidemic, and somebody died the week after I left to go home. Everybody just got sick. I remember I got sick the week before I left. They were putting people who had the disease in the same units where people are supposed to be isolating because they're trying to go home, or they're isolating because they just got there. They were putting everyone together. So, the COVID lockdowns definitely got bad.

There's also supply chain issues. In Illinois, the commissary suppliers just dropped the contract, so they haven't even had commissary in Illinois state prisons. As far as general trends in the prison system, another huge thing is the ban on books and literature and magazines, and the digitization and the copying of mailed stuff. That is another huge thing that's happened in the past three years that is just an absolute tragedy. They just want to go more corporate, with Amazon and Walmart. And the consequence of that is now a lot of people can't send books individually, even in places where ordinarily you could, like at a low security place. Also, the Books to Prisoners groups are no longer considered authorized vendors. I do Books to Prisoners, and we just get that shit all day, every day. We're going to battle with them. Given everything else that's been going on in the world the past two years, a lot of people might not think of prisoner access to literature as high on the list, right? But of course, it means everything to us.

Another big thing is the drug problem. And I don't want to give rise to the system's sensationalist arguments about the war on drugs. I don't want to give any credence to their sensationalism about that. But I will say that it has absolutely been a huge difference in the past five or six years, particularly because of the proliferation of synthetics. When first getting locked up, people are always smoking weed and making wine and stuff, and they are always trying to catch them, of course, and lock them up. People are always trying to cope. In a general sense, maybe there's something wrong with drugs and alcohol, sure. But in the other sense, it's a little bit more innocent than the shit we have now. People aren't going to cope. You're talking about a desperate, stressed out population of folks who are going to try to find ways to deal with the pain.

But K2 kind of took over the system, and everybody was messing with it.[3] Every dimension of life is actually kind of absorbed by it now. After a while, I saw that people were writing home and asking for money, people were getting debts and getting stabbed and beaten up borrowing money, which is now the main reason why people get in trouble. It just kind of undermined the convict code, and it undermined solidarity. And then I saw the damage it was doing to people. People were getting zombified, and it was definitely

---

3. K2, or spice, is a synthetic marijuana with effects that can be more unpredictable and dangerous than cannabis. The prevalence of K2 in prisons has increased, leading to increased scrutiny, mail restrictions, and conflict.

a very different animal than marijuana. So now you've just got people who are strung out.

You hear all the talk from cops about the drug epidemic in prison and how we have to take the mail away [to prevent drugs from entering prisons]. In reality, they don't give a damn. Like, it's almost a joke. And I've been to several places where they just sit there and laugh and watch people just fuck up and fall out, and almost every day someone is carried away in a stretcher. Almost every day, and they're just laughing. I don't want to see people get locked up in the hole and get charges; I don't think that's a solution to this problem, of course. So, I just think that has played a role in eroding inter-prisoner solidarity. It keeps people preoccupied and caught up with this thing that obviously isn't furthering or helping anybody in any way. Every prison I've ever been in is completely dominated by that shit.

I mean, look what they did in the 1960s and 1970s; they've always done this, right?—historically used vices as a means to control the population. We spend more time fighting each other or fighting our own battles than realizing who the enemy is. And Pfizer is the one with patents on all these synthetic cannabinoids. Why would they even make this stuff? I mean, the pharmaceutical companies are the biggest drug manufacturers in the world, right?

The biggest accomplishment is just walking in a way that reflects what you truly believe. Helping people and the relationships that you build over years, they just circle back too. There's little stuff too. I was a GED tutor my first bid, and I was in the class but I also helped people individually. This one time they had a graduation, and they had everybody who was graduating stand up, and I realized I worked with a lot of people over the years. So that was cool. I typed motions and grievances for people. I wasn't a lawyer, but I would often help if I could, mostly just typing and giving my opinions. I've definitely filed a lot of grievances over the years. Most of the time, sadly, they don't work, but sometimes they do, and people get love. There is nothing better to fucking see than someone go home because they made something happen, they did the work, and they did it right. To be able to help them in any way, even if it's just by typing something, is cool. Generally, just speaking up for people.

I played bass and was in band programs too. One thing I realized when I was in Kentucky in a band program was that the cops were all white, and they basically had all the music equipment, and the only bands playing were white metal bands. I played in bands, but that was fucked up. There was another group of people from DC that were into Go-Go.[4] The feds have the DC people, who are kind of a special category in the federal prisons. So anyone who is locked up in DC, doing any kind of time, goes to federal prison. So there's a group of DC people—the DC car was kind of notorious, and they wanted to play in the band program. But the cops erected all kinds of stupid-ass rules basically to prevent them specifically from playing. One of the rules was that you actually need to have two or three people in the band who are playing actual instruments. So they wanted me to play just to be able to meet the requirements. So I did, and I kind of went to bat for them, and the cops didn't like that at all. They didn't like that at all; they hated this group of people. They kept trying to get them to not be part of the band program, and they kept using stupid, two-sided rules as far as rules applied. They'd let it slide when some other band broke some drumsticks, but then when the Go-Go band broke drumsticks, they kicked them out of the band program. So I filed paperwork and went to bat for them. There were a lot of little successes like that.

We were talking about that last inch that they can't take from you, so every time that you are able to express that, and to buck and to get over on them in any kind of way, is a victory. It's a small victory, and you have a lot of small victories. Even something as mundane as the everyday ongoing conspiracy of prisoners to steal from the bosses, right? Everybody's got each other's backs; everybody just works with each other to get over on them. And there is a sense of satisfaction in a job well done.

Sometimes it can be a little bit more bold. At MCC [Metropolitan Correctional Center] New York, we actually had two hunger strikes. At MCC, they had three elevators—one for visitors, one for staff, and one for prisoners, and the prisoner elevator was broken for a week or two. So what they did was have a prison-wide lockdown, and they kept everyone in our cells, denied phone calls, denied visits for everybody. So we were just in our cells. At the time, I was actually in a dorm type of set-up at MCC; one of the floors is kind of like six dorms. Then during the day, they opened the doors

---

4. Go-Go is a call-and-response type of funk music that originated with Black musicians in Washington, DC.

so everybody in the dorms could hang out in a smaller area together. But at night and in the morning, they locked us in this room with twenty-six people. There's six rooms with twenty-six people in each. They had the old style bars where you could sit there and yell at other people in the dorm and stuff. We were in downtown New York, so a lot of people had visits. People wanted to be able to use the phone. It was ridiculous. The elevator was broken, so we couldn't even use the phone. What the fuck? We can't even call our people and tell them that they can't come visit. I was like, "Man, fuck that." So the food trays come, and every single person refuses them the first time. Everybody did. Even the orderlies refused to hand out the trays of food. The captain had to come up. He was pissed, and everybody was just yelling at him. Eventually, they let us out and let us use the phone, although they still didn't allow us any visits.

Politics and Prison Dynamics

So, I participated in the drug program RDAP.[5] It takes nine months to start with, and then you can earn up to a year off of prison. The whole thing is a tough question: would you rather do easier time but more time, or would you rather do harder time but less time? For me, the sooner I could get out, the sooner I could get back into it, the sooner I could rebuild relationships with my friends and family. I mean, hell, everybody's in prison with you, right? Who wouldn't prefer to do easier time? But it's a year off your sentence [if you do the harder time]. I'm not trying to say anything about the importance of drug therapy and stuff like that because it is an alternative to incarceration.

But the main thing about it is it's more than just a drug program; it was actually more of a security ass-kissing contest. It really was a straight-up bootlicking thing. Plus, I was in a low security place, so the caliber of inmate, I mean, there were straight up rats and bootlickers. And in a program like this, they're rewarded and protected because it really is a dog-eat-dog situation. Only one out of every three people are graduating, so you basically have to sink somebody else and shit like that. I was probably at the worst one, like

---

5. Residential Drug Abuse Program (RDAP) is a Federal Bureau of Prisons approved program of therapy related to substance abuse. Reduced sentences are often offered to incentivize prisoners to participate in RDAP.

the worst one. I was skewered repeatedly, and that was with me trying to play along. If you would listen to me, you would even think like, damn, this guy is fucking a mockery of everything he stands for. And so I felt kind of fucked up. I never did anything in any substantial way that would compromise that. But, nevertheless, I felt like a puppet going up there and playing along and talking the talk. I didn't feel good about it, but I ultimately thought that it would earn me a year off prison. Ultimately, I could return to the struggle and then make more of a contribution into people's lives in a meaningful way, instead of me just sitting around for another year just doing nothing of any substance. Well, I mean, I was doing stuff, but I could be doing easy time where I do my own shit, or I could go to this program and get out of here earlier. So I put up with that. I didn't like everything that I had to say, and ultimately it didn't work out for me, and I ended up getting kicked out.

But during my time there, I like to think I made a contribution and difference to the scene because of the way I went out—everybody saw it for what it was. It was an ongoing, sad thing, man. Like every day somebody gets up there, and they just destroy somebody, and somebody gets kicked out, almost every day. And then you're dealing with people's actual lives. It's not just like, "Oh man, I got kicked out of the program." Instead it's, "Oh, man, my out-date got set back a year." So, you're dealing with real people's lives. And then there are people who are really straight-up bootlickers who are going around door-to-door making sure you aren't breaking any of the little rules. Man, I got set back so many times.

The whole time I was inside, my whole thing was trying to walk in a way that matched what I believe. I didn't feel completely good about myself, with RDAP and whatever; in retrospect, I guess it was also just a waste of time when I could have been doing something productive.

In general, I look back at my life and my tactics and ask, "Am I being the most efficient or productive? Am I fucking squandering an opportunity?" Then again, life is stressful, man, life is painful, especially in jail, so people do what they have to do to get by.

I definitely had a lot of cops mess with me over the years. A lot of times they don't like you, and they'll just wait for the opportunity to fuck with you. On the one hand, ACAB, hate all cops, but on the other hand if you're going to be seeing them and working alongside them (I worked in the kitchen at a lot of places), there might be a cop who's maybe not the biggest asshole.[6] He is an asshole in that he's going to pepper-spray you if he has to—this one particular cop actually did pepper-spray a bunch of people—but nevertheless, since I was a little cordial, he would let me slide on certain things. He would look the other way. On the other hand, you do also have to call out the assholes, and that comes at the cost of them not letting you slide.

Remember, though, that the first chance they get, they're going to crack your head. That's happened to me multiple times. When I was in Kentucky, I was working laundry, and I was beefing with this cop who was just the biggest asshole. I called him out one time, and I embarrassed him in front of all the prisoners, repeatedly. During the uprising in 2020, he was so bold that he would feel comfortable saying some obnoxious stuff, saying, "I would blow his noodle off myself," in reference to George Floyd.[7] He was a piece of shit, man.

I've filed grievances and had case managers tell me straight up, "You want to keep filing grievances? I'm just going to fuck you over. What do you think about that? I'm going to boost your points. I'm going to send you to a max. Is that what you want? You're going to make enemies." I told him, "I just want to be very clear. Are you telling me that you're going to retaliate against me if I file these?" He said, "I am. What're you going to do about it?" It's just naked, raw power, man. Anyway, I was a prolific grievance filer, all the way to DC, all the time. Mostly about mail stuff. I would say most of the time, it's smarter to just duck them and not let these cops even know you. But you have to push back too, right?

The main thing, I think, is that the system is a catalyst, just a factory for manufacturing white supremacy. One time—the saddest thing in the world—my first time being locked up, there was a young kid about my age from Wheaton, the western suburbs of Chicago. I talked to him at first, and we had been to some of the same places. But then I saw the white boys kind of roll up on him from afar, a whole group of them go and start hanging with him, kicking it with him. The next thing you know, the kid shaves his

---

6. The phrase "All Coppers Are Bastards" originated in England in the 1920s, was shortened to "ACAB" by striking workers in the 1940s, and was popularized in the US during the punk scene that emerged in the 1970s. The acronym is also often written as "1312," the numerical representation of the letters in English.

7. George Floyd was a Black man murdered by Minneapolis, Minnesota, police officer Derek Chauvin on May 25, 2020. His death sparked worldwide protests.

head; he's getting tattoos. Then he's not talking to me anymore. Just think about things like that, right? I went and sat next to him once, and he told me, "They said I can't sit with you anymore, man." I said, "You're just going to do whatever the fuck they tell you? Why?" And he said, "It's just how it is, man." It's sad.

I mean, all white people are racists, in a sense, but when that kid came in he wasn't like that, like, he wasn't a Nazi. But nevertheless, he just became that way. Maybe it was because he was young and needed protection or maybe it was just the pressure. There's this sense of uncertainty, and you just become a sponge when you're first there because you want to survive. It's very, very different with the white cliques versus other groups that may be self-organized based on race or affiliation. Very different, 100 percent different. All the feelings of life of white resentment and the bullshit sense of reverse racism is magnified there. A lot of white people feel like they're the minority and they have to protect each other and organize themselves. I've also heard a lot of people say they weren't racist before coming to prison but prison made them racist. There's a lot of racist bullshit in there.

Prison tends to cause a lot of people to lose faith in general human nature. Because you deal with a lot of broken people, and the system just breaks and breaks and breaks people further. Generally speaking, prisoners are overwhelmingly against police and prisons, and there's definitely a sense of pride in defining yourself in opposition to that and defining yourself as a convict that's true to the code, that's down.

In the feds, there's definitely a sense of fear that you just can't beat them. For one, during trial there's no shot, almost never. Nobody ever goes to trial, and everybody who does gets crushed absolutely. Which is a terrible, sad thing. So the consequence of that—not to mention the cooperating thing, which is much more prevalent at the federal level than the state—is that you're dealing with a lot of people who really see the system as unbeatable. The best thing to do is keep your head down and try to avoid the shots and just play the game. A lot of people really just want to keep their head down and do easy time. If you want to make a stink against the cops, know that the retaliation is real. So, a lot of people try to avoid that, especially if they have things going on, like side hustles.

And then there's another set of people who really kind of internalize and justify the logic of imprisonment. They're bombarded by being told, "You've fucked your life up. You did this. You need to get your shit together." Some people will even thank prison for saving them, saying, "Where I was in my life, I could have died." I mean, there's a very real sense of that too, and that's kind of a consequence of society in general.

Some people feel like they deserve to be in prison. At the same time, there are plenty of moments when authorities push too hard, and when they go too far, that's when people start talking about it, and other cars start talking together, that's what they fear the most.

Sometimes that's when they'll even throw concessions, which is like a sense of victory. It's a protracted tug of war, and ultimately I don't know what it's going to take to win the overall thing, but in these battles most of the time they win, but we have moments where we win too.

I hung with Connor Stevens [of the Cleveland 4], and I hung with Jerry Koch, the grand jury resister, in New York.[8] I got along very well with both Connor and Jerry. I also did time with Olajuwon Davis, from St. Louis, who was arrested during the Ferguson uprisings. It was an FBI entrapment to blow up the [St. Louis] Arch with the New Black Panthers. He's one of the most brilliant and going-places type of people I've ever met. He was a real deal. I played in a band with him, and I was in the drug program with him. He was very well loved, very talented, very intelligent. He's going places. I mean, almost everybody I messed with was political, was into revolutionary stuff. But they were people who had either become politicized in prison or politicized in the world. There was a sense of solidarity, for sure. Connor and I ran together for Running Down the Walls one year, along with another friend of ours.[9] We supported each other, and there was definitely a sense of bonding.

To the extent that I was able to participate politically from prison, it was basically writing articles and tweets and stuff like that. I wrote a lot of articles about what was going on in prison and my reflections of life outside. Just commentary from afar. I was lucky enough that a lot of people really did

8. Connor Stevens was one of the Cleveland 4, four Occupy Cleveland activists who were arrested in 2012 and accused of plotting to blow up a bridge after being coerced by an FBI informant. Jerry Koch was a grand jury resister who was imprisoned for his noncooperation. His story is included here.

9. Running Down the Walls (RDTW) is a 5k noncompetitive run/jog/walk/roll held annually since 1999 to raise awareness and funds for political prisoners currently held in North American prisons. See glossary. Find one or start one near you.

reach out and try to amplify my voice. *Wildfire* published some of my articles, and we'd publish things on Twitter and my support site.[10] I tried to the best of my ability to keep our Twitter account running, and later on during the grand jury thing, me and my brother did a podcast.

Everybody doing some amount of time is inevitably going to be in the hole at some point. Whether it's because of something they did or didn't do, or whether it's just simply because of being in transit or whatever the case may be, they're going to end up doing hole time. So I did spend months here, months there, months here, months there. A little bit more than a year probably, in total. You kind of get used to them doing the worst thing that they could possibly do to you. You get used to the idea that they could just literally take everything from you, even your clothes, your letters. Whatever meager possessions that you're able to amass, to surround yourself with, things that are familiar or are yours, know that they're going to take that from you entirely, put you in a completely different place with no understanding of when you're going to get out or anything like that. I mean, it is a constant struggle against time.

But just like in regular prison, in the hole you develop a routine. I read a lot. I loved getting absorbed in books. You have to go about it with humility too, because at this point they use solitary with so many people in prison. Oftentimes, it's not something special that's happening to you; it's something that they do to everybody. And so when we complain and speak out about solitary, it's often not just a personal struggle. It's more like complaining about generalized conditions, that solitary is used as general policy. It takes a strong mind to survive it, but it comes down to that last inch; if you don't let them take that last little bit of you, then you'll be all right.

I don't have any regrets for doing the things I did to get me here. I look back pretty fondly about the ways that I fought back the whole time, and that I did good for the most part and walked the way I believe. I learned lessons along the way, but I would like to think that I reached a lot of people and developed relationships with people that are lasting beyond the time that I was in jail. I correspond with a lot of people still that I knew inside. I always look back and think, "Did I pull this off with the most precision? Could I

---

10. *Wildfire* was a newsletter focusing on solidarity with US anarchist prisoners, support for prison rebellion, and antiauthoritarian struggle against prison.

have done it better?" It's always important to reflect on your actions and see if you met your goal and what things can be improved. I'm always looking to see how I could be more effective. I think I did a pretty good job, I would say.

Looking Forward

I was very fortunate to have been very well loved and supported every step of the way, especially this [latest] time in prison. People went to my court dates, had rallies at the jail, sent me birthday cards, and I got letters from different ABC groups and books from Books Through Bars.[11] I was always very well taken care of. People were always helping me amplify the voices of projects that I was working on. So, those are all the things that you can ever possibly imagine in solidarity work.

In a sense, people aren't going to be really free until we tear down the system. People's only hope is to tear the whole prison system down. There are no appeals left in the equation. It's all or nothing for most people. I had a lot of cellies who were lifers, pretty wise folks. It also has to do with the system's attempts to make their atrocities invisible. They try to hide the shit that they do on the inside to people on the outside world, and they try to prevent the people on the inside from speaking out to the outside world. So us undermining that in any sense, just making it visible to people, is undermining it. And I think we do that very well.

Think very carefully and completely though before you do something, and accept the consequences. If you're going to be involved in this type of work—even if you aren't even doing anything illegal—nevertheless, we know what we're up against. Be very real and clear about what type of consequences you could have, and accept those. That way you're not completely caught off guard. Also, study other people's cases. That's something that we do pretty well.

Before you get involved, just understand and think through your actions very carefully and what it means to yourself and other people if you were to be caught. Keep your head up and remember that even the

---

11. Books Through Bars (BTB) are informal groups that send free books and information to incarcerated people. Find a BTB group or start a books-to-prisoners group near you.

non-direct-action-type stuff—what you do every day, the small interactions, and walking in a way that reflects what you truly believe—is tremendously important.

Kojo Bomani Sababu

Kojo Bomani Sababu (Grailing Brown) is a New Afrikan Prisoner of War currently serving a fifty-five-year sentence for his involvement in a bank expropriation on December 19, 1975.[1] He was subsequently charged with conspiracy for an alleged plan to use rockets, hand grenades, and a helicopter in an attempt to free Puerto Rican prisoner of war Oscar López Rivera, who was convicted in 1981 of seditious conspiracy for his part in struggling for a free Puerto Rico. Kojo has served over forty-five years in more than ten federal penitentiaries, including Leavenworth, Lewisburg, Marion, and ADX Florence.

Prison Life

I was not prepared to spend this much time behind concrete and steel. Psychologically, I've always been strong, so no problem there. Throughout the years support grew and then decreased. It is pretty much stable on the family front.

No [prison] time is tolerable. In the 1980s and early 1990s, the programs existing in the institutions gave you the opportunity to have true leisure. These places [now] are warehouses of human flesh used for misery,

---

1. According to former political prisoner Sundiata Acoli in his essay "A Brief History of the New Afrikan Prison Struggle," "We use the term 'New Afrikan' instead of Black to define ourselves as an Afrikan people who have been forcibly transplanted to a new land and formed into a 'new Afrikan nation' in North America. But our struggle behind the walls did not begin in America."

inundated with young men without any guidance. My quality of life has gotten worse. I have hypertension, diabetes, I can't exercise, and I need hip and knee replacements, both on the left side of my body. I also have a prostate problem. But through it all, I manage gracefully.

My most pleasant moments have been when I'm with like-minded people. The best times were with the following: Jihad [Abdulmumit], Oscar [López Rivera], Ray [Luc Levasseur], Mutulu [Shakur], Sekou [Odinga], and many other comrades, like those in May 19th [Communist Organization] and Ohio 7 [defendants].[2] We had great discussions and much warmth.

Since being imprisoned, I lost my wife, sister, two brothers, three aunts whom I loved dearly, and an uncle. Coping was not hard. I knew I could not change the results, nor would I be allowed to attend funerals. The amount of rage, lack of morals, low education levels, psychological problems, and hopelessness surrounds you daily. You must navigate around this always or get with it.

My proudest achievements inside included teaching a few people how to read and helping prisoners overcome doubt in what they can achieve. It's a great feeling to have someone thank you for making them see a different alternative than incarceration.

Politics and Prison Dynamics

You are always faced with a situation that may run counter to concepts you live by in prison. Racism is a normal product of federal prisons; it is a tactic used by employees to maintain control. Keeping people divided into gangs or other social groupings denies prisoners the ability to unite on issues regarding

2. May 19th Communist Organization was a revolutionary anti-imperialist organization dedicated to acting in solidarity with and following the leadership of national liberation movements inside the borders of the US and around the world. The name refers to the birthdays of Malcolm X and Ho Chi Minh and the date of the death of José Martí. May 19th worked with Black, New African, Puerto Rican, Mexicano/Chicano, South African, Palestinian, and other groups fighting to free the land and for independence and socialism, and analyzed the US as being a white settler-colonialist state. The group organized white people to join in anti-imperialist solidarity in a number of projects including the John Brown Anti-Klan Committee and in support of political prisoners. The Ohio 7 were captured defendants and members of the anti-imperialist underground organization the United Freedom Front (UFF), including Levasseur and Jaan Laaman, both of whose stories are included here.

their imprisonment. Racism is paramount in prison. You cannot hide from it. It will confront you at every level of confinement. Wading through rough waters in this swamp is normal. Progressive people in prison do not allow racism to ruin ties. When the tension is in the air, people stick to their base.

My stints in Marion and ADX commenced as a result of disciplinary hearings. They find you guilty and make a referral to the regional office for placement at administrative maximum institutions. Once transferred to those prisons, you are scheduled for a review at yearly intervals. Marion replaced Alcatraz; ADX replaced Marion. Seemingly all these institutions are now using mind control, behavior modification, and ideological control programs.

Looking Forward

Outside support is essential to the political prisoner. There is a need to remain connected to your roots. It keeps the PPs [political prisoners] energized and abreast with matters confronting the movement, and they could contribute insight on matters. PPs should exchange information that may become useful in resolving problems.

The prison reform movement died many years ago. It attached itself with many people inside that were no good. Needless to say, we still have to have a strong movement to abolish these places. Organizations that stand up for the rights of the oppressed are faced with imprisonment, so their quality of life in these places should be better than what we have now.

If you become a person in confinement, you should first realize this is a serious affair. Do not destroy any ties with family, friends, kinfolk—you'll need an outlet, a pressure valve. Nothing makes you feel better than a hello from someone not within arm's reach. Don't be antisocial, but be careful when you talk to or get involved with others. Study. Take advantage of all this free time and apply yourself to things that are useful to you.

Keep supporting PPs who are confined. Subscriptions to magazines, books, and newspapers make time pass much more easily. Stress is a functional part of separation from opportunities you once held. You will be commanded to do some of the most absurd things. Understand this is a life you have no control over, but you can control your responses.

Laura Whitehorn

Laura Whitehorn served almost fifteen years in high security federal prisons for her involvement in the anti-imperialist armed actions that culminated in the Resistance Conspiracy Case of the mid-1980s.[1] She served time at the Baltimore City Jail, the DC jail, the high security unit at FCI Lexington, FCI Alderson, FCI Dublin (then called Pleasanton), and the high security unit in Marianna, Florida. Laura was involved in Students for a Democratic Society (SDS), the Weather Underground Organization (WUO), the May 19th Communist Organization, Prairie Fire Organizing Committee (PFOC), and many gay rights and AIDS support groups.[2] Since her release at the turn of the century, she has been involved in a number of causes and is a cofounder of and organizer with Release Aging People in Prison (RAPP).[3] Laura edited and wrote the introduction for *The War Before: The True Life Story of Becoming a Black Panther, Keeping the Faith in Prison and Fighting for Those Left Behind* (Feminist Press, 2010).

---

1. The Resistance Conspiracy Case started in 1985 when seven anti-imperialist activists were charged with bombing military and corporate targets in the US throughout the early 1980s. See glossary.

2. Students for a Democratic Society (SDS) was a predominantly white student activist organization that rose rapidly in membership between 1960 and 1969 before splintering. One of the groups that resulted from the dissolution of SDS was the Weather Underground Organization (WUO), a militant clandestine organization that carried out bombings of corporate and government targets throughout the 1970s in solidarity with Third World communities inside and outside of the US.

3. Release Aging People in Prison (RAPP) is a New York–based advocacy and education organization created and led by formerly incarcerated people that works to free incarcerated elders. See glossary.

Prison Life

No matter where I was, I exercised, and in some places it was really hard. At Baltimore City Jail, it was ridiculous but fun because it was on the roof. From the roof you could actually shout, and people from the neighborhood would come. And then we were all singing, "The roof, the roof, the roof is on fire. We don't need water, let the motherfucker burn!" It was a ridiculous way to exercise: you had to run around it probably twenty times to make a mile. But exercise was something I did wherever I was, including just running in place in my cell.

I felt mentally prepared for a few reasons. One, I had done jail time in Pittsburgh, Allegheny County Jail, and in Cook County Jail for political protests of different sorts back in the 1960s and 1970s. So, I already knew that jails and prisons were the belly of the beast, that they were full of Black people, many of whom had ridiculously petty cases. In Baltimore City Jail when I was there, there were women who were in there because they couldn't pay a bail of $50. So, I was ready for the community that I walked into, and that was really important. Because of my politics, I had some grasp of the role of prisons and jails, so I was ready for that. And because we were doing illegal things when we were underground, it wasn't a *surprise* to be arrested, but it was a shock, totally a shock.

There wasn't that much of a support system in Baltimore when I was arrested because my dear late comrade Marilyn Buck and my still-current comrade and friend Linda Evans had just been arrested in New York at the same time. Susan Rosenberg and Tim Blunk had been arrested up there almost a year earlier. So, there wasn't anyone in Baltimore who could come down and see me and stuff. But I had support. I felt support from the people in New York, and then I was able to create support in Baltimore. That was back when you still had phone books, and I got the phone book from the chaplain's office and I went through and looked under "committee," and I wrote letters to all of the support committees asking them to pay attention and to come visit. And CISPES (the Committee in Solidarity with the People of El Salvador) did; they sent people in, and I met some of the Catholic left people that way too, who came in and visited me.[4]

---

4. The Committee in Solidarity with the People of El Salvador (CISPES) is a grassroots

In our case, because we were white, because we were from a movement that already had some coherence, and because Linda and I right from the beginning were out lesbians, we attracted support that we tried, over and over again, to make more general and to make apply to the Black prisoners in particular. There was some success but not enough. I think we had more support than most political cases from the beginning. Our families all gave us support as well.

The first thing that happened was that I formed friendships and was so embraced by the other women. And of course, the fact that my case in Baltimore was in the news, and that it was clear that we had done actions in solidarity with the Black Liberation Movement, Puerto Rico, Central America—people were really curious about me and also reached out to me *immediately* with support from inside the jail, even though the guards were ordering them not to come near me. So, they said *fuck that* and just came around me, supported me, brought me food. When you get arrested, you have nothing. They brought me everything.

I hate being told what to do, so getting used to the prison routine was hard. It was such a learning experience for me because I was the only white incarcerated person for most of the time that I was in the Baltimore City Jail and a lot of the time I was in the DC jail. I had to learn which of my attitudes about authority were legitimate and when to stand up and help give voice to the complaints of all of us in the jail, because I was used to doing that. But then I had to realize that some of my fury came from expecting to be treated better than that—from the assumption ingrained by white privilege, that I would be treated more humanely. I wasn't used to being treated so brutally, as opposed to all the Black women in the jail with me who had been treated this way all their lives. It was really a learning experience for me.

I also learned that I had social standing in the world that was different from the social standing of the guards who had direct control over me, but who were Black and mostly not college-educated. That was something that dawned on me after a while. At first I felt like, "Yeah, I'm standing up, and I'm getting away with that." And then I realized it was because there's still a social standing issue here. I think for white people in prison, that's generally

solidarity organization that has been supporting the Salvadoran peoples' struggle for social and economic justice since 1980.

a reality. You still have white privilege. Without that, I think I would have been in the hole even more than I was. And I would have been beat down much more often.

I was in very bad conditions in the Baltimore City Jail—they had me under twenty-four-hour lockdown at first. For the first month, I didn't get out at all. All the security around, even with all of that, which was not pretty and not pleasurable—at the same time, I realized that I had connections outside. I was held in pretrial detention, and Filiberto Ojeda Ríos, from the Puerto Rican struggle, had been in preventive detention for years.[5] Yet through legal connections, I was able to get an op-ed in the *Washington Post* about the issue. So, you know, those things don't go away just because you're a political prisoner. I may have been treated worse, but at least someone on the outside knew about it.

It's so funny: the conditions and the food at the Baltimore City Jail and in the DC jail were so fucking horrendous. By the time I got moved out of the Baltimore City Jail, I had gone from probably one hundred and ten pounds when I got arrested to weighing eighty-nine pounds because the food was so hideous. There were roaches and mice. It was really unbelievable. No heat and no hot water a lot of times. But I actually liked it better in those places than I did when I got to MCC in New York and to Dublin.

Because in the feds, a lot of the women prisoners were embezzlers or tax evaders, stuff like that, but there was a sense of entitlement, of "I shouldn't be here." And the way federal law worked, the only way you could get any break on your sentence was by snitching, so there were quite a few snitches in MCC in particular. There were enough people like that to make that an actual kind of culture, whereas in the city jails and county jails, people had more of a collective attitude of struggle, resistance, and community. I mean, you did hear that *some* in the city jails, but less often.

I was in Dublin with the *independentista* political prisoners from Puerto Rico, Marilyn Buck, Linda Evans, and later Donna Wilmott.[6] For a few years, we had an amazing collective of women political prisoners. We had that

---

5. Filiberto Ojeda Ríos was a Puerto Rican militant who cofounded the Boricua Popular Army, better known as Los Macheteros, and its predecessor, the FALN, to struggle for Puerto Rican autonomy. In 2005, Ojeda Ríos was killed by the FBI outside of his home in Puerto Rico.

6. *Independentistas* was a term used to describe Puerto Rican independence fighters.

revolutionary community, and we were able to affect the culture of the prison but also have relationships to movements on the outside. When I was moved to FCI Lexington, all of the DC women were there because there was no federal prison in DC and no long-term facility for women, which they built later. There was a different atmosphere and collectivity and sense of resistance there too. You find joy and community wherever you can. I was very fortunate that I was not in Florence or in Marion, in some of the men's isolation places that were more brutal and isolating.

There was one moment that jumps to my mind in terms of losing hope. I had this dear friend at Lexington—she had also been in the DC jail, it was a DC case, although she was originally from North Carolina—and her name was Amira Cooper. For some reason, some universal power, we just loved each other enormously. We were best friends. We spent hours talking together, sharing our lives, which were so different, and everything. She was my heart, as they say. This is 1990, I guess. And for people who had AIDS, we—the political prisoners—did a lot of HIV work, but it was AIDS. Somewhere in there, the virus was discovered as the cause of AIDS, but remember there were no effective HIV treatments yet. People were sick; they were dying hideous deaths. There was terrible, terrible discrimination from the institutions. I mean, it was just horrible. So, everywhere we went, we all created AIDS support and education. And we created that at Lexington, where all of the women in the federal system who had AIDS were sent because it had the hospital. We had created what we called the A-Team, A for AIDS, obviously.

But Amira and I were two of the people in that group, and she was fierce and great and amazing. One night, right before count, I was in her cell and I wasn't supposed to be there. She had a single cell because she'd been there a long time. And one night, right before the nine o'clock count, she said to me, "Laura, I just have to tell you, I have AIDS. And no one knows." At that point, it was a total death sentence. And then they called count and I had to clear the unit. I went up to where I lived, which was a big dorm, and I went into the bathroom and threw up from my guts. I cried and cried, and I missed count, and I got written up for it. Luckily, the guard knew something had happened, and Amira got him to tear up the shot [disciplinary infraction]. But at that moment, I felt like there was no hope because all these people were dying and we couldn't fucking do anything about it.

As a movement person, someone who had been fighting for all these different movements for so many years, I felt like we just didn't know how to do this, we didn't know how to save people that we loved. The same thing was going on already on the outside, so I had a body of grief in my heart from all the people on the outside that I knew who were dying. And then, I'm happy to say, she later won an appeal and got out on this compassionate release thing that the people in DC did for people with HIV. She lived a little bit longer, and then she died while I was still in prison. So that was a moment.

I think the other was when I heard that Kuwasi Balagoon died.[7] I was in solitary in MCC New York and had gotten written up. That happened to me a lot in the first five to seven years, until I learned how to do the same things without getting caught, how to operate clandestinely in prison. I was in the hole, and it was December 13, 1986, Marilyn Buck's birthday. I wasn't in general population, but she was, so she could make a phone call. She snuck to my cell and told me Kuwasi died. That was another moment where it was just really hard because again it was AIDS, and we had no sense of a movement that would really be powerful and antiracist and give a shit about people in prison, about Black people, Black queers, Black women. At that point, the movement that was supporting people with AIDS, which was a great movement, was really still defining AIDS as an issue for white gay men and straight men, and not white women, let alone Black people.

As far as the AIDS work that a lot of us political prisoners were working on then, when we all were sentenced and sent to where we were going, it became easier to communicate those things. But, yes, we did very similar work. When I was together with Marilyn [Buck], Susan [Rosenberg], Linda [Evans], and Silvia Baraldini in Marianna, Florida, there we were able to do a lot of good AIDS work because we had so many connections on the outside, and people would come visit us who were doing work on the outside.[8]

---

7. Kuwasi Balagoon was an anarchist and lifelong activist who was involved with the BPP and the BLA. He was a defendant in the infamous New York Panther 21 case, he escaped from confinement numerous times, and he was imprisoned from 1981 until his death of pneumocystis pneumonia, an AIDS-related illness, in 1986 at age thirty-nine. There is a collection of his writings called *Soldier's Story: Revolutionary Writings by a New Afrikan Anarchist* (PM Press, 2019).

8. Silvia Baraldini is an Italian activist who supported Black liberation and Puerto Rican independence and was imprisoned in 1982 for grand jury resistance and aiding in the prison escape of Assata Shakur. After being transferred to Italy in 1999, Baraldini was released from prison in 2006.

I lost my father while I was inside. I couldn't be with him as he grew ill and died. That was hard. I so appreciated how my sister not only took on his care but helped me connect to him during the decline. And Susan's father, Manny Rosenberg, that was a big loss. He was diagnosed with cancer and died really fast. He was a wonderful, wonderful man who really threw down for political prisoners and was very connected with the Puerto Rican prisoners, in particular. There's so many people, I can't even remember all of them. Mike Riegle, a queer leader who died of AIDS and had been a friend.[9] And then inside, especially at Lexington, women were just dying of AIDS every week. I grieved, and I would go out and run if I could, and cry there. I also, I guess, turned my grief into anger. I started doing artwork around AIDS because I was so infuriated when the government came out with that stupid red ribbon stamp, when they were actually doing nothing. So that started me on creating, and that helped to bring some artwork. Ceremonies with people inside were important, all kinds of memorials, candle lighting, just holding each other— and when I say holding, I don't mean physically. In most places, we weren't allowed to physically hold each other, so we were holding one another's grief.

I was arrested in 1985, and I got out late in 1999, and that was the beginning of what's called mass incarceration. And for women, the numbers went up by 800 percent or so. For example, when I was first in the federal prison in California, I was in a cell that had been built for one, but it held two people. I came back after a few years when I was sent there again, that same cell had four women in it. A tiny cell. And when I got out, some of those cells had five women in them, and the TV rooms were converted to dorms. So there was that.

The quality of life, of course, became more punitive; things were taken away. In the beginning, when I was locked up in the feds, you could get clothing from home. But by the end, not only couldn't you get clothing from home, but you could only have a certain number of things. They would do shakedowns all the time and do that. There were also supposed "reforms" that were actually forms of repression. The system would institute programs that we had been doing ourselves, but now the programs were headed up by staff and there was a prohibition against us meeting together without staff.

---

9. Mike Riegle was a journalist, gay liberationist, and prisoner rights activist who wrote for the anarchist paper *The Fag Rag* and *Gay Community News*. He was a part of the Redbook Prison Book Program and advised the American Friends Service Committee (AFSC) and the AIDS Action Committee on the concerns of prisoners. Riegle died in 1992 after a long struggle with AIDS.

All to make it harder for incarcerated people to organize and resist, even to learn together without supervision.

The other thing about it was—and this was true in the beginning too but not the same massive numbers: I was in with women from California, which meant there were a lot of Indigenous women who had federal crimes because they're committed on a reservation. They were some of the most stand-up people because they were convicted of violent crimes. Whereas the white women in federal prison, a lot of them were [in] on sort of financial crimes and such. The Black women were the victims of the drug war. So, there were women I was in with who were in their twenties and thirties who were serving double-life sentences for some bullshit drug conspiracy.

Thankfully, through a lot of advocacy and struggle on the outside, some of them have gotten out now. But at the time, the people I was with, my friends, they had kids, or they didn't yet have kids. And I really could see the fabric of genocide. You're taking oppressed communities, and you're removing an entire generation, and a future generation, because the numbers were so huge of incarcerated women. That was really when I understood mass incarceration from the inside, and not just a matter of numbers but also as a strategy by the state to repress resistance, to keep communities from fighting back by destroying the fabric.

And then, of course, when I got out, I could see that by walking to Harlem and seeing how the housing stock had just been depleted because so many people had been sent to prison, and then their families got the burden. I saw that and I felt it. The quality of life went down. Mass incarceration created the basis for gentrification and ethnic cleansing.

When I first was arrested, because they stacked charges, I was facing a total of seventy-eight years. The other women thought that was an unbelievable amount of time. By the time I left, if I had done seventy-eight years, it would have been par for the course. People were facing hundreds of years of sentences. I think that kind of blew me away.

Mostly, everything I saw just sort of affirmed what I had thought my entire life, since I was old enough to notice that Black people were being segregated in New York and lynched across the country. In the federal system especially—even though it's the most racist, patriarchal, piece-of-shit system—they have to let you celebrate Black History Month and Women's History Month. So, from early on, I was part of these committees in different places. The Black History Month committee, for example, which was like five Black women and me. And in that, I was able to use my connections with people on the outside to get things in.

The best was when we showed [the 1971 documentary] *The Murder of Fred Hampton* in Lexington, I think. The guard who was assigned that night, luckily, was a total idiot, because I told him it was a mystery story about Black people. So, it's for Black History Month, and we were able to show that. Then in Lexington, which was full of the poorest, sickest women from DC and elsewhere, we created a Black History Month show that was like an Oprah Winfrey show where people played the first Black women to do whatever, to work at NASA and all this very kind of petty bourgeois sense of what success is. This was my great honor, when we performed the show, instead of having to play a slave catcher, I got to play Gerda Lerner, a white woman who wrote a book called *Black Women in White America*.[10] It's hysterical; it was a bullshit role they created just for me. But the joy was, I sat there in the auditorium, watching this play and realizing how revolutionary it was that this group of women had come together and fought with the administration and created this powerful show. The administration almost closed it down at the last minute because some of the racist white women went to the warden and said, "This is anti-white." Amira again came and got me and said, "Come on, white person, you can support us." We went to the warden and I gave him my white-person word that the show wasn't anti-white. So, being part of that creative experience, it really felt like something was being accomplished because the way that everyone felt the next day was different.

Politics and Prison Dynamics

In our case, the Resistance Conspiracy Case, through a lot of really hard legal wrangling with our lawyers—especially Alan Berkman (one of my deceased codefendants) and Linda Evans, both of whom were really brilliant on being able to understand the law (Linda still serves that function in the case to try to release Dr. Mutulu Shakur, in particular, but also in Ban the Box)—we

10. Gerda Lerner was a radical historian and writer whose work was prominent in the 1960s. The book *Black Women in White America* chronicles over three centuries of Black women's contributions to history.

were able to fight our case.[11] We were able to have a situation where we didn't go on trial, appeals were going up to the Supreme Court, and Alan had developed first Hodgkin's lymphoma and then a repeat of Hodgkin's lymphoma. He was really, really ill. At different points, he almost died.

Finally, we were in the DC jail and were looking at going to trial. Because of Alan's treatments and the radiation, he was paralyzed from the waist down, and he was deathly ill. At that point, there were two federal medical centers for men, one in Springfield, Missouri, and one in Rochester, Minnesota. They were as different as day and night. Rochester had the Mayo Clinic right there, and Springfield was a butcher shop.

We had been discussing taking a plea deal, and I had been totally opposed to it because we wanted a political trial, and our position was, "Yes, we had done these things, but the government was so violent and illegal that we had to." I was the person who was the most opposed to even considering a plea bargain. And one night I was in my cell in the DC jail, and a friend of mine who worked in the infirmary came down, and she told me Alan was in a dire condition. Then the next day I walked into our codefendant legal meeting and I said, "I'm ready to deal. I'll take my whole forty-five years, I don't care." It was hard.

I look back, and I think, I didn't even give my fingerprints when they wanted to take my major case prints. When I was arrested, I fought that for like three years because it would help them. I wouldn't stand up in court. I don't have a problem with those sort of, I guess, performative gestures at certain points. But I was dead set against a plea bargain, and I had to do it because if we had not done it and had stayed in that jail, and he had been sent to Springfield, I definitely thought he would die. I don't know if that's true, but that's what I thought. That was hard for me. By the way, we wrote a whole position paper about why we did it to try to explain, and we sent it to our comrades in Germany and Italy (the Red Brigades and the Red Army Faction).[12] And we got a letter back from the Italians saying, basically, "What the fuck is wrong with you, explaining that? Of course you did that. Revolution is about love. There's nothing wrong with that."

11. Ban the Box is a campaign that fights to remove the check box in hiring applications that asks if applicants have a criminal record.

12. The Red Brigades were an armed and militant Marxist-Leninist organization active in Italy primarily during the 1970s. The group made a minor resurgence in the 1990s and 2000s.

[I was in conflict] with other incarcerated people, especially in Lexington, at Dublin, and at Marianna, where there were white women who were either anti-abortion people or members of biker groups that were racist. There was this one woman in California when Linda and I were first there in 1987, who would make these pretty notecards. She would make notecards and sell them to other prisoners. A lot of the women really liked her because she would give them cards for free if they needed one for something. This one woman one day came to me and Linda in the yard and said, "Why are you so mean to this woman?" We'd say, "Because she's a fucking Nazi." So, sometimes it was on that level.

Other times I had some physical confrontations. I had physical confrontations with bullies a lot at different times, especially in the DC jail and then in California. When I was first there in Pleasanton, it was coed. That was right before AIDS totally blew up and they stopped having coed prisons. It was still coed, so the guys who were there were all snitches (they'd get sent there because the prosecutor had said, "Give us some information and we're going to send you to a prison where there's three women to one man, and you're going to have a good time"). They were horrible, and I had a lot of confrontations with bullies and snitches there who were men.

I hit and I got hit, there were physical confrontations, but I never got the shit beat out of me, which was kind of fortunate for me. I'm little, so when I stand up to a large person, sometimes it takes them aback. One person even said to me, "You're not scared of an ass whipping?" And I said, "No, I'm scared of a lot of things in my life. But I grew up with very strict parents. I got a lot of whoopings." But, again, it's different if you're Black because you're more vulnerable to being physically abused by guards and punished if you fight back. And it's different in the men's prisons, where physical confrontations can be generally more violent.

I remember talking with Alan about this when we got to the DC jail. I was talking about the little Nazi enclave of women and how we'd challenged them, and he said, "In a men's prison, you have to handle it really differently because you can get knifed." It just was different. Because for me, I was really fortunate that things worked out that way. But in women's prisons, there was also violence, and especially sexual violence by guards, or the constant threat of sexual abuse by the guards.

For me, one of the hardest things was being pat-searched every day by male guards. I actually got written up once for "attacking," a guard. I just elbowed him to get his hands off me. That was a constant—standing up, avoiding, and confronting the sexual abuse of women in the system. It happens every single day, and it's not even seen as abuse. It's just what they do. Strip searches, group strip searches where you're with five other women and you're stripped, not by men, usually by women guards, but still. That was one of the things I had the hardest time with and had the most confrontations with guards over, personally.

There was one time when being Jewish was a bone of contention, and that was in Marianna, Florida. When I got there, Marilyn, Susan, and Silvia Baraldini were already there. Susan and Silvia had been sent there from the Lexington high security unit for women, which is an experiment that the government tried and failed at. Marilyn was probably just sent there because she was high security. I got sent there as punishment for a rebellion that we did at Lexington, where we just all gathered in the main area and wouldn't go in for count, which is, of course, the worst thing you could do. When I got sent there, you did an intake, and it always asked you what religion you were. And usually I put none because I'm not observant. I didn't think it was important to say. But there Marilyn said to me she noted that she was Jewish (even though she wasn't) because there was a lot of antisemitism amongst the guards and the staff there. So I said, "Okay, well, if you can do it, I should do it too." So I did it, and we fought for certain things like getting matzo for Passover. They had an Easter pageant in the chapel there where some of the prisoners performed and said the Jews killed Christ. It was really bad there.

Then I had a cellmate who was one of the Black Hebrew Israelites, which is a very small religious organization.[13] She and I were friends and, because she was Jewish, she also got the matzo for Passover. You had to take your matzo with you to the cafeteria for meals, and she came and joined me at my table. She had forgotten her matzo so I gave her some of mine. And the chaplain wrote me up for giving away something that I had that only Jews could have. He looked at her, and he saw a Black person that couldn't be Jewish, even though he knew, because he had the list of Jews, which were

---

13. The Black Hebrew Israelites are a group of African Americans who believe they are descendants of the ancient Israelites, though many of their expressed views tend to be racist and antisemitic.

like five. He couldn't put it together, so to me that was a really clear example of racism. But I never got called names for being Jewish.

I got shit from guards for being a lesbian. There was one guard in particular in the DC jail who absolutely hated lesbians. When she would strip-search me, she would make me stand there naked, she would leave the room, she would do all this shit. She would poke my breasts really hard. There was also a guard at Lexington who, when he was pat-searching me, grabbed my breasts really hard and squeezed them. It was painful, and that's the guard that I elbowed. It came out that he was doing that to all the out dykes on that compound.

The main thing about being an out lesbian for me was that I could support the young women who were having their first lesbian relationships while they were inside. On Sunday, the chaplain would preach that if you're gay, you're going to hell. And young women would come to me crying, saying, "I'm going to hell." I don't know the Bible, so I'd have to say stuff like, "Well, does God create people he hates?" But even by embracing them, it played a role, and also I stood up for that politic.

I already talked about being in with a whole group of us anti-imperialist and *independentista* political prisoners in Dublin. But during my years in prison, I was also inside with some of the Plowshares prisoners, and that was really cool because we all quoted Frederick Douglass, "Power concedes nothing without a demand." But we advocated fighting in armed struggle, and they said we have to destroy those arms. It was really interesting and I learned a lot from some of them.

I loved being in with the Catholic left women. They really knew how to work the media. This one time, we had no water for a while. They gave us porta potties and a bottle of water a day, and we were all furious. Now this one woman from the Catholic left calls the media, and because of her status as a Plowshares person, she was able to reach someone, and she got the water fixed.

I think Liz McAlister was in with Lolita Lebrón and Marilyn [Buck], I think in Alderson. Also, Dylcia Pagan was there at the same time, and I think Assata Shakur at one point.[14] Assata was there, I think, when Marilyn

---

14. Assata Shakur was a member of the BPP and the BLA who was imprisoned from 1973 until 1979, when she escaped from prison and was later given political asylum in Cuba.

was there in the seventies. I think that might have been before Liz's time. In California, we would do programs in the chapel together where Marilyn, Linda, and I would bring a certain kind of view, and the Catholic left people would bring a different kind of view, both about how to embody political principles. It was a great chance to learn and teach.

As far as being housed with my codefendants, when we were in DC together, it was because we were on trial. But when we were in the other prisons, at that point there was only Dublin, California, and Danbury. They hadn't even opened Tallahassee yet. And then on the lower security level, there was Alderson and all these low level places, but there weren't other FCIs for women. Obviously, when they started to lock up two million people in this country, that changed quickly.

Then there were times when I learned about performative principles— things that were being performed but not really enacted. There was this one woman whom I really loved. We were in Dublin, and there was this part of the compound where there was grass and a sign saying "Don't Walk on Grass." She told me, "I'm going to walk on the grass because I shouldn't follow any of the rules here." And I said, "If you're not going to follow the rules, when you get brought into the institution, you have to refuse to give your name, refuse to give your information, and get put in the hole. Do your whole time there. You can't pick and choose." And then I went back and I thought about myself and how I, at times, had picked and chosen where to make a stand because it just felt like something I wanted to do, treating resistance sort of as an emotional outlet. So, that changed me. I learned so much in my years in prison.

The night I was first arrested, I was put into this horrible cell in Baltimore City Jail, and it was hot as hell. It was May, the cell I was in was over the laundry, and I couldn't sleep. I lay there, and I thought two things. One, you better fucking believe in your politics, girl, because now you're going to do life in prison for them. So, you better figure out right now how you want to do this. That one was kind of easy. And then the other thing was—you know how people say they can take everything but my dignity?—well, I thought to myself, if they start taking my sense of humor, they've won. Because that's what keeps me going.

Just being able to look at life and see the absurd and find some kind of joy in that. You feel like you've been part of a movement that you thought was going to win, and then we didn't win. Instead we got all this repression as a result, and all of that. Susan and I, especially in Marianna, used to just make up stories, make up screenplays for television. I mean, we didn't really write them, but I think that really helped to alleviate some of the grief and some of the fury. We still laugh about those made-up TV sitcoms we thought of back then.

But the first thing we were all doing was the AIDS work. David Gilbert and my dear friend, cofounder of RAPP, Mujahid Farid, they were two of the three men who started what later became PACE (Prisoners for AIDS Counseling and Education).[15] I think we all did that because of where we found ourselves and what we felt about it.

There was this moment when I was in Lexington when the Rodney King beat-down happened, and I was getting some newspaper [coverage], I think it was the *Guardian*, some left activist newspaper.[16] And Barbara Smith—whom I had known back in Boston, and who taught me a lot about the difference between what white lesbians and Black lesbians face—had an article saying all these white left organizations are issuing statements condemning blah blah blah.[17] And she said stop making statements that just say you support what *we're* doing and start organizing against racism yourselves. Taking us back to SNCC and what Kwame Ture was saying, we don't need you to organize the Black community.[18] And I thought, what am I doing? And I started to write for publications on the outside. After a while, I had a column in *Prison Legal News*, which was started by an incarcerated man and still exists today. I wrote articles and statements promoting antiracism in white spaces. This could never have happened without the support of people on the outside. Being in Dublin, California, we were thirty to forty minutes

15. Mujahid Farid served thirty-three years in New York state prisons and was denied parole nine times before he was released. He then cofounded Release Aging People in Prison (RAPP) with former political prisoners Laura Whitehorn and Kathy Boudin.

16. Rodney King is a Black man whose extensive and brutal 1991 assault by the Los Angeles police was recorded and led to international condemnation. The acquittal of the officers involved led to the 1992 Los Angeles riots.

17. Barbara Smith is an author and activist who was a leader in defining and establishing the field of Black women's studies in the US. Barbara and her coconspirators in the Combahee River Collective are credited with originating the term "identity politics," defining it as an inclusive political analysis for contesting the interlocking oppressions of race, gender, class, and sexuality.

18. Kwame Ture, formerly known as Stokely Carmichael, was a prominent Black leader and organizer with the Student Nonviolent Coordinating Committee (SNCC), an organization started in the South in 1960 that was a catalyst for pushing the Civil Rights Movement forward.

from Oakland, and we got visits all the time from activists out there, especially women activists who were doing work on Mumia Abu-Jamal's case.[19]
That was one of the first things we did, even back in DC, when he [Mumia]
was facing the death penalty and people had not heard of him yet, we got
the word out. Alan Berkman alerted us as to what was happening to Mumia.

We did a lot of collective artwork around Mumia and sent that out for an
art show called Art Against Death or Art Against the Death Penalty. Again,
it was because we had connections on the outside. We also tried to get the
attention of the movement around HIV, to the situation of people in prison
with HIV. That was also an antiracist struggle in many ways. There's a guy
who was a grand jury resister, Bob Lederer, who, with other people in New
York, was very open to that argument and tried to help from the outside.[20]
He was consistent with his work.

Bonnie Kerness is a dedicated activist from New Jersey who's done a
lot of work against solitary for many years.[21] A few years ago, she asked me
to contribute to something called "Survivors Manual: Survival in Solitary,"
put out by the American Friends Service Committee. The one I always talk
about is making a schedule for yourself and sticking to it, so that by the end
of the day, you don't fall into depression. Instead, you feel like, "Okay, I didn't
do much because I'm limited, but I did something."

The actual control unit I was in in Marianna, Florida, was a trip. It was
created after a very powerful struggle had succeeded in closing the high security unit for women at Lexington. One thing that happened that helped fuel
the campaign against the Lexington unit was that church groups were able
to tour the facility, and they could see the outrageous conditions. So the
new control unit was, as we thought of it, tour-proof. It looked very nice, we
could wear our own clothes, there were privileges that were supposed to

19. Mumia Abu-Jamal is a journalist, author, and former member of the BPP who has been
imprisoned since 1981. His death sentence was overturned in 2001, but supporters have been
advocating for his release from prison ever since. As of 2023, Mumia remains in prison.

20. Bob Lederer is a journalist, longtime queer antiracist and anti-imperialist activist, and
member of the grassroots collective Resistance in Brooklyn. In 1985, he was a grand jury resister
and political prisoner, and was a cofounder of the group Queers United in Support of Political
Prisoners in the 1990s.

21. Bonnie Kerness is a lifelong activist and organizer who has been a human rights advocate on behalf of prisoners since 1975, working as coordinator of the American Friends Service
Committee's Prison Watch Project.

make us forget we were in a tiny controlled place with no contact beyond the hundred women there (and the very many guards, of course).

At the time, comrades on the outside were agitating against control units, and quite naturally they focused on Marion and the other prisons for men. And they defined control unit by the conditions—twenty-three hours in-cell, for example. We wrote them to argue that it's actually the goal of the control unit rather than the conditions that define it, because if the goal is to crush revolution (as a warden at Marion famously admitted), they can try to achieve that goal through a combination and variety of conditions.

In general, physical brutality is more commonly used against men in prison because with the difference in size and number of incarcerated people, women in prison can often pose less of a physical threat to the institution. So you have to look at things other than physical conditions to see how the system functions. If you only look at what happens in men's prisons, you end up obliterating the realities of incarceration for women.

I wish I had been less arrogant. I wish I had figured out sooner what I was taught after I got out—by Eddie Ellis, former Black Panther who died, very important in the prison movement in New York, and from Farid, whom I mentioned before, and from Jose Saldana, who's now the director of RAPP—that we had to build more of an ideological connection between political prisoners and the situation of prisons.[22] I mean, we were all abolitionists before we knew that word because we're revolutionaries, and abolition is revolution—you can't just remove one huge aspect of state violence without confronting the system as a whole. But I wish that at that point I had been able to open my eyes and really see what mass incarceration was and how intimately it was connected with the repression of the Black Liberation Movement in particular.

I saw these pieces of it, but it wasn't until years later when Chokwe Lumumba—the late, great lawyer and mayor of Jackson, Mississippi—and I were in New York and were talking after a presentation he gave.[23] I

---

22. Eddie Ellis was a former member of the BPP and a former political prisoner who never stopped fighting for prisoners' rights. Jose Saldana is the formerly incarcerated current director of RAPP.

23. Chokwe Lumumba was a radical human rights lawyer prominent from the 1970s onward. He also served as second vice president of the Republic of New Afrika (RNA) and was later elected mayor of Jackson, Mississippi.

was talking about mass incarceration and how I knew it played a role in repressing communities. He said, "Look, first they did COINTELPRO and they destroyed revolutionary Black organizations and organizations from other national liberation movements. Remember that J. Edgar Hoover said Black youth should know that if they want to be a revolutionary, they'll either be dead or in prison. That was a serious plan, and mass incarceration has made that a reality."[24]

Not everyone in prison is a revolutionary, but if you can destroy communities and undermine their economic and social health, you can turn people against each other, you can prevent another era like the seventies with Black Consciousness. It was right in front of my face. And yet, when I got out, I started doing work on political prisoners that *isolated* cases of political prisoners from the overall situation and role of prisons in the United States. And it took some years. I mean, there was part of me that got it. In my AIDS work, working for *POZ* magazine when I got out, I was able to make some connections, but it took years. Plus, now working with family members of incarcerated people, I have a much clearer sense of how mass incarceration undermines and destroys families and whole communities.

RAPP really started in 2013, and I got out in 1999, so that's a slow learning curve. I don't see any problem in saying political prisoners are a particular class of incarcerated people and that one of the key roles of prisons is to incarcerate people who are rebels or who threaten the system in some way. I still believe that. But there's something about making a [connection] between political prisoners and the rest of the prison population that I wish I had gotten sooner.

Looking Forward

Outside support is utterly critical. People should listen to what the incarcerated people want. In the beginning of the pandemic, when people were dying in prison, RAPP did some of the first rallies. We actually did them in person outside Sing Sing and other prisons. And we always made sure to

---

24. COINTELPRO was an illegal and top-secret government counterintelligence program that was most prominently orchestrated by the FBI from the 1950s through the 1970s to discredit, neutralize, and eliminate subversive individuals and organizations.

communicate with people inside and say, "Are you going to get shit if we're outside doing this? What's the administration like there?"

Part of why we started RAPP was because we were hearing from the people inside that they were not able to get out due to the parole system, the way it worked in New York, and could we do anything to change that. So, listen to what people inside want. I always say to activists, "Do what's needed and not what you feel like you want to do." Sometimes that means doing very unsexy things like fundraising, and people don't want to do it because it's not like doing a rally.

I really feel that we need to understand that the one place in the US where people know about political prisoners is in the joints. I found this out when I started doing work with RAPP. When we started RAPP, we would go to these meetings at a place where a lot of reentry housing is. There would be a room full of like forty-five mostly formerly incarcerated men on a Saturday morning, who had gotten out, and the rest of us would be either advocates, family members, or formerly incarcerated people from elsewhere. We would start by going around the room and everyone could call the name of one person they wanted to bring into the space. Sometimes it was like Malcolm X or something. And guys I had never known would say Herman Bell, Jalil Muntaqim, David Gilbert, and they knew them through their practice inside.

That was something I knew myself because all of us—most people who are political prisoners—are doing something for their community when the community is inside. Read susie day's book about the lives of Eddie Conway and Paul Coates [*The Brother You Choose: Paul Coates and Eddie Conway Talk about Life, Politics, and the Revolution*].[25] Eddie went in and was like, "Okay, I'm in prison, I'm not doing anything." And immediately he became a mentor and a leader in there. When I was in Baltimore, I was in the women's jail and was hearing about Eddie Conway because of that. I think that putting those cases in the context of trying to end the system of permanent punishment, the racist prison and policing systems, is important.

Political prisoners are political prisoners because we are revolutionaries. So, to build a movement of support for political prisoners *separate* from

---

25. Eddie Conway was a former member of the BPP who spent over forty years incarcerated as a political prisoner in Maryland. Paul Coates was his friend who campaigned for Eddie's release and started the publishing company Black Classic Press in order to get books to prisoners. susie day is a journalist and Laura's partner.

the politics that we started with . . . In other words, look at the Ten Point Program of the Panthers. It was like, Black people shouldn't be in prison, Attica, you know, tear down these fucking prisons. To only focus on political prisoners separate from that, I think, is a mistake. That's what we tried to do with RAPP by looking at the actual mechanisms that are preventing the release of people inside. When we started, there were five or six political prisoners in New York State, and now, while very sadly some of them have died, the rest have now gotten out.

We can free political prisoners and have everyone out and nothing else changes, or we can free political prisoners and have—like in New York, all these other people getting out on the same pressures that we put on the parole board that allowed for the release of Herman, Jalil, Seth [Hayes], and David—a lot of other people who had violent crimes against police—and the cop unions had sworn that they would all die in prison—and we were able to get them out. It can be done. Same thing in Pennsylvania, with Maroon [Shoatz] and MOVE.[26]

I think people are doing amazing work. We all say all the time that there should be more unity, more of a central free-political-prisoners effort, but it's hard because there are so many distinctions in how the political prisoners could be released—I mean, some we have to push parole, some compassionate release, et cetera. And I do think politics is local, meaning a struggle needs to be centered in and strength gotten from the location, so if we want to actually get people out, it kind of makes sense that the work gets localized rather than centralized.

But if we can unite more in the way George Jackson said (Jose Saldana has been quoting this recently)—"Settle your quarrels, come together, understand the reality of our situation, understand that fascism is already here, that people are already dying who could be saved, that generations more will live poor, butchered half-lives if you fail to act. Do what must be done, discover your humanity and your love in revolution"—then we can

---

26. Russell Maroon Shoatz was a former member of the BPP and the BLA who spent forty-eight years in Pennsylvania prisons before being granted compassionate release in 2021 and dying less than two months later. The MOVE organization was founded in Philadelphia by John Africa in 1972 as a spiritual, back-to-nature group with a revolutionary ideology. MOVE faced police abuse from the start, and nine of its members spent decades imprisoned as political prisoners before seven of them gained their freedom. See glossary.

make the most use of all the groups.[27] For instance, the Jericho Movement has a great directory of political prisoners. I do think we're beginning to share and learn from each other's strategies, though, and that's a really good thing. Forcing the state to release people is a huge, hard task, so we need each other.

Don't snitch. Don't see power as those who are the biggest and meanest. Understand power as a collective process. Let us know you're there because there are people all over the country who are now aware. You don't put millions of people in prison and keep it a secret. That's the downside for the United States of their policies.

This is one of RAPP's principles: do not throw anyone under the bus. Jose [Saldana] talks all the time about how there are classes inside, of cases, and that sexual abuse and sexual abuse of children is at the bottom. As a crime, you can say that, but as a person who committed a crime, if we throw people under the bus, then our whole claim of being humane, of everyone deserving to be seen . . . Something that Mutulu Shakur always said when we were in MCC together for a minute, was, even the guards. Don't look at the uniform and think, Okay, I'm not going to try to reach you. People change, people's minds open.

Know that there is life in prison and life after prison. You're still alive when you're in prison. It helps to be able to find some way of feeling that every day. Herman Bell and I talk about that a lot. We both always found a tree somewhere that we could see out of a window or that was in the yard and sort of enjoy it. Look at the beauty, look at it changing, and have some kind of sense of knowing this is not permanent. This prison is not permanent.

I'd like people to understand how hard it was for susie [day]. How hard it is for a lesbian who has a loved one, because there's no recognition. Now, it may be different, but certainly back then, it was more restrictive. If your husband came to visit, you were allowed to kiss, to hold hands, at the beginning and end of the visit. For us, though, it was not permitted.

I want people to understand what the family members go through. RAPP now has community leaders who are family members, mostly Black and Latinx women who were isolated before they met us. They didn't know

---

27. The quote is from George Jackson, *Soledad Brothers: The Prison Letters of George Jackson* (Chicago: Lawrence Hill Books, 1994), xxv.

other people who had family members. We found them through leafleting in their neighborhood or something, then talking with them, and now they're our community leaders. The pain they carried every day; they are people whose loved ones will fucking die in prison if we don't win our demands for RAPP. I think of their courage. They don't quite get the same notice that the incarcerated people do because, of course, they can go home. They can go to McDonald's; they can cook dinner; they can do all those things.

But the trauma of having someone inside and not knowing from minute to minute whether they're alive. Did they not call because they were in the hole, or did they not call because the line was too long? When Sekou Odinga was still in, I remember talking with déqui [kioni-sadiki], when Sekou had pneumonia at one point.[28] His friend was calling her to report because Sekou was too weak to leave his cell and call her. She couldn't talk to him. She couldn't be there with him. I think about when my father was dying, I couldn't be there with him. Seeing it from the point of view of millions of people on the outside, and the courage that they have to stand up, and what we as a movement, if you're political, if you're a political person, what we have to do for the families in terms of love and existence and respect, is huge.

But really, don't throw people under the bus. If RAPP's initiatives restricted the benefits of going to the parole board when you're fifty-five, no matter your sentence, if we cut out people with certain kinds of cases, especially cases involving cops, we would've gotten it passed last year. It's such an easy bill. But then we'd be building the system, creating a new "undeserving" group of incarcerated people whose cases involved cops. I think we always have to remember, reforms that don't change some fundamental piece, that don't organize masses of people to understand the need to destroy the prison system, only make it harder for the next round.

On the other hand, I would say to abolitionists: Remember, when struggling around conditions that the people who are suffering under those conditions, they are the people who will make a revolutionary movement. Those people inside, and those getting out, that's the movement. So we need to fight for their humanity while they're inside along with fighting to get them out.

---

28. déqui kioni-sadiki is a tireless coalition builder, organizer, and educator and has served as chair of the Malcolm X Commemoration Committee. She waged a successful campaign for the release of her husband, Sekou Odinga.

Eric King

Eric King is an anarchist political prisoner who was arrested and charged with an attempted firebombing of a government official's office in Kansas City, Missouri, in September 2014 in solidarity with the protests following the police murder of Michael Brown.[1] In 2016, Eric accepted a noncooperating plea agreement and was sentenced to ten years in prison. Since his arrest and subsequent incarceration, he has been held in solitary confinement for years on end and has been assaulted by both guards and white supremacists. He has faced unprecedented mail bans and restrictions and has served time in numerous federal prisons, including USP McCreary, FCI Florence, USP Leavenworth, and Florence AdMax. Eric is a member of the Fire Ant Collective and has published three zines—*Battle Tested* (Causerie Publishing, 2015); *Antifa in Prison* (Radical Paper Press, 2019); and *Pacing in My Cell* (Radical Paper Press, 2019). His sentencing statement is included in the book *Defiance: Anarchist Statements Before Judge and Jury* (Detritus Books, 2019).

Prison Life

I wasn't mentally prepared in any way. I had to learn a lot of things on the fly, and a lot of it was painful and difficult. I knew prison was shitty, but I

---

1. Michael Brown Jr. was an eighteen-year-old Black man murdered by Ferguson, Missouri, police officer Darren Wilson on August 9, 2014, leading to increased protests against police violence.

175

wasn't prepared for the mental attacks, the lack of any control. It was horrible. Support was super-limited at first. I wasn't a part of any mass movement and didn't have any relationships with big radical groups. The first letter [from a supporter] was from Denver after about three days, and I ignored it because I thought surely it was a scheme. I called the number after a couple of weeks. Support grew slowly. I still have friendships with those first people (when I'm allowed calls and emails, that is).

It was hard to adapt to prison culture. I was very snobby. "I'm a revolutionary. I do what I want!" This didn't last long, but at first it was a challenge because we reject racism, we reject these divisions the system uses to keep us powerless. But, if you live in a shark tank and act like a turtle, you'll have all sorts of issues.

If I had to pick a "best time," it would be the twenty months at Florence. This was the longest stretch out of the SHU in my entire bid. I got to spend every Saturday and Sunday with my wife and kiddos, which is so big. I had a great routine, made long-term friends, had phone and email access, read amazing books, and stayed out of the way. Until it ended, it was the best time I'd done. Family access makes time tolerable.

My happiest moments are almost exclusively visits. Family days at Florence, where we could do activities and eat together. Playing card games with my wife, shit-talking with the little ones. Seeing real friends get released were super-good times. I got to listen to Kansas City's football team win at the Super Bowl back here in segregation. That was lovely. Being cellies with Jaan [Laaman] for five really great days was amazing as well.

I had done yoga moderately on the streets, but at Englewood I had an amazing teacher who I spent hours with every day. Dr. Joel was very patient and an enjoyable person. I was able to take that to Florence to actually teach it, and I have stuck with it since then through these SHU years.

At CCA [Corrections Corporation of America] I learned Scrabble, and I can't tell you how involved in this game I can get. I honed my skills there, went to Englewood, and got beat multiple times a day by my massive Hawaiian game partner, who taught me all the U words. Then I became a monster at Florence! I won three institution holiday tournament titles (not to brag) and got to feel like I am better than those around me, which is a prize in itself. Daniel [McGowan] recently got me a Scrabble dictionary, which I love!

I've lost hope many times in prison: My first time in segregation (nine months at CCA), while in holdover at Leavenworth, the first year in the Englewood SHU while pretrial. I'd like to say I just bit down and got through it, but that would be a lie. I cried. I got very violent. I got countless write-ups trying to cope. But over time, my wife helped guide me out of my wretched funks. Friends stuck it out and upped support. The hopeless times have been beaten by forcing myself to think of hopeful times. Sometimes you can do it on your own, channeling the strength of those before you. Other times, you need family and friends to hold you up, call it out, do whatever it takes to bring you back. Where there's love, there's hope.

I have lost family while locked up, and it really sucked. The one which crushed me was my brother dying. He died in a house fire in December 2017, and I still don't feel I've dealt with it. We were locked down, and I just cried and cried. My poor cellie must have been so uncomfortable. But his stepbrother had died two days prior! Trying to talk about it—and understand what are very complex feelings—has helped, but there are tears left to shed.

What's shocked me the most is the very casual attitude toward extreme violence. The beatification of those who "have a body" (killed someone). It is expected that you will engage in violent acts, and if you aren't up for it, then violence will be brought to you. I've worked my way up in custody, so I've seen it at low, medium, and penitentiary level, and the pen level still shocks me. I'm up for whatever, but beating someone's head in because they *didn't* feel like beating someone else's head in? For changing the channel? For wearing shower shoes (instead of boots) to the shower? Feels a bit over the top and underdiscussed. It's stupid as hell.

The number of convicts who support "law and order" politicians was also confounding. Along with the visceral hatred towards women, gays, and transgender people, you'd think there were droves of transgender wizards roaming the states cursing everyone, being the cause of every problem on earth. It still shocks and sickens me.

My proudest achievements have been growing my relationship with my family through very hard times. Allowing myself to be open, vulnerable, honest, and to not close myself off to being sad or happy, or to criticism, loving, call-outs. I feel I've strengthened my politics and intellect. I'm very proud that I've never [stood by and] watched someone be victimized for their sex or gender, no matter how risky or hairy the situation was. So, really I'm proud of growing as a person and being decent in a world that can punish decency.

Politics and Prison Dynamics

I find myself in conflict with my ethics every day in prison. Sitting with a bunch of snaggletooth racists in the chow hall and the TV day room sucks, but you do it because to do otherwise would result in your head getting kicked off. And it wouldn't cure prison racism. Having to fight other prisoners makes me sick also. It's doing the state's job. But you do what you must to keep things smooth. You aren't going to change prison, but you can try and not let prison change you.

It seems I've had nothing but conflict this entire bid. As a left-wing radical, you can get it from all sides: white gangs/racists and the admin at the same time (they are often the same, it seems). It's always played out in violence. That's how everything in prison ends up. There's been times just being "antifa" has resulted in fights with prisoners—sometimes orchestrated by SIS [Special Investigative Supervisor] (hello, McCreary). Sometimes being an outspoken anarcho-prison-hater has resulted in getting attacked by staff (hello, Florence and Englewood SHU). Being different in an environment that craves conformity leaves you open to many issues, and you either fall in line or you get dragged into the broom closet by a lieutenant or try to calm your breaths while being strangled during your inaugural four-pointing [being shackled in four-point restraints]. In recent times, the whole antifa thing has caused countless confrontations with staff, resulting in outrageous mail, phone, visit, and email bans.

I've navigated racism in prison very delicately. I've had friends and interactions with people of all races, but you live, eat, watch TV, and workout with "your race," and it sucks. I've been able to teach and take classes with other races and gamble/play cards with everyone. I've had some issues for being an "n lover," which has resulted in tension and violence. When you're known to be antiracist, some watch and critique your every move. Some people have their whole lives built around politicking and hating. The big issue for whites is Blacks. Having a walk and chat with Indigenous people or Mexicans doesn't raise the same eyebrows. Once you're established as a "solid white guy," the scrutiny lessens greatly. I don't think I ever established that. Some don't give a shit at all. A bro of mine would workout with the Crips and let people know, "If you don't like it, come stop me." He was 6'3", 230 pounds. At a medium [security prison], folks weren't willing to push that line. At a USP, he may have been beaten off the yard, maybe stabbed.

I've done time with more right-wing "political prisoners" than our mob. I've been celled up with two Bundy people. I've been friends with many Islamic fighters of various degrees. One, Talib, I shared a good friendship and respect with. He's got twenty-eight years for plotting a federal court-house bombing. We're not so different, LOL. At Florence, I was with a reformed Army of God member, who suffered great guilt for his actions. Then at McCreary I got to be cellies, then friends, with long-term freedom fighter Jaan Laaman. Wait until you see his list of "who's who" he's done time with. Jaan really looked out for me right out of the gate, and it was an educational and inspiring five days that have had an impact on my life ever since. It inspired this entire project! Cleveland 4 comrade Skelly was there also, but we didn't get a chance to meet.[2] But, by all accounts, he's a wild, great guy (and a great pillow maker).

When I first got locked up, I fell back badly, mostly out of being over-whelmed and fearful. Then, when you get your footing and start finding your voice, it changes. At Florence, I had a lovely project going of having amazing portraits done of long-timers. We only got three done before they got me out. In the last few years, I've done tons, and it's felt amazing. Organizing barricades, trashings, setting up mini-riots and group hunger strikes for basic rights. When I had mail, I was signing folks up for IWOC like hotcakes.[3] I was not the founder, but I was at ground level for Fire Ant, which is an anar-chist collective between anarchist prisoners and comrades and friends in the free world. This is a really amazing project that I'm blessed to be a part of. [People in] Maine and Bloomington coordinated together with Jennifer

2. Joshua "Skelly" Stafford was one of the Cleveland 4, four Occupy Cleveland activists who were arrested in 2012 and accused of plotting to blow up a bridge after being coerced by an FBI informant.

3. The Incarcerated Workers Organizing Committee (IWOC) is a prison-led section of the Industrial Workers of the World (IWW) that works to abolish prison slavery and fights to end the exploitation of incarcerated workers.

Rose and others to bring it to life, and I'm so impressed with its creation and continuation.[4]

Organizing and resistance comes at a cost. I've gotten an absurd amount of disciplinary write-ups, losing months and months of good time. Even perfectly legal things can lead to increased monitoring and harassment. I've been given write-ups for writing to IWOC and leading "group-led demonstrations," for writing poems that NYCABC put in their newsletter (they were referred to as a "terrorist organization").[5] There is always a great deal of risk/threat by pushing the line forward inside. I've really focused on sharing what happens behind bars, putting out writings that call out the violence, racism, hypocrisy, and shadiness of the prison and its administrators. Right now, I'm organizing with a long-term friend and supporter to put together a book honoring the lives of political prisoners while they are (or were) inside. [You're reading that book right now!]

It's always risky business, though. I've been given shots (write-ups), put in the SHU, physically attacked, had my phone and mail taken for years, all for calling out their naughty behavior. I've been inspired by things like Victory Gardens and Certain Days and Fire Ant, which join up outside comrades with folks inside, with creative, tangible results.[6] It's empowering and everything the prison system despises. Honestly, I really wish there were more link-ups between us inside and those outside. It's a very difficult thing to pull off, which makes those who do pull it off that much more impressive and admirable. Something like Certain Days links free world, state, and federal prisoners and has been going on for years. It's a huge project that I admire greatly. Prison is another front to the same struggles, and the more we can build together, the better.

I think a few may agree with me, but minus the lack of visits and daily

4. Jennifer Rose is a trans anarchist prisoner, jailhouse lawyer, organizer, and Fire Ant collective member who has been in prison since 1990. Her story is included here.

5. The New York City Anarchist Black Cross (NYCABC) is the New York chapter of the ABC, an anarchist political prisoner support organization.

6. The Victory Gardens Project (VGP) was formed between political prisoner Herman Bell and outside supporters in rural Maine as a mutual aid project of growing and distributing organically grown produce in oppressed communities and providing political prisoner education. The Certain Days: Freedom for Political Prisoners Collective was formed in 2001 and creates an annual calendar to raise awareness and funds for North American political prisoners. Certain Days was originally cofounded by New York state political prisoners Herman Bell, David Gilbert, and Robert Seth Hayes, and their outside supporters.

showers, long lockdowns start feeling like little vacations from the nonsense of prison life. You can catch up on books, magazines, and letters. You get to finally sleep in, slack off on your fitness (a little). I've been blessed to either have a good cellie or to be single-celled during lockdowns. With a bad cellie, it could be very bad.

The violence inside that causes the lockdowns is really gross to me (except rare occasions, on staff). I cope with it by not engaging except when absolutely necessary. I don't spend all day reminiscing about "this guy getting booked" (stabbed) or "that guy having such and such" done to him. And I don't politic. It's not my business what a man in another case is doing. By having a small ego, not needing to impress or prove myself to anyone, I can avoid having to partake more often and having to constantly hear about it. There is some trauma and PTSD which will need to be worked out in the future.

If I could change anything about my prison time, I would have been smarter sooner. I showed my hand way too early, so staff and prisoner enemies knew what buttons to push. I also foolishly waged my battle against prison in a way that left me open to being destroyed. These small, unwinnable battles are something I still make the wrong choice about sometimes, but I'm learning and feel much smarter and more prepared every day. I'm proud of the stances I've taken, the ground I've stood on, but my tactics weren't always bright.

Looking Forward

I realize how important outside support is more and more every day. With every new restriction, I see why the bureau is so terrified of seeing people backed by real support. I don't think I've ever been more supported than right now. Even though I haven't had mail in over a year, some folks have really turned up for me. Some people have really stood up for me, refusing to let me be buried and forgotten. I get all the books, mags, and articles anyone could want. I know that my name is being kept alive and my writings and updates are being shared with the world. My support team are some of my closest friends; they work with my wife and fight like hell to represent me and keep my mind and spirit alive and thriving. It's a wild sensation to feel as if your support is growing even though you are side-lined. It says a lot.

But more needs to be done. I feel the feds/police have the force to nul-lify any extreme actions. I have these unrealistic hopes . . . sectarianism, fear, and all-talkery will ensure there is never a unified front. There are some unre-lenting people and groups who do everything possible to stand by and lift folks up inside. But I'm not sure we know *how* to tear down the system right now or have the structures in place to support two million freed people.

I've seen *a lot* of this recently, and I feel it's the most important thing that outside support should do as much as possible: outside advocacy. Spreading the word, getting unfamiliar folks interested, mobilizing people to partici-pate in support-oriented activities. Ask prisoners what they need or want. I was four years into my bid before Daniel [McGowan] and Josh [Davidson] told me I could ask for things; that I could be demanding. We see pics of the protest in the North of Ireland in support of the prisoners, because their support built a connection to the populace in those areas. This is hard in the US because of how spread out we are. But we see it with Running Down the Walls. So, why can't we have days of protest, marching, et cetera? Make us visible, make my mom know who Oso [Blanco] is and who Sundiata [Acoli] is.[7]

The drug situation [in prison] is ugly and sad. I don't give a fuck about drug use, but people base their entire existence around it, and it makes them compliant tools. You can't resist or care if you are demobilized on your bed drooling after smoking some K2. They allow it in because it creates a gang power structure, where the prison's alleged "warriors" are just state operators, keeping order and smashing anyone who makes the admins uncomfortable. The bureau very cleverly keeps making BOP life more and more shitty, ensur-ing escapism in zombie-making drugs is more likely, thus ensuring further control. A prison full of Jaans would terrify them, so they fill the cells with drooling, easy-to-handle clowns, which isn't terrifying at all.

It really depends on the custody level, but prison will test your char-acter. It will reveal where you stand and what you are capable of enduring. I'd say you don't have to jeopardize who you are and to also be aware of

---

7. Sundiata Acoli is a former member of the BPP and the BLA, and a former New York Panther 21 defendant, who was a political prisoner from 1973 until he was paroled in 2022 after forty-nine years at the age of eighty-five.

consequences. I'd say, "This situation is going to really suck, but you can and will make it beneficial to your life. Don't let them control you. Fight to win."

Prison really sucks, and there are a lot of trauma-inducing events we can't talk about. We absorb this brutality and cruelty, and, even if it's normalized, it still takes its toll. We are living inside a Proud Boys rally every day of our lives.[8] We need real outside connections. Friendship is a desperately needed commodity. We need to be kept alive outside while having our lives inside recognized for what they are: a daily resistance against a system built to crush us. Please hear our stories, feel our victories and losses. If we have families, please give them love also. They are suffering every day as well.

---

8. The Proud Boys are an exclusively male organization founded in 2016 whose members include white nationalists and neo-Nazis. They participate in violent, racist, and anti-LGBTQIA+ actions. Several Proud Boys members are facing sedition charges in relation to the January 6, 2021, attempted coup at the US Capitol.

Rattler

Rattler (Michael Markus) was arrested on October 27, 2016, at the ceremonial resistance camps at Standing Rock. These camps were convened in North Dakota by Native peoples and their allies who gathered there to stop the Dakota Access Pipeline. Collectively, these Indigenous resisters are referred to as Water Protectors. Over eight hundred Water Protectors were arrested defending this sacred land, many the result of widespread police sweeps at demonstrations with scant or no evidence to link most individuals to any crime. Rattler was charged with civil disorder and using a fire to commit a felony, and he spent twenty months on house arrest before serving over two years imprisoned at FCI Sandstone for his resistance at Standing Rock.

Prison Life

I was prepared mentally. The way I looked at it was, they're locking me up because they're scared of what we're doing. And I was told they were actually just afraid of me in general. But I was mentally prepared, and I felt that at least I was going to prison for something that's worthwhile. If this is something that has to be done, then I'm ready to do it. And when I got out, I was ready to do it all again.

I went in there cheerful. I went in there with my head high and my fist in the air. I walked through with that attitude, and I walked back out the same way, head high and fist in the air. Carrying that attitude in there, it tended to lighten the mood for a few of the guys, so it was helpful to them.

You're supposed to be learning something while you're in there, but the only thing it's teaching me is that when you get people to follow you and stand beside you and behind you, that scares them. So, we're doing something right for the people and not for the corporations. This is what we were doing, fighting for the people.

I stuck out like a sore thumb because I refused to adapt. It's easier in a minimum security place because there's a lot more people and it's not so racially divided. Not as bad as it is at higher level security places. But generally, I would sit with the Natives. But I had bunkies who were Black, Mexican, white, and I would go sit with them too. Sometimes I'd go in and instead of standing there waiting for a place to sit, I just looked for the first open place to sit and sat down. I didn't care where it was.

I never lost hope. There were times I wished I could do more. Being inside, I couldn't do anything for the people, so what I did to continue what I was doing was talk to the guys inside. Before we got locked down because of COVID, I would be walking out in the yard and, during the whole week, I probably talked to between twenty and thirty guys. They would come to me and start talking to me about their problems. So, I would sit there or I'd be walking around, and, next thing you know, guys would come up to me and start talking about their dreams, their kids, stuff going on within their lives. And I'd sit there and talk with them. That was me basically just doing what I could to help everybody out.

In one way or another, it was the same thing we were doing at [the Standing Rock] camp. We're just trying to help people heal. So, when I was inside, I decided that one thing I could do to "help the people" is talk to them and listen to them. Some of the guys I talked to said they were going to look for a place to help out like that. I guess you could say I turned them into protesters. They said they wanted to get involved in protests against the KXL and Line 3 [pipelines].[1]

I taught a few of them [other prisoners] that we've got to quit looking at them as their crimes. This is the time to wipe the slate clean and start all over and become a better person, no matter what they did. Just look at them

1. The Keystone XL pipeline extension was initially planned in 2008, but, after growing legal challenges and protests by climate justice advocates, Keystone XL construction was canceled in 2021. Line 3 is a pipeline extension first proposed in 2014 and completed in 2021. Legal and grassroots efforts to thwart the Line 3 pipeline continue as of 2023.

as a human being and try to help them. I don't know if it held or not, but I tried to instill less prejudice in there, just by talking to other people and not discriminating based on what charges they had. I think that having them hopefully carry that on, to look at everybody as a human being, is something that kept going.

One of the things that shocked me is that I had at least four guards tell me that I should not have been in there. They looked at my charges and what I was in there for, and they told me I shouldn't be in jail or in prison.

I got two different letters, one from North Carolina and one from Berkeley, California. Both were from second graders, and the kids all drew me pictures and told me thank you for fighting for the water for us. And that right there is what made it all worthwhile for me. That's the most inspiring part about doing all this.

Politics and Prison Dynamics

I did have one situation that got me thrown in the hole for the weekend. I left my unit without my ID card once, and I was asked to show it at the chow hall. So, I ran back to my cell and got my ID. It was during my Sun Dance, so I was fasting along with everybody that was dancing.[2] It was my third day of fasting, but I would get in line at chow and then give my tray away to other prisoners. I think it was a lieutenant that stopped me and asked to see my ID, and I said, "It's a good thing I went back and got it, because I know how the Gestapo likes their paperwork."

Well, he tells me to repeat what I had just said, and since I was joking when I said it, I said it again. He kind of flipped out at that and demanded my ID and told me to button up my shirt. Then he told me to go into the lieutenant's office. So, I go in there, and I wait for him, and then he tells me to go into the next room. A little closet. There are no cameras in there. Then he gets in my face. He starts yelling; I start laughing. He kept getting in my face, yelling. I told him, "I know what you're trying to do. You're trying to get me mad, and it's not going to work."

---

2. A Sun Dance is a Native ceremony, originally prohibited by colonialists, in which the community gathers for prayer, healing, and personal sacrifice.

So he yelled some more and then told me to leave. I went to the gym for a while and then got called back to the lieutenant to sign some paperwork. The captain was there and started yelling at me. Then the lieutenant arrived and joined in. I said, "That's a bunch of bullshit." Then they told me they were putting me in the hole, and they cuffed me and brought me to the hole.

I was there for three days, for the weekend. They threatened to force-feed me because I wasn't eating, I was on a fast. Then they made the chaplain come in to verify that I was following Native practices. And then Monday they let me out of the hole. I didn't even get a write-up for it.

I wasn't really able to be politically active while locked up. Everything was censored coming in, but I could mail anything going out. I did send letters to people and shared things over the phone. But being monitored on the phones and being recorded, it's kind of hard to actually be actively doing anything. I wouldn't say I was able to stay politically active. I'm a person of action, so I like to be there physically. I'm not really good at technology; being a keyboard warrior was never really my thing.

I saved every letter I got. During the first year I was there, I averaged three letters a day that I was receiving and responding to. When I started on the second year, it kind of slowed down, where I was only getting maybe four or five [letters] a week. But when I first got there, I was getting three or four letters a day, and I wrote everybody back. I was going through books of stamps.

Looking Forward

If you're going to be doing this stuff, with what the government is doing, everybody has to be prepared to go to prison for what they believe in. It's good to know that there are people out there who are willing to sacrifice themselves to do the same thing.

If you feel that you're going in for the right reason, then be proud of what you did. If you're going in there for standing up for your rights as a human being, standing up for the earth, even protecting your family, then be proud of what you did. Now, if you're going in there for selling drugs and you need to get yourself straight in your mind, I know you're probably doing it to support your family, but you're tearing other families apart at the same time.

Don't look at people as the color of their skin, or even the colors they wear. Look at them as human beings. You don't need to approach them, but at least be cordial, be nice about everything. Just treat everybody well. Be courteous to people, and generally you'll get along well that way, at least at a minimum security [prison].

Ray Luc Levasseur

Ray Luc Levasseur was a member of the United Freedom Front and the Sam Melville–Jonathan Jackson Unit who spent over twenty years in prison.[1] The group known as the Ohio 7—Ray, Patricia Gros Levasseur, Barbara Curzi-Laaman, Carol Saucier Manning, Tom Manning, Jaan Laaman and Richard Williams—were working-class revolutionaries charged with actions against US military facilities, recruitment centers, and corporate headquarters. These actions were done in solidarity with the people of South Africa and Central America, who were bearing the brunt of US imperialism. Ray spent twenty-one months imprisoned in Tennessee State Penitentiary in Nashville and at Brushy Mountain State Penitentiary in Petros, Tennessee, between 1969 and 1971, before spending twenty years imprisoned from 1984 to 2004 for his actions with the UFF. Ray has published three zines—*Family Values*; *Letters from Exile*; and *The Trial Statements of Ray Luc Levasseur*—all of which are to be republished by Kersplebedeb and Burning Books in 2024.

---

1. The United Freedom Front (UFF) was a group of working-class revolutionaries who engaged in armed struggle against US imperialism in solidarity with freedom struggles in South Africa, Palestine, and throughout Central America in the 1980s. Actions done by some of these same people during the 1970s were done in the name of the Sam Melville–Jonathan Jackson Unit. Sam Melville was a political prisoner who was murdered in the aftermath of the September 1971 Attica uprising. Jonathan Jackson was murdered in an attempted kidnapping at the Marin County Courthouse in August 1970 in an attempt to free his brother, politicized prisoner George Jackson.

Prison Life

When I was in the first time in 1969–1971, I was not in the least prepared for the ordeal, partly because while on bail I remained in a fog of denial about getting carted off to prison. I did have some support from friends, but I was largely on my own. But I was a street fighter, Vietnam vet, and had had my first taste of political activism in the South, so I quickly got into survival mode. When in survival mode you fight the system, anyone that comes at you while you're trying to live a principled life. Being shell-shocked wasn't on my agenda, but the cumulative effect of 1969–1971 stays with me to this day.

During that first bid, I never did adapt to prisons steeped in white supremacy and Jim Crow segregation. I crossed the color line and did most of my time in the hole, supermax, and death row. (Although I was doing a five-year sentence on a marijuana charge, I was celled on death row as a problem prisoner.)

When I went to prison again from 1984–2004, I was very mentally and physically prepared. I considered myself a captured combatant (although for political reasons we called ourselves "political prisoners"). I considered death and prison occupational hazards of a revolutionary.

I/we had some measure of support (personal and political) as soon as we were captured. The level of support gradually increased through several high-profile trials and the formation of small defense committees. Once we received long sentences and were carted off to various prisons, the defense committees ceased to exist—replaced by an informal network of supporters. While the level of support we received was substantial, it never reached the level it could or should have been (a dilemma common to the majority of long-term political prisoners).

During my second bid, I was held in Maine State Prison (Thomaston, ME), Metropolitan Correctional Center (NYC), Walpole State Prison (Walpole, MA), USP Marion (Marion, IL), ADX Florence (Administrative Maximum) (Florence, CO), and USP Atlanta (Atlanta, GA).

The majority of my time was in solitary, segregation, and small group isolation. The first five years, our trials displaced much of the regular prison routine. The next ten years were mostly solitary, where the routine/structure is more simplified than in general population; for example, you eat in your cell, leave your cell in restraints, don't work a job, and so on.

During my second bid, I was older, wiser, hardened; I was not so easy to shock. I was prepared for battle and survival. That said, there was plenty to be disturbed and troubled about. At some point, I was disturbed that I *wasn't* more shocked about blood and guts (when this happens, you need to reflect on survival, yes, but not at the expense of letting your humanity slip away).

When it comes to my survival, I do whatever it takes for as long as it takes, as long as it doesn't violate my basic values and principles. I can adapt to a lot of routine/structure while hating and undermining it. Prison is an intense microcosm of larger society. Any part of prison culture I found, I either ignored or opposed it.

A typical routine is based on time, place, and conditions, and routines can be disrupted or altered by factors beyond one's control. The connecting threads in my routines: maintain physical strength and conditioning; nurture physical and spiritual health; if it moves you, embrace your spiritual connections; read, write, and study; network with the outside world.

I never lost hope while I was in prison. Hope springs eternal. Definite low points, but I never hit bottom. The struggle for me was to avoid succumbing to the acute cynicism that prison breeds.

Yes, I lost people while I was locked up. I internalized it, like I do with most hurt and stress. I began losing friends and family from the earliest days of my imprisonment, and it's continued since my release with the passing of Richard Williams, Tom Manning, and others.[2] That Tom and Richard died in prison left me with an emotional wound that will never heal. It also left me with a sense of failure in not being able to get them out.

In max security, you're not going to any funerals, memorials, or celebrations of life. In prison, I paid my respects through the written word—letters and tributes. After my release, the letters and tributes expanded to attending memorials, funerals, sharing that life and death with sons and daughters, friends, family and comrades, planting trees of life, scattering ashes facing the dawn, prayers at sweat lodges, and so on. Back in the world and being able to closely share life lived in struggle has provided some degree of restorative balm.

---

2. Richard Williams and Tom Manning were members of the UFF who were captured in 1984 and subsequently died while still incarcerated, Williams in 2005 and Manning in 2019.

The quality of life in prison has gotten worse—in quality and quantity. More shit on a much larger scale and, until more recent years, less "conscious" prisoners to continue the struggle. Prison is a microcosm of the larger society. The negatives of the larger society are intensified inside. In my time (1984–2004), I saw the pinnacle (for now) of mass incarceration by design, supermax prison expansion, and expanded use and abuse of solitary confinement. During this same period, there appeared to me a decline in conscious prisoners and organized resistance (compared to the height of the prisoners' rights movement in the 1970s).

In the past fifteen years, there's been a small rollback in numbers of incarcerated people, more signs of organized resistance inside (the Pelican Bay strikes are an example), and more former prisoners involved in anti–mass-incarceration work. That's all to the good, but the actual conditions of life inside remain horrendous. For the uninitiated, it's worth looking at the monthly *Prison Legal News* (and other sources) for a sense of just how degrading, dehumanizing, violent, and corrupt the American gulag has become on a massive scale.

The system is designed this way, and it's gotten worse because of its sheer size, entrenchment, lack of accountability, longer sentences, and damaging effects felt far beyond steel cages used for social control.

My proudest achievements inside were my political advocacy through my writing and pro se representation at trials and the positive impact I've had on other prisoners I did time with.[3] It starts by setting an example: how you carry yourself, what you say and how you say it, mental and physical discipline, avoiding the traps (drugs, gambling, predatory behavior, etc.), demonstrating kindness without weakness, utilizing political education and consciousness-raising. My political writing circulated widely among prisoners so I was well known as someone who resisted the system with whatever weapons could be had, be [they] guns or pencils.

By "positive impact," I mean having some part, however small, in seeing the mindset of some prisoners evolve from clueless and/or reactionary to conscious, with a new political perspective on their situation vis-à-vis the prison industrial complex and its role as an enforcer of class

---

3. The legal term "pro se" refers to self-representation in a court of law, directly translated from Latin as "for oneself" or "on one's own behalf."

and white supremacy. That kind of change in a person is a beautiful thing to see.

Politics and Prison Dynamics

When I arrived at USP Atlanta, they dragged me out in seg [segregation] for months, where horrible civil rights violations prevailed. I began documenting these violations and a cover-up in GP [general population] that involved an asbestos-contaminated section of the prison. All this was happening when the prison was scheduled for an ACA [American Correctional Association] accreditation inspection. The administration became aware that related information I was sending out about the situation was being published. I was walking a tightrope because any confrontation with the administration over conditions, or any confrontations with reactionary prisoners or guards I encountered in seg, risked having me returned to ADX. A movement lawyer-friend offered to negotiate with the administration. That negotiation resulted in an offer: drop the seg and asbestos issues, and they'd release me into GP. So, I dropped the issues.

That's always troubled me. I rationalized it by avoiding a return to ADX and setting the stage for my release four years later. You can't win every battle, so you have to be strategic about which battles you pick. Underlying your decision is your prison sentence. Someone doing one to five [years] might decide differently than someone doing ten to fifteen, who may decide differently than someone doing twenty, thirty, forty.

The best defense for a political prisoner against potentially hostile individuals and groups is to gain their respect. I did that with groups, and mostly so with individuals. A lot has to do with how you carry yourself inside. I had no serious problems with groups or gangs—and I was around the heaviest gangbangers in the federal system. They have a sort of begrudging respect for those who challenge the prison, are fit to defend themselves, and who are not profit-motivated.

I was in conflict with guards and administration from 1969 to near the last couple years of my 1984–2004 bid. Physical assaults, suits, disciplinary charges, and so on. I have zero empathy for anyone making a dollar off the Amerikan gulag.

In 1969–1971, the racial tension at TSP [Tennessee State Penitentiary] and Brushy infected all aspects of life there. Ubiquitous and pernicious. Lots of KKK mentality. Racial barriers were real. There were problems as soon as I crossed the color line in the segregated mess hall and hung out with Black prisoners. (My codefendant was Black also.) I was threatened by guards and the administration for not staying with my "own kind." After stints in solitary, they transferred me to Brushy Mountain, where James Earl Ray and his admirers were.[4] Brushy was an early supermax and spin-off of the convict leasing system.

Once a week, we boxed in a makeshift ring. My choice was to fight the baddest racist white boys in the ring or take my chances sans gloves whenever someone wanted to go at me. I opted for the ring, which earned me a measure of respect. The place was so racist, I was the only white to box with Black prisoners. I was in a fight with a white dude who came at me within a week of my release. If I'd been there any longer, I don't know if I'd ever have been able to walk out in one piece.

When I was in from 1984 to 2004, I wrote and spoke against racism wherever I was, emphasizing solidarity as the prisoners' greatest weapon and racial conflict as prisoners' greatest weakness. I tried to carry myself accordingly. Interracial relationships: political prisoners are an interracial group and always gravitate to each other wherever they are. Associating with "conscious" brothers. The worst racial violence was gang-related, which I managed to avoid. Prison being prison, racism is always present, either overt or covert. One has to be ready for the worst to manifest itself without warning.

Circumstances (including trials) allowed me to spend various amounts of time with Tom and all my codefendants. Also with Oscar López Rivera, Filiberto Ojeda Ríos, Mutulu Shakur, Sundiata Acoli, Alan Berkman, Ed Mead, Kojo Bomani, Bill Dunne (and, because of particular pretrial circumstances at MCC-NY, Marilyn Buck, Laura Whitehorn, Susan Rosenberg and Linda Evans). These were opportunities to share ideas, provide mutual support, share resources, develop trial strategies, develop political prisoner support, and to various degrees foster closer personal relationships.

After the trials were concluded, I was always separated from

---

4. James Earl Ray was convicted of the 1968 assassination of Martin Luther King Jr. He escaped Brushy Mountain State Prison briefly in 1977 and died behind bars in 1998.

codefendants. To be around other political prisoners inside was a source of strength and well-being for me. When I wasn't around another political prisoner, I more acutely felt the loneliness of the long-distance runner.

I was able to do some political work while imprisoned. Pertaining to 1984–2004, it began with representing myself pro se in court proceedings/ trials, the defense/support committees that were formed, published political writings, media interviews, and the never-ending politicizing among prisoners.

Violence in prison is inevitable. It's a fact of life and death in cages. Political consciousness-raising means discouraging needless violence between prisoners and encouraging a view that identifies the real enemy. I don't really know how best to cope with "casual" violence. What I did do was try to keep from being one of its victims. One thing I did was to always be armed. Since the one weapon you have with you 24/7 is your body, I kept my martial arts skills honed and kept my strength and conditioning at a high level.

I've been in SMU (seg units), MCC (high security unit), Harford FDC (small group isolation), Marion (supermax), and ADX (supermax). I was sent to Marion and ADX as an administrative transfer because of my political beliefs/associations (i.e., not a disciplinary transfer). I've done disciplinary time in seg, but mostly I was kept in seg or administrative hold, not disciplinary. MCC and Hartford FDC were small-group isolation units. My placement in these units was administrative, not disciplinary.

Comparing these units/prisons to general populations is like comparing apples and oranges. There are common threads but substantive differences (the most profound and damaging being the level of isolation.)

Looking Forward

Outside support is essential. Without it, already isolated and vulnerable prisoners become increasingly isolated and vulnerable. To a lesser or greater degree, I always felt supported, though the level of support for our group never reached the level it should have. Supporters need to embrace PPs as "our" political prisoners. This personal/political connection with the imprisoned is a powerful motivator.

There's always more to be done as long as there are political prisoners, and as long as cages are used as a method of social control. There's a sort of pecking order that's existed for a long time, whereby some PPs receive extensive support while others receive little. Attempts to address this issue by uniting various support groups under one banner have failed or had limited success. Somewhere in the future, there needs to be greater unity in effort.

There's an old guerrilla adage: "recruit or die." Outside support groups need to expand their numbers with an eye toward improving the quality and increasing the quantity of their work.

I think there is, generally speaking, more unity among prisoners now than in 2004 when I was released, albeit still far short of what it needs to be to mount more serious challenges. It's encouraging to see so many former prisoners involved in political activism—more than I've seen since the height of the prisoner rights movement in the 1970s. More former political prisoners have been politically active these past twenty-five years because a relatively large number were released during this period, and they retained their core values, did not forget those left behind, and organizing/advocacy is in their DNA.

Read *Soledad Brother: The Prison Letters of George Jackson* and other books by activist prisoners. Realize that you're entering a danger zone and the best body armor you can have is the respect and support of others. Remember that life in the gulag is still *life*. Affirm life, defend life. Reject the worst that imprisonment brings to bear.

Elizabeth McAlister

Elizabeth (Liz) McAlister is a founder of the Jonah House in Baltimore and has been involved in antinuclear Plowshares actions and other acts of resistance for over fifty years.[1] She is the widow of Philip Berrigan. In order to raise their children and maintain the Jonah House, the two often took turns serving prison terms for their acts of nonviolent civil disobedience. Liz McAlister was involved in the Harrisburg Seven case, where she, Philip, and five others were charged with planning to kidnap Henry Kissinger. Most recently, Liz was one of the Kings Bay Plowshares 7, seven Plowshares activists who entered Naval Submarine Base Kings Bay in Georgia on April 4, 2018 (the fiftieth anniversary of the assassination of Martin Luther King Jr.) and performed symbolic acts of disarmament. Liz served twenty-eight months at the Alderson Federal Detention Center for Women in the 1980s, and she spent seventeen months imprisoned in Georgia for her actions with the Kings Bay Plowshares 7. She also served numerous other sentences for her activism, usually for six months at a time or less. According to Liz, she served a total of "maybe five and a half" years in prison for her direct actions.

Because of Liz's late-stage dementia, she was joined by her daughter, Frida Berrigan, who graciously helped to clarify certain dates and locations. Frida published *It Runs in the Family: On Being*

---

1. The Jonah House is an intentional Catholic Worker community established in Baltimore, Maryland, in 1973 by Liz McAlister, Philip Berrigan, and others.

Raised by Radicals and Growing into Rebellious Motherhood (OR Books, 2015), in which she talks about growing up with her parents in and out of prison.

Prison Life

One of the things that I found absolutely essential for survival in prison is to take the time to be alone and to pray. So, I would make that an absolute priority. I knew that without that I wasn't going to be able to walk that walk. It was needed as much as breathing, practically. That was the beginning of every day and the end of the day and at periods throughout the day.

Do you adapt to it, or do you just try to walk your own walk, around or in the midst of it? There isn't any kind of culture that is attractive. You have to create whatever you want to have supporting you. You have to do your daily praying and your daily interacting with different people and keep the head and the heart as alive as possible. Not to do that is to just allow yourself to go to pieces. You need to work at it every single day. You need to develop the kind of friendships where you can have a serious conversation with somebody. Once you start something like that, it just becomes so clear how important it is to other people as well as oneself. You have to work at it, and you can do that all the better with others.

You're trying to find people who will take a walk with you on a daily basis and do more reflecting together, do some praying together, do some reading together, share things that we've come across that have meaning and that lift us up and make us think beyond ourselves into the world we're living in and how we can make a difference.

As far as jails themselves, I don't think one is more colorful than another. What do you do with it, and how do you spend your day? That's what makes a big difference. You spend your day doing some good reading, doing some good interacting with people who are willing to interact on some kind of serious level. Talking with them, reading, and things of that sort are super-important to keep in your head.

Frida: In Alderson in 1984, 1985, and 1986, Mom was there with a number of her codefendants: Clare Grady, Jackie Allen, Sister Anne Montgomery,

Suzanne Schmidt, and Kathleen Rumpf.[2] And then other Plowshares people came in and out. Mom worked on the grounds crew, so she was outside every day. There was a camp aspect to Alderson, at the time anyway, that seemed very attractive. They could do knitting and art projects and work in the greenhouse and all of that, and so that may have made it better. But there was a little bit of looseness around the edges of the institution that allowed for that.

When Mom was sentenced for the Kings Bay Plowshares action and her codefendants started going off to jail, many had bonded out before trial, and Mom didn't. When they started getting sentenced, the judge was very clear that they weren't going to the same institutions. So, everybody's serving their sentences very much alone. They're very far away from one another. I think that would stand out for a number of reasons as a somewhat positive prison experience. There were contact visits and that sort of thing.

Liz: I don't think I ever lost hope inside. What was important for me, and I think is important for anybody doing time, is to have one's own schedule for the day. And prayer is essential for survival. I knew that, and I took that very, very seriously. It's what gets you through. You begin the day with prayer, and you intersperse prayer throughout the day in order to just keep on keeping on. There are no solutions that we can do that are on our own: we need that spirit, we need that inspiration, we need that prayer. We need the prayer of others, and we need to pray ourselves. You are walking into something that could be very, very destructive without that.

I have lived long enough with people who've been in and out of jails and prisons, and I have been able to do some sharing on what one needs to make it, and to not just make it but to grow with it, to grow from it. Maybe even help to make a difference in the time that others are doing. Because you get together, and you talk about things that are important to talk about, and you boost one another up, you keep the conversation alive, you keep it going, you keep it about things that are important, things we should be thinking about and talking and praying about. There was a lot that went on that was very life-giving for me, and I'm sure it was for other people as well.

I think good interactions with other people are always a source of joy. To see people who have been down in the dumps, who are able to talk and

2. Clare Grady, Jackie Allen, Sister Anne Montgomery, Suzanne Schmidt, and Kathleen Rumpf were Catholic Worker and/or Plowshares activists who served various terms of imprisonment for their civil disobedience and direct action protesting nuclear and military targets.

interact and smile, and even to get a good laugh, that's a joy. It's rich. It says that our interaction with one another as inmates makes a radical difference, or can make a radical difference. So keep it up, keep it going. Because if people can keep that alive, then we can make a difference.

My mom, Elizabeth, died while I was at Alderson. I was able to get a furlough to attend the funeral. I think that was in 1985.

Frida: She was quite elderly, and perhaps Mom went into prison having said goodbye, and sort of made her peace with that, with her mom. But it was still a loss and a hard way to experience a funeral. For a big Irish family, everybody's gathered, and Mom came in with two marshals. I was little at the time, so I don't have very strong impressions of them personally, but they were present throughout the funeral, the burial, and the ceremony. I don't think she was handcuffed, but they were keeping a close eye on her the whole time. I think it affected the whole family. It certainly affected my aunts and uncles to see that.

Liz: I think prisons have definitely gotten worse. Some of the things that are somewhat humane get cut short, and then in the next year they get cut shorter. They keep doing this. It comes down after a while to it being on your own shoulders to come up with things that you can do with the other inmates that can make a difference to our lives there together. There are other inmates who respond to those opportunities with energy and enthusiasm. It makes a difference, and it's a good thing to be doing.

The time when one's head is active and also interactive with other people, well, you need that so much in those settings, because they are radically impoverished. Anything like that that you have going is really going to come from the inmates; it's not going to come from any other source.

Walking into a jail cell and being surrounded by people that you don't know, trying to develop relationships, it's rich and rare. What becomes clear is that these are other human beings, and they are not home, and they are in some strange place, and they're trying to make it. What can we do, what can I do, what can I say to this person, that's going to be a source of life and joy rather than a put-down? How can I develop that? And when you can begin developing that, it can get very, very rich, and very, very good. It's clear that's something the others want as well. They really, really respond to one another, respond to anybody who is going to initiate a conversation that has some life and wholesome loving spirit to it, rather than bitching and complaining.

When you can share something and people get a laugh out of it, it's so great. It creates an atmosphere where others will do some reading that they'll want to share too. To keep it alive as much as you possibly can, that's what you're trying to do. But also to be willing to just sit down and listen to what another is walking with, and, if you have some insights, to share them. But mostly it's a matter of listening and being empathetic and sympathetic. Maybe empathetic more than sympathetic.

Politics and Prison Dynamics

You live out your principles in prison the same way that you try to live them at home. It's a different geography, but you can still greet people. You can still ask them questions that can bring out either something they're wrestling with or something they're joyful about. If you can do that for people, that's a gift, that's a joy.

People need to be listened to. You need to take time to hear what they're struggling with. I mean, everybody's struggling with being where they are, but it has different dimensions to it depending on what family they've left behind, what situation their family is living in, who's taking care of children if there are children (there usually are). Are the children keeping in touch, are the people who are caring for the children keeping in touch? These make huge differences in people's ability to do time, knowing that their kids are okay and well cared for. It makes a huge difference. If that isn't happening for some people, then once in a while it's good to sit down with them and help them write a letter. Doing this helps people maintain relationships with their children. What's going on? What are they reading? Is somebody reading to them at night? Is there something I can send that you can read?

I had friendships develop with people of color, with people of different races. It takes a lot of work, but it's a good thing to do. It's a good thing to embrace. I found it enriching to be able to walk with somebody whose whole upbringing, whose whole faith commitment, is different. It's good to respect that, to learn about that, to hear about that, and to see that, yes, of course, that's a different approach than I take, but it's an approach that this person is using that has managed to bring her to this point in her life and is carrying her through this experience in ways that are beneficial. So, right on.

At Alderson [in the 1980s] there were also Puerto Rican *independentistas*, somewhere between two to five individuals, who were doing something like thirty- to fifty-year sentences. The three years I served then, or single-year sentences, were small potatoes in comparison. It was an embarrassment of riches. I think it wasn't accidental that I wasn't imprisoned alongside other political prisoners. I think that those locking us up wanted to keep certain elements apart from one another as much as possible.

You try to begin each day anew and afresh and try to bring as much caring for others into that as you can. Being open to asking a question here and there of another person, and then being willing to sit and listen to the answer, becomes very, very important. To ask a question and then not pay attention is a turnoff. But to ask a question and then tend to it and then come back with a follow-up question the next day or so is really important. The women need to be listened to.

Looking Forward

Outside support is a source of life; it's a source of love. You're in touch with those who love you and with those you love. Those who are doing the work you would be doing if you weren't in jail. It's so, so rich. With those relationships and friendships, you can get through anything.

One of the things that could make a big difference is writing to prisoners and asking them [what they need]. Ask what would be useful, what can I send you that would be useful in their situation right now. Obviously, it's not going to be something that will enable them to escape; it's going to be something that is a source of enriching the spirit, enriching the soul, enriching the mind. Those are the things that are the most needed in that situation. Share books with those inside. The kind of reading that you can get into and that can make you think, make you pray, make you reflect and grow. Those are absolutely essential. It's an atmosphere that isn't going to give you any of that, so that's got to come in some fashion.

Frida: I wonder about looking at the economic arguments for prisons and making common cause with the prison guard unions and the support staff unions. Honestly, COVID provides an opportunity for that, and maybe some of this work is already happening—I'm not deeply involved in the abolitionist movement. The prisoners' lives were 100 percent expendable with COVID. But guards' lives didn't appear to matter all that much more. Some really good reporting was done on guards getting sick just as much, or almost just as much. And they relied on getting protective gear from their friends and family and GoFundMe campaigns, not from the industry that is making so much money off of these prisons. Does that provide an opportunity?

It costs $80,000 to imprison a person for a year, and it costs this much to have somebody on house arrest, so there's the whole argument about giving compassionate leave to people because of COVID. But that took so long. We'll never know how many people who work for the prison-industrial complex died of COVID, because they work for the prison-industrial complex. Just like we won't really ever know how many prisoners died. We're not going to know that. But this us-versus-them scenario has been set up. It ties into gerrymandering, the way our political maps are drawn, where prisons are built. They really just play on white-versus-Black and urban-versus-rural and the urban boogeyman.

And prison guards don't get rich. I mean, I guess it's a good living, but it sounds like an awful living, really. So, some sort of common cause there seems like a fruitful line for somebody to pursue. I don't think you pursue that by saying, "Let's abolish prisons," but I think there's a way somewhere in there for the abolitionist movement.

Liz: I don't think there's unity amongst prisoners today. I think that's something that people, prisoners, should be very, very careful about. A lot of inmates are constantly looking for things, and they'll find it wherever they can find it. And it's understandable, and it eases the pain for a while, but then you have to look for more again. And there are people in jail who spend all of their time looking for when and where and how they can get the next fix. I just find that so tragic that that's the way some people feel they have to spend their time. But there it is, and that's part and parcel of what you're living with 24/7. There are some who are constantly looking for where they can get the next fix.

I have been in a very privileged position, from time to time, of being able to invite people in who can bring things inside that are a benefit to all the inmates. That is a good thing to be able to do, and it's really important to do it *but* not own it. Just, you know, this is coming, but we're not asking how it's coming. It's coming, use it, love it. There are some who catch on, and they know, and they come to you and ask if you can get ahold of x, y, or z. And then you try to find a way to get ahold of x, y or z. There are so many people who are willing to send things in, to bring things in, that can be brought in. If you're in a position to know those people, then it's a good thing. But get it out to others in the jail as quickly as possible, make it available to others. Let them know it's not mine, it's not personal, it's for whomever wants to use it.

I think the big thing to know is that you're with other human beings, and they're breathing, and they're in pain, and what can I do to carry some of that with them, to lighten it for them, to make it less burdensome for them. Tell a good story from time to time. Bring in some books that people would like to read. Many of us have folks who send books to us, so send in what people in the jail or prison want to read. Try to get some things in there that would be a source of rest and recreation for them, uplift for them, insight for them, or just a good way to spend a couple of hours of an afternoon. Get friends to send books. It's a gift.

Malik Smith

Malik Smith (Meral Smith) is one of three political prisoners known as the Virgin Island 3. Malik Smith, Hanif Shabazz Bey (Beaumont Gereau), and Abdul Aziz (Warren Ballantine), were charged with murdering eight people in the US Virgin Islands in 1972. During the 1970s, a movement to resist US colonial rule began to grow in the Virgin Islands, growing into a small-scale Mau Mau rebellion on the islands. Malik has served time in over ten different federal facilities, both in the US and in the Virgin Islands, during his over forty-eight years of incarceration. At the time of this writing, all three of the Virgin Island 3 are imprisoned at the Citrus County Detention Facility in Lecanto, Florida.

Prison Life

From the 1970s to the early 1990s, the way I did time was much different than now. In the feds, I had a job in the UNICOR clothing factory, where I operated different types of sewing machines.[1] I made pants, shirts, and jackets for the prison system and for the military. I also worked making blankets and towels. I am a tailor in the true sense of the word, because I can make pants, shirts, jackets, and other stuff once I have the proper sewing machine.

---

1. UNICOR, or Federal Prison Industries, Inc., was established in 1934 as a prison labor program for those incarcerated within the Federal Bureau of Prisons.

In the feds, I went to the dining room for each meal. But at Marion and all private prisons, the food is brought to you. At least in these prisons you can have your own twenty-one-inch TV. One thing about me, though, is that I've been able to adapt or modify the conditions as needed.

When I first came to prison at twenty-two years old, I was a very experienced young warrior, being that I was well-read as a revolutionary and had experience in some of the civil rights marches in America between 1967 and 1969. I listened to many of the Black Panthers and Black Liberation Army leaders at the time, especially Fred Hampton, Huey Newton, Elaine Brown, and Malcolm X, though he was taken earlier on.[2] In fact, I was in North Carolina when MLK was killed in 1968, and I witnessed the KKK and other bad white boys in action. So, in a way, I expected to be imprisoned someday, and I was somewhat mentally prepared, even though this is my first and only conviction.

In my early days I had a lot of support, especially my four sisters, and I still do. But after all these years in the struggle, most of my supporters seem to believe that no relief will come. In fact, at times I myself wonder what is really going on with those judges and politicians because if you saw [the film] *The Skyjacker's Tale* about police brutality and the false confessions they used to convict us, we should have been released a long time ago.[3] Up to this day, over forty-eight years later, no one has ever said they saw any one of us at the scene of the crime, and none of the weapons or bullets they said committed the crimes had our fingerprints.

Our main support groups now are the Jericho Movement and the ABC groups in Philly and New York, and our family and a few friends. I never expected to be in prison this long, no matter the crimes.

It was not hard to adapt to prison routine or structure because I was well-read and had some life experiences at an early age where I could go through or overcome just about anything. Prison culture in the feds, at Lewisburg, was very ordered and strict. You get respect by giving respect,

2. Fred Hampton was a charismatic leader of the Chicago branch of the BPP, assassinated in his sleep in a COINTEPRO operation. Elaine Brown was a national leader of the Black Panther Party in its later years.

3. *The Skyjacker's Tale* is a 2016 documentary chronicling the infamous 1972 Fountain Valley massacre and the subsequent hijacking of a plane to Cuba by codefendant Ishmael Muslim Ali.

and you mind your own business and don't talk about what others do. There was hardly any snitching like there is today. In those days, a man could get seriously hurt or killed for snitching. In fact, during the 1970s and early 1980s, there was an average of fifteen to twenty killings a year at Lewisburg. A lot was due to a race war between the Aryan Brotherhood and Blacks, especially those from DC. Maybe that's still going on now.

The happiest moments were when I went back to the Virgin Islands in 2009. The way time is done down there is much different than in America. That was the first time I ever used a cellphone. It's not legal, but just about every prisoner had one. I used to have home-cooked food and all kinds of fruits and drinks brought from outside. And the women working there were very good to me. In a way, I was like a hero coming back home, even though they did not know me personally but heard about me because of the case I'm in prison for. Plus, by that time, I'd been smoking marijuana since 1986, and it was in abundance there. So, I was like in heaven. Then I was able to go outside on a tour around the island with six others who were in the Virgin Islands with me, and I was able to see some of the changes that took place since I left. Another time, I went out to a youth program where I offered some advice on how to avoid coming to prison and listened to what they had to say and answered their questions. In fact, I did that twice, and we had a group of elders who had been in prison a long time who used to go to the Youth Rehabilitation Center (YRC) and hold workshops with the youngsters there, including girls. That was a hell of an experience to hear the mindset of boys and girls fourteen to fifteen years old. They see life much different than how I saw life growing up.

The quality of life in prison now is much worse than when I first came in. In this day and time, there is no loyalty in friendships, and it's a dog-eat-dog world among most in the young generation. Yes, there are some true and loyal youngsters, but on the whole you have to watch your back from even your best friend or brother. Then, the way things were run in prison back in the 1970s, 1980s, and early 1990s, it's worse now. There are a lot more restrictions and lockdowns today. Plus there are video cameras and listening devices everywhere. There are hardly any programs for a prisoner to learn any skills. Being this is a detention center, there are no programs here at all, but even in the other private prisons we've been in there's not much for a prisoner to learn, except development on paper. In fact, all the self-development programs offered here I used to teach in the feds and Virgin Islands prisons.

Being that I came to prison young and followed the teachings of the Honorable Elijah Muhammad, leader of the Nation of Islam, and I was exposed to the Black Civil Rights Movement in the 1960s and early 1970s, and I grew up under the teachings of the Leadership of Elders in my village, I decided early that I will do my best to make sure that other family members and friend's children do not fall victim to prison life.[4]

Politics and Prison Dynamics

I have had conflicts during my time in prison, but only twice did it lead to physical confrontation with other prisoners and once with an officer. The way I live my life and carry myself allows me to deal with things and other people, mentally and spiritually, and the fact that I established a reputation early in my time, that I am serving a lot of time and am fearless about defending myself, it seems that status has served me well. One of the incidents with a prisoner was hand-to-hand combat that I won easily, and the other was really messed up because I had to defend myself by stabbing him several times, almost killing him. That happened in the late 1980s, and it seems, even with his size and his reputation, I got the best of him, and my status and reputation was enhanced. Then an officer and I got in a hand-to-hand combat in the visiting room in December 1995, while I was trying to get some ganja to celebrate the holiday season. Though I had him under control, I was bum-rushed by at least twelve other officers in a matter of minutes, and I suffered some serious pain during that confrontation. Because of that incident, I was sent to Marion lockdown unit in 1996.

Racism thrives in prison, and even though at one time I have spoken out against white people in power and authority, I never had any problem with regular white people. In fact, most of the people that have been my best advocates and supporters are white women. Believe me, most of the racial conflicts I have in prison are from administrative staff. Many times,

---

4. The Honorable Elijah Muhammad was the leader of the Nation of Islam, a Black nationalist religious and political organization established in 1930.

when white women visit me, officers have harassed me in the visiting room, terminating and suspending my visits for hugging or kissing. There were a few who even questioned one woman on how she could visit me when I am in prison for killing white people and serving a lot of time.

I have done time with many political prisoners and have pictures at home with many of them, like Sekou Odinga, Sundiata Acoli, Veronza Bowers, Jaan Laaman, Tommy Manning, Leonard Peltier, Bill Dunne, Kevin Rashid Johnson, and I am sure others whose names haven't come to mind here. All the men mentioned above and I are friends, and we were involved in revolutionary or political work at one time or another. When I arrived at Marion, I went through the entry shakedown and was put in E Unit, where I met the famous John Gotti, who was living upstairs from me.[5] Jihad Abdulmumit (now out) is one of my biggest advocates and supporters. It's been so long since I've been around those men that particular memories are hard to come to mind. But Sundiata Acoli and I were living in the same unit, a few cells apart, and we shared reading materials and poems we wrote. Plus we worked out together sometimes. Though prisoners with revolutionary mindset talked and worked together, there were not many organized actions available. Sometimes when we had certain group programs and we had outside guests, many of us gave speeches, but most actions were behind the scenes.

If I did not rely on the advice of my attorneys and some family and friends expecting justice from the courts, I would have escaped or died trying to escape earlier on in my life. But now that is too late due to my health and age. Listen, I am not guilty of the crimes I was convicted of, but I am guilty of assisting fugitives before these crimes took place (three are my codefendants). They manufactured evidence and fabricated testimony and claimed that I confessed after being severely brutalized by the police. To be real, I still can't understand how after all these years have gone by, no one has truly stood up and really challenged all those bullshit lies they told about me. Even if I did what they said I did, there is no way I would confess on myself then wait on those who imprisoned me to release me.

---

5. John Gotti was the leader of the New York-based Gambino crime family who orchestrated the 1985 murder of his predecessor, Paul Castellano. Gotti was imprisoned in the early 1990s and remained behind bars for the remainder of his life.

Looking Forward

I don't think enough is being done to support our political prisoners, but I don't see any way the prison structure in America will be torn down. Our supporters need to take more direct approaches to those in authority, like holding mass demonstrations all over America, confronting those in authority personally, letting them know exactly who should be released and show them why. But in a capitalist society with class culture, there is no way prisons can or will be torn down. Human nature itself will direct a person who is hungry to take food or other items to get what's needed to satisfy that hunger, and, based on the laws of society, those actions are criminal and require imprisonment. This is a society where there are so many guns and other weapons, and racial, political, and economic conflicts, that violence will take place and those in authority will make sure there is a place to lock you up. There might be some reforms and leniency, but prison will be here forever unless they start executing you right away for committing a crime, without a trial. I don't believe we'll ever reach that lifestyle, but prison isn't going anywhere. Though I do believe that public support applied directly can help get some political prisoners released. I look at all the demonstrations for George Floyd and the Black Lives Matter marches, and even though some changes were made, the same problems still exist. The way I see it, the oppressors will always have a prison system to keep the rebellion among the oppressed in check. They also have a system to keep resistance and demonstrations in check, like blackballing some, intimidating some, putting some in prisons, and killing some.

It's a hell of a fight to be in, supporting and advocating for political prisoners, and I for one truly appreciate those who are involved. But as I said, I believe that more direct and stronger physical approaches or confrontations are needed in these times. At seventy years old and with my health problems, prison life is not for me, especially after I have already been in prison for over forty-eight years.

The best advice I can give to anyone coming to prison today is do your best to get your release as soon as you can. Study your case carefully to determine your best options and be truthful to yourself about the approach you choose to take. Those two approaches are based on my own trials and errors in my own efforts. If there is no easy way out and you have to serve a few years, look for educational or vocational programs and self-development programs that you'll be able to use to get out sooner and use once you are released. Though there are not that many programs offered in prisons today, I believe the federal prison system is the most beneficial. One of the main things to keep in mind is always to be mindful of who or what you become involved in. Life in some prisons can be rough and tough, violent, and, in some, life can become so easy you become complacent and don't do all you need to do to prepare yourself for release.

The main thing I want people to know and keep in mind is that no matter what happened in my life, I have always conducted myself in an upright, honest, and trustworthy way, always dealing with others with respect and fair play. Not to say that it was an easy ride, but I believe the moral principles I was brought up with, and the principles I learned from older prisoners early in my time, helped me a lot. There were times when I got involved in selling and using drugs, but I made sure not to become addicted to any of them and not to victimize those who were. In over forty-eight years, I never informed on anyone or checked in the hole due to fear or anything else. I want people to feel the vibes within the words that I have written and know that at no time will I ever give up or surrender trying and working to be released from prison. Even if anyone believes I am guilty of the crimes I'm in prison for, I believe I have served enough time. The fact is, no one ever testified that they heard me or saw me commit those crimes. Though weapons, bullets, and other "evidence" were presented, none had my fingerprints or were connected to me personally. The only evidence used to get this conviction on me is a "confession," which was prepared by the police, who brutalized me for at least three days before I signed it. All of this is documented. Plus four of the jurors filed affidavits after our trial saying how they were threatened, intimidated, and forced to vote guilty.

What's so bad about all this is that high government officials were there and knew what happened and haven't done anything to correct it, only because seven of the victims were white people and the crimes took place on Rockefeller's property. That is the bottom line right there.

David Campbell

David Campbell is a lover of language and the arts, who was two weeks away from moving to Paris to study French translation when his dedication to combat the alt-right drew him to a protest. At the protest, a brawl broke out in which a fifty-six-year-old intoxicated alt-right man was knocked unconscious. Cops stepped in and broke David's leg in two places. The District Attorney's office filed gang assault charges against David, who took a noncooperating plea agreement. He served eighteen months at Rikers Island, coinciding with the outbreak of the COVID pandemic. David translated *Revolutionary Affinities: Toward a Marxist Anarchist Solidarity* (PM Press, 2023), a sweeping history by French authors Olivier Besancenot and Michael Löwy.

Prison Life

I went to an antifascist protest in January 2018 in Manhattan. The alt-right was celebrating the one-year anniversary of Trump's inauguration so there were a lot of alt-right guys in suits and black bloc folks.[1] At the end, around ten thirty at night, it turned into a brawl that lasted only a few minutes. I got caught up in it, but I didn't start it.

There were no cops around when it first happened, but at some point during the course of this brawl, a cop came around the corner. We got

---

1. The alt-right is a loosely affiliated white nationalist movement that became prominent in the United States in the 2010s. The black bloc is a tactic used by militant protesters who wear all black and shield their identities.

surveillance footage later, and his body language is very clear. The cop did a double take (turns his head), and then he launched at the first person in black bloc that he saw. It was me. I didn't say anything. He grabbed me from behind and threw me to the ground. When he did that, he broke my tibia in two places, the second-largest bone in the body.

There was a guy on the other side who had been knocked out, and he was lying on the ground. Instantly, it became this narrative about how I had stalked him or tried to kill the man. All kinds of crazy allegations were made that I didn't know about until I got out of the hospital. In the hospital, I was handcuffed to the bed, and at one point I was shackled to the bed with my nonbroken leg.

Finally, after four days, I got arraigned. My friends posted bail, and I got out. I went home and learned about these wild allegations. I saw the right-wing tabloids, and later I got the documents with the really crazy allegations that the cop was making. All that stuff was thrown out in court, but the original narrative put forward by the cop is still held up as an example by the far-right (like Andy Ngo) of how the left-wing is unhinged, violent, and dangerous.[2]

There's an entry in an index of Andy Ngo's book that came out last year with my name in it. It says, "David Campbell tried to kill an old man with his bare hands in the middle of the street." What actually happened is I got caught up in a brawl, and I kicked the guy that was on the ground twice. That's not that bad, but it's not great. Even though most people agree with physical use of force against fascist folks, the guy was on the ground, so I probably didn't have to do that. I wasn't thinking clearly. I was pissed off, and it was kind of hectic. When I did that, it enabled the DEA to get me on a gang assault charge.

Gang assault is this crazy law that's been on the books since the Giuliani-Pataki era. It basically says anytime you're in a group of three or more people, if you're involved in a physical fight, you're all responsible for each other's actions. It's a three-and-a-half-year mandatory minimum. You don't have to prove that you know each other. Even though I was the only person arrested, they could see there were other people on camera. I

2. Andy Ngo is a conservative journalist, provocateur, and a right-wing media personality who resides in Portland, Oregon.

didn't know anyone that I was with, and I wasn't interested in finding out if I knew anybody. I resisted my case for about two years. Ultimately, I took a plea [deal] to eighteen months, and I served twelve months in Rikers from October 2019 to October 2020.

I was in jail, not prison, which I know is confusing because those terms are used interchangeably by a lot of people. Jail is such a short-term facility and there's so much turnover. Rikers, in particular, is so poorly organized at the institutional level. The institutional time blocks that you have to organize your routine around keep changing. For example, yard was at 2:00 p.m. for about three months and then the next day it changed to 7:00 a.m., overnight. If you want to go outside and work out, you'd have to start getting up at 7:00 a.m. It forces you to change whatever else you built in your schedule. I developed about a dozen different routines during my time behind bars because things kept changing. They also randomly rotate people around between housing units.

I had a lot of support going in and knew that routine is really important. I knew from the start I wanted to really seize the time and structure it in a way where I was doing things that matter to me. It was important to me to go to the yard because I got to go outside and exercise. Even though I could exercise in the dorm, I felt a little more free to do my own thing in the yard. It's also the only place where there's a pull-up bar, so there's certain things I couldn't do without going to the yard. Working is huge in jail in terms of breaking up the routine, so my job was important, as well as working on writing and translation projects, reading books and letters, and responding to letters.

I had a lot of support. I was aware that I was going into a situation that I couldn't possibly be ready for. I did a lot of preparation and spoke with a lot of former political prisoners before I went in. I had a shit ton of support with my defense committee, the radical community in New York, and friends and family. I don't think you can really prepare for it because it's just so weird. There's nothing that can really prepare you for it.

Jail is much closer to street culture in terms of the hood or homeless people, addicts, and boosters [shoplifters who sell stolen goods] and stuff like that than prison. I think there's a lot of crossover with that in prison too, but jail is very much like that. I was trying to figure out what the hell was going on around me. I couldn't understand half the stuff people were saying because they were using jail slang or coded language. I couldn't sleep well the first few weeks. I couldn't get physically comfortable anywhere. I would go to my SOD [Special Operations Detail or Special Operations Division] job in the morning. Sometimes, instead of taking a bus, I'd ride around in a church van. Sitting in those seats in the church van was like being on a crappy couch with an ottoman. A few minutes is incredible. So, yeah, jail took some getting used to.

I think the best advice I received before I went in was "Mind your business, stay quiet, and just observe. Once you think you have it figured out, just remind yourself that you don't have it figured out. Stay quiet. Observe some more." That was very helpful. And also, it sounds very cheesy, but I'm a big believer in the power of human connection. It is a real thing. I believe in that very strongly. My background is in theater, which helped. I also had some indication from other people who've done time to just go up to people and be real. Don't present yourself like a pushover, but say something like, "Look, it's my first time and I'm just asking straight up, can I use that phone right now?" People respond to that because you're putting them in a position of authority. You're deferring to them. So I did that a lot, and that helped a lot too.

In the big picture, my time was not that long. I made my peace with it before I went in. I actually made my peace with doing longer. The DA sat on three and a half years for about nine months and decided to cut it down. When I originally took my plea, it was supposed to be for twenty-four months, serving sixteen, but then I got eighteen, serving twelve as kind of a bonus.

A few months before I moved, I was going through all of my notebooks from jail. I was struck by how funny the shit in there sometimes was. You just get used to everything, and then something happens, and you find yourself laughing at it. Your body's craving some laughter, so there were a lot of funny moments.

In terms of a best time or easiest time, it was hands down during the first lockdown. It sounds crazy, but I was in a very specific situation where three-quarters of sentenced inmates on Rikers Island walked out the door overnight after public pressure and a strike we did inside to release people due to COVID. I was not among the three-quarters of people who left. I was in the one-quarter that was stuck there. I was in a forty-eight-bed dorm and thirty-six guys just walked out, give or take. So there were just a dozen of us left. We all got along pretty well. There was no beef over dumb shit. There were plenty of phones, plenty of toilets, plenty of TVs, and plenty of showers.

There was not that much noise. All of the guys that walked out just left all of their stuff—mattresses, pillows, blankets, commissary stuff. Because what do they need it for? They were going home, so fuck jail. I'm talking months and months' worth of commissary food. A lot of the guys who were important in the social hierarchy would pick someone to give their shit to. They were like, "You're a cool dude. Have all my shit." That happened to me. We all got along, and we had plenty of space and plenty of stuff. All of these COs were getting sick or calling out sick, and they weren't enforcing shit like they usually did.

We were also "on quarantine" and stuck in the dorm for sixteen days, which sucked. But, honestly, I had a great routine, and it was comparatively very enjoyable. It was much more chill than what it had been like before that because a busy dorm is kind of crazy. So, actually, the way things turned out for me during the first wave, in particular after everyone was released, was kind of nice for a bit.

Conditions definitely got worse with COVID, besides my personal first-wave experience, where it was pretty sweet because it cleared out the other inmates. So many things got way worse with COVID. Disruption of services like visits, mail, yard, programs, healthcare, even food. Endless and arbitrary lockdowns. Jails and prisons are using the pandemic as a catchall excuse to delay or reject whatever they just don't feel like dealing with.

On the outside, when people talk about whether little inconveniences that we've lost due to COVID are going to come back, there's always a question of customer satisfaction. Like whether this or that service that was cut due to COVID will come back because it made the customers happy, and businesses like to keep their customers happy. That's just not a factor in jail. They don't give a fuck about you, and you have to fight for every square inch of dignity. Even just to get it written on paper, it doesn't mean they're going to abide by it. So it's sad to say, but I think that it's going to take a lot of work to get conditions behind bars back to where they were pre-COVID.

I practiced my Spanish grammar. I speak fluent French, and I've spoken decent Spanish for years, but I always just learned it on the job and never really studied the grammar. So I got a lot better with my Spanish grammar and also kept my French alive while I was inside, which I'm really proud of. Now I'm in grad school in France for translation, which is pretty huge. There weren't any French-speaking inmates there. There were a couple of people who spoke different French patois, Creole languages. There were a couple of guards that were French speakers, but you cannot speak to a guard in a language that other people don't understand. That's not good. So I had a few French-speaking friends who would do video visits. I would call them, and we would practice that way. Other than that, it was on me. I would do grammar exercises. I worked my way through an entire book of advanced French grammar, one chapter per week. I tried to make one of the books I was reading a French book. I would sit there at my bunk and just read out loud to myself so my muscle memory for pronunciation didn't get mushy. It's not really a new skill, but I'm a nonnative speaker, and for a whole year I kept that alive. I'm really proud of that because it's allowed me to be where I am in my life now.

I also did a lot of working out. I got way bigger than I'd ever been, which was kind of fun. I learned a lot about working out. For years I did a little exercise, but I learned some really wild exercise shit in jail that I really enjoyed.

Honestly, the level of solidarity shocked me the most. There's a lot of solidarity in Rikers. People share things. They take care of each other. It's often cloaked in this machismo, but there's a lot of solidarity and real kindness. That was surprising.

I was also surprised by how "buddy-buddy" people often are with guards on Rikers. It might not be like that elsewhere. I know that definitely flies in the face of what a lot of people on the left, including myself, would like to believe about incarcerated folks, but it takes a lot of work to just be standoffish with people all the time. You live in close quarters with them, and you depend on them for everything. When you need toothpaste to brush your teeth or toilet paper to wipe your ass, guess who you've got to go to? The guards. If you want to go to your visit, to the library, to the yard, to chow, or to the clinic, you have to go through them. They are the gatekeepers, literally.

Furthermore, on Rikers, a lot of the guards come from the same neighborhoods as the guys that they lock up. A lot of those guys know each other on the street. A lot of them are even family. After my release, I met up with this guy I'd met inside. We were just chatting, and he was talking about how a captain at Rikers was his aunt's stepfather or something. It sounds like a pretty distant connection, but apparently he used to see the captain at some extended family barbecue every year, and they knew each other. There are a lot of people like that. They grow up together, or they know people who did. Even if they don't know each other personally, they have the same reference points. I even met a handful of guys who knew me or recognized me from my neighborhood in Brooklyn while I was locked up.

There's a line: don't be a snitch. People let you know if you're crossing a line, but because people are not staying for very long, they're less hard-line about the code of silence than they might be in prison. The twelve months that I did is long for that facility. Rikers is a quick, quick turnaround time, so these guys are focused on the street. They're not really going to buy into that hardcore *omertà* thing.[3] Like, people are generally suspicious of you if you spend too much time chatting with a guard, and especially if you're chatting with a guard alone, but in general, it's totally okay to chat with guards.

There is a very pronounced sense of us versus them. There are prisoners, and there are guards. When we went on strike during COVID, that came to the forefront. At the same time, there's also "he's a cop, but he's all right." There's a lot of that.

There was also a moment when I looked back, and I realized I'm up there now socially. It's not like I was the gang boss in the house, but I had the corner bed. The layout of the dorm was one corner bed with two windows and no neighbor on one side. That is prime real estate. I had the corner bed for the last five months of my bit. It's not like I was going around fucking motherfuckers up to get it. It's just because people are chill. If you play your cards right and you're patient and you ask nicely, people just see seniority. They see how long your beard is. They see how fucked up your shoes are. They see how much commissary and how many books you have. They can gauge how long you've been in. Not everybody gives a shit, but there's a sense of, "I show up in this house, and I don't know where to go or what to do. I'm going to ask that guy, how do things work here?" Before you know it, people are coming to you and asking you questions. It's surreal. So, I'm proud that I was able to move up socially over time.

Politics and Prison Dynamics

It's not that my time was easy, but I wasn't in a supermax. I didn't have to stab

---

3. *Omertà* is a Southern Italian code of silence and noncooperation with government officials and legal authorities.

anyone based on race to survive. It was nothing like that. Rikers is totally different. There were things that I was not happy about. I went in ready to fuck somebody up if I had to, or do my best to fuck somebody up if that's what it took, even if it's over something stupid, because those things really matter. You can't leave, so the other folks that you're locked up with see everything and it follows you. Certain words are fighting words. For example, you can't tell someone "suck my dick" on Rikers and not expect to fight. I think it's the same behind bars in most places. I got that impression from stories people told me about their time upstate. And if you back down from someone telling you that, it's going to follow you.

There was this big, scary guy who moved in a couple of beds down from me, maybe a month before I went home. He was kind of an asshole with me. I was kind of freaked out and kind of pissed off. I didn't want to get caught up in something a few weeks before I went home. This other guy told me he was in the 5 [housing unit] with him, which is another one of the buildings on Rikers. He told me, "I was in the 5 with him and this guy told him, 'suck my dick,' and he backed down, so don't worry about him. He's a pushover."

I went in knowing that your reputation really matters a lot, but I didn't have to do anything crazy like that. Ethics are, to some degree for me, dependent on the situation. I know that moral relativism can get dangerous. There's a slippery slope. But in jail you do what you've got to do to get by, and it doesn't mean you take pleasure in it. It doesn't mean that's who you are. Obviously, if you do something repeatedly over years and years, it can have an impact on you, and there's some sort of philosophical discussion to be had there. But, in general, I was ready to do what I had to do to get by. Fortunately, I didn't have to do anything really fucked up. Certain things I'm not super happy with, but I didn't have to do anything really crazy.

I had zero fights, and I'm really proud of that. I took my inspiration from Daniel McGowan, who had no fights in seven and a half years, and from David Gilbert, who had no fights or tickets in forty years.[4] I was like, "Well, if they can do it, I can do it." That was something I was conscious of going

4. Daniel McGowan is a former Earth Liberation Front (ELF) political prisoner. His story is included here.

in. I didn't want to do that shit and there are ways to back down from a fight if someone crosses that line and uses this sort of language I talked about a second ago. You can always say, "That's not worth my good time." Among guys who are serving sixteen months max—sixteen months was the longest sentence where I was, and there were very few guys serving that much—it really makes a lot of sense that something is not worth your good time.

You could win small battles by filing a grievance. I was like the nerdy white guy in whatever housing unit I was in. People who didn't even know me would just come up to me waving paperwork in the air like, "Yo, help me out with this." Obviously, I'm the guy to handle paperwork because objectively, statistically, if you tallied up the number of experiences dealing with bureaucracy and filling out forms and the amount of reading of documents that each of us had done, I would probably come out on top. It's a skill set. It's "that's the guy you go to." I went to pretty much everyone else for everything concerning daily life at Rikers because that was a skill set they had and I didn't.

When I had conflicts with guards, sometimes I could win by following the paper trail and standing on that. Sometimes but not always. With other prisoners, sometimes I would lose my temper because it's a very stressful environment. I've always had a bad temper, but I've gotten better about that over the years. I got better about that even during my time in jail just because you can't really flip out. People will fuck you up because you're ruining other people's experience. When I had conflicts with other prisoners, I just tried to be aware of them physically when they were around me and not let them get behind me. I'd keep an eye on their hands, especially if they're reaching for something. I'd make it hard for them to cut me. And then, honestly, it sounds kind of crazy, but I would just go up to people and try to clear the air. It happened a couple of times where afterwards I was like, "Listen, man, I'm sorry I reacted that way. It was early in the morning. I'm really stressed out because I thought I was going home this week."

A dude attacked me with a mop stick once. The dude was my friend, but he flipped out. I'm fairly confident that I could have fucked him up. I'm not a martial arts master, but I'm bigger than him, and I know how to defend myself. I just didn't let him hit me with the mop stick, and I was like, "Dude, let it go," and the CO intervened. In general, I just tried to be like, "Listen, let's drop it. We can always fight. We shouldn't." He didn't talk to me for two days and insisted he was going to kill me. Then one day he just stood up and said "It's all good, Papi" and wrapped his arms around me. He was kind of insane. He did that with a lot of people. But the point is, you could go to people after the fact and be like, "Listen, my bad, I'm stressed out. I know you are too. Let's just drop it." That tended to work.

It is integrated at Rikers. It's not segregated at the policy level. That's probably surprising for people. I think most people in most facilities deal with some sort of racial segregation, but even before I went in, I talked to people who served time in different places and it's not always like what you see on *Orange Is the New Black*. In some places it is.

I made sure pretty much all the white people that I met knew what I was in for so they wouldn't try to appeal to white racial solidarity with me. I was very clear with them about what I was in for because I felt safe doing that at Rikers. I could get away with that. Just about every time I met a white person, I would be like, "I'm in for beating up a Trump supporter. Do you like Trump?" Because I felt comfortable, not because I'm a tough guy, but you do have to play that part a little bit in jail. It's not who I am, but I felt comfortable doing that, to give you an indication that betraying white supremacy in there was a nonissue for me, which is great.

Then you had this sort of clustering with Latino folks, but it's not so fluid. There's a lot of Puerto Rican folks, children of Latino immigrants, and people from Spanish-speaking families that—regardless of their legal status or citizenship status—don't speak a lick of Spanish. There are plenty of those people. There's white-passing Spanish people and a lot of Dominicans who could be identified as Black depending on who you ask. So it gets really fluid. Is someone who's a fourth-generation Puerto Rican in the Spanish section or not? What about a guy from a Guatemalan family who speaks no English? They decide. It's very fluid.

The vast majority of folks incarcerated at Rikers are Black, so Blackness isn't really a practical criterion for cliquishness. It's more often based on affinity, friendship, and gang affiliation. But, even then, gang affiliation could mean anything. I met Puerto Rican Crips.[5] I met Chinese-American Bloods.[6]

---

5. The Puerto Rican Crips are Puerto Rican members of the Crips (Community Revolution in Progress), who were formed in Los Angeles, California, in the late 1960s and early 1970s.

6. The Chinese-American Bloods are Chinese members of the Bloods (Brotherly Love Overcomes Overrides and Destruction), who were formed in Los Angeles, California, in the late 1960s and early 1970s.

I met a Black American guy from Jersey City who was a Latin King and a white Greek guy who was a Latin King.[7] These are people I've met, real people, so it's super messy. As much as I can say I had a clique or a crew on Rikers, it was mostly folks of color. I had a few friends who were white from my time inside, but race was largely a nonissue, especially in my case. I think my having been sentenced for fighting with the far-right resonated with people. It helped me a lot.

And again, you also have to understand that most of the cops, most of the COs, I mean, on Rikers are working-class people of color. A lot of them are immigrants. Even if they're enforcing a white supremacist prison system, they're not doing it with as much gusto on certain points.

Even if they don't have a really developed political consciousness, a lot of people would be happy to share anecdotes with you about anything. One guy had a huge Los Macheteros tattoo on his forearm. He claimed to have been involved with Los Macheteros in Puerto Rico. It was a pretty old tattoo, but who knows—maybe he just liked them. I don't know.

Writing is such a personally fulfilling thing for me, and I'm really grateful for the reception my writing got while I was inside. I've continued to get shit published since I got out. It helps to normalize this stuff and to get these stories out there, whether it's my own or somebody else's. So I wrote stuff, some of which got published. I wrote about our strike for *Hard Crackers*, and then I think the Certain Days calendar was the first place I got picked up after that.[8] I was so stoked.

When I went in, I wanted to just get in and get out. Besides sharing my beliefs with people or sharing literature like zines or books, I wasn't planning to rock the boat. I didn't want to lose any good time. That mostly held true. When COVID hit, I helped organize a strike, which was huge. I think it contributed to getting a lot of people released. I'm very proud of that because it was a real risk. I broke with the rules I established for myself about not rocking the boat, because the game completely changed. It wasn't clear if they were

---

7. The Almighty Latin King and Queen Nation, or the Latin Kings, is one of the largest Hispanic and Latino prison gangs in the United States, founded by Puerto Ricans in Chicago in the 1950s.

8. *Hard Crackers* is an online and print publication that is guided by the principle that in ordinary people there resides the capacity to escape from the mess we are in, and a commitment to documenting and examining their strivings to do so.

literally leaving us to die or not. Now we know more about COVID, but at the time we had no idea. There was panic in the air that first week COVID hit.

As for violence, if you don't have beef, it's probably not going to affect you. I had some small beefs with people. I had beef with this one guy in particular. He was more of a prison guy. I was kind of worried about it, but nothing ever came to blows. You can compare it to being a gentrifier like myself, living in a neighborhood that's traditionally the hood. Especially if you're a white person moving into a working-class urban neighborhood from somewhere else or if you have a different educational or socioeconomic background, you live your life in a neighborhood where the violence has not really changed for the people that grew up there. In New York, sometimes there's a little shrine with those votive candles that appear out in front of your bodega because someone got shot there last night. It's sad. But in terms of anxiety management, those things are not coming for you. They don't really affect you because you're not involved in the world of the beefs that are being aired on the street, gangbanging, drug dealing, fucking somebody else's girl. You live in that, and it's around you, but it's not really coming for you. It's kind of like that with violence on Rikers for guys like me.

Also, you're not allowed to practice martial arts on Rikers. There are cameras everywhere, so they really enforce that. I know in other places this is not the case. A lot of people upstate told me the prison actually gave them boxing gloves. At Rikers, they didn't do that. I wasn't able to practice martial arts. One of the ways that I would handle my anxiety about being attacked is I would walk through the steps in my mind. I'd plan what I would do if I were walking down the main hall and somebody bum-rushed me out of the side hall, which does happen. I would walk through it in my mind, like right arm comes up, foot goes back, step left, strike left hand. That was super helpful for me. No matter where something might go down, I felt like I already had a visualization of it.

A lot of people carry bangers on Rikers. I don't know if this term is used elsewhere. There are shanks, but they're very rare, especially among sentenced inmates like myself who were more chill because they were going home soon. In comparison, detainees might be in for graffiti, or for armed robbery, or for first-degree murder. It's one big house. So detainee culture on Rikers is different from sentenced inmate culture on Rikers. That is true in terms of violence and the things people use to carry out violence. Sentenced people mostly use bangers, which are very small. They're for slicing, not so much for stabbing. It's just to scare somebody off. People also cut each other on the face and the hands. Mostly, I think guys just don't want to seem like they're not ready for a fight. It gives them a sense of security, like a comfort blanket. People make bangers out of all kinds of stuff.

There was a point, I think in August 2020, about two months before I came home, where things were noticeably getting more violent. It's very hard to come by statistics in there. All of the newspapers have stories about Rikers ripped out. Rikers, cops, COs, the state prison system, the feds; all that's ripped out, so it's hard to come by concrete information. A lot of stuff is just based on feel and rumors. "Oh, I heard somebody got cut in this dorm the other day. Oh, I heard somebody went to the clinic. He was sliced up from this dorm." It's just rumors, so it's hard to gauge. There was a point when it was clear that everybody believed things were getting more violent. I think it was because the courts opened up and there was a whole bunch of new blood coming. There were those of us that lived through COVID and had been weathering the lockdown behind bars, and then all these new people showed up.

I was researching for a writing project recently, and I found a graph of violence over the past two years at Rikers, month by month. There was this huge spike in August 2020, and I knew that's when it started. The people around me were arming themselves, so I got a hold of one of those little plastic tags on a bread bag. I sharpened it on a wall and I kept it in a place where there was plausible deniability. I could say it wasn't mine. I never had to use it.

I was very aware of the security blanket phenomenon of bangers, but I didn't have beef, so I never wanted one, because it's also a huge liability if you get caught with it. You can lose all your good time or worse. This was two months before I went home. I thought it was kind of dumb to risk it. On the other hand, things were kind of wild, and I was so aware of the fact that I knew very little about jail culture. I'm not just being humble—in there it's a security issue. I didn't know if shit was going to pop off as some sort of free-for-all. I doubted it. But I was perpetually reminding myself that I needed to be careful. At the time, being careful meant having something on hand that I could use to defend myself if needed, but which I could also deny was mine if I got caught with it.

Looking Forward

There's a lot of research that shows that people who are well supported and maintain ties with people that they are close to in the outside world do better coming back and reintegrating once their time is done. It also makes you feel like you're not forgotten when you're doing the time. It's literally uncountable the number of times I heard comments about the amount of mail I got or the number of visits I got. It is kind of sad. At the time, it's just banter, but, once removed, I realized guys are saying that because they never get mail. Not a single piece. Not a birthday card. Some of the guys never call anybody. They sell their phone calls to other guys, like the guy who doesn't have enough phone calls to hang on the phone with his girlfriend all day because they limit the number of calls you can make.

I just think about how much stress and conflict would be eliminated for everybody in there if people on the outside gave support. Like, "Yo, we love you. We hear you. We miss you. We can't wait to see you again. Keep your head up. Stay cool, and don't do anything stupid." That's essential.

Supporters should just make sure they ask prisoners what they actually want or need.

Another thing to keep in mind is that jail is unfortunately super homophobic and transphobic. I had to ask a couple nonbinary friends to "butch it up" when they came to visit me because people notice who visits you, and all it takes is one homophobic comment to drastically change your social life in there. Another comrade sent me a zine about the George Jackson Brigade that had a lot of stuff about militant organizing among gay prisoners printed on it in very large font. I had to find a way to get rid of it because even that can be very dangerous in jail.[9]

Something that formerly incarcerated grand jury resister Jerry Koch told me is that your time behind bars is not just lost. This period of time does not just disappear from your life. I knew that, but I couldn't really fathom it for whatever reason before I went away.

There are certain things you can do in there that are very rewarding and enriching for you and your personal growth that are very difficult, if not

---

9. The zine mentioned is titled *Queer Fire: The George Jackson Brigade, Men Against Sexism, and Gay Struggle Against Prison* (Untorelli Press, 2014).

impossible, to do out here on the outside. I mean, people pay good money for meditation retreats and detoxes and shit. Tech bros will pay good money to get away from it all, and there's some overlap there. Even for me, I served all my time in a very noisy dorm. I never had a cell to myself where I could just do a prison ashram thing. Even then, in a noisy dorm, I adjusted. I got used to it and tuned out that noise, and I was able to read, write, study. People would get into fistfights around me and I would think, "They're not going to knock over my stack of books that I'm using to translate. It's fine." And just keep going.

So, time is not wasted. It's not going to disappear. You can do things, so have a list of projects to accomplish. Have a list of things that you want to get done, that you can only get done with nothing else to do. That's really important.

The hype about life behind bars is often worse than the actual living. Even if you get into some serious shit, it's like anything else—you bite your tongue and deal. You just jump in and start swimming. You can handle it one day at a time.

You may come out with some quirks. I mean, I always, always scan the tops of barbed wire fences now because I'm looking for a break. It's just a game, a way of having control mentally. Where would I make a break for it? In there, I had nothing else to do, and lots of barbed wire to look at. Also, if I'm in a crowd, I look at people's hands, especially when somebody's hand goes down to their pocket. I notice much more now if someone is carrying a little pencil or something. I don't know if I would have noticed that before because I never asked myself.

A lot of my fear about going away was that I would be traumatized and shell-shocked. It's a real fear. But try to go in with an open mind, and don't judge it. Remember that the conditions are not that dissimilar from the conditions that people go through living in the International Space Station or in the Arctic research station or in ballistic submarines. Obviously, those experiences are socially valorized, unlike doing time. But the experience of incarceration has objective similarities in some ways. For me, it's helpful to draw those parallels, because it demonstrates that it's not impossible to do this. That's what I would have said to pre-incarceration me or to someone going in now.

I got to say, I feel like I learned a lot. I think you'll learn a lot too, if you're going in or know somebody who is going in. You'll learn a lot of things that a lot of people won't get, and that's okay. There's a lot of humor in there. There's a lot of tenderness and solidarity in there that is hard to explain to someone who's never lived it. Even in places where shit is crazier than where I was, there's a lot of that.

Also, there are people behind bars who have done bad things, but most of them absolutely do not need to be there. That's not anything new, but I cannot say that enough. On that note, I'm just devastated that when I was locked up at Rikers, three-quarters of us could just go free, and no one seems to be taking that fact as the indicator of the needlessness of the jail and prison system that it is. I think about 13 percent had been rearrested six months later, some abysmally small proportion. Now it's back to being an overcrowded shithole. It's like, they literally let everyone go overnight, no questions asked, not that long ago, and things were fine. Why are they not doing it again? So, yeah, some people behind bars have done really bad things, but they don't need to be there. They really don't.

Xinachtli

Xinachtli (Alvaro Luna Hernandez) is a lawyer and community organizer from Texas. Xinachtli was recognized nationally and internationally as the national coordinator of the Ricardo Aldape Guerra Defense Committee, which led the struggle to free Mexican national Aldape Guerra from Texas's death row after being framed by Houston police for allegedly killing a cop. Xinachtli's human rights work has been recognized in Italy, France, Spain, Switzerland, Mexico, and other countries. In 1976, Xinachtli was wrongfully convicted, and he was paroled in 1991. Subsequently, in 1997, he was sentenced to fifty years in prison for defending himself by disarming a police officer who drew a weapon on him. The trial evidence clearly showed Xinachtli was the victim of witch hunts and a police-orchestrated conspiracy to frame or eliminate him. While imprisoned, Xinachtli has helped countless people with his jailhouse lawyering, and he is also an inside member of the Certain Days Collective, which produces a yearly calendar to raise funds and awareness about political prisoners. In total, Xinachtli has served over forty years in numerous Texas state prisons, usually in solitary confinement, where he continues to fight back against his imprisonment.

> "In memory of all liberation martyrs that gave up their lives so we all can be free. The loss of their lives was not in vain. We continue where they were extinguished by the forces of racism, state police power, and terrorism."
>
> —Xinachtli

Prison Life

When I first entered prison in January 1976, I was totally apolitical. I was twenty-two or twenty-three years of age and had no social or political identity, as a by-product of having lived under neocolonial rule. I was born on May 12, 1952, in Alpine, Brewster County, Texas, about ninety miles from the US/Mexico military-imposed border, a colonial subject of various colonial wars against Mexicans, and against the Mexican National Territories, in the 1800s that spanned the entire US Southwest, from "Tejas" to California. I was born in a racially segregated society and forced to attend racially segregated public schools. I lived under an all-white police force and saw an occupation army that patrolled and controlled our Chicano barrio with an iron fist. And a racist, brutal Alpine sheriff named Jim Skinner, who was sheriff for over forty years in Alpine, with a record of racist brutalities and murder of young, unarmed Mexicanos/Chicanos, never serving a day in jail.

Although I was not political, I now describe myself as a natural anarchist, due to the fact that I was a bona fide antiauthoritarian and despised racist police who brutalized our barrio with impunity, resulting in many physical fights I had with police, which resulted in me being pistol-whipped by cops and thrown in jail with my head all stitched up. I did manage to get my licks against the cops, one time kicking a city cop on his chin, splitting it open, and was charged with police assault. However, because I was just an underage juvenile, I was never sent to Texas prisons then.

I became politicized in prison and suffered extreme forms of state repression, including beatings, false disciplinaries, horrible food, prolonged stays in solitary confinement, denial of parole, and being imposed with the label Security Threat Group (or "gang member") to justify solitary confinement and isolation from the rest of the prison population. This is a policy and practice that continues today here at the McConnell Unit, as I am in a cell block housing the mentally ill, with extreme mental problems, and beyond reach of getting them engaged in the struggle for the defense of their human dignity and their human rights, behind white Amerikkka's iron curtain, where suppression still remains the order of the day. My incoming and outgoing correspondence and legal and political writings, essays, letters—all critical of institutional racism, of colonialism, capitalism, imperialism, and fascism—continue to be denied.

It was very difficult to adapt to the prison routine, especially in 1976 when the Texas prison system was severely overcrowded. We were sleeping on the floor in packed cages, under the control of an inmate guard-and-building-tender system of brutal inmates empowered by racist, brutal wardens, armed with knives to control prisoner behavior and thought. They were given special privileges in return, like a special cell, or extra food at all times of the day and night.

I think it was Karl Marx who once said that it is not for us to merely interpret the world but to change it. For it is true men and women who make history. My revolutionary politics and my spiritual and intellectual growth and development, and my, if you will, ascendency to the heights of a life of dedication and commitment to the freedom struggles to change the world are what has kept me sane, alive, and never, ever losing hope. For we, as the most oppressed class, are also the most advanced, scientifically. Dialectical materialist history is on our side, for we are gravediggers of the old capitalist order and delivering a new one, like a midwife delivering a newborn, but here, from the ashes of the old, rotten, corrupt, and bankrupt society, "pregnant with social revolution." So, I have accepted my "scientific role" as the vanguard in the United States, inside and outside, who will fill in, in our columns of soldiers and guerrilla fighters, like those in the Lacandon Jungles of Chiapas, fighting for a better world, free of capitalist, imperialist oppression.[1]

Nothing has shocked me, to see the racism and the sheer brutality on the inside, that has resulted in loss of life and limb to many prisoners, especially those murdered by inmates, with guards' complicity. As an innocent man, I knew the system was dirty, cruel, and rotten, but seeing with my very own eyes wardens and prison directors engaged in these atrocities, sanctioned by established politicians, was certainly a shock, at the very least. But I was prepared to deal with these issues, for I experienced the brutalities of local police in my hometown of Alpine, Texas, when I was eyewitness to the cold-blooded murder of my sixteen-year-old friend, Ervay Ramos, shot in the back by racist Alpine cop Bud Powers on June 12, 1968. I was with Ramos that tragic night. The racist pig never served a day in jail. The Ramos murder was reported by the US Commission on Civil Rights in its 1970 report

---

1. This is a reference to the Zapatista Army of National Liberation. See glossary.

entitled *Mexican Americans and the Administration of Justice in the Southwest* (US Government Printing Office).

Politics and Prison Dynamics

I was suspicious of all whites, but my study of law and prisoners' rights, and finishing my education through my own self-help remedies, led me to the study of religion, political science, and true history, which led me to the study of the history of revolutions, like the Cuban Revolution, and the Black Panther Party, leading me to "meeting George Jackson," which forever changed my life. I became a new man, seeing things differently and thinking outside the box, coming to despise the US government, white supremacy, colonialism, capitalism, imperialism, and fascism. I still underwent many changes in how I saw women, other races, capitalism, and the US flag, and I embraced a revolutionary belief system that today, in 2021, sustains my sanity and the strength and power of my ethics and convictions to dedicate myself to the struggle to change this racist, oppressive US society into a better world. It is an ongoing struggle because I have lived under a racist and oppressive system that has many persons entrapped in that vicious cycle of self-destruction, drug usage outside and inside, and resorting to criminal and gang ways that serve and benefit the capitalist economic system, reinforcing the division of races and classes, pitting one race against the other and one class against the other, to sustain the system as we know it.

Certainly, one cannot avoid conflicts inside with other racial groups, within our own race/ethnicity, and with the prison administration, in struggle against a very racist and oppressive prison system we brought down to its knees through the sheer power of prisoner unity and determination, facing all sorts of obstacles and a policy and practice of state-sanctioned violence and terrorism against those of us who stood united to bring about many changes or reforms of the prison. But not stopping there and going beyond the mere struggle for prison reforms, but coming to the realization that the prison system in Amerikkka is an integral part of capitalist society, or a pillar thereof, as one part of the racist, violent, and coercive state apparatus that enforces capitalist class rule, provides surplus commodities of infusion to the capitalist production forces (such as the commodity of law, lawyers, the

legal profession, printing presses, law book companies, and an entire industry that is based on mass incarceration of capitalism's surplus populations
of the poor, the unemployed, and the "reserve army of workers" that must
commit crimes in order to survive, or to sustain self-destructive habits the
same system instills in people living under capitalist rule).

What has kept me alive, sane, and always in survival mode is my firm
belief that I am serving the cause of justice for the most poor and oppressed
segments in US society, and so I never lose hope and always manage to find
light in the darkness of these racist, dark dungeon cages I am thrown in,
knowing that I never assaulted the Alpine pig sheriff on July 18, 1996. He
assaulted me, and I only disarmed him in self-defense, one of the most
revolutionary acts any one single person can accomplish, in disarming the
racist armed violence and attacks against those like me, in a long line of
cases, targeted by the forces of COINTELPRO, the brainchild of J. Edgar
Hoover, ex-FBI director, to suppress social movements and prevent the rise
of a Messiah that can unify and electrify the movement on behalf of the
poor and oppressed in Amerikkka. So, I shake off whatever setback I may
be hit with, like the recent passing of my dear mother, awaiting a decision
by the parole board whether to release me or not [Xinachtli was denied
parole]. No matter what decision they pick, I will continue the struggle no
matter where I find myself, in barbed wire communities or behind the iron
curtain of Amerikkka's notorious "Guantánamo Bay Prison," the William
G. McConnell Unit, named after a racist and brutal police chief who ruled
Beeville, Texas, with an iron fist for many years.

Looking Forward

When the prison knows that prisoners have strong outside support, I have
seen them with my very own eyes back off or be more reluctant to unleash
the unvarnished brutalities of its terrorist violence and brutalities against its
captive population.

My advice would be, in Texas, to expect a racist and brutal prison regime,
especially if you are Black, Chicano, or Native American, and get involved
with jailhouse lawyers and demand your basic legal, democratic rights. You
will face intense repression that may include beatings, false disciplinary cases,

relegation to solitary confinement for long periods of time, horrible food, lack of adequate medical care, no educational, religious, or other self-help programs other than the ones you work to develop with existing "leadership" that is into it (and not into the holy-roller mentality of seeking salvation in religious dogma, or the pie-in-the-sky faith the prison system supports because it serves their own purposes of maintaining good slaves.) As long as there exists this capitalist political economy, there will be prisons, for the prison is a pillar of capitalist class relations. Prisoners coming into the prison must discover their humanity and open their eyes beyond the social conditioning we are all subjected to as subjects of a racist and oppressive patriarchal system.

What has sustained and kept me alive has been my revolutionary belief systems [which] I came to discover through jailhouse lawyering, and from those that came before me, to bring me in, teach me the ropes and guide me in the right direction, to begin seeing myself, the world, and the dialectical sciences that [are] the destiny of us being the most marginalized and oppressed segments of US society. Because of our condition under neocolonialism, capitalism, imperialism, and bourgeois fascism, we are the motor force for change, and [we] are the vanguard elements that eventually will lead a social movement from within, demanding changes, and a new society, a new political-economic system that does not exploit the labor power of the workers, and can provide true freedom, justice, and equality that the current capitalism system can never provide.

If released in the near future, I will begin by organizing podcasts and other internet social media outlets to get the word out and speak about my experiences, hoping to organize a speakers' bureau network where I can travel the nation and the world doing presentations on the many topics that need true clarification, from criminal injustice to prisons, human rights, colonialism, the death penalty, the labor movement, the prison movement, and social revolution.

David Gilbert

David Gilbert is a lifelong anti-imperialist who was captured and imprisoned as a result of an attempted expropriation of a Brinks truck in Nyack, New York, in 1981.[1] He was sentenced to seventy-five years to life but his sentence was commuted by outgoing Governor Cuomo, and he was released from prison after nearly forty years in November 2021. Though he spent short stints at MCC-NY and other federal prisons and jails, David spent the majority of his forty-year incarceration at the six maximum security men's prisons in New York (Attica, Auburn, Clinton, Comstock, Wende, and Shawangunk prisons). While in prison, David was a cofounder of the Certain Days Collective, and he also helped pioneer AIDS awareness programs that saved thousands of lives in prisons across the country.[2] David wrote numerous zines, including *Our Commitment Is to Our Communities: Mass Incarceration, Political Prisoners and Building a Movement for Community-Based Justice* (Kersplebedeb, 2014). He also wrote three books—*No Surrender: Writings from an Anti-Imperialist Political Prisoner* (Abraham Guillen Press, 2004); *Love and Struggle: My Life in SDS, the Weather Underground, and Beyond* (PM Press, 2012); and *Looking at the U.S. White Working Class Historically* (Kersplebedeb, 2017).

---

1. This refers to the October 20, 1981, attempted robbery of a Brinks truck in Nyack, New York, in which a guard and two police officers were killed, followed by numerous arrests and subsequent murders of underground operatives and their supporters.

2. The Prisoner Education Project on AIDS (PEPA), a model AIDS peer education program, was created in prison by David Gilbert, Mujahid Farid, and "Papo" Nieves at Auburn Prison in New York following the death of Kuwasi Balagoon, one of David's codefendants.

Prison Life

I wasn't really mentally prepared, but I did have a lot of support. Both support from our small but staunch political movements on the outside, and also from fellow prisoners who respected our commitment to the struggle against racism and for social justice.

Prison routine, while annoying and insulting, was not that hard for me because I have a lot of self-discipline. Prison culture was a change for sure, but I had some good guidance from political prisoners, ex-Panthers, as well as politically conscious prisoners.

The best sense of community was at Auburn when I was there from 1983 to 1987 because there were other political prisoners there, also one or two prisoners who had been in the Attica uprising, and a general sense of prisoner solidarity. My best programmatic work was at Comstock in the 1990s when we set up and ran a very effective peer education program on AIDS. I also did a lot of tutoring of men working to get high school equivalency diplomas. My best relationship to nature was at Clinton in the Adirondack Mountains, near the Canadian border. There was a hill in the prison yard where you could stand and look out at the mountain greenery and see a lovely lake.

Naturally my happiest times were on the trailer visits, those forty-four-hour visits in little trailer homes within the prison grounds, with my son. The trailers are such a blessing for maintaining and strengthening family love and bonds, but unfortunately only four prison systems in the US provide them. Next to the trailers, my happiest moment was a morning in Comstock when I headed out to a visit, and as I walked through the school I saw our peer educators doing an AIDS class in every classroom without me there to lead the work. And in every classroom the students were paying rapt attention.

Since prisoners were allowed to get TVs in their cells in the late 1990s, there has been a certain dumbing down of the population. Due to broader changes in society and at least in New York state prisons, there's been a decline in political consciousness and in a sense of community, although that's not completely gone. We lost the best program prison had to offer—college—in the 1990s, but it has come back in the last few years. Also, there seems to be less violence among prisoners than when I first came in.

I don't remember if anything really shocked me; we had been in solidarity with prison struggles for years, so I knew a lot about prisons. What surprised me the most was that even within that most repressive structure, people found ways to form small communities or social networks and to take various initiatives, some good, some not so good, not controlled by the authorities.

What I was least prepared for were the various social protocols. Like you don't go onto a particular weight court, or hang out at a particular table, unless you are invited by the group who kind of ran or hung out in that area. There were also protocols in the mess hall, like don't turn your back on anyone. But these weren't much of a problem for me because I got guidance from ex-Panthers, Teddy Jah Heath, may he rest in power, and Jalil Muntaqim, who happily is now free.

Naturally, being able to parent from prison has been super important. After that my proudest achievement was doing pioneering work back in the 1980s to establish peer education programs on AIDS in prison. Our work saved many lives and became a model for similar programs in other prisons, both in the state and nationally. It was also an example of dealing with crisis through education, organizing, and mobilization from below.

Politics and Prison Dynamics

I think there were many situations where I would see an injustice, most often racist, and didn't feel able to intervene. So, it's hard not to do something, although there were also times [when] I was able to act. I dealt with that by trying to focus on the best ways to be strategic in doing something about the overall injustice of this system.

When I first came in, and during a few subsequent periods, I got a fair amount of petty harassment from the COs. Nothing as severe as a beat down or planting a shank in my cell, but efforts to set me up on various tickets. But I was able to parry those efforts, and after a while the harassment stopped. There've been very few problems with fellow prisoners; mainly I was treated with great respect, even by most of the white guys. In New York State, whites are only about 15 percent of the prisoners, so while many might be white supremacists, it's not acted out in a physical way. There was one situation where a particularly vehement white supremacist group wanted to move on me, but it was put in check by the other white guys who had a lot of respect for me. So, mainly or overwhelmingly, I haven't had to worry about violence from other prisoners and even from the COs.

When I first came up, the prisoners were pretty segregated, and white guys were cautioned not to hang out or have friendships with Black or Latinx prisoners. But no one was going to say that to me, and it wasn't a problem for me. Even with the segregation, there was a fair amount of solidarity, and people would come together around issues of prisoners' rights and safety.

Early in my bid, I typically was with one or two other political prisoners, all of them ex-Panthers. In the 1980s, there were about fifteen of us, and back then only eight or nine Max A prisons [the highest security prisons in the state]. The friendships with various political prisoners were especially precious, with a strong bond and valued political discussions and even occasionally a common project such as a political prisoner calendar.

Also, political prisoners who were at the same prison as me provided crucial support for our AIDS education projects, which started because of the death of my codefendant and best friend, Kuwasi Balagoon. When we were getting the first project going at Auburn in the 1980s, the administration did a lot to try to foment opposition to us by various prison groups. Nuh Washington, may he rest in power, who was so widely respected, played a major role in putting those divisions in check and building support for our project. Once we got it going, he actually completed the first training for peer educators in prison anywhere. Later, when I had a program going at Comstock, Herman Bell played an important role in supporting our effort to see that people did not get vested, did not go off track, because of the prevailing and harmful conspiracy theories. I was able to continue political work in many forms: efforts on AIDS education, prisoner rights issues, and lots and lots of political writing. I got lots of invaluable feedback from the outside and also from other prisoners.

One always wishes to have done more or better in providing emotional support for loved ones on the outside, for organizing against prison injustice, for engaging in political work. But overall, I feel pretty good about how I did my bid.

Looking Forward

Outside support is super-important. I know some people endure without it, but it was invaluable to me. Outside people will not always be able to come up with the answers, but the caring and support still matters. Not nearly enough work has happened on either supporting political prisoners or prison abolition, but the efforts people are making are terrific and make a big difference.

People facing prison, particularly men's prison, have been inundated with the media portrayal of a very macho, violent culture. Without denying that this can be a problem, it's important to remember that the key to how you do in prison is human relationships—how you carry yourself, how you relate to other people, and being a person of principle are all more important than being a big bruiser.

The movement needs to understand that even though the majority of prisoners are men, there are many women in prison who face major obstacles and forms of abuse. So, our movement has to pay attention to the reality, needs, and struggles of women in prison.

The injustice of the prison industrial complex is not just about the over two million people held in cages but also the impact of that on our families and communities. That's why my pamphlet about the criminal injustice system was titled *Our Commitment Is to Our Communities*. That's why our struggle to free political prisoners and to abolish the whole punishment paradigm is an essential part of the struggle against white supremacy.

Susan Rosenberg

Susan Rosenberg spent sixteen years in high security federal prisons for her involvement in the anti-imperialist armed actions that culminated in the Resistance Conspiracy Case of the mid-1980s. Her sentence was commuted by outgoing president Bill Clinton in 2001. Susan was imprisoned at the Lexington high security unit at FCI Lexington, the first maximum security prison for women in Marianna, Florida, and FCI Danbury, and she also spent time in the DC jail. She was involved in the May 19th Communist Organization, the Puerto Rican independence movement, the movement to Ban the Box, and the successful fight for the release of longtime political prisoner Dr. Mutulu Shakur.[1] Susan published the book *An American Radical: Political Prisoner in My Own Country* (Citadel Press, 2011).

Prison Life

When I was first arrested, I was held at MCC-NY for almost a year before being transferred to a prison. I had political and legal support in New York while I was on trial. I had movement lawyers, and at that time there were several other political cases going on that enabled a number of us political prisoners to associate with each other. When I was transferred to Tucson, I was held for a year with three other women (including Alejandrina Torres,

---

1. Ban the Box is a campaign that fights to remove the check box that asks if applicants have a criminal record from hiring applications.

a Puerto Rican POW) in an all-men's prison.[2] I was not prepared for that. I spent the year trying to deal with the completely repressive conditions. Alejandrina and I were set up when a guard placed a knife in our cell, and as a result of the disciplinary punishment we were sent to the experimental high security unit in Lexington. We were the only women there for the first three months. It was extremely hard to live in prison in those conditions. I was considered the highest-profile prisoner that they had ever had (which was ridiculous to say the least) and was constantly shackled and chained, even to the showers.

When we were in Marianna (Marilyn Buck, Laura Whitehorn, Silvia Baraldini, and myself), we were able to organize together and began one of the early HIV/AIDS peer advocacy efforts. The same kind of organizing happened in Danbury. While on trial in Washington, DC, for the Resistance Conspiracy Case, all of us in that case organized the first HIV/AIDS program and were, despite the utter criminalizing attempts by the administration, able to fight the horrendous conditions inside the DC jail.

At Lexington in the experimental High Security Unit, Silvia Baraldini, Alejandrina Torres, and I made an agreement that, despite our internal conflicts, issues, and challenges, we agreed that fighting the state, the BOP, and the prison authorities was primary over any issues between us. We stuck to that and were able to put together a united front that enabled us to resist the torture we were experiencing. There the outside support was the most important because they refused to be quiet about the conditions we were in and were encouraging us to survive. It was not "kumbaya" (if you will) but it was life-saving and effective.

There were very hard and bleak moments. When I was at Lexington SHU (which was a form of torture) for almost two years, it was extremely difficult. When I was sexually assaulted by staff at Tucson FCI, it was also very hard. What shocked me the most was the utter contempt and cruelty, the utter disregard for human rights, the deep hatred and misogyny towards women, the relentless degradation by the institution's rules and staff of individuals' very humanity.

The only time I was really able to practice anything collective was when I

---

2. Alejandrina Torres is a Puerto Rican freedom fighter who was a political prisoner for decades due to sedition charges based on her involvement in the Fuerzas Armadas de Liberación Nacional Puertorriqueña.

was in general population. I became a writer and poet inside. When in population, I was able to get a master's degree in writing from Antioch University. At that time, I was the first woman to obtain a master's degree at that prison. It was done through independent study and prison visits with different instructors and professors. It was actively opposed by the institution, with only a few individuals from the prison that helped make it possible.

My happiest times were during visits, during times with sister prisoners, running on the track, teaching, and organizing as a prisoner peer advocate. Becoming a writer was one of my proudest achievements. And obtaining my degree. But above and beyond those things was the successful organizing of a collective of other women prisoners to teach a course on Black history. This is detailed in my book, *An American Radical: Political Prisoner in My Own Country*.

Politics and Prison Dynamics

The idea of accepting incarceration and accepting the conditions of life as dictated by the prison system was a never-ending conflict with my personal ethics. Living inside prison was a constant time of acquiescing to a greater power. Every day was a day of constantly making compromising decisions not to rebel. I was with white supremacists and abortion bombers, and there was a lot of conflict with them. I went into prison with a "prison jacket" of being BLA (even though I was white and never in the BLA). This meant that I was able to build community with my Black sisters inside. It allowed me to live inside the most repressed but most beautiful community.

This community has faced both historical genocide and slavery and all the more current forms that those original circumstances evolved into. The lowering of the expectations of life, whether in terms of education, or family relations, or human solidarity was one of the most profoundly denigrating things to bear witness to. Women struggled to overcome those things even in the very worst of circumstances and conditions. Women built communities and units and "families" and continued to try and find love and connection. Women wanted to learn what they didn't know; there was a continual expression for freedom and multiple forms of resistance. It happened in big ways and small ways.

Far and away the most difficult things to deal with were the guards. I tried to find sympathetic humans within the guards, and, when I did, I urged them to quit.

Racism is the main way that the authorities keep control. That and fear. As an antiracist white in prison it was important to stand up to racist attacks on individuals and oppose prison policies that targeted women of color. The issue of language was also a sharp-edged tool that authorities used against Spanish-speaking women prisoners. The forced high school equivalency learning was in English, and those that could not pass the tests were denied good time to their sentences. This was a huge attack on all Latinx women prisoners. The denial of religious rights to Native and Indigenous women was another form of racism. Fighting for religious rights was another thing that I struggled to support. I helped dig pits for Native American sweats that occurred at Danbury after much organizing and legal struggle that Native women waged.

I was at MCC when Mutulu Shakur and Marilyn Buck were on trial. At that time, Geronimo Pratt, David Gilbert, Sekou Odinga, the Puerto Rican Macheteros, and others were all at MCC. It was an amazing experience to be with all those prisoners at the same time in one prison. We were able to meet together and plan trial strategy and use the time together for political and spiritual solidarity. [IRA political prisoner] Joe Doherty was there, and he was a great comrade to us all.[3] The ideological links between the IRA, the Puerto Rican independence movement, and the BLA were also part of the mix. Also, I was in Marianna, Florida, with Laura Whitehorn, Marilyn Buck, and Silvia Baraldini, and we were able to be together in that prison.

My experience was in solitary, in men's prisons, in the experimental high security unit for women, and the first maximum security unit for women prisoners. These were all completely different from the general population that I later experienced. I was directly designated to those units; it was not for disciplinary reasons that I was sent there. All these experiences were not comparable to general population.

---

3. Joe Doherty was a former volunteer with the IRA who escaped Ireland during a 1981 trial and was subsequently captured in New York in 1983, after which he fought an ultimately unsuccessful nine-year legal battle against extradition and deportation. He was imprisoned alongside numerous other political prisoners while in the United States.

Looking Forward

Being part of a movement meant that I almost never felt completely alone. I had a lot of support from the movements that existed at that time. I had great support from my parents, and they in turn organized others as well as supported other political prisoners. There was a group of lawyers who engaged with me and with all the political prisoners at that time who were critical in helping us defend ourselves from all the different state attacks. This included Susan Tipograph, Judy Holmes, Soffiyah Elijah, Nkechi Taifa, Mark Gombiner, Chokwe Lumumba, Lynne Stewart, Jonathan Lubell, Mary O'Melveny, and others for sure. It made all the difference in how doing time could happen.

I think that now the political prisoner support movement is more fractured and individual than it was during my imprisonment. That is something that the state has been successful at—reducing people to individuals, and individuals have different strategies for release. However, I work on Dr. Mutulu Shakur's legal and political defense and have for the last decade, and it is in the last few years that various groups have come together to create a strategy to obtain his release [Mutulu was released on parole in December 2022]. I think getting our elders from that earlier generation out of prison is a huge political priority for all social justice activity. So many of our comrades have died while in prison. So, work in defense of the elders and work in defense of more recent political prisoners. Join the efforts. Link any other work with the fight to defend those who have been imprisoned.

In the midst of terrible repression and oppression, keep your heart open. Keep learning from the people around you and from the outside as much as that is possible. Build unity wherever you can in all the multiple conflicts that emerge. Stay fit. Don't eat sugar. Keep connected to the outside if possible. When you get out, get as much help as you can. Needing help is not something anyone should be ashamed of. Prison is part of the struggle for a new and different better world. Every movement in the world has always had and will continue to have people imprisoned. It is the nature of the struggle. It is a part of the overall struggle for radical change. It is both harder and clearer how to fight white supremacy and racial violence in prison. I think that is something that all prisoners (particularly white ones) need to play a role in.

I also believe that the explosion of women's leadership in the Black and Brown and POC movements has changed the nature of the movement(s). Linking prisoner solidarity work that recognizes the advances that women have made against sexual violence and against the police violence against communities is crucial. And I believe that all our work can and needs to be directly linked to prison abolition and community control of policing. The fight for human rights is international, and in that there is great strength. The recent International Human Rights Tribunal that charged genocide against the US government in its policies and practices against Black, Latinx, and Indigenous peoples made it clear that American prisons are on the front line of that genocide.

Daniel McGowan

Daniel McGowan is a former member of the Earth Liberation Front who spent more than five years in federal prison—part of that time in a high security Communication Management Unit (CMU)—as a result of prosecutions commonly referred to as the Green Scare. Daniel spent the majority of his incarceration at FCI Sandstone and at the CMUs at USP Marion and at FCI Terre Haute, as well as six months at a halfway house. He has been involved with political prisoner support for most of his activist life and is currently a member of the Certain Days Collective, New York City Books Through Bars, and numerous political prisoner support committees. He published *Exposing "Little Guantánamo": Inside the CMU* (Eberhardt Press, 2009).

Prison Life

I was very much on the idea of preparing for prison by talking to people who had done time and by educating myself on stuff. The truth is that the materials that are out there about prison—whether it's these federal prison handbooks or otherwise—they're just the standard party line about what it's supposed to be like. But the BOP, the Bureau of Prisons, is completely different from what they say on paper. So, I thought I was prepared, but I clearly wasn't. I think it's hard to prepare yourself for the sort of deprivation that exists in there and to prepare for the kind of way you have to be to get by.

I tried to do my time as productively as possible. At Sandstone, I had to go to my job, which was in psychology. I was an orderly, so I just had to sweep and mop pretty much every day to keep the bathrooms clean. Then once a week, the bus would come in and new people from different compounds would have to get a psychology assessment, like a two-minute assessment. We had to give them forms, but that was pretty much it.

At the CMU, there's no work call and no free movement outside the unit. So, essentially your whole life is in your housing unit, except for a few areas where you can actually move, like recreation or education. But it was always just a series of cages, like the rec cage. We had a TV room, and the laundry was in the unit. It was mostly the same, but my vision of doing my time was to be as productive as I could no matter what. So I would focus on doing more educational pursuits during the day. When I did have coursework or education courses, there was lots of reading and writing, so I would do that. I did a few correspondence courses when I was inside. Writing a few letters during the day, working out, playing basketball, things like that to keep busy.

In some ways, I feel maybe people need to accept the fact that they're in prison and their impact on the outside world is going to perhaps be lessened. It's hard to participate in the movement when you're in there, other than writing. I felt like I had a lot of good support, but it's hard to adjust to the rigidity of the system. The way you relate to people in there is completely different than out here, and I'm generally an inquisitive kind of person with a lot of questions and at times strong opinions. On the inside that doesn't always work out so well because it's perceived as being nosy or in people's business. So I had to check myself with that and keep my judgments to myself more.

The adjustment period in prison is sort of like being on a very uncomfortable plane. Your first year is tough. When you're first ascending, you have a period of getting used to everything in there—the social mores, the rigidity of the system, the politics. Then you become acclimated, and you just kind of cruise for a while. Then your last year is kind of tough because you're getting ready to leave that world. The transition is tough on both sides.

So, for a while I thought Sandstone sucked. Then there was a period of time where I thought, "It's not going to get better than this. I have a cush job, I get visits all the time, I get a shit ton of mail, I get a lot of books, it's not a violent place (not a place that I have to deal with Nazis all the time), there is karaoke, floor hockey, basketball, all of these programs." But at the end of the day, all of that is a distraction from the fact that you're in prison, you're away from your family and your friends, and you're totally sidelined and not able to participate in anything meaningful.

I never lost hope. I had moments when I came close to losing hope, though. When I was first arrested, I was at MCC New York, which is now closed and has no one there. It's a shitty, mostly pretrial facility, and I got taken to 9 South. You get off on a floor, and then you go up a tiny little stairway. It feels like a half floor almost (reminds me of *Being John Malkovich*), and this is the "terror wing." I got taken to the long end of this hallway, and there was a generator near my room. They put me in what's called a dry cell, which is a cell with no access to water. There was a camera on me at all times, and it was like the SHU, or the segregated housing unit. I heard people chanting, doing prayer call, and I realized I was surrounded by Muslim dudes, probably people with so-called terrorism cases because this was around 2005. I remember thinking at that point it was pretty dire. It was December 7, it was cold, it was snowy, it was right before Christmas, which is a time of year that I really like, and I couldn't believe that this was the start of what was going to be a fucking crazy part of my life. I negotiated with myself and thought there was no need to get hopeless. If you get life in prison and things look horrible, you can kill yourself at some other point, but you don't need to do that now. That was basically a coping mechanism so that I didn't lose hope.

But I would never say I lost hope. It's hard to relax in prison, even when you have those good times. You may laugh, but you always have something on your mind—that you're in prison. That's why in prison photos, people are often very serious because the idea of making it seem somehow good is tough for people to stomach, the idea that you're going to send out a picture with a big, fat grin on your face.

I had a happy moment pretty much every weekday when I went to mail call. There were some moments that were just so ridiculously overwhelming. I'd be walking back to my cell with a handful of books. I happen to be very lucky; people were very supportive, and I have a lot of people who care about me, and they sent me books and letters. Some days I would get like five letters. I'm very appreciative of that. And honestly, five letters from my good friends are very different than ten or fifteen letters from strangers. Mail call was always a time [when] I was happy.

I would love getting visits too. You get all dressed up, you iron your clothes, take a shower, shave, you do whatever you need to do. Going to the visiting room is called "going to the dance floor." I was definitely always in my sweats and not particularly concerned about how I looked. I had a short buzz cut for most of my time. But I would gussy up on that day. People were just blown away that I was seeing people that weren't my wife or my mother and my father. It would be friends coming to visit. You go through and have a strip search and take all your clothes off and then put them all the way back on, and then, as soon as they crack the door, there's that moment when you're looking for your visitor. That's always a really good moment when you see them.

There's one moment that I thought was great: I think it was the US Sentencing Commission that adjusted some crack sentences. Either that or Obama did something. But they were furiously calling people's names out on the loudspeaker at Sandstone. I think it was this thing called Drugs Minus Two, which just meant that the guidelines went down like two years. So what happened was people were suddenly eligible for time served. They were calling people to come to R&D, which is Receiving and Discharge. When you get called to R&D, either you're leaving or a package or something came for you. There were all these fucking people who got called and went home. I think twenty-five people went home that day, including a guy who I ate lunch with that day. It was mind-blowing. So there were moments like that. I knew I wasn't going to get any relief from the crack law. I mean, I have what the government considers a violent case, arson and terrorism, all that stuff. I knew I was not going to get any play from anything the whole time I was in there. But it's always really nice to see people go home.

There was a guy in my unit that made like fifty crocheted elephants for a cancer hospital for kids, and I thought that was amazing. If I had the skills, I would have done that. One thing I did was be the instructor for the greeting card class. We got a lot of contact paper and laminate, and this guy taught me how to make cards that had a door to it and stuff. So, I made a lot of homemade cards, a lot of them, of course, because I sent them out.

I read more books and magazines than I care to name. Because I wasn't able to do courses, I would get interested in certain topics, and I would research and read a tremendous amount about it. I'm looking at my bookshelf right now, and I can see some of the topics. I spent months studying and reading everything I could on the environmental and conservation move-ment. I read a ton of ethnographies, from sociology, everything from *Gang Leader for a Day* to Émile Durkheim. I read a ton about the Irish Republican freedom struggle. I read every prisoner memoir that I could get my hands on. Any kind of prisoner—if a prisoner wrote a memoir, I read everything about it. I went through a period of time where I read all the classics that I could possibly find. Those were pretty easy to get through the interlibrary loan program. I exhausted everything by authors that I like, like Dave Eggers. I read a bunch of mass market paperbacks. I read everything from James Patterson, Patricia Cornwell, David Baldacci, Daniel Silva, Harlan Coben. I read a ton about the Black Panther Party, the Weather Underground, and the Black Liberation Army. I read tons of biographies. I read all the James Bond books. I was reading so much, and I would get ideas with everything I read, and I would then just ask for those books from the outside or ask for them from the library. I read a ton of graphic novels. Every graphic novel that I liked from growing up I reread. And then I read a shit ton of X-Men, Batman, Watchmen, all that stuff.

I did that just to try to keep my mind as active as possible and to come out of prison smarter, so to speak. I don't think reading makes you smarter. I think being discerning and having that sense of discord in your brain, trying to make sense of the different things that are in there, how what you're read-ing makes sense with reality. So, not parroting what you read but using what you read as fodder or as a tool to sharpen reality. I think sometimes people read things and then just replicate it. That's not what I was trying to do. But I was trying to occupy myself, so I would read nonfiction mostly during the day, then I read fiction at night when I was tired. I feel ultimately it was pretty fruitful, but in a lot of ways it was just to help pass the time because I had so much time available.

And I could share the books too, though people didn't always love the political stuff. I remember at Sandstone I was at my job, and I was reading the Durruti biography by Abel Paz that AK Press put out about fifteen years ago.[1] It's a huge book, maybe three or four inches wide; it's like a weapon. If

---

1. Buenaventura Durruti was a Spanish insurrectionary anarchist who played a significant role in the Spanish Revolution and worked with the Federación Anarquista Ibérica (FAI) and the Confederación Nacional del Trabajo (CNT) before being killed in battle. The book men-tioned is *Durruti in the Spanish Revolution* (AK Press, 2006).

you put it in a pillowcase, you'd be able to knock someone out with it. And I was reading it and trying to explain to this guy why I was reading about this, and it was mind-blowing to him. He was like, "Why are you reading this book?" It made no sense to him. He would be more interested in reading a get-rich-quick book. And I'm reading this book about this Spanish anarchist, and he doesn't know what anarchist means. But when I was at the CMU, a lot of people had higher education levels, and so I would be able to share books, especially if it was about current events and was meaningful to people's lives. And the potato chip books, the beach reads, were in high demand.

At Sandstone, I actually donated all the books to the library. I read so much nonfiction, and we didn't really have a nonfiction section in the prison library, so I established the nonfiction section. I brought like fifty books. Then when I was at CMU, they wouldn't let me donate to the library. We had our own internal library, which was fed from the institution library. So since I couldn't donate the books, I sent them home. I sent home about fifteen to twenty copy boxes full of books, about $17 a box to ship home. When I came home and went to eat one day, I looked down and under the kitchen table was like half of the boxes. In time, what I did was, I took them out, and I donated about half of them to Books Through Bars in New York City, and I have the rest of them here. Every once in a while, I'll be at Books Through Bars, and a book from like eight years ago that I donated is still there, which means that that book is probably never going to get sent out. But, yeah, I donated as much as I could.

I lost my mom when I was in prison. She passed away in December 2009, while I was at Marion. Usually at some institutions you can go out on a furlough, like a day pass, to go to the funeral. And then some places they do this thing where they'll let you go out, but you have to pay for the marshals to guard you, and you're chained the whole time. I didn't do that. I was at the CMU at Marion, the Communication Management Unit, and, given my case, I didn't even make the request because I thought it would be denied. Why get your hopes up? Plus, I didn't have the money to contribute to fly back to New York City and essentially be a fucking sideshow at my mother's funeral. So, I didn't do it. I butted heads with the warden, and I got her to give me a bedside phone call with my mother. I was able to talk to my mother when she was partially conscious and say goodbye. Then when she passed, I was able to get a call with my sisters. Usually on the compound the chaplain would arrange all of this. But instead I had to draw on outside support to force the BOP into having the fucking compassion to let me say goodbye to my mom. That definitely sucked, and I don't wish that on anyone.

Also, my codefendant killed himself when we were in the very beginning of our case.[2] I was at Lane County Jail at the time. I remember I got woken up at three o'clock in the morning; I was in a maximum wing. They moved me into the SHU and put me on suicide watch because my codefendant, Avalon, had killed himself in a county jail in Arizona that night, apparently. They didn't tell me who it was, of course, because they don't care. They just moved me, put me in a gown, and I was put on a fifteen-minute watch, where a cop would walk by every fifteen minutes to check on me. That was December 21, 2005. I was in this fucking gown with this tiny blanket and it was super cold in Eugene. It was damp in the jail, and I had to be there. I was there for like ten days. Finally, when the doctor got back from New Year's break, I was let out. I read *The Jungle* by Upton Sinclair, which was one of the worst books to read in that kind of state because it was so depressing. There was no book cart; the guard just brought me a book. I also read *The Road* by Cormac McCarthy when I was in prison. Now when I see it at New York City Books Through Bars, I always say to not send this book to someone—it is too depressing. I mean, I'm nobody's nanny, but, seriously, it's depressing.

What I saw in the CMU that I didn't see in general population were people who worked for the BOP coming back from Afghanistan and Iraq and then being in a unit of mostly Muslims and expressing hostility to the Muslim population there in all kinds of ways—by disrespecting people's Korans or prayer rugs to comments under their breath to bumper stickers on cars. All kinds of really shitty things that the government can try to say was just "First Amendment," you know? It was kind of gross, and I saw a lot of that. It's weird, I'm not a Muslim, but I just thought it was disgusting, like the way they were treating people.

One thing that was shocking was just how easy it was to become numb to the horror of what goes on in there and how you have to consciously fight that in order to not become a robot. It's like that time in school when

2. Bill Rodgers, or Avalon, was a codefendant of McGowan's and over a dozen others in the FBI's Operation Backfire, which targeted activists related to the ELF and the ALF. Many of these individuals were arrested on December 7, 2005, including McGowan and Rodgers. Rodgers was found dead in his jail cell on December 21, 2005, the winter solstice, of an apparent suicide.

someone falls and everyone laughs at them, but it's that to the extreme. Everyone has their own problems, and so it becomes incredibly atomized and insecure, individualistic. And the prison staff and the bureaucrats, and also the system itself, is all about making you just like an atom, like an individual. The idea of any kind of collective struggle is anathema to them. I mean, they're petrified of that, right? So I think that was shocking, how fucking cruel people can be, how fucking shitty they can be about other people's circumstances.

I was also shocked to see the changes in sentencing. There was reform coming. I was watching how people sentenced for meth were getting mandatory minimums of thirty and thirty-five years, and I didn't understand how that was possible. Also shocking was just how many people were in the BOP that were from Mexico, for instance, that were convicted not of actual crimes but of crossing a line in the desert that the US government has decided is a border. That was really shocking.

A lot of the stuff I wrote about in my blog when I first got in was about me adjusting to prison and basically learning about how fucked up the world is. I mean, I had no experience with meth or people that sold or produced meth. It's not as cool, so to speak, as *Breaking Bad*, right? It's just people with really bad teeth and really crazy stories, talking about how fucked they were in their case. And, unfortunately, sometimes talking about what they want to do when they get out, which is not always the smartest thing. I think to myself, you're trapped in the cycle of "I'm going to do it better next time." On some level, it's like, what else are they going to do? So who am I to judge? All that shit was shocking and eye-opening.

Politics and Prison Dynamics

I was dragged into the lieutenant's office once. Well, there were a few times. One time, there was a fight at the CMU, and all of us were dragged in, stripped down, and they checked if we had any marks on us. The person who ended up getting in trouble was a Muslim guy, and the Muslims asked the non-Muslims to write cop-outs, to write letters to the staff, saying that this person is a good person, he's a calming person in the unit, and we would appreciate if he could come out. So that was strange because I wasn't snitching, but I felt like, I'm sending off a cop-out, a kite to the cops, advocating for someone.[3] It definitely was like crossing some racial, maybe ethnic, lines that are pretty uncommon in prison.

I definitely had a few conflicts with prisoners. I got into a pushing match in the CMU over the TV, but it was really just tempers between decent people. It was between me and a Muslim, which was a fucking big deal with the other Muslims because I was totally unsanctioned. I didn't have a crew or car; the whites in the unit were old-timers and a Nazi. And so this guy was telling me I couldn't be getting into a fight with a Muslim. And I told him, "I'm not trying to get in a fight with anyone." I remember having this ridiculous conversation where I had to talk to the imam and basically say, "It's cool. Everything's cool with us. We made peace." He was actually a friend, and he's out now and we're still friends.

But, other than that, there's tension and shit, there is a bit of a dog-eat-dog world there. I just made sure that people didn't touch my shit or step to me or anything like that.

As far as conflicts with guards, I didn't get into any physical conflicts, but there's always this derision. I caught a lot of shit. I'd get things like, "McGowan, how do you wipe your ass and go to the bathroom when toilet paper is made out of trees?" Stuff like that. Or, "How do you justify getting so much mail?" And I'd ask if they understood the concept of recycling and how that works, that I don't actually use toilet paper that comes from trees. I mean, I do here because I have no fucking choice, but . . .

I would always go to great lengths to try not to use too much paper. I wrote so many letters on the back of old fliers because I was trying desperately to not use paper. It would also save me money at commissary. But there would be tons of old fliers after an event, and I would grab those. There was one recycling bin in the cop's office and in the library, and I would literally have a bag of fucking paper and I would dump it in there. But it looked so suspicious—I was essentially sneaking to recycle. I mean, it was ridiculous.

Racism is just like a fact of life in prison. The politics about it are really intense, and you can get yourself into a lot of shit. I basically fucked with whoever I wanted to. At the low security prison, it's less of an issue. But

---

3. A kite is a message or note that is secretly passed between prisoners or between prisoners and guards.

people are pretty fucking racist. And you'll hear all kinds of crazy shit. I learned new words in prison that I didn't know before. I was in the CMU with an old Nazi, a pagan that was in for like twenty-five years. He and I would sometimes get into arguments, but it was pretty chill. I always had to remind myself that this guy was accused of assassinating someone, so I should probably act accordingly. He considered me a communist. He knew Ray Luc Levasseur from Marion or from ADX twenty years ago. He'd say, "You're a communist, just like Levasseur." It almost seemed pointless trying to explain to the Nazi that I'm not a communist. For the most part, we got along, though. He tried to tell me that Hitler was a vegetarian, which I told him was the most cliché, Nazi thing to say. And technically not true, but, also, who cares? It doesn't matter to me.

For the most part, this is pre alt-right, this is pre-Trump. So it's like simmering racism. You'd see some shit like when I was in transit. So, when you go into any DOJ [Department of Justice] facility, the president and the vice president are on the wall, and when I went back to Marion in transit once, they [hadn't put up an] Obama photo. It was like four months into Obama's term, and it was still just blank. I remember thinking to myself, that is so fucking obviously racist.

The whites are like garden variety racists in federal prison. They're good-old-boy peckerwoods. They just have regressive ideas. They don't think of themselves as haters. They're not politicized, necessarily. They just are acting it out. Being from New York, I would obviously seek out people from New York, and none of those people from New York were white. If I saw somebody on the call-out sheet that you check in the morning and they had an 053 registered number [meaning the Eastern District of New York], I'd be like, *Oh, that's a homie.* At Sandstone, it ended up being a lot of sex offenders who got arrested at JFK Airport for sex tourism, or their computers had porn on it. Those weren't my homies, because they were just people arrested at JFK Airport, which is ironically very close to where I grew up. But, yeah, not people that I necessarily wanted to fuck with.

The CMU was full of different people; it was a mixture of Muslims who were entrapped by the federal government. There was no case, they were just approached by FBI agents or whatever in order to do something, usually something against people. Those people were kind of hard to do time with because they had such a sense of outrage at what happened to them, and they were very much stuck in, whether they were innocent or not. They were clearly fucked with and entrapped, and so I understand their sense of outrage, but it also makes for a very singular, narcissistic thing. Whereas the guys who were arrested pre-9/11, they had already done a lot of time and so were pretty acclimated to the prison system. So, they had a sense of perspective. They had already done time at ADX. They'd already done time at a compound. They were used to dealing with Americans and cultural stuff, whereas some of the guys that were entrapped were straight up coming from the street. It was basically street, county, compound. They saw everything in CMU as so horrible, whereas some of the guys who had been in ADX said it's not actually that horrible. You'd be surprised—we don't have to deal with this, we don't have to deal with that. You don't have to wear boots to the shower. You don't have to fight. You don't have to carry a knife. So, those guys were harder.

As far as the guys who had been in for a while, I was friendly with one of the people who was in for the World Trade Center 1993 incident, somebody who was actually in custody at the time that that happened. He was convicted of the conspiracy but was not actually involved. He is doing a life sentence. I was in with people that were in for basically fundraising, for just doing charity. I was in with four of the five members of the Holy Land Foundation, and I got along really well with a few of them.[4] I didn't know most of them, but I knew two of them. The two men that I liked are doing sixty-five-year sentences.

I was in with the Somali pirate. His last name is Muse. [He] is a really funny kid who just learned English from TV and was really interested in pop culture and sports stuff. He was very goofy. He would just throw the basketball all crazy because he had no idea how to play basketball. He was very cool and very generous, always lending me magazines and stuff. I was in with John Walker Lindh, the so-called American Taliban.[5] He seemed like a nice guy but didn't really talk to most people. A lot of people I knew were convicted of material aid to support terrorism.

---

4. The Holy Land Foundation Five are five former leaders of a Dallas-based Muslim charity (the Holy Land Foundation) who were unjustly convicted in 2009 of funneling millions of dollars to Palestinian militants. Each of the five were given sentences of between fifteen to sixty-five years in prison. See glossary.

5. John Walker Lindh is an American-born man who was captured in Afghanistan when the US invaded in 2001, and he was sentenced to twenty years in prison for aiding the Taliban. He was released from prison in 2019.

But there were those people, and then there were Sovereign Citizens, people that put out billion-dollar liens on federal judges and are part of that whole Posse Comitatus, right-wing thing.[6] And that's interesting because it's multiracial, so you get Black folks on that tip, you've got white folks that are on that tip, some of them are part of the Moorish Science Temple, and they take different names and stuff.[7] So they were a pretty interesting group.

I was in the CMU with some people who were accused of going into training camps for Al Qaeda and for the Taliban. And then you have these random groups of people. I was the tree hugger; Andy [Stepanian] was an animal rights person.[8] There was a Native American man who they thought was going to blow up the Sixth Circuit Court of Appeals or Seventh Circuit Court of Appeals. There was a guy who was part of what they called the Dixie Mafia, like a southern gangster who had done a bunch of time at Angola in the 1970s.[9] Like I said, you had a bunch of these Sovereign Citizen types who are filing false liens and refusing to carry driver's licenses. Some of them are vaguely right-wing. The Montana Freemen people were there.[10] You had some people who had used phone and communications to send threats to people. You had a few high-profile sex offenders like this one con man who actually died in custody. He was some sort of a Mormon who was married to young girls, basically thirteen-year-olds. And he was Jewish by birth but apparently was a Christian. He ran a ministry called Tony Alamo Ministries, and he made all this money. It was really fascinating. He was a weird person.

Other people in the CMU at Marion who I knew included a FARC arms dealer and member and a Russian arms dealer.[11] There was a guy from

6. The Sovereign Citizens Movement covers a wide range of right-wing activists, tax pro-testers, conspiracy theorists, and armed antigovernment militias that spawned, at least in part, out of Posse Comitatus, a far-right, white supremacist, armed group that gained traction in the 1960s and 1970s. The practice of filing bogus liens against the property of government employees ties up time, money, and resources in an act of antigovernment protest.

7. The Moorish Science Temple of America is an Islamic organization founded by Noble Drew Ali in 1913 that teaches that human beings are capable of being redeemed.

8. Andy Stepanian is a former animal rights political prisoner who was a defendant in the SHAC [Stop Huntingdon Animal Cruelty] 7 case.

9. The Dixie Mafia is a southern-based criminal organization that was most active in the 1970s and recruits heavily in prisons. "Angola" refers to Angola State Prison in Louisiana.

10. The Montana Freemen was an antigovernment militia that started in Montana in the 1990s. Several of their members received prison sentences after an armed standoff with the FBI. Their founder died in prison in 2011.

11. Fuerzas Armadas Revolucionarias de Colombia (FARC) is the People's Army of

Baltimore who was accused of calling in threats and killing witnesses—I have no idea whether he did it or not, but he had a life sentence.

I was in with one of the Fort Dix Five, one of the Albanian brothers.[12] I was with some PFLP [Popular Front for the Liberation of Palestine] people who were accused of taking down airplanes.[13] There is the case out of JFK Airport, that guy that was accused of wanting to blow that up. I was in there with him. I mean, I don't know about the veracity of most of these cases. You know, most people said they were innocent. I was in there with a codefendant of the so-called Millennium Bomber. I was with the imam from Albany, Yassin Aref, who was entrapped. The Virginia jihad case, the paintball case. Adham Hassoun, whose codefendant is José Padilla.[14] Yeah, just lots of lots of different people.

Tsutomu Shirosaki, with the Japanese Red Army, was at Terre Haute when I was there, and he was in contact with *4strugglemag* and the Certain Days calendar.[15] I used to get the New York City ABC updates and distribute them to people, and people liked those because it was all information about prisons and stuff. But political organizing was kind of tough. I would often ask that my crew do benefits that benefited forest defense and things that I was in for, basically. It's just hard to be politically involved. I wrote for magazines, I wrote articles, I wrote letters, I tried to be involved in political back and forth, basically. But it's super challenging, and there were times that it was much harder than others, you know?

I didn't really have a lot of lockdowns. Sandstone was locked down a few times because of severe snow. I was always in the SHU when I was in transit,

---

Colombia that was active in armed struggle against the state from the mid-1960s until 2017, when they disarmed in favor of more legal tactics.

12. The Fort Dix Five are five immigrant men who were convicted of planning to attack a US military station at Fort Dix, New Jersey. As of 2023, four of the five remain in prison.

13. The Popular Front for the Liberation of Palestine (PFLP) was a revolutionary socialist Palestinian nationalist organization founded in 1967 that was most prominent in the 1970s when it engaged in airplane hijackings and sensationalist actions with other revolutionary groups around the world.

14. Adham Hassoun and José Padilla were arrested in 2002 and in 2007 were convicted of conspiring to commit murder and fund terrorism. Hassoun was released from prison in 2020, and Padilla is scheduled to be released from prison in 2026.

15. Tsutomu Shirosaki was imprisoned in the United States until 2015 for his involvement in the Japanese Red Army (JRA), an armed and militant Japanese revolutionary organization that was active for thirty years starting in the early 1970s.

and that sucked because I'd be two weeks here, two weeks there. When I went to Oklahoma, I almost invariably was in the SHU because of my case, and I would leave there with the black box on. The black box is a device that goes over your handcuffs and really limits your movement. We were locked down for half the day after bin Laden was murdered by the Navy SEALs, which happened to be my birthday, in Terre Haute. You don't really have much of a choice; you just deal with it. You just try to work out, you try to get up, you try to not be in bed all the time. That's pretty much it.

I experienced being in segregation while I was in transit, which is definitely annoying. I probably did about one hundred days in the SHU then. Besides that, I was only in the SHU for like one day when I was in general population at Marion. They said I tried to circumvent the mail monitoring on the phone somehow. They put me in the SHU and then drove me to Terre Haute, the other CMU, the next day. So I was only in the SHU overnight. But mostly I was in the SHU, what they consider Ad Seg [administrative segregation], when I was in transit. I've been at the transit centers for weeks at a time, moving from point A to point B.

At the CMU, people were much easier to talk to, and I had more in common with them. They were very politically engaged and were fighting their cases. But everything was just tighter at the CMU. When I first got there, you got one phone call a week, and it was only fifteen minutes. So, the communication is severely sharpened, whereas on the compound you can use the phone like three hundred minutes a month. And then for December, around the holidays, they give you like an extra one hundred minutes. And so that's one thing. And then with visits, at Sandstone I was getting two visits a month, two weekends a month, so like thirty-two hours. And then at CMU you can only get four hours a month, and it was noncontact, and it was in this tiny little space. So it was just completely bogus.

And at the CMU you don't interact with everyone. You just interact with the people who live in your housing unit. This could be twenty people, could be fifty people. Everybody comes to you, so you're completely dependent on the food coming to you, the commissary coming to you. At the CMU, for commissary they just come with bags, and you get what you ordered, hopefully. It's always a problem; you always get shortchanged. So, everything is in the unit. And in order for you to leave the unit, like to go to dental or medical, the whole compound has to shut down while you are in the hallway.

I think it was inevitable that I was going to end up at a CMU because the CMU was criticized for basically being a Muslim unit. So here I was, a non-Muslim at this place in the Midwest. I think a major problem for them was that I was doing this education program, so I was using their computers. The funny thing is it was a sociology degree, and I was basically being critical about stuff I was involved in and trying to find a different way of handling environmental resistance. But they just couldn't read that, and they saw it more as just being pro ELF. But that's not what I was doing. In fact, my papers would have fucking ultimately ended up pissing off people, I think, in that I was critical and I was trying to come up with other ways of doing things that were not necessarily destroying shit belonging to your enemies. So, I was disgusted by that, that they used that against me.

I think the only thing I would have [done differently] was, when I went to court, I asked the judge to assign me to a local prison, and the judge doesn't have the capacity to do that. My lawyers should have known that the judge has no say, because judges are in the judicial branch and the BOP is in the executive branch. So, I wish I would have just been a little more ambivalent about that. People told me they're not sending you near your house, and you need to get over that. Susan Rosenberg told me, "They're going to fuck with you so bad, you just need to get used to that." And I was like, "Nah." I was believing what they said in the paper, like it's not like that. Now, oh my god, I've told her numerous times just how right she was. Because she said, "They're going to fuck with you. They're going to look at you as a race traitor. And you just need to know that, and the BOP is full of shit." And I was really naive, super naive, you know? So, I think I would have just had my eyes a little more open, had less hope that things would change. I mean, I spent a lot of time at Sandstone thinking I just want to get closer to home. But, meanwhile, what I ended up getting was transferred further from home and also to a worse place.

Looking Forward

For me, outside support kept me grounded; it kept me connected to my life back east. I think outside support is essential. How would you get money on your books, and how would you get visits without outside support? Visits are important, letters are important, books are important. I think most political prisoners read a lot, and I think it's important to have outside support. Also, when medical issues come up, when transfer issues come up, if people are fucked with by the guards, it's always important, I think, for people to have someone to reach out to. Otherwise, you're just in there on your own. We've seen what happens when people are forgotten about—crazy shit happens to them, and then no one even knows. You just search the inmate locator one day and find out they died. That's happened to me multiple times. It's kind of crazy.

I felt supported 100 percent, all the time. The truth is that the system is set up in a way to make you not feel supported. It's set up in a way that basically you have to have faith that people support you. You really have to believe that the support is there even if you don't see it because they can hold your mail or put you in transit where your mail can't catch up with you. And you don't actually know that you're being supported.

I think some people get a lot of support because they're well known, and other people don't get as much support. And I think it begs the question of why people get supported in the first place. I don't think political prisoners should be supported because they're elderly, per se. But what has happened is that the prisoners from the 1970s and 1980s [get most of the attention]. The general political prisoner list is roughly thirty to thirty-five people right now. But when it was one hundred, there were always people who were never going to get that much support. And I ask, why is that? Why? Our basis for support should not be about how old or infirm the person is. The basis should be rooted in supporting movement people because you're in agreement with what they did, or you're in agreement with their values and the movements they come from, or that they're coming from your actual movement itself. And why would we not support the people that come from our movement?

So, is enough being done? You have high-profile political prisoners like Mumia Abu-Jamal and Leonard Peltier, and now you have a much smaller political prisoner list.[16] But, I don't want to presume that Mumia and Peltier are getting a ton of support. I mean, it certainly seems that they are, but

---

16. This is a reference to the fact that many long-term political prisoners had either been released or died behind bars, and incoming political prisoners are less frequent now than in the 1960s and 1970s.

what something looks like is not always what it actually is. Then you take people on the list now, like Joe-Joe Bowen or Bill Dunne or the Virgin Island 3, and those people aren't getting any kind of level of support. And I think it's challenging in some ways why. Joe-Joe is on a life sentence. He was already in prison and killed a warden of a prison, so maybe people feel like it's just not worth supporting him. I don't know. Not to say he doesn't get any support. He was in the SHU for like twenty years, and the Abolitionist Law Center got him out, I believe.[17] So that's great. But, I think it's always hard to tell who's getting supported and who's not. There are a fair amount of the younger prisoners who I find didn't get a lot of support. Does Eric King get a lot of support? I don't know. It's a disparate group of like twenty people around the country that support him.

I think a lot more could be done as a baseline for the people inside. Make sure they have money on commissary, make sure they have books and letters, make sure they have visits, work with them on publishing things together. Things like that are important. I think any aspect of doing political prisoner support should be concerned with the freedom of the people there and understanding that not everyone is going to get out. I don't believe that everyone on this list of thirty people is going to get out, and I think it's foolish to think they will.

I think you need to work on campaigns that will lift all boats. I think a lot of the work that happened in New York State with Release Aging People in Prison (RAPP), Parole Preparation Project, and many other groups, created a situation that got political prisoners out.[18] I'm specifically thinking of Herman Bell, Jalil Muntaqim, Sekou Odinga, Maliki Shakur Latine, Robert Seth Hayes.[19] All these people got out on parole. A lot of that has to do with the fact that the parole board composition has changed dramatically. There are more parole commissioners, there are way less people in prison, and I think that people actually have a fairer shot at parole. They're not just getting

---

17. The Abolitionist Law Center (ALC) is a law firm based in Pittsburgh, Pennsylvania, that focuses on political cases and support of political prisoners who have spent decades in prison. Attorneys with the ALC have worked on the cases of Mumia Abu-Jamal and Russell Maroon Shoatz, among many others.

18. The Parole Preparation Project (PPP) is an advocacy and support organization in New York that works to ease the parole release process for incarcerated people serving life sentences.

19. Maliki Shakur Latine is a former political prisoner from the BLA who gained his freedom after decades of incarceration with the help of the above-mentioned organizations.

denials over and over, and that has to do with advocates. That doesn't have to do with the governor doing better; it just has to do with advocates.

I would want the past me to understand and to be reminded of the fact that people on the outside have lives and are dealing with real things and real issues themselves, and that the world doesn't revolve around you. There are moments with some of the newer prisoners, in the way that they engage people on the outside, that make me feel like some new political prisoners are forgetting that people on the outside actually have lives and jobs and are not able to drop everything they're doing just to meet their needs. That so much of what they need to do needs to be on their own, to be a little more self-sufficient about stuff. There's definitely times when I feel like there's a certain amount of narcissism that takes place. So, I would want younger me to realize that the world doesn't stop because of this super intense thing that's happening in your life, and that you need to do what you can on your own to be self-sufficient and ask for help when it's needed but not rely on people as much as I did. I'm pretty sure that I was a big drain on people. I gave a lot, but I also asked for a lot. And it was, I think, pretty challenging. And I'm experiencing this now, not necessarily with someone I'm working with, but I'm adjacent to a few situations where I'm watching people on the inside ask what I might consider too much from those on the outside. I don't think it's a situation where we have to do exactly what people ask us to. It should be a mutual working relationship. Sometimes it becomes one-way, and I think that's wrong. People should be more mindful of that dynamic.

Since I've gotten out, as a recipient of such good fortune and solidarity, I've tried to pay it forward. My goal is to be a force of fucking will, someone who got out of the system and refused to give up, who continues fighting for people's freedom, for people to be treated properly, and for us to be able to support captives from our movements. The experience of being in prison extracts something from you. People that get out are not to be treated like delicate flowers, but there is a cost that you pay, and people need to deal with that when they get out. They need to deal with how prison affects personal relationships and how you view everything.

I think political prisoner support has gotten pretty refined in recent years. Part of that is because of less people in prison, in general, but also less political prisoners. There's been so many people that have gotten out in the last five to ten years. But I feel like what's happening is people think the support is covered, you know? But in my interactions with even some of the high-profile political prisoners, I realize that there are way less people involved than anyone thinks. Even people like Sundiata Acoli and Mutulu Shakur have very small crews. Sundiata is a New Jersey prisoner held at the feds, and it's very challenging to get him out. We're asking the New Jersey state governor to commute his sentence against the will of the full law enforcement community. So, it's really challenging. I support those efforts to get Mutulu and Sundiata out [Sundiata Acoli was released from prison in June 2022, after nearly fifty years behind bars, and Mutulu Shakur was released in December 2022 and given just months to live due to late-stage cancer].

I also think that there is a basis for supporting newer prisoners, people like Jessica Reznicek (a Water Protector), Daniel Baker (an antifascist political prisoner), and Daniel Hale (the whistleblower being held right now at CMU Marion). I think that just because there's not a large amount of political prisoners entering the system, they shouldn't be forgotten. My fear is that as the list [of political prisoners] gets smaller, the people that worked on the campaigns of people who were freed will retire. A lot of the people who are involved are in their sixties and seventies, so I'm fearful that those people will retire. And then what will happen to the newer prisoners, you know? Part of my efforts in the ABCF is to grow the ABCF with younger folks so that we have new collectives made up of people who are not all forty-seven years old like I am.

Linda Evans

Linda Evans was an anti-imperialist political prisoner for sixteen years, and before her imprisonment she was involved in many organizations, including Students for a Democratic Society, the Weather Underground, and the May 19th Communist Organization. She was captured in 1985 and convicted for her part in the Brinks expropriation and also in the Resistance Conspiracy Case. She served sixteen years in prison before her sentence was commuted by outgoing president Bill Clinton in 2001. Linda was imprisoned at various jails, including the DC jail and FCI Dublin. Since her release, she has cofounded All of Us or None, a grassroots civil rights organization of formerly incarcerated people and their families, and she works tirelessly with California Coalition for Women Prisoners, the Drop LWOP Coalition, the Immigrant Defense Taskforce of North Bay Organizing Project in Santa Rosa, and the successful campaign to free Dr. Mutulu Shakur.[1] Along with her partner Eve Goldberg, Linda wrote *The Prison-Industrial Complex and the Global Economy* (PM Press, 2009).

---

1. All of Us or None is a grassroots civil rights organization of formerly incarcerated people and their families. The California Coalition for Women Prisoners, the Drop LWOP [Life Without Parole] Coalition, and the Immigrant Defense Taskforce of North Bay Organizing Project in Santa Rosa all work to challenge mass incarceration and improve the lives and chances of those behind bars.

Prison Life

We were surprised by the FBI so we had no real opportunity to get mentally prepared. I don't think it's possible to be mentally prepared to be arrested while you're trying to evade the police. We had some support from close comrades who helped us—great support from radical lawyers, who defended us in court, but little support from the broader political left.

I hated never seeing any distances—and so many prisons I was in, all you could see past the razor wire were more prisons. It was the same at Dublin. There's no way I could be comfortable with someone controlling every tiny detail of my life—buttoning the top button of my shirt, being required to wear a bra, being subjected to searches whenever some cop felt like it.

Every day I walked the track or lifted weights. Eventually, at Dublin, the rec director bought some sewing machines, and I learned to quilt, then spent time in the rec barn quilting. We created an AIDS education group called PLACE—Pleasanton AIDS Counseling and Education (FCI Dublin was previously named FCI Pleasanton). The group was inspired by ACE [AIDS Committee for Education] at Bedford Hills women's prison in New York State, which was also started by political prisoners—Kathy Boudin and Judy Clark.[2] Work for PLACE was ongoing—we were an official club while they were legal in the prisons, so we held meetings, organized Prisoners Fight AIDS Walkathons, distributed an educational comic to every cell, and brought the AIDS Quilt to FCI Dublin. So every week I might have work associated either with PLACE or with other activities.

No prison or jail is fit for human beings. Putting people in cages is never a solution to our society's social problems. Yes, people develop relationships and even families while they're inside that continue beyond the bars; we create our own social dynamics to make any institution even vaguely tolerable, I would say survivable. For me, being with those comrades was an honor and a privilege—because we supported each other in maintaining our political relationships with movements outside, and we had similar worldviews, which reduced the isolation everyone feels in prison.

---

2. Kathy Boudin and Judy Clark were political prisoners who spent decades in prison before gaining their release. Both were incarcerated as a result of the failed Brinks expropriation mentioned in the footnote above.

The presence of my comrades made it tolerable to the degree it ever was. I did years of time with Dylcia Pagan, Carmen Valentín, Lucy and Alicia Rodriguez, Marilyn Buck, and Laura Whitehorn. During our trial preparation, all of us on trial had day-long legal visits together. My cellmate Ida McCray Robinson was also a political prisoner, locked up for hijacking a plane to Cuba.

I was on trial with Marilyn Buck, Susan Rosenberg, Laura Whitehorn, Tim Blunk, and Alan Berkman in the Resistance Conspiracy trial—so we were all in the DC jail together for over a year. The DC jail was and is full of Black people who can't post bail, who are waiting for trial or for transfer to federal prison. All the Resistance Conspiracy defendants were placed in solitary on different living units; the men's units were told that Alan and Tim had tried to kill Jesse Jackson in order to turn the other prisoners against them. But the solitary cells were simply locked cells at the front of long tiers of cells, so people were curious and talked to us whenever they could. We all connected with other people inside the jail, and eventually they knew who we were and why we were there—that we were political prisoners. People supported us, shared contraband coffee, and showed us how to make smoke-less fires from toilet paper. They shared dog-eared paperback books, and we shared information about HIV/AIDS, which was newly discovered and ravaging the Black community.

Our lawyers petitioned the court for the right for us to have day-long visits together to prepare for trial. We had decided that Alan would represent himself so we would have a direct voice in court. This also allowed us to visit together without an outside lawyer coming in. The DC jail was required by the court to put aside an unused classroom for this purpose, and most days we left our cells and spent many hours of the day together analyzing the boxes of evidence the state planned to use in their case against us. Not all of our time was spent on trial preparation, of course. For example, Tim Blunk, an accomplished artist, taught us all how to paint sunsets (we had some paints or markers to mark up the evidence.) Because we were held in solitary and on different units for so many months, this time together was really precious. We had been arrested a few years before and subjected to individual trials in various jurisdictions (for me, two trials in New York, one in Connecticut, and one in Louisiana). Now we were back together being tried for the Resistance Conspiracy, so it felt like an opportunity to explain our politics to a broader audience.

The small number of women's prisons prevented the US government from effectively separating the women political prisoners. Alejandrina Torres, Silvia Baraldini, and Susan Rosenberg were all housed in an experiment in small group isolation at FCI Lexington. Laura Whitehorn was being held in solitary at FCI Alderson. The rest of us—the remaining Puerto Rican women POWs, the anti-imperialist women prisoners, and a Plowshares prisoner—were housed at FCI Dublin. Ida McRay Robinson was also a political person, a member of the Republic of New Afrika who was convicted of hijacking an airplane—but Ida didn't call herself a political prisoner. She knew who I was and rescued me by claiming me as a cellmate—Ida lived in a coveted two-person cell, and we became lifelong friends/comrades.

At FCI Dublin, as soon as our cells opened in the morning, Marilyn Buck mentored a young Black woman who hadn't graduated high school and had two life sentences plus forty years. They huddled in a corner of the unit lobby over their books every morning until work call. Marilyn's love and friendship meant that young woman had the chance to learn, reflect, and transform herself. Today that young woman is free because of a clemency grant from President Obama, and she just testified to Congress.

My happiest moments inside were the collective achievements we achieved, like all the AIDS education and service I was engaged in and the walkathons and fundraising we did inside for AIDS services and the Oakland Children's Hospital. Friendships with the other political prisoners and others also.

My father died while I was locked up. I was allowed time off work, and I walked the track a lot. Grieved that I couldn't be with my mother. Generally, I deal with stress and grief through action. I have tried to integrate the slogan of the Vietnamese into my life: "Hatred into energy."[3] I didn't meditate or do yoga in prison, but those are also excellent ways to deal with stress. I was really lucky to have lots of visitors, which kept me connected with life and the world outside, introduced me to new ideas and new people, and helped me feel relevant. Many of these visitors form my chosen family now, as we developed deep, meaningful relationships through the visits.

------

3. This is a line from a 1966 song by Luu Nguyen and Long Hung called "The March of Liberation."

I feel confident that both Alan and Marilyn would want their lives celebrated through action to fight white supremacy and build a society based on equality and liberation.

In women's prisons and jails, community is generally very vibrant and strong. The resilience and real community that women create collectively was remarkable. People are usually greeted with offers of shared commissary and hygiene items until your commissary account opens, shared food, cautious questions, and lots of shared opinions and advice. Because medical care is so abysmal in prisons and jails, women take care of each other when we're sick. A friend of mine was diagnosed and was receiving chemotherapy in an outside hospital. Between her treatments, she was extremely sick, vomiting and unable to hold down food. Helping her survive the chemotherapy required a lot of care—shifts of friends checking on her, getting ice, or cleaning her cell.

Another way we built community was through our HIV/AIDS awareness organizing and other educational efforts that also build leadership skills and friendships. Some of these efforts actually benefit the institution, so wardens may be inclined to allow them as a way to keep people occupied and positive. At FCI Dublin, prisoners formed a Council Against Racism to combat white-preferential hiring at UNICOR (prison industries) and to request translation of important prison documents into Spanish. We also organized an international festival with performances of music and poetry from every country with someone on the compound. But we lost our staff sponsor, and the club was disbanded by prison administration. Eventually, all the "inmate clubs" in the federal system were disbanded and are no longer allowed.

The AIDS work was crucial at that time to break through the stigma attached to being HIV+ and to educate people who were in such close contact with each other that they weren't in danger. It was empowering, gave people something important to do to help others, and connected us with the outside world in a significant way—showing that women in prison could share their time, energy, and resources to fight AIDS and support people living with AIDS.

Politics and Prison Dynamics

Everywhere I went I was friendly to everyone, inclusive in every way, and never tolerated people saying racist things in my presence. PLACE was always associated with counseling and services for the entire population.

I'd be surprised if any long-term prisoner wasn't in a SHU at some point—it's impossible not to break one of their stupid rules just during the course of life. Life in SHU was unbearable—not solitary confinement but living in a four-person cell, twenty-three and a half hours a day, never knowing who would be put in that cell, including people with emotional problems and people who were detoxing from drugs. While in SHU, I stopped my cellie from committing suicide—but she obviously needed trauma-informed care she wasn't receiving.

During a regular prison day, you can maintain your own schedule as long as you go to work and allow a million indignities. You can possibly cook your own (very limited) dinner, take a walk or run on the track and enjoy some fresh air, possibly have control over the lights in your cell. Within the *huge* limitations of the prison and prison regulations, you can determine some aspects of your life. In the SHU, you are at the total mercy of the guards, including a request for a simple cup of hot water.

Looking Forward

To maintain one's sanity, political commitment, and hope, nothing is more important than outside support. People react to prison differently, and some people get really depressed inside. Contact with the outside—with people who know and love you and support you for your actions—[is] critical reinforcement for our political identity. As political prisoners, we are captives, captured by our mutual enemy on totally alien territory—and prison feels like another planet for everyone. Outside support reminds us of the outside world, our families, the reasons we are in struggle and took the actions that led to our imprisonment.

I felt supported both as a political prisoner and as a lesbian political prisoner. Naming myself as a "lesbian" political prisoner was a serious political decision for myself at that time because I was fearful that coming out would further erode the very little political support that we had. Of course, what actually happened was increased support and the opportunity to reach out to the lesbian and gay community with anti-imperialist, antiracist politics, which we tried to do both in DC during our trial and afterward in partnership with Out of Control: Lesbian Committee to Support Women Political Prisoners.[4]

Occasionally someone would say they had mailed us something or had accomplished some task we requested of them when it wasn't true. We would wait for the mail, or the expected outcome, with no way of verifying whether something had happened as we hoped. Absolute honesty is key in relating with people inside.

Little analysis has been done of who our current political prisoners are. There's an older generation of political prisoners that the state refuses to release—Leonard Peltier, Mutulu Shakur [released in 2022], Mumia Abu-Jamal, Ed Poindexter, others listed on the Jericho website—and others more recently incarcerated for other political actions, some taken outside of supporting political movement structures or struggles.[5] Partly because of the nature of state versus federal incarceration and the fact that defenses must be mounted on behalf of individual people, the political prisoner support movement is decentralized. De facto unity of purpose exists—FREE THEM ALL! Free [fill in the blank name] and all political prisoners! But the legal *work* of getting people out has been prioritized above building a unified and powerful support movement for all the political prisoners.

Above all, be humble and respectful. Listen a lot, and let your empathy guide you. Look at going inside as an opportunity to experience what millions of people experience along with you—captivity and how to survive it. Maintain a goal of coming out stronger and smarter about life. Learn about the direct oppression of the state apparatus. Learn about other people coming from backgrounds different than your own.

THANK YOU to the many, many people who supported me during

---

4. The Out of Control: Lesbian Committee to Support Women Political Prisoners (OOC) was a self-supporting committee formed in 1987 to organize resistance to the Lexington Control Unit for women. The ten women of OOC struggled for ten years to expose the brutality of this federal penitentiary, culminating in a lawsuit and the closure of Lexington.

5. Ed Poindexter is a former Black Panther who has been wrongfully imprisoned since 1970. His codefendant, Mondo we Langa, died of medical neglect in prison in 2016, and Poindexter's leg was amputated in prison in 2023 after decades without medical attention.

the sixteen plus years I was in prison, when I got out, and ever since. My life partner, Eve Goldberg, is someone who visited me in prison! We fell in love and now have lived together in freedom for over twenty years. I developed lifelong friendships with other political supporters who visited me in prison and with some wonderful women I met inside. I learned enduring life lessons about oppression and resistance—subjected to the total bodily control of imprisonment, we built community, took care of each other, and broke every stupid rule that we could. Prison is another place to learn about why we so desperately need a political, economic, and social revolution in this country.

Herman Bell

Herman Bell is a former member of both the Black Panther Party and the Black Liberation Army, and he was imprisoned for forty-five years. Herman was captured in New Orleans in 1973, and eventually he, Jalil Muntaqim, and Albert Nuh Washington were convicted of attacks on police. Herman was also implicated in the San Francisco 8 case and pleaded guilty to a lesser offense. He spent five years imprisoned in the federal system, in the Marion control unit for two of those years, before spending decades in various New York State maximum security prisons. While imprisoned he was committed to community work, and he is a founding member of the Victory Gardens Project and the Certain Days Collective. He was released in 2018, after his eighth parole hearing.

Prison Life

I had never had an acquaintance with prison in and of itself before [my arrest in 1973]. I was in a county jail just briefly in my young life. I had heard conversations about prisons and prison conditions and all of that. It's not like I encountered something unexpectedly. But there's a difference between a county jail and a prison. They have two different rhythms. Prisons are really dangerous places. There's a culture, and it used to be more strict back in the day. If your name becomes dirty in the prison, you got problems. Like if you're a snitch, if you're a coward, and on and on and on. It's almost in some ways like a big schoolyard. Those things come back to haunt us behind bars. So, anyway, it's an interesting and a dangerous place. You have to keep your wits about you in prison, otherwise you'll be consumed by prison. It eats you, it eats at your soul, it eats at your very being. And the longer you're in there, the deeper the bites, you know?

I think I was mentally prepared. Even so, the actual living that experience out is different than what one may have imagined it to be. You're living it, you're breathing it, and you're feeling it. You feel hungry. Hunger is something that's really real. How do I eat? Where's the food? And the people holding the keys are the ones holding the food. It kind of really shrinks things in many respects. So in theory, yeah, this is what's going on and this is how I see myself carrying out my day-to-day life under those circumstances. But to live it, I must say, my dear brother, is different.

My adjustment came, I think, largely through observation. I just surveyed my surroundings, my environment. I took note of who was who and what went on, and I paid particular attention to those who sometimes asked too many questions or who had a reputation of being an informant. Eventually you encounter individuals who are the movers and shakers on the tier or in the prison itself. That's part of the culture. And when you do, you size them up, you determine if this person is decent or not, what kind of leader he is or enforcer he is. Because they had enforcers in there too, very dangerous men.

You observe a lot of the so-called extralegal illegal activity going on in the jail. It's like an orchestra because there's so much drama that's really going on. Then there are issues that come up in the prison culture that require some accounting. For example, when guys want to strike, [they] lock down in their cells in protest. As you proceed on your journey, you take it all in, and you learn from it. As I reflect on it now, I was probably more like a fly on the wall, an observer, and doing it within the context of my social consciousness and my politics.

But you run across some interesting people in prison because you've got all walks of life inside the prisons, whether you're in a federal prison or a state prison. And some people you grow fond of; you acquire a certain amount of respect for those people. For some, you walk around a corner and you run into the man you always thought you were. There's some significant revelations that go on in that place. It tests your very fiber every day if you're going to survive all of this, though.

The guys that run things, they're always lurking about looking to bust you and throw you in the box and just prolong your agony and time in prison and damage your reputation. They beat you up. But I've seen some really kind gestures performed by people in there too. I met some really decent people in there.

Usually they bounced me around a lot. Every two years, they transferred me from one jail to the other. They could do it, and they did it. So when I got in these cells, I always looked for some pictures, some posters. They would only let you have posters of a certain size. I used to use those posters—like a seascape, some meadow or whatever—as my escape. I could go hang out for a moment and transport myself—beam me up, Scotty—and it helped a little bit. Your daily life and your day-to-day routine, these things have to come about in order to survive. Because if not, not only the cell will eat you up, you will go insane. So you have to have a routine.

In the early to mid-1980s, I was at Clinton [Correctional Facility in] Dannemora. They threw me out of Attica, and I got sent up to Clinton. It was the wintertime too, and it was cold. Clinton is in the mountains, maybe fifty miles or so from the Canadian border. It gets so cold up there at Clinton that when you are out in the yard, there is such a silence that it's almost deafening. Everything just shuts down. I had heard about Clinton when I was in the feds because some New York guys were telling me about the winter sports that they have up there in the jail. They told me they even ski at Clinton! I'd heard about skiing and seen pictures of skiing, but I had never skied. Some parts of the prison are flat, but it sits on the side of a mountain, almost like a cone. There were service roads that go down like inclines, and so you get your skis and you huff and puff and go up to the top—no ski lifts there—and you get in your skis and then you go down. That was cool. In prison, it's good to take your mind off things, and skiing helped. Everybody did it because the prison gave you skis and boots. They didn't give you any poles, though. My first time on skis, I'm going down, and I was told to keep my feet straight, and there's this guy in front of me. He's going slow and I'm picking up speed. I'm going downhill, and this guy is in my way and nobody had told me how to stop. So I fell. At least I stopped, right? So I picked up my skis and I went back to the top and I asked someone how to stop on these things.

The other joint where I went that was kind of soft was Eastern. Some called it Napanoch. I got sent there from Shawangunk, which was not far from Eastern. Shawangunk was kind of modeled after Marion in that Shawangunk had a fence with this razor wire as the perimeter. There are no walls or towers. It had an attitude, Shawangunk did. And so I managed to get out of there and wound up in Eastern. Eastern at that time was like the mecca of the New York state prison system. Eastern was soft. I heard about it and said, "Count me in!" They always threw me in these dungeons, these bad places, where you're miserable. So, I went to Eastern.

So, I got into the reception area at Eastern, and it was like I peeled off a layer of skin. I didn't realize the amount of tension that I was under at the other jail. There was a tremendous amount of tension there because we had locked the place down for a whole year, locked it all the way down. So we were all locked in our cells. Basically, the state had the walls and we had the prison.

I never lost hope that I would get out. It was unthinkable. It never crossed my mind. What did cross my mind is that they would hold me inside for so long that getting out wouldn't matter that much. That's the reality of it. In that movie *The Shawshank Redemption*, this guy named Jake, they had him living inside so long that he just couldn't relate to the outside world at all. It was alien to him. People give up hope when you hold them in confinement for so long. And when you give up hope, you have nothing left. Sometimes people just go and lie down and never wake up, and that's a sad commentary. It says something about the state of the human condition because we could do better, and we can be better people. This whole business with these prisons, these jails, those things have to go away. We have to make it so they go away. But people have to feel it, though, too, because our loved ones are in these places. It's true, you have people that have done some really, really horribly mean things to people—that is true. But they weren't born that way. They weren't born to do that. And that's no justification either. It's sad.

There was a tiny little piece of joy in there in regards to people's kindness toward one another inside. It's touching when you see it because you know that it's genuine. Most people are destitute in prison, and the only means of making it inside is from what few pennies a state job may pay, or if he's handy with some kind of craft and can sell something. Other than that, a person like that has absolutely nothing. No loved ones, they may have all passed away. That happens too. So, there's no one there, no visits, nothing. That person may have something, and he unselfishly shares what he has with someone else. To me, that's like a giant. You see that, and you celebrate that, and that also gives you hope that we aren't all bad.

In a way, it was like the baby boomers suddenly appeared in human society. At the end of the war, there was an explosion of births. The population just ballooned, and I'm a product of that. Prior to the crack epidemic hitting the prisons, the things that prisoners did in order to survive, including leaning on snitches, were pretty much firm and well respected. Guys had established a pattern that enabled them to survive with some modicum of dignity. Guys used to take pride in how they dressed with creases in their pants when they had visits. I've heard people say that sometimes they go into a prison visiting room and the prisoners look nicer than their visitors. Guys used to really tidy up when they went to visit their loved ones. They made moves out of sight of the guards that were admirable, very smooth. And it worked well until this explosion of young people coming in—crack babies really. When they came in, they would carry razors in their mouths, and they would spit the razor out and slice each other up. All of that came from the young people coming in. That created a lot of tension. It's like a new kid on the block, but he's no good because he's too young and impatient to learn. So, you have to keep them at a distance and maintain a firm line with regards to them. Sometimes in prison you have to be firm. They eventually learned to stay in their lane and carry on a lot of what they do, but among their own crowd. But in the process, they brought a lot of heat on everybody else because we had to put up with that bullshit.

So, I saw the change—almost like the passing of the guards, where the old traditions of surviving inside were slowly giving way to this new population that's coming in. It was heartbreaking to see, especially in New York State, which is where I was in all of these prisons. Everywhere I went, I saw nothing but Blacks and Puerto Ricans inside. I wish prison on no one in truth, but that's what I observed. It was very hurtful to see.

I also observed society's failures in other ways too. Our society has failed these young men in terms of being more supportive in their nurturing and upbringing. Basically, these kids had to survive the best way they could in an environment that was very hostile in many ways. So there was a change, and I imagine there's a continuous change, but I can't say today what it's like there now.

Guys have shown me some respect inside the joint. That has been a constant thing with me, in that throughout my imprisonment, I always thought that I had to comport myself in a certain way because this is what I want people to see as one who represents our struggle. So I maintained a very firm posture in that regard, unwaveringly. I think somehow that caught on. People saw that and they observed the consistency in that, and they respected that. So I got a lot of respect inside the prisons. I like to think of it as not because of what is said of me but what is thought of me. If you add all that up, I'd say that's something I feel really good about.

We were on the front line, and we have to be consistent in that. People appreciated that because, in some ways, I think they saw themselves in us except that we just happened to be in different circumstances. I remember when I went to the parole board, just before I got notice that I was going to be released (it was unusually long before they sent notice), every time the guys would leave the block and then come back in the evenings or afternoons from their programs, they'd pass my spot, and they would ask me, "Did you hear anything yet?" I'd say, "No, I'm waiting too!" They were asking me as if they were waiting for a decision too because in their minds if I got out, they *certainly* would get out.

Politics and Prison Dynamics

I never even thought of having a physical conflict with anybody inside, and I'm really, really glad that I never did. I can't recall having to raise my voice, for the most part. We probably wouldn't be speaking here today had I not encouraged myself to find a better way around things. I always was a peacemaker whenever I could be, as opposed to instigating. The guards will play you and will try to intimidate you, and they will use the least pretext available to assault you. And when they do it, they do it in gangs. It's not one or two of them, it's a gang of them. Except for the latter part of my imprisonment, I never had a confrontation with a prison guard. I mean, they've gotten some looks from me, but I've never had a direct confrontation. And I am so happy that I didn't because I wouldn't be here speaking with you today.

I have met a few guards who were on duty who I regard as decent. I thought of them as decent, and I thought of them as being well raised by their parents. The reason I did so is based on my observation of how they treated other men, if they treated them with appropriate respect and kindness. Not in a paternalistic way, but I think it's because that's just who they are. That's how they are. I think the whole world can applaud that. I respect that. I've received respect from them too. I mean, they may not like me— some of them probably hated my guts—but they didn't go over the line with regards to me because it's just the way it is. I live a certain way, and I'm not going to change. And I'm no tough guy. I'm a softie.

In New York, Dave Gilbert and I spent six months, maybe a year, together at Comstock. Jalil [Muntaqim], my codefendant, and I never spent time together. They always kept us separate. Sometimes he'd get on the same transportation that I'd come in on and they'd put me in the same cell that he had just left. The only time I spent with Jalil in New York was in 1995 or so when we were brought down to the city for a hearing on some technical matters related to ballistics. So they brought us down and I think we spent about five days together then. It was Jalil and Nuh [Washington], my other codefendant, and we spent about five days together. We'd have legal conferences, so we were able to hang out that way. But other than that, since the time that we were sentenced, we were scattered.

And then, when the San Francisco 8 case came along, Jalil and I got sent to California and spent time with other comrades. We were there for almost two and a half years. Oh, that was a miserable place. I suffered more in that jail than in any of the other places I'd been. It was miserable. They turned on the air-conditioning on our floor, and it was always chilly up there. But that was nothing compared to the rest of this stuff. There were guys there swept up off the street who were on psychotropic medications, and they would stay up for five days in a row without going to sleep. That was their thing. So we had to fight all this, read our court documents—we're exhausted. Those guys sniffed instant coffee and did all sorts of things. Even the guards weren't tough enough for these cats! I complained to everybody, and they still wouldn't move me. I spent two and a half years there. You think I wasn't ready to get up out of there?

I was at Marion with Peltier and also Rafael Cancel Miranda, one of the Puerto Rican Five.[1] Rafael was teaching me how to play guitar. That was my

---

1. Rafael Cancel Miranda, Lolita Lebrón, Andrés Figueroa Cordero, and Irvin Flores

early Marion experience. I liked both of those guys right away. Rafael, of course, had his history, and he'd done a long stretch in Leavenworth, Kansas, and then, in the latter part of his imprisonment, he came to Marion. So he was finishing out his years there. I think he was sentenced to twenty-five years, but there may have been extenuating circumstances. As if to say, well, according to the law, you're not going to get out. I think it was Jimmy Carter who released the Puerto Rican Five. I used to correspond with Lolita Lebrón as well and sent shout-outs to the remaining Puerto Rican Five. They're really wonderful people, very upstanding.

This other brother and I started this cultural group in Attica. This was actually in 1979 when I came to New York State prison, and it was called the Afro-American Cultures and Studies Group. It was a Black studies class. We started that, and it was very popular among the guys. You couldn't get any more [students] in the classroom. It provided light and sustenance, encouragement, a sense of self for a good many of these young men that they found newly discovered, as it were. These were young guys, for the most part, guys our age who identified with the struggle and appreciated knowing and learning even more about it.

Then I played football with these guys because I felt that football was something universal that guys could relate to in a way similar to Victory Gardens, with food as a means to bring people together. Nobody's going to beef over food unless maybe it's the taste. So in playing sports, football in particular, guys could identify with me. They'd feel like I'm the guy they can go talk to. It was a good way to get close to people inside. And eventually you might sidle up to me and strike up a conversation, and so on and so forth. That worked for me in two ways, in that I could approach these guys without them feeling talked down to, and I found myself in a position in relation to them that I could also scold them for the things that I see them doing and things that they should be doing for themselves and their families.

Since you're in [prison], make good use of the time that you have. You owe that to yourself and to your family. Go get your GED. Go to some kind of vocational program. But you're not going to hang around here and let me see you just sitting around doing absolutely nothing. It ain't happening. I

Rodríguez were imprisoned for attacking the US House of Representatives in 1954. Oscar Collazo was another Puerto Rican imprisoned for a failed assassination attempt on president Harry Truman in 1950. Together they were known as the Puerto Rican Five.

used my presence and my time doing things like that. And passing on books, checking up on people to see whether or not they read them, and then go and collect my books.

I had a gang of these guys running backward and forward, so there was a connection. This is kind of like ongoing political work that never really ceased with me, and I dare say David and Jalil as well. We moved on in our journey. I like to think that I have grown as a result of the experience. I wasn't stagnant. I didn't feel like I was unproductive. And then eventually I got out.

Certain Days actually sprang out of the community we had in Victory Gardens. I wanted to create a calendar that would be supportive of political prisoners but also to serve as a kind of repository or a reminder of important names and important dates in our history. I also envisioned it to not only look professionally produced but to *be* professionally produced. That was important. To get the project going, I talked to Tynan Jarrett, Helen Hudson, and I can't even remember all the names, but we had a core group. We talked about how this thing is going to go, I explained some of the things that I especially wanted to see because it's a reflection of us and our can-do attitude towards anything. Then, of course, it would be a source of pride because we produced it. It wasn't you. We produced it. This is ours.

The hope was that it would gain a special place in people's hearts in the community. My sales pitch was always, "If you don't have a Certain Days calendar in your home or in your office or wherever you happen to be hanging out, consider yourself a square. And nobody wants to be a square." So we got it going, and it's still going. And I take great pride in being a part of creating that calendar. It's a beautiful calendar, and people who have the calendar or who on occasion speak of the calendar, they love the calendar too. They speak highly of the calendar. So I say, kudos to that.

All things considered, I didn't do bad. I did okay. My lifelong passion is to be the best person I can possibly be and treat people with respect, and in the process try to be the living message that I bring.

Looking Forward

I think that folks should think about community projects, think about that long and hard. I think folks should maybe even envision organizing a community center because you can get the people there. You start out with the kids because the adults are going to follow the kids. When you have the kids, you bring them up to speed, turn them into little gardeners or whatever. But I think that that will help solidify the community.

I think prisoners will always be prisoners, and prison guards will always be prison guards. I hope in the process of being prisoners, since they are prisoners, that they try to be the best people they can be and care for one another. I think that's important. It's just as important for people to be concerned about family members of those who are imprisoned and their children. They shouldn't be forgotten because they're doing time right along with their loved ones. I think overall, when we talk about support, we need to rethink all those things because there's only so many people to do so many things. Whereas oftentimes things that need to be done go undone simply because there's not enough people there helping to provide the services needed. It doesn't require a lot. We don't have to have a whole lot. We can just take a little bit, do a little bit. That's okay. You get somebody else to pitch in, and we're good. We've got to go in that direction. If not, we'll just be spinning our wheels.

I ran across this quote the other day that says, "The process of liberation is irresistible." That's strong, it's irresistible. So eventually we're going to get there unless these fools let go of some of these nukes and do us all in. But we keep the faith and keep moving on.

I think the activism out in the communities and the streets is going to intensify because the social contradictions are going to intensify. So there will be those who are imprisoned. Don't be faint of heart. The struggle doesn't end when you happen to be in prison. By the same token, you have to be cognizant of your environment because we're all human and we are all susceptible. We all have our demons. But we also have our strengths.

There are younger people out there now who are getting their law degrees because you're definitely going to need legal assistance in some form or fashion. We were fortunate at the time that we were in prison because there were a fair number of radical lawyers out there holding us down, representing us. So, as things intensify, we're going to need more people like that on the front line fighting for our loved ones who have been imprisoned. By the same token, folks got to do what they got to do, you know? This is a protracted struggle, so let's not get too serious about ourselves.

Jennifer Rose

Jennifer Rose is an anarchist and trans womxn who was originally sentenced to seven years in prison in 1990 on charges of armed robbery. Jennifer has been incarcerated in over a dozen California state prisons. Since becoming politicized during the 1991 Folsom Prison strike, Jennifer has become a talented jailhouse lawyer and prison activist, engaging in protests, strikes, and other forms of direct action. While imprisoned, Jennifer was charged with additional offenses and sentenced to multiple twenty-five-years-to-life terms and has survived over a decade in solitary confinement in the Pelican Bay SHU. Jennifer is active in anarchist organizing, continues educating and mentoring from behind bars, and is also a member of the Fire Ant Collective.

Prison Life

How does one prepare for brutality and torture? Or Jim Crow racial segregation? I was offered "support" by racist skinheads and woodpiles [white crews or affiliations within prisons] as a white-identified prisoner from Orange County, which I'm ashamed and regretful to admit I went along with initially. The "mandatory program," or racial segregation, was strictly enforced by the state policy and prison gang politics. I had to defend myself from sexual abuse, guard brutality, and racialized gladiator fights. It was all pretty scary and traumatizing.

It's hyper-vigilant, militarized, racist, sexist, toxic masculinity, and dehumanizing. It was disorienting, violent, and unsafe. The reality is pretty ugly and worse than most people could imagine. I did what I had to; I stood my ground, fought back, and resisted my captivity by going to the law library and filing grievances. I became a jailhouse lawyer and began corresponding with social justice advocates, abolitionist groups, the Anarchist Black Cross, and *Love and Rage* newspaper.[1] This is what led to my eventual politicization as a revolutionary prisoner and my total disassociation from the racist whites, for which the AB [Aryan Brotherhood] put a hit out on me for being antiracist.

I loved being involved and having played a part in the 1991 Folsom Prison food strike [and] the 2011 and subsequent prisoner hunger strikes, which reached from across California to Guantánamo Bay to Palestine. More recently, I was able to play a part in the annual #NationalPrisonStrike with my Fire Ant comrades, Sean Swain and Michael Kimble.[2] In 2016, I was viciously attacked and seriously injured by four pigs twice my size at Kern Valley State Prison. Since then, the last five years spent at Salinas Valley have been some of my best years. I was proud to play a part in cofounding the Fire Ant Collective in 2017 and have been able to focus on my college studies and self-development while continuing various organizing work and writing projects.

Now I'm an undergrad student at Blackstone Paralegal Studies Program, Coastline College, and Hartnell College, Rising Scholars Program. My daily routine includes schoolwork, letter writing, legal advocacy, my clemency campaign, and parole prep for my next board of parole hearing in July 2025. My boyfriend and cellmate of two and a half years, Peter, is solid and a proud Black man incarcerated on an LWOP [life-without-parole] death-by-incarceration sentence for a youth offense as an ex-gang member from the LA area. I also participate in rehabilitative programs and self-help groups offered within the prison, while doing poetry workshops and writing mentorship with Empowerment Avenue, Prison Renaissance Project, and Prison Journalism Project.

I became a jailhouse lawyer advocate and politicized and revolutionary prisoner/abolitionist early in my incarceration. I've litigated pro se in

---

1. *Love and Rage* began in 1989 as an anarchist newspaper and became a network of local collectives of anarchists and antiauthoritarians in the early 1990s.

2. Their stories are included here.

federal civil rights cases and state court criminal cases and habeas corpus proceedings. I've been successful in obtaining three settlement agreements (for $1,000, $3,000, and $20,000), and won a writ of habeas corpus in 2002 resulting in my release from Pelican Bay SHU after ten years of solitary confinement. I'm also certified as an inside organizer by Initiate Justice and am doing similar work for TGI Justice Project and Prisoner Correspondence Project.[3] I'm the transgender rep for my facility—Inmate Advisory Council (IAC), a member of the IWW/IWOC, and National Lawyers Guild. I have done Legislative Advocacy work to repeal extreme sentencing laws and advocate for #MassRelease and decarceration.

Besides my college/paralegal studies and my coming out as trans/queer, I have told people that my proudest achievement is the collaborative work of cofounding and contributing to the Fire Ant Collective, with Robcat and Bria, Eric King, Sean Swain, Michael Kimble, and Nadja with the Bloomington ABC crew, all of whom are part of what I consider my Fire Ant family. I also have been proud of building up the Red Roses, a direct action trans feminist prison collective, and our work with TGI Justice Project and Black & Pink toward queer/trans/womxn liberation and prison abolition.[4]

I've definitely lost hope while in prison. As an abuse and torture survivor, I can look back to 2002 and 2003 when I was actively suicidal after over a decade in solitary confinement. At that time, I had been through so much insanity, had been both implicated with and simultaneously targeted by the AB and skinheads, but in reality was coming out to my therapists as a trans woman and antiracist with absolutely zero support.

Other than my pen pal correspondence at GIC of Colorado, ABC, APLAN/*Green Anarchy*, and others in the revolutionary abolitionist movement, I was at the deepest, darkest moment of despair with seemingly no

---

3. Initiate Justice is a collaborative effort by people in and out of prison who advocate for criminal justice reform in California. The Transgender Gender-Variant & Intersex (TGI) Justice Project is an organization that works to end human rights abuses against transgender, intersex, and gender-variant people, particularly trans women of color in the California prison system. The Prisoner Correspondence Project shows solidarity by connecting gay, lesbian, transsexual, transgender, gender-variant, two-spirit, intersex, bisexual, and queer prisoners in Canada and the United States with similar communities outside of prison.

4. Black & Pink is a prison abolitionist organization supporting LGBTQ and HIV-positive prisoners that organizes a pen pal program, distributes a prisoner-written newspaper, and provides Know Your Rights educational materials to those incarcerated.

hope and no light at the end of the tunnel.[5] I had begun to convince myself that death [might] be a better alternative than a miserable life in long-term solitary confinement at Pelican Bay SHU, surrounded by psychopaths and haters. I attempted suicide by cutting my neck and hanging myself. I was then removed from Pelican Bay SHU per the federal court injunction in *Madrid v. Gomez* and was twice placed in the Department of Mental Health (DMH) at CMF Vacaville to undergo acute psychiatric care and recovery.

The queer/trans prisoners in California have gained significant legal and legislative reform victories/success, including uniform, statewide medical policies for "treatment of transgender persons," an expanded and updated *Care Guide: Gender Dysphoria*, which conforms to "standards of care" (World Professional Association for Transgender Health), with supplemental *Guidelines for Evaluation of Sex-Reassignment Surgery Requests*. This was the result of landmark court decisions in the cases of two incarcerated trans womxn, Michelle Norsworthy and Shiloh Quine, who both have spent decades serving and surviving life sentences. They have both completed their surgical care and moved to the women's facilities!

Other victories include obtaining gender-appropriate clothing, feminine cosmetics/hygiene products, and an "Authorized Property for Transgender Inmates" matrix for trans womxn in men's facilities and trans men in womxn's facilities. These are limited "reasonable accommodations" compared to cisgender male and female prisoners due to separate/different prison cultures and "security concerns" between male and female institutions.

More legislative reforms, which I actually had some input/involvement with drafting, include S.B. 310, the Named Dignity Act (which streamlined the legal name and gender changes for incarcerated transpeople to ensure reentry with proper identity cards and documents), and S.B. 132, the Transgender Respect, Agency, and Dignity Act, which addressed PREA [Prison Rape Elimination Act] loopholes and noncompliance, or nullification, by clearly mandating statutory rights and duties applicable to *all* transgender, nonbinary, or intersex prisoners based on their stated preferences.

---

5. The Gender Identity Center (GIC) of Colorado is an organization that formerly provided support, direct services, and safe spaces for communities in need. The Anarchist Prisoners' Legal Aid Network (APLAN) organizes and supports anarchist prisoners and produces a newsletter of the same name. *Green Anarchy* was an anarchist magazine and anticivilization journal produced in the Pacific Northwest between 2000 and 2008.

But what good are laws and legal rights which can routinely be ignored or nullified and are routinely violated by the pigs with impunity? It's an uphill battle, with rare and limited success. What has changed since the COINTELPRO assassinations of Bobby Hutton and Fred Hampton and George Jackson?[6] Not much. Hundreds of political prisoners like Leonard Peltier and Mumia Abu-Jamal remain in prison, along with a whole new generation of anarchist and antifascist prisoners, journalists and whistleblowers, along with migrant womxn and children asylum-seekers or refugees.

Politics and Prison Dynamics

When I first came to prison, I was not yet "politicized," as a white-identified (part Native/Cherokee) young person. I didn't see any options but to go along with the mandatory program of strictly enforced Jim Crow racial segregation that existed in California prisons as a matter of state policy at the time of my initial incarceration in 1988–1989. I made the mistake of falling in line with the white racist program of the AB and skinheads, which I had grown up around in the suburbs of southern California. Big regrets, and I've long since changed my personal stance as an openly antiracist white who associates mainly with the Black & queer/trans prison communities, and [I] am double-cell housed with Black or queer/trans cellmates to avoid the annoying racist/homophobic haters.[7]

My first year or two, I had a couple racial fights but only out of necessity of self-defense. I've been attacked and targeted by other prisoners due to an ongoing gang or "racial" conflict when I was in New Folsom ASU in the early 1990s.

But nearly all of my conflicts after that point in my incarceration were with pigs as part of the prisoner resistance (e.g., cell extractions and beatings, barricading and sabotaging ASU control unit cells, and attempted escape from the courtroom). Most of these incidents were resisting solitary confinement torture and prison captivity. Some incidents resulted in

---

6. Lil' Bobby Hutton was the first and youngest recruit to the BPP and was killed by the police before his eighteenth birthday.

7. "Double-cell housed" refers to two prisoners being held in a cell meant for one. This is often done because of overcrowding but also for punishment or to incite conflict.

additional prison terms for assaults or weapon possessions, including my twenty-five-years-to-life sentence under California's "three strikes" law.

In more recent years, I've been in fights or riots either in self-defense or community defense (of Black and queer/trans comrades, friends, and sisters) against hate-motivated racial or transphobic gang violence such as the 2015 prison riot at Kern Valley, where I rode with a dozen Black prisoners against some gang members (white and Mexican) who targeted my sis Jasmine Jones, a Black trans womxn.

Also, in March 2017, I was in a fight with an individual here at Salinas Valley who killed an incarcerated trans womxn, Carmen Guerrero, in 2013 at Kern Valley.[8] He's now on death row. These days I do my best to avoid conflict and violence with any prisoners or officials. I've made a commitment to nonviolence and prisoners' humxn rights advocacy.

I'm no longer part of the "white" car; I'm part of the multiracial queer/trans car (or family). I don't even identify as white because I'm part Cherokee/Native. And there's only one race—humxn! I'm currently in a three-year long intimate relationship with a Black cisgender male cellmate, and I associate mainly with the Black and queer/trans communities with no problems. Of course, this is on an SNY (Sensitive Needs Yard) yard. If I was on a GP (general population) yard, I'd probably be killed by the AB woodpile or skinheads, as a "race traitor." Fuck racism!

My "politicalization" began with learning about abolitionist struggles from before the Civil War against white supremacy and the African slave trade in the antebellum South's plantation system, and continued with becoming a jailhouse lawyer and prisoner humxn rights advocate.

Then I participated in the 1991 Folsom Prison Food Strike protest against proposed visiting regulations by CDCR [California Department of Corrections and Rehabilitation] to cut our visits from four days a week (Thursday through Sunday) to two days (weekends and holidays). This resulted in me being targeted for placement in the hole, or Ad Seg [Administrative Segregation] control units, or solitary confinement, and a bogus rule violation for "inciting" (i.e., writing to the local ACLU to provide counter-info about the protest and subsequent lockdown conditions). In fact,

---

8. In 2013, Miguel Crespo was housed with Carmen Guerrero for just eight hours before he bound, gagged, tortured, and murdered her in their shared cell.

the pig Sergeant Remple is the one who violated rules and the law by illegally opening and obstructing my confidential legal mail. For that reason, my rule violation was dismissed after spending two months in punitive segregation, in spite of which I was placed in a more restricted facility at New Folsom rather than returned to Old Folsom.

Around this time, I began corresponding with the Prisoners' Rights Union (PRU) in Sacramento, the Anarchist Black Cross, and *Love and Rage* (an anarchist newspaper) in New York. This was the beginning of my development and political education as part of the revolutionary prisoner movement. I wrote inmate grievances and filed writs of habeas corpus and civil rights lawsuits—most of which were summarily dismissed until I won a couple of monetary settlements for $1,000 and $3,000 in the US Eastern District of California for brutality and an auto accident injury in an illegally modified prisoner transport vehicle without seat belts or safety compliance. Then another legal victory when my petition for writ of habeas corpus was granted in Del Norte County Superior Court, ordering my release from Pelican Bay SHU after more than ten years in solitary confinement due to violation of my due process rights by a classification committee!

I was proud of these wins and also encouraged that I now realized it was possible to sometimes win significant legal victories and political battles that advance our collective revolutionary struggles for liberation and prisoners' humxn rights against slavery, torture, unjust systemic racial oppression, gender violence, and class-based social divisions or inequality.

When it comes to extended lockdowns, one has no choice but to handle it and cope with it. The best way I learned to survive the harm and trauma of prison torture and violence is to always stay productive and engage in positive self-development (e.g., educational and rehabilitative self-help programs), physical exercise routines, some form of self-care or spiritual study and practice like yoga, Taoism, or Native spirituality and traditional cultures. It takes time to learn how to navigate, avoid, and cope with the everyday casual, random violence of prison captivity. At first I simply embraced it, but as we age, we mature, we find wisdom, and we reclaim our humxnity.

Some of us will never fully recover from the harm and trauma caused by our prison captivity, especially as survivors of abuse and torture who spent many years and decades in long-term solitary confinement, control units like Pelican Bay SHU, or who suffered beatings and brutality by the pigs, or who were shot at with semiautomatic assault rifles during gladiator fights, and/ or witnessed the murders of other incarcerated people by gang members or guards. I'm working on my own trauma, healing, and self-care practice.

My first time in control units was in Folsom ASU, where I spent a couple of years before I was transferred to the Pelican Bay SHU, where I spent the next decade. At first, it was depressing isolation in nearly 24/7 cell confinement with little or no property. Then it became dangerous when I experienced the gladiator fights, and guards shooting, maiming, and murdering incarcerated people for unarmed fistfights. Prisoners stabbed and sliced each other with weapons. I eventually learned to survive this state-sanctioned terror and torture. I entered Folsom ASU in August 1992, engaged in a lot of individual and collective prisoner resistance by barricading or sabotaging our cells in protest, fighting back against guard brutality, and jailhouse lawyer advocacy in the courts.

Looking Forward

Outside support is crucial to prisoners' sense of humxnity and inherent self-worth, especially if they don't have any family support or friendship. I haven't always felt supported. When I first came to these slave plantations at California Institution for Men (CIM) in Chino, I was not prepared for the cold, hard reality of gun towers, razor wire, and inhumane conditions of confinement behind those concrete walls and steel bars. Most people in 1989 American society would probably be surprised that Jim Crow racial segregation was still strictly enforced per state policy and under threat of violent retaliation by prison gangs or prison officials of the CDCR. At that time, I didn't have any outside support, and I was feeling alone and vulnerable as a young, feminine-looking "white boy" with long hair from the Orange County suburbs, just south of Los Angeles.

Also, I feel prisoner supporters need to understand or do more to connect with incarcerated people or POWs/political prisoners on a genuine friendship level or a humxn level. Stay consistent and solid in responding to the prisoners' letters; don't just slack off and become nonresponsive without explanation. Inquire about their health and safety, living conditions, and material support needs. Real solidarity is shown by actions, not just words.

We have our own problems, and we're not trying to hear about others' problems in the "free world."

I think that there should be a well-funded legal team of progressive lawyers and humxn rights advocates pursuing every legal remedy or obscure technicality that could open up a pathway to freedom! Every prisoner supporter should consider ways they could help revolutionary prisoners organize solidarity campaigns or support teams of committed comrades, family members, movement attorneys, humxn rights lawyers, and legal advocates who might be able to petition international humxn rights agencies—such as the United Nations and Inter-American Commission on Human Rights—to address issues of state-sanctioned terror and torture of political dissidents and to respond to the needs of political prisoners for solidarity actions and campaigns, online fundraisers and petitions, material aid support, and trauma-informed care. Also, POWs/political prisoners and other incarcerated people often become starved for intimacy with another persxn for love and affection that is mutual to share with someone as a lifelong partner or lover.

My advice to those entering the prisons/slave plantations/POW camps is to maintain your individuality and self-autonomy. Begin your educational and rehabilitative self-development by reading abolitionist newspapers, building community and dialogue, educating family and friends, and learning the law and legal remedies through consulting jailhouse lawyers. Learn how to be a self-advocate. Avoid bullshit, bullies, drugs, and gangs, and limit your interaction with pigs and prisoners alike. I'd want "past me" to not learn the hard way about autonomy and authenticity of being, to come out as queer and trans sooner in life, to understand the One Life, One Humxnity of This Living Earth, Mother Nature. The "beautiful idea" of anarchy ("without rules") and autonomy of land/space. No law but natural law!

My life inside is not typical, as a femme/queer/trans womxn in a men's prison. It's been a hard struggle yet increasingly rewarding. It's not without heartache and hard-fought steps forward. I've enjoyed the affection and intimacy of lovers, the authenticity and genuineness of comrades and friends who continue to act in solidarity with me and other anarchist prisoners through letter writing, material assistance, mutual aid funds, advocacy, and organizing. I'm so proud and hopeful for the potentialities and continued development of the international anarchist and antifascist actions and insurrections!

Ed Mead

Ed Mead was a member of the George Jackson Brigade in the Pacific Northwest during the 1970s. As a result, he spent thirty-five years of his life in prisons around the United States, eighteen of which were due to his political activities. While in prison for his part in the armed struggle of the GJB, he helped to found Men Against Sexism at Walla Walla State Penitentiary in Washington. Ed served time in numerous state and federal prisons, notably Marion, Arizona State Penitentiary, Washington State Penitentiary (Walla Walla), and Brushy Mountain Prison in Tennessee. In addition to the George Jackson Brigade, he has also been involved with the Prairie Fire Organizing Committee, the Attica Brothers Legal Defense Committee, the National Lawyers Guild, *Prison Legal News*, and *California Prison Focus*.[1] Ed wrote *The Theory and Practice of Armed Struggle in the Northwest: A Historical Analysis* (Kersplebedeb, 2007) and the book *Lumpen: The Autobiography of Ed Mead* (Kersplebedeb, 2015).

1. The Attica Brothers Legal Defense Committee was a diverse group of Attica survivors, their families, formerly incarcerated people, lawyers, law students, and others that sought to provide some sense of justice to those prisoners traumatized by the massacre at Attica prison in 1971. The National Lawyers Guild (NLG) was founded in 1937 to provide legal assistance to communities that need it most.

Prison Life

I had such a time alone. Unlike many other political prisoners who had hope of being released one day, I had no hope. One of the first things I did was to dismiss my appeal. And so there were only two directions for me to go. One was over the wall, and I was working on that all the time. And the other was up against my captors. I did a lot of that, so they transferred me a lot. As a result of that, I was in a lot of prisons in a lot of states. I never adapted, so that was my problem. The prison is just really a sick environment, and I always figured that if you adjusted to it, what did that make you?

There were good times, and there were bad times. There were some of the worst people I ever met and some of the best people I ever met. And when dealing with the worst people, to get on that list, you had to be someone trying to kill me. What I would do during those times is direct myself, and as many of those as I could bring along, and smash them up against the administration. When my friends and I are in struggle with the prison administration, it's very difficult for these reactionary, Aryan Brotherhood types to attack us from the rear. It exposes them as the collaborators that they are, and they don't like that kind of exposure. So in the end, they generally wind up helping us, not that they want to but because of circumstances.

I learned how to use computers in prison. I had a computer in my cell, and with a pair of tweezers and nail clippers, I would tear it down to the motherboard and put it back together, like a sixteen-year-old kid in their first car—just trying to squeeze a little bit more out of it than it was willing to give. And so when I got out, I was able to get a job in the computer industry and make enough money to live okay when I retired.

Prison has gotten worse because of constant budget cuts, staff shortages, food quality—just everything got worse. They're charging you to get medical attention; just every step of the way they're squeezing money out of you and your family.

I have two proudest achievements. At just about every prison, there's ways that you distinguish yourself in the prison's hierarchy, in the pecking order. At Marion federal prison, for example, they sell regular T-shirts in the commissary, but the T-shirts they call wife-beaters are contraband. So if you have a wife-beater, then you're somebody. At another prison, say Brushy Mountain, they issued jockey shorts, and if you wore boxer shorts, then you were cool. At Walla Walla, the way you established yourself was by raping vulnerable or gay prisoners. That was a well-known and widespread practice. Young, vulnerable prisoners would come in, and they would be glommed onto by predators. They would be sexually abused and then sold to another cell full of people. So, I organized Men Against Sexism at the Washington State Penitentiary at Walla Walla. That put an end to the prisoner-on-prisoner rape and the buying and selling of prisoners. We did that through a whole lot of means, including six homemade shotguns. That was my second-proudest achievement.

My proudest achievement was at the Arizona State Prison in Florence. There are very big industries at that facility—many industries. The first thing I did was organize a group called the Committee to Safeguard Prisoners' Rights, or CSPR. We put out a statewide newsletter that went to prisons all over the state, we filed litigation on behalf of prisoners with mental challenges, we did a lot. But we also won paid vacations for industrial workers. We were getting ready to launch an initiative that would have increased prisoner pay, industrial pay, by 100 percent. The Aryan Brotherhood kind of ran the joint, and this was a case where they had to join us. In this particular instance, we had dual power, and the prisoners walked proud. They had a sense of themselves and their strength. Of course, that situation was intolerable to the pigs, so they yanked me out of there, and the next day I was on my way back to Washington. The Committee to Safeguard Prisoners' Rights slowly went downhill—because it was a mass organization, it wasn't a cadre organization—and finally dissipated. But that moment of dual power, when it could go either way, was my proudest moment.

Politics and Prison Dynamics

Okay, personal ethics. I arrived at Washington State Penitentiary in Walla Walla in the late 1970s. And because I was part of a group that had bombed the headquarters of the Department of Corrections in the state capital, they locked me up immediately. It was called the IMU, or Intensive Management Unit. As I'm being processed, booked in, there's a kid in front of me, about twenty years old. I don't talk to him, and he doesn't talk to me; we're each in our own drama going through this. So, they give us some coveralls and he gets put in cell 11. I get put in cell 10, a filthy cell, dirty, dirty water, fecal matter smeared on the walls, boogers on the bars, just nasty. So I'm there bemoaning my fate, and a gang of five or six prisoners tried to get into the cell next to me, after this young kid. It's pretty obvious they want to rape him. There is a guard down at the end of the tier trying to open the kid's cell. Well, the kid sticks a book in between the bars and prevents the door from opening. The predators try and grab the book, he pulls it out, the guard tries to open the door, he sticks it back in. This goes on for a little while, and I'm having a terrible crisis of conscience. I know I need to say, "Stop, you villains, what you are doing is wrong," or something else equally stupid. But I'm afraid they'll come to my cell next. So, I'm struggling with this dilemma when the predators go down to the end of the tier and get pitchers of hot water to throw on this kid. That doesn't work, either, and the guard tires of the whole thing, and so it's over. And I'm just disgusted with myself and the situation. In eighteen years of confinement, that was my moral crisis.

Of course, any time you're trying to move, no matter what direction you try to move in, you're going to run into conflicts. And if you're a progressive or communist, there's only one direction for you to move and that's up against the administration. Well, the administration's first line of defense is the racist groups like the Aryan Brotherhood. And so there's conflicts with these groups. As far as conflict with the administration, that goes with the territory. Unless there's a point of conflict, there exists a state of class peace. There can never be a revolution as long as that condition exists. So, our job as communists is to develop that struggle, to develop that conflict. In the process of doing this, we make enemies of those who have administration-sanctioned perks. They have the drug business and things like that. You come in conflict with that element. So, not only are you facing bitterness from the administration, you're also facing bitterness from your rear.

The struggle against racism and sexism on the inside is an ongoing issue. At the US prison at Marion, the mess hall was segregated—the Blacks ate on one side, the whites ate on another. I tried to integrate it: I had my Black friends eat with me on the white side, and I and two of my white friends would eat on the Black side. One of my two friends showed up once, the other one never showed up, so it was just me. I got death threats. So I just ate on the Black side for the rest of my time over there. The struggle against racism is a constant one. The contradiction between the keepers and the kept is the primary contradiction. Racism and sexism are sub-issues that you work on all the time, but they aren't the primary issue.

So here's the thing, from our perspective, you fight the class enemy from wherever you find yourself on their soil. So it's not time-out when you go to prison; you continue your political work in whatever form that might take. Whether it's publishing an underground newsletter for prisoners or whatever. For most of these prisoners on the inside, the political prisoner is the only communist these people are ever going to meet or ever going to see. That's a big responsibility on our shoulders to be the kind of people that generate respect because of the work that we do.

If you're an activist on the inside, you do a lot of hole time, and that comes with the territory. When I was transferred out of the hole at USP Marion, they shipped me out on the fifth day of a hunger strike. Shit on the walls, feathers torn out of pillows, papers lit on fire. I mean, we were down to our underwear in a struggle in a lockdown. Your one human power is what you and those in that unit have, and that's what you're throwing up against them. I was transferred out of there and sent to Leavenworth, where I had a whole tier to myself. That's where Mark [Cook] and I were able to hook up again. So, yeah, we do a lot of hole time, and, even when we're in the hole, we still resist. Flooding, fires, noise, any advantage we can use, we fight even from the hole. If you're not making them lock it down, you're doing something wrong. It's right to rebel. Don't adjust.

Looking Forward

There are different kinds of outside support. The best outside support I had brought me pounds of gunpowder, ammunition, and a pistol. Things that I could use, and not mere hand-holding. That was my definition of outside support. So, there are different definitions of outside support. Listen to the prisoners. What do they need? If you're lucky, you won't be listening to a prisoner like me.

Things are really, really bad. In the mid-1970s when I went to prison, there was no homelessness. People and communities hitchhiked across the nation without fear. Since then, the fear has just penetrated every level of society. As that happened, the homelessness increased, the disparity in income, everything has gotten worse and worse. Yet the left is totally atomized and appears powerless. We're on the verge of going to war in eastern and western Europe right now. Where's the antiwar movement? I'm not even talking revolution here. And if I was talking revolution, where's that at? It's sad.

The prison is a microcosm of the outside. And everybody's looking out for their own self-interests. I don't think that they're unified at all against the administration. I communicate with a lot of prisoners, and the most advanced, the most progressive prisoners, do not see themselves as the little motor that starts the big engine of social change. Their mindset, when talking about outside support, is to write to this legislature for this change. They're looking for other people to do what needs to be done and don't see themselves as the focal point of change. The big problem is that they're looking for someone else to do their struggle for them.

Jerry Koch

Gerald "Jerry" Koch is an anarchist and legal activist who in 2009 was subpoenaed by a grand jury investigating the bombing of a Times Square army recruitment center the year prior. Jerry refused to cooperate, and in 2013 he was imprisoned, ultimately spending 241 days in federal custody at the Metropolitan Correctional Center (MCC) in Manhattan and the Metropolitan Detention Center (MDC) in Brooklyn. Since his grand jury resistance, Jerry has taken up the legal profession as a way to assist those who, like himself, have come up against the criminal legal system.

Prison Life

What's weird about a federal grand jury is it's just like a quirk in the legal system where coercive detention is actually allowed, explicitly. Which is both draconian and Kafkaesque, and both of those are words that tend to be overused but I think very definitively apply in this instance. How it works for a subpoena to a federal grand jury is you come in and refuse to testify. Your strongest argument is actually the Fifth Amendment against self-incrimination. Even though I didn't know anything about what they were nominally investigating. The whole thing is secret. They don't have to tell anyone what's going on. Your lawyer is not allowed in there. It's just a total black box.

Obviously, grand juries have a long history of being used against activists and anarchists going back really to the second Red Scare, arguably going back to the first Red Scare and all the anti-anarchist stuff in the 1910s. But you really started to see it come to the fore during the McCarthy era, then against the Black Panthers and other activists in the 1960s and 1970s. Then, of course, later with the Green Scare and the targeting of antiracists and antifascists, anarchists, and activists. But, point being, I refused to cooperate.

I had an old Reagan appointee as the judge, and he was furious at me, screaming at me in court. Like he was personally offended by my existence. His later order ordering my release, a big chunk of it, was just him personally insulting me. Then they told me I'd be put in jail unless I cooperated, and I said, "Well, do what you got to do." But with a federal grand jury, because you're not charged with anything or even suspected of anything, you're in until you cooperate or until the grand jury expires. In the feds, grand juries are impaneled for eighteen months regularly. Special grand juries can actually be extended up to, I think, thirty-six months.

You're in until the grand jury expires. You cooperate or this other rather ironically named Grumbles motion works, which is an argument basically that it's so clear you're never going to cooperate that the coercive detention has now become punitive.[1] Because there's just no chance of coercive detention working, which is ultimately what got me released after eight months and seven days.

But with a grand jury, because you're not charged with anything, you don't know how long you're going to be in for. There's no sentencing guidelines because you're not sentenced to anything, which adds an emotional difficulty to it. I mean, look, anyone doing time, there's a lot of emotional difficulty and pain. And in comparison to many, I did comparatively short time. But it's really difficult to have no idea how long you're going to be in for. That lack of surety to fall back on is kind of a second little extra twist of the knife.

So I was taken in by the marshals, and at first I was in MDC Brooklyn, which is a rather infamous facility. It was called Little Guantánamo by some folks who were in there. I was in the SHU for a little while by myself and then with a cellie. Then I was in a different unit, and they started to get pissed after the first two weeks because I wasn't folding immediately.

---

1. A Grumbles motion (named after the 1971 case of Don and Patricia Grumbles) is a "Memorandum of Law in Support of Motion to Release" arguing that one's continued incarceration is punitive.

Then they moved me at like five in the morning, with no heads-up, to MCC in lower Manhattan, which, if anything, is perhaps an even more infamous facility. For a long time it was where they kept really high-level terror suspects. It is this just hellish little high-rise in lower Manhattan. Now it's really famous because that's where Epstein killed himself.[2] But it has a long history of holding political folks. I was there for the rest of my time in gen pop [general population]. Then in the SHU for a little while. For gen pop, they put me into a unit known as the snitch unit. I was surrounded by people who were cooperating and didn't have super great feelings about my refusal to cooperate. They clearly did that purposefully.

There was a lot of really encouraging and supportive activism around my incarceration. Folks were doing demos [demonstrations] outside of the facility and all sorts of really cool stuff. The administration of that facility started to get really pissy about it and started to actually follow my support website. It got to the point where they would know that a demo was coming, and they would preemptively put me in the SHU by myself for five days with no explanation, no nothing, which was really scary because I had no idea how long I was going to be there, on top of not knowing how long I was going to be in prison for. That was pretty nasty and a pretty scary part of prison.

Then they put me back in gen pop, and that's where I finished up the rest of my time in jail, until this Grumbles motion worked, and then they abruptly cut me loose in the middle of a blizzard in late January in Manhattan with no heads-up. No one knew I was getting out, not even my lawyers. The marshals just kind of dumped me in the lobby of the courthouse. I asked if I got a phone call, and they told me to go away. So, I called my mom collect from the vestibule of the federal court, and I'm like, "I think I'm out. I don't know what to do."

I just stood there trying to figure out what to do for a while, and the marshals were standing there with their hands on their guns, just staring at me. I'm dressed in my 3XL marshals jumpsuit, no ID, nothing, standing in federal court. Everyone's there in a suit. No one gets released directly from the MCC. So everyone's just like, "What the fuck are you doing?" I eventually got sick of waiting there with all these people just staring at me, so I went

---

2. Jeffrey Epstein was a financier who was arrested in 2019 and charged with running a sex trafficking operation that catered to wealthy and prominent people around the world. He was found dead in his cell at the Metropolitan Correctional Center in August 2019.

outside. I didn't get to say a proper goodbye to my friends in the unit, since I didn't know I was getting released. I stood outside of MCC for a while, just waving in the hopes that folks inside could see me and know that I wasn't leaving them behind or abandoning them. I did that until I was just shaking so bad from the cold that I couldn't do it anymore.

Then I booked it, and I just ran, which probably looked really weird that a person in prison gear is just running full speed away from a federal prison. I booked it through lower Manhattan to my lawyer's office, in a blizzard, wearing shitty, thin sweats and the little prison shoes that are like knockoff Vans (they call them Patakis in New York for the ex-governor). I showed up at my lawyer's office, and the people there were very surprised because they didn't know I was being released. I think their first thought might have been like, "Oh, Jerry escaped! What the fuck is he doing here?" So yeah, that's how that went.

First, obviously, prisons are really scary. When I went in, Jeremy Hammond—a very well-known and amazing political prisoner—was also in MCC. Actually, when the marshals took me in from the courtroom, the judge had ordered me to MCC but then decided to take me to MDC. I tried to argue with the marshals because I wanted to link up with Jeremy at MCC. That didn't work at first, but, actually, later we ended up meeting each other and started becoming friends. I can't say enough good things about Jeremy.

As a white guy, people assumed that I would run with the other white guys. I made it very clear that that's not how that worked for me at all. People tried to call me "white Jerry" and I was like, "Not happening, no. I'm just Jerry." That's just not going down. I'm lucky that in New York feds, there's not a lot of neo-Nazi shit. Of course, there's some. One CO actually asked if I was Aryan Brotherhood and I said I was actually the exact opposite.

I ended up rolling with a pretty diverse crew, with some Bloods-adjacent friends, some Latin Kings folks. Then I got in with the Muslims because my cellie, whom I spent most of my time with, was a very devout Muslim. Then there was one Triad guy and one or two other white folks.[3] I ended up having a good crew, and I'd be able to go to some of them if I thought I was going to have a problem or thought I was in danger. I could ask them to watch my back. That's kind of routine.

---

3. The Triads are a Chinese organized crime syndicate.

I had great support. I have an incredibly supportive community here. There's a really good anarchist scene in New York, so I had a ton of support in that respect. I don't think anyone's really prepared. In some ways, the hardest day of the entire thing was the twenty-four hours before I went in because it felt kind of like you're facing a firing squad and you just don't know what's going to happen. Of course, at that point, you're running through every worst-case scenario. And you face that shit. But once you're in you learn how to deal with stuff, whereas, before, you're running through all the worst-case scenarios about prison.

I was friends with folks who had done time. I talked to a friend of mine, Dave, who had done some time. I talked to Daniel McGowan a lot about it, because he had just gotten out. I had done some support work for him, then meeting him in person right before I went was pretty weird. But I'd actually done noise demos outside of MCC before I went to MCC, so there was a very weird reversal. I've since done a lot of noise demos outside of MCC and MDC, and now I really know what it's like when you're in there—what you can hear and what you can't hear, stuff like that. For a lot of noise demos, you've really got to keep the chants simple. Complicated chants are hard for folks to hear.

I'd done political prisoner support and a lot of jail support and arrest support for a number of years before that went down, especially for the radical and anarchist community here. I spent so much time in court before then that people thought I was a lawyer. Now, ironically, I've become a lawyer.

At first, there's definitely a learning curve. But once you get a crew, you have folks to work out with, you have a workout schedule, you have time when you're just reading and writing letters. There's folks you cook with when you make food after dinner because the dinners there are disgusting and it's not enough calories to really survive on. People don't understand that commissary is actually a necessity, not just a nice plus.

I was in facilities that are predominantly pretrial. MDC and MCC are interesting because they're both jails and prisons because you can also serve your time there if you're doing much shorter time or at the end of your bid. I preferred MDC, but I was there only for like two weeks. It's possible I just never got the real nastiness. I was in the SHU there, and the SHU there had a shower. I'm a very clean person, so that was nice. The first night they leave you alone, and you cry for six hours and then fall asleep out of exhaustion.

My first cellie there was a Russian mob guy who was really nice. He helped explain stuff to me. We were talking about ourselves, and I told him I'm a radical, and he asked from which side. It just never occurred to me that people inside might think I'm far-right when I say something like that because from our communities when I say radical, it's very clear what that means.

A lot of folks don't realize that "short-term facilities" and jails are really brutal. People think about the upstate prisons, but there you have a proper yard and slightly better food and stuff. I mean, you can't make generalizations quite like that. I'm not trying to fall in the trap of saying my time was harder or easier than someone else's. Everyone does their own time. But of the two, I guess MDC was better-ish. Also, fuck MCC, I hope that shit collapses in on itself.

But I was in some ways lucky because I was in for something that was a very easy decision. Refusing to cooperate was a really quick, easy decision. I never second-guessed it, even at my lowest. And I never have since. The consequences are brutal, but I would make the same decision again in a heartbeat.

When I was contacted by one of my old lawyers for the second grand jury, he said, "You've been subpoenaed." The first words out of my mouth were, "Okay, I'm not going to cooperate." So, I had that to fall back on and draw strength from. It's kind of perverse to say that I was lucky, but in comparison to a lot of other folks, it was like, I know what I'm here for. It was the right decision. It's an easy decision. I'm never going to put someone else in a cage. And I had an incredibly supportive community and family, with some caveats. I mean, there's moments of hopelessness; I think anyone who says they don't have moments of hopelessness is probably putting on a stronger face.

Being inside for noise demos was really amazing. The first one, it was like a fucking monsoon outside. People are in these thick-ass raincoats, and there's still like fifty people outside chanting with banners. Inside everyone was asking me who are you and why are these people here? That was a really great feeling, knowing these people really have my back.

The real moments of beauty are seeing people work together and find each other and learn from each other and understand that we have a common foe, which is the prison system. People refusing food together, people teaching each other, people just hanging out together and having both easy conversations and sometimes really hard conversations. Prisoners aren't the revolutionary subject or whatever; they are people just like everyone else. I don't want to put anyone on a pedestal. I don't want to lionize people, whether they are political prisoners or anyone else.

That said, there are some true moments of beauty and solidarity and care that I saw inside. It was all the more meaningful that people were doing this while being in this hellish situation—while being brutalized and tortured physically, psychologically, and emotionally—and still getting through each day and talking to each other and supporting each other. There's a number of moments of beauty; it's just hard to convey because beauty trapped inside concrete and rusty steel isn't what most people would think of as beauty.

I think of myself as an empathetic person, but I do think that that was heightened and developed while being inside. It's also what set me on the path to being a lawyer. I did legal work for years before doing my time, and I was always, like, "Fuck lawyers, I'm never going to be one. I'm never going to legitimize this system." Doing my time and looking around, I realized the best way I can think of to get these folks out is to be a lawyer. If I thought that there was a different best way to do that, I would do that.

It's not exactly the most radical thing, right? It's the rearguard of any kind of social change. It's harm reduction. But I think of it as putting myself and my abilities as a shield in front of our clients. Not to be self-aggrandizing, it's the client that matters, not us. But you protect them as best you can from the worst excesses of the state. So I came out with that skill, although it took me a number of years to accept that. I came out and was really fucked up for a while, and then I was a teacher for a few years, and I ended up going to law school. So obliquely, I guess I got that skill out of it.

Overall, I think I gained more friends and comrades. You see the truth of people when you go away. Some people are there for you and then are abruptly not; they're just in this for the show. For some reason, people think that supporting folks inside is a thing to show off with. There's this weird power dynamic in doing support. No, they are the person doing the time; we're just here to help. But there are folks who went to bat for me from all over the world, some of whom I met later. I was pretty lucky in that regard.

There's the violence too, and the threats of violence and all that stuff. I experienced some of that, and I dealt with it. I was pretty lucky that, by the time I was really dealing with the nasty parts of that, I had a good crew who would watch my back. I was threatened with stuff, and I stood up to them, and I was like, "Nah, it's not going down this way." But seeing people being brutalized, being taken advantage of, is tough. Even when you think you're prepared for it, seeing it, trying to help, and then not necessarily always being able to help I think is kind of surprising.

I knew that people were going to snitch, but I didn't expect the extent to which people were snitching on each other all over the place, especially in the feds. A lot of people cooperate, and they purposely put me in the snitch unit to deny me as much solidarity and support as I would have had in other units. That was kind of hard, and you don't really realize it's the snitches who run the gambling, it's the snitches who run the drugs, it's the snitches who run the unit, and all this kind of shit. And how many people are trying to jump on each other's cases all the time, calling up other people's prosecutors to be like, "Oh, I talked to this guy."

One of the most brutal things I found was this one guy who was snitching on his entire family, which is really crazy. He was in with his cellie, this guy named Bodega, who was fighting his case. I thought they were a crew. It turned out every time Bodega was leaving the cell, this guy was going through all of his legal paperwork in the cell and calling the prosecutor and going through his papers. That's both surprising and unsurprising. But you're never really prepared for it.

Politics and Prison Dynamics

I got threatened by some other inmates and obliquely threatened by guards. I thought I was a tough guy going in, and then I realized that what a real tough guy means is you end up doing life in the SHU. You end up doing life in the hole because you're going to get arrested for something and then you're going to be in and you're not going to be able to take any shit from anyone, ever.

But I was able to stick up for myself. I got threatened by this guy who I later found out had some bodies on his case, like murder stuff. I got pissed with him about something and I told him to come to my cell where I screamed at him a bunch, which made him back down. Only later did I realize that was a dumb fucking idea.

Another time this guy threatened me for sticking up for another guy who, I think, was being sexually assaulted. He threatened me with some nasty shit, and I had to make sure that I was not in parts of the unit for a little while. I had to check in with a couple of people and be like, "I need you to watch my back." But I was able to get through it without having to get in physical fights.

Society is racist as fuck; prison, even more so. Shocker, I know. I was able to deal with that by saying, "Look, I don't run with the white guys. That's just not what I'm about." Once people knew who I was, what I was about, and respected me, then I made friendships. I was able to run with folks from all sorts of different crews. Often in jail, color sticks with its own or looks after its own. People kind of crew up by race, ethnicity, skin color.

One of the really cool things in the feds, at least where I was, was when there's new people in the unit, people take up a collection for them because they haven't been able to get commissary yet. Seeing that was always really amazing. People just giving stuff that the new people are going to need that you have extra of and not expecting anything back. It's really beautiful. Often it's the Muslims taking care of the Muslims, and so when I would throw in for the new Muslim guys, that would surprise people. It was kind of expected that the white folks would take care of the white folks. So we would do the collection and I'd bring it to the new people and say, "Look, I'm bringing you this stuff because you're going to need it to get started. There's this assumption that white people are going to look after white people, and I need you to know that that's not what I'm about. I just want you to have this stuff because you're going to need it. But this is not a 'we are allies by virtue of our skin color' kind of deal."

Obviously, I witnessed a lot of that kind of stuff. A straight-up race riot almost happened over a missing domino [game tile]. But I was able to make friends and hang out with a lot of nonwhite folks from different groups and crews. I was able to be an antiracist, an antifascist, an anarchist—that's why I was there, after all—and I talked about that shit. I think people could kind of see that when looking at me, and I think that made things a little easier for me.

Obviously, the system is structurally racist, the legal system is structurally racist, prisons are structurally racist, and they really try to get folks who are incarcerated to perpetuate that stuff. Just like any group of people that exists in there, not everyone, not even necessarily the majority, but just any group of people, that kind of stuff exists. It's hard to see those things play out.

I talked to folks about stuff, and I think I turned a few folks on to anarchist ideas. Setting up a lending library, including a political section, I think was really good. I corresponded with a lot of folks outside. Some of my support committee set up something called Inside Out. At the time it was a reading circle where different folks inside would read and write reviews and then communicate with other folks who were reading the same books and writing reviews and stuff. I think that project kind of trailed off. I wasn't organizing riots and shit, but I would like to think in my own way I was doing some political work. But a lot of my time was spent trying to be a really good boy because the grand jury stuff was just so weird.

Having some of the more aggro texts, like the Ward Churchill stuff, for example, or Sean Swain, passing that kind of stuff around inside would shock people.[4] They would read it and say, "You can't say this!" Like [Churchill's] chickens coming home to roost in a 9/11 essay.[5] Pass that essay to Muslim folks inside, and they're like, "No, you're not allowed, you can't have this, you can't say this." But it's also just other political texts like *No Gods No Masters*, which is like a great starter, and other anarchist history stuff.[6] Sharing the Anarchist Black Cross news, since they do a lot of support. They're some amazing folks. People should check out ABC. They'd send me the updates, and passing those around to folks inside really turned a lot of people on to anarchism and political organizing and connecting with others who were doing time. The first time you pass it to people, they're like, "What the fuck is that?" And then by the second or third time, they're like, "Wow, this is awesome. Let me get that next."

I think it's good for your support committee to be friends but not family. It should be political comrades. My mom wasn't on my support committee, but I think, just in general, it's better for family not to be involved because

---

4. Ward Churchill is an author, historian, and activist who has published significant books on government repression.

5. Churchill's book, *On the Justice of Roosting Chickens: Reflections on the Consequences of U.S. Imperial Arrogance and Criminality* (AK Press, 2003), includes an essay published on September 12, 2001, that claims that the four suicide plane attacks orchestrated by Al Qaeda the day prior (9/11) were retribution for the violence and imperialism of the US government.

6. *No Gods No Masters: An Anthology of Anarchism*, edited by Daniel Guérin (AK Press, 2005).

they have enough stuff. Also, folks who are involved in an intimate relationship, or partner, should not be part of the support committee. You want that to be a separate thing because there's so much emotional stuff happening there.

Looking Forward

Don't lionize or valorize folks in prison. They're people just like any other people who have needs, who have hearts, who have imperfections. Political prisoners aren't superheroes; they're just people, and they need help and they need conversation just like other people.

Commissary is really important, like I said earlier, making sure people have money on the books. It's not extra money to go shopping with. It's not the equivalent of ordering in rather than making food. These are necessities, really. Understanding that prisoner support, and political prisoner support especially, is in it for the long haul. I think it's tough, and certainly I'm guilty of this as well, of getting into stuff full speed ahead and then after a while realizing that the day-to-day of this is actually a lot of work. That's one of the reasons I have so much love and respect for ABC. They've held it down for years and years and years and will continue to. So, I think those are all parts of it.

I would highly recommend looking into your local Anarchist Black Cross. They not only organize letter writings but also disseminate really up-to-date info on how to support political prisoners. I also like a lot of the discourse that was happening here in New York during the George Floyd uprisings around "no new jails." Noise demos outside of prisons are a huge way to support folks inside and send direct messages of solidarity to folks trapped behind those walls. Honestly, the New Year's noise demo here in New York is among my favorite events of the year. If you haven't been to a noise demo, I can't recommend it highly enough.

If you're heading to prison, remember: one, you're going to get through it. It's going to fucking suck, but you're going to get through. Two, whatever you're imagining in the days right before you go in is probably worse than what's actually going to happen. Some bad shit will happen, but whatever you're doing to yourself is probably worse than what's going to happen.

I developed a method which seemed to work for me, and I've walked and talked other people through this, and it seemed to help them because I've done support stuff for a number of other folks after I got out. I call it the Firsts Method because you're not sure how to start your time right and how to get through that first week. That first week just seems like it's going to go forever. So, the way to think about it is to just get to your first _____. Get to your first meal; get through your first full day; get to your first shower; get your first piece of mail; get to your first rec time; get to your first game of spades. Then get to your first workout, your first commissary. Then get to your first whatever it is, whether a legal visit or being able to send mail. Just plot it out by you getting your first _____ and then you think about what's the next first _____. By the time you've covered all the firsts, you've got your routine. And that's the way to think about it. Don't think about it as only being in for two days when you've got years and years and years ahead. Think about the next first thing, and by the time you've gotten through all the possible firsts, then you know what's going on.

I never get this quote right, but my old cellie told it to me, and it goes something like, "Someone's talking to another person, and the person's brother is going through hell in prison. And the question is: How does your brother do that? How do they get through it? And the answer is because they have to." At first, I didn't really understand that, and I reflected on it a lot. You just have to get through it because you have to, and the meaning of that, I think, is hard to really conceptualize if you haven't had to do it. But that's how you deal with an impossible situation. You get through it because you have to.

Michael Kimble

Michael Kimble is a politicized prisoner and an anarchist from Birmingham, Alabama. At the age of twenty-one, he and a male friend were holding hands in public one night and were violently attacked by a known racist and homophobe. Kimble defended himself and his friend, which resulted in the attacker being killed. He is serving a life sentence (with parole as an option) and has now been held in Alabama's prison system since 1985. Michael was assaulted by Officer Thomas at Easterling Correctional in June 2021 and had both arms broken in four different areas. Michael has served time in seven different prisons in Alabama. He is a member of the Fire Ant Collective.

Prison Life

I've served thirty-six years to date and became politicized while in prison, first as a revolutionary nationalist, and then I became and embraced anarchy in 1994 and have been on that path ever since.

It was difficult for me to adapt to prison routine and structure because I've been used to doing basically what I wanted to do on the outside. And even though society is structured in a way similar to prison, prison is more direct as far as control is concerned. Even to this day I've been unable to adapt to the strict regime and hierarchy of prison. I've always been a rebel.

I've always made it a cardinal rule to fight against adapting to prison culture, which is death.

Around 2014–2019 at Holman [William C. Holman Correctional Facility] was the best time, and the resistance that had sprung up there against the forces of control made things more tolerable. And 1994–1998 at Donaldson [William E. Donaldson Correctional Facility], the solidarity and camaraderie made things more tolerable. Collective struggle has, in my experience, created relationships of solidarity that last from one prison to the next and for many years.

In the last thirty-six years of prison, I've learned how to do woodwork, hobbycraft, leatherwork, read music, learn Swahili, and go jogging. But now there are so many restrictions on hobbycraft and leatherwork that it's not even worth doing at most prisons. Here at Donaldson, there are no outlets for either. At most prisons, you must be assigned to a faith-based dorm to participate in hobbycraft.

Politics and Prison Dynamics

I've had verbal and physical conflicts with other prisoners. I've had to stab a few prisoners in self-defense. I've had conflicts with the Southern Brotherhood (SB), a white supremacist prison gang.[1] And most definitely had problems with admin where I was placed in lock-up and have been assaulted on numerous occasions by guards and have taken the initiative against guards. The outcome has been lock-up, more time, et cetera.

I've navigated the racial tension through confronting it. I've never been the victim of racial violence from prisoners, but I have been the focus of racial violence from guards who hated my activism on the inside. I ran across a couple of antiracists years ago at one prison, but the only antiracism going on is simple survival.

Richard Mafundi Lake and I were very close for many years.[2] We also

---

1. The Southern Brotherhood (SB) is a large and deadly white supremacist prison gang based in Alabama.

2. Richard Mafundi Lake was a longtime organizer and activist against police brutality who was imprisoned in the post-9/11 period when anti-Muslim hysteria was rampant. He died in prison in 2018.

had family relations. Mafundi was a mentor to me and many other prisoners. He's transitioned now, and I really do miss him. And the struggle is less without him.

I'm constantly doing some work to educate, agitate, and organize, and I do try to involve those comrades on the outside. *Fire Ant* [a zine and collective] is a project that emerged from anarchist political prisoner Jennifer Rose networking with free-roaming anarchists in the so-called free world. It's to generate material support for anarchist prisoners who may or may not have material support from the outside. In my case, it has been a big help so I can go to commissary to purchase things to supplement the awful food being served and also help others who find themselves in debt and can't pay. This has been able to stop some of the violence and also made it possible for me to make phone calls, send emails, and fund social/cultural events on the inside in efforts to build solidarity among prisoners.

To be truthful, I think *Fire Ant* can be better. This is our (locked down anarchists') publication and an avenue to educate people on what's going down in the prisons and what we think needs to be done. It gives us a voice, and I don't think we are putting much into it. So, I'd like to see it just a little more. All of those involved are excellent writers and I'd like more content from them. I learn from them, and I'm inspired by them.

Looking Forward

Outside support is so important because the system will fuck you over if they see you have no support. To have outside support can mean the difference between life and death.

Stay away from the gangs and educate [yourself] as much as possible. Use prison as a university, and use this time to mend broken relationships.

My life is in constant danger from other prisoners and guards. It really is. My life is one that screams against the injustices on the inside and that brings me constant pain. Understand that I'm constantly in danger, that this shit is real. Understand that being an anarchist only escalates my pain because I'm always bucking these backward notions from prisoners and guards alike.

Bill Harris

Bill Harris was a member of the Symbionese Liberation Army and was arrested in the mid-1970s, along with other members of the group following the kidnapping of Patty Hearst. After eight years of imprisonment, Bill was released. In 2002, due to new forensic evidence, Bill and other members of the SLA were again arrested and charged with a 1975 murder during an SLA bank expropriation. Bill was sentenced to seven years in prison and was released on parole in 2006. Bill served his sentences in California in various county jails, including LA County Jail's Sirhan Sirhan unit, the San Quentin Adjustment Center, and CSP Solano in Vacaville, California.[1]

Prison Life

In a way, it's like getting thrown into the briar patch. The harder they did things, the more things opened up for us to attack them and to eventually win most of our cases, really. It's a miracle that any of us got out, but there is that white skin privilege. I had two prison sentences, twenty years apart. They totaled eleven years, seven months, twenty-six days of actual time. I did just under eight years starting in 1975 and then just under four years starting in 2003.

---

1. Sirhan Sirhan is a Palestinian man convicted of the 1968 assassination of US politician Robert F. Kennedy in Los Angeles. He was granted parole in August 2021, though his release has been blocked by Governor Gavin Newsom.

I was housed all over. First night in jail I spent in the San Mateo County Jail. After that I got transferred to the Old Courthouse Jail in LA. I spent a year there, first in what was called the "Sirhan module," along with my wife. The first time I did time, I was in the LA County Jail, then Palm Hall SHU at California Institute for Men, which is like a reception center from LA County. We all went straight to the hole. Emily [Harris] went to death row; Russ [Little] and Joe [Remiro] were on death row before they were even arraigned.[2] They even got taken out of the cell one night and put down in the gas chamber and were threatened with being gassed for some silly shit. A lot of weird things happened to us back then.

In county jail, the sheriffs are horrible; none of them go to heaven. They're all going straight to fucking hell. I was in the courthouse jail too. Then San Quentin Adjustment Center. I went from Palm Hall, which is the same thing as Chino, and then I went to San Quentin and spent about the better part of three years in the Adjustment Center. I had to sue them to get out of there, since we hadn't done anything to earn isolation. Everybody's in there for killing other prisoners or doing something seriously bad on the mainline. And we hadn't done shit; we hadn't committed any offenses yet. I think I got busted with a joint one time, but I didn't even get a DA referral. But the guy next to me was Geronimo Pratt. Geronimo got busted with a joint, and he actually had a trial. So again, there's that white skin privilege. That was at the Adjustment Center at San Quentin.

Then ten years later, the second time, I was at Sacramento County Jail, DVI [Deuel Vocational Institution] in Tracy, and I did the rest of my time at CSP [California State Prison] Solano in Vacaville, California.

Because they always came down hard on us, that opened the door for us to respond. And they really weren't ready for us. First of all, they didn't know how to deal with anybody who went pro-per ["in propria persona," to represent oneself]. And they allowed us to have cocounsel of our choice. I was interviewing some of the best lawyers in the world who wanted to come work for free for me as my backup counsel, as my cocounsel, with me running

2. Russ Little and Joe Remiro were Bay Area radicals and early members of the SLA who were captured and given life sentences for the 1973 murder of Oakland schools superintendent Marcus Foster. Little was retried and acquitted of the murder in 1981, but, as of 2023, Remiro remains incarcerated, denied parole more than ten times, the final SLA member to remain behind bars. Emily Harris was Bill's codefendant and wife at the time.

my own case. Imagine that. No lawyer would do that today. But because they were going to come down on us so hard, and because we were all educated, and because we had good lawyers that we got to help us . . . I mean, check it out, I was my own lawyer for a year, and I had Leonard Weinglass for my cocounsel because he was representing my wife.[3] What a deal!

It was wild and crazy back then, really. There are so many things that gave us an edge. And when I got busted, it just so happened they [codefendants Russ and Joe] were on a change of venue in the LA County Jail, so when Emily and I got busted we got shipped to LA right away to get us away from [Patty] Hearst because the Hearsts were trying to sever her off and get her a good deal. So, we ended up in the same jail with Joe and Russ down in LA. We ended up together, and, the next thing you know, they wanted to keep her [Emily Harris] across town in Sybil Brand [Institute], the county jail for women, and they got me in the Old Courthouse Jail. So, when I go pro-per, I tell them you've got to bring her over here every day. To solve that problem, they brought her and kept her in the jail with me. Back in the briar patch.

That's what really got me into the whole concept of the criminal justice system because I really had no plan to have a trial. I thought they were going to kill us, like they did our comrades in LA. I didn't even have a lawyer in mind to talk to when I first got busted. I couldn't afford a lawyer. Luckily, everything worked right. We got put together at a time where we could strategize, instead of being isolated and played off against each other.

I'd already been visiting, so I was mentally prepared. I knew what to expect, but it was more than I expected. But by knowing what I expected, it helped me navigate what I didn't expect. Plus, I had been in the USMC [United States Marine Corps] in Vietnam. The fucked-up racial drama in the military prepared me for prison.

Everything was just unique. Everything was hard just because it was us. Then, when we responded, they didn't have remedies for some of the stuff that we did, like going pro-per and things like that. The *Faretta* decision came down right before we were getting busted, which is the decision that allows you to be your own lawyer. Now most people would be foolish to do such a

---

3. Leonard Weinglass was a criminal defense attorney and constitutional law advocate. He represented many radicals over his long career, including the Chicago 7 defendants, the Cuban Five, whistleblower Daniel Ellsberg, White Panther Party chairman John Sinclair, political prisoners Kathy Boudin and Mumia Abu-Jamal, and many others. Weinglass died in 2011.

thing. But what could we possibly lose? We'd already been monsterized and Mansonized.⁴ So, when we become effectively involved in the court process in front of a jury, not some enigma sitting at the defense table, and we can handle the theater of the courtroom, we don't look so fucking crazy and weird and mean as everybody's portrayed us to be. And it really works to our advantage because the jury is going, wait a minute here, they told us that and it's really this. Why would you try to frame a guilty guy when you can just do it legit and probably win? That's how you end up with OJ [Simpson] and stuff like that.⁵

I had political contacts when I first came in. Otherwise, I was so totally out of pocket I wouldn't have survived five days. I was five foot and six inches, 145 pounds, hella good shape, but I was around these monsters, just huge fighters. Many of them are oddly twisted. Anyway, I was really lucky. I had great luck. I had a good reputation. I never fucking backed down. I never did the easy shit. I demanded that I get to relate to whomever I wanted to relate to, whether they be white, Black, Brown, Asian, or Indigenous. And I always got that privilege. That's huge. And I was consistent; nobody could ever say that I took a side. They knew my politics were that I was antiracist, but when things are going on politically, that's how we unify to get guards' boots off our necks. I was one of the few people who could handle that. There weren't many white guys doing that shit. Most white prisoners were too scared to go that direction; it's too isolating and dangerous, and maybe they wouldn't survive taking those stands.

It's funny, even while I already knew people in the prisons and visited, I assumed that there were much more solid individuals, more people of integrity, in prison than there really are. I learned right away that's just not true. And then, as a private investigator who [subsequently] worked on a couple hundred criminal cases, who's read hundreds of incident reports, I learned that most everybody talks to the police. Everybody's fucking talking to the man! This was a big change because, before, you didn't do that. The criminals that are successful, they understand the arena. They know they're

---

4. "Mansonized" is a reference to Charles Manson and his Family, a California-based cult, many of whose members were convicted for the brutal murders of nine people in the summer of 1969 with the intention of causing a race war. Manson's involvement in these murders received unprecedented international attention. He died in prison in 2017.

5. OJ Simpson is a former football player and actor who was acquitted in an internationally publicized trial of the 1994 murder of his ex-wife, Nicole Brown Simpson, and her friend, Ronald Goldman, in Los Angeles.

going to get busted. They know they have to have an exit strategy. They know they have to have a bondsman. They have to have a lawyer they can work with. They know they're gonna get busted because, first of all, they're not a mystery to anybody. The cops know about them—they're mostly just getting by because the cops aren't good enough to catch them. But they're going to, even if they have to make shit up, so they have to be ready for it.

Nowadays it's not like that. Guys don't know what they're going to do once they get busted, they just don't have a clue. Another thing that made it easy for me was that I understood the criminal justice process, and so I was really an asset. Like lawyers going to prison, nobody's going to get nasty with that lawyer because he's got value, because he can do legal work for people inside prison. He can actually train and help other people figure out shit. So, in my case I wasn't a lawyer, but everybody knew I got myself out of shit. I should have been buried under the prison, and I'm not. I'm in prison for a while, but I'm going home. That's always valuable, somebody telling the truth about what to do. So that made it easier as well.

We fought back, and we fought in every way we could. We had nothing to lose. So in that way it really worked to our advantage. We wore them down to the point where they couldn't do what they originally tried to do. And now there was a trend, and so it became scary in a way, if you're the district attorney who's getting approached by these powerful backdoor motherfuckers, and at the same time sees that we're prevailing in some of these cases that we should lose. Part of it is because we're charming, the jury likes us, and we're not acting crazy in the courtroom in front of the jury. We save that for when the jury is gone. I could antagonize the fuck out of the judge when the jury wasn't there. The DA used to hate that shit because I would be obstreperous when there's no jury there, and then I'd be very charming when the jury's there, and they had no idea what an asshole I could be. We had literally nothing to lose. It was a gift almost to be able to proceed that way. Now, if I was Bobby Seale, I'd have been bound and gagged and kicked out of court.[6] I got beat up a few times in court, but I never got totally banned from the courtroom.

---

6. Bobby Seale cofounded the Black Panther Party in Oakland, California, in 1966; was a defendant in the infamous Chicago 8 case following the police riots at the 1968 Democratic National Convention; was charged but ultimately acquitted in the New Haven Black Panther trials in 1970; and ran an unsuccessful campaign for mayor of Oakland in 1973. He continues to be active and influential as of 2023.

It was an easy transition for us; we weren't youngsters. I was thirty when I got to the pen. It's different than being a kid, and it's different if you've got people that you know in there, even if they're not your race, because that's always a challenge. I was pretty much a "gang of one" the whole fucking time, and I had serious enemies who definitely wanted to kill my ass, people who were in league with the guards and who were white nationalists in one form or another. That was a challenge.

It was both hard and easy. They make it hard, but we had advantages, so it could have been way worse. I know a few white guys for whom white privilege didn't help them all that much. Because if you don't choose to ride with the whites, you're on your own; it doesn't matter. The Blacks aren't going to back you necessarily. They're going to admire you from afar and say this is one crazy peckerwood here. He's cool, but he's crazy. It's a challenge. You've got to be really on your toes to maintain your principles.

You know what prepared me for prison more than anything else? Vietnam. The USMC and Vietnam prepared me for prison because that was worse. That was actually worse. I got to Vietnam in June of 1966. Imagine this. It's June 1966. So, the beginning of the second year of us being there in great numbers. I'm in the Marine Corps, and there's not that many guys, a much smaller force than the army. They were desperate to get people, so they even came up with a two-year enlistment, and they started snatching people out of the criminal courts in the big cities.

Back then nobody knew anybody that went to jail. The prisons had hardly anybody in them. It was long before fucking mass incarceration. Back then, they didn't see prisoners as an asset or prisons as a way to make money. You had to spend money to keep people locked up. As a matter of fact, in some states, particularly in California, being Black didn't get you sent to the penitentiary. It got you sent to the county jail. You filled up the county jail, but it was mostly white guys, a few Mexicans, and Blacks in the prisons back before the 1960s. There weren't that many people in because they had to spend a lot of money on you. Even now, you could send a guy to Stanford for the same cost of keeping him in fucking prison every year. So go figure.

When I was in Vietnam, it was worse than prison because there was all the self-segregation. There's all kinds of race drama, because most of the white guys are from the South, and most of the Black guys got sent to Vietnam because of some court case where the judge gave them an offer before they even got arraigned. You could do two years in the Marine Corps or one year in County. Take your choice. So, I'd say eight out of ten Black guys that I met, who were from mostly major cities in the US, had that option. They're just as disgruntled as any draftee. And, on top of this, it's the middle of the Civil Rights Movement, which was on the television for everyone to witness. Most of the military bases are in the South, and so there's all this great racial tension anyway, and everybody's armed to the fucking gills. So, if you think prison is gnarly, those casual companies were the shits man, because there were fucking murders and shit all the time. I was a gang of one because I couldn't ride with the white supremacists. And I wasn't Black or Brown. So, I got grudging respect from some cats, but I didn't have real comrades.

So, I was prepared for prison. I'd felt I'd already been there, I'd seen how bad that could be, and Vietnam was really much worse. I was twenty-one and scared as shit. I never was as scared of the Vietnamese as I was of the fucking Marines. I got shot at more times by Marines, not counting mortars and shit. I wasn't a grunt, so I wasn't in the bush all the time. And I wouldn't have volunteered for that shit because I already was an antiwar person before I left Vietnam. I quickly and seriously became antiwar while in Vietnam.

Because of the time, they hadn't really prosecuted many middle-class or lower-middle-class, educated white revolutionaries. They'd been dealing with Blacks most of the time, and other people of color. They hadn't caught any of the Weather Underground [people] yet. We didn't get tortured with cattle prods like those cats, like the Panthers and the BLA revolutionaries who got busted in New Orleans. We always thought they were going to do all that shit to us, but they never did. White skin privilege really is a big deal. It was very obvious to me that we got treated differently, but part of it was because there was so much notoriety that they didn't want to get caught fucking around.

I got beat up there a number of times by sheriff's deputies and a court bailiff, but we found ways to move it to our advantage. Really, if you've read the books on how to struggle with power, if you've got some insights into it, there are ways to maneuver. And besides, they didn't separate us that well. To save them money and to make it easier to control us, they put us all together. That's the only time I've ever heard of political prisoners getting their own little space during that time we were in LA, which made it easy because we mostly won all of our cases there. It made it easier for us to navigate the system. And we had the privilege of getting a lot of lawyers wanting to help us. And we were in California; we weren't in some other fucked-up state where the criminal justice system is horrific. So, we benefited anyway, and it made it easier for us to win, made it easier for us to get to the point where they wanted to deal our cases out. It didn't hurt at all that the whole Hearst empire was also behind this, in a kind of back-assed way, because to help her their efforts also helped us. So it was easier to navigate a cruel, unfair system.

Reagan was governor of California when the SLA started. Jerry Brown got elected right after we got busted, which didn't help because the FBI came up with a COINTELPRO move right away, saying that we were going to kidnap [Brown's] sister and a busload of prison guards' kids at Folsom to get Geronimo [Pratt] and a whole bunch of other people out of prison. They did a lot of things trying to set us up, but it never worked. The good thing was we weren't on most prisoners' bad sides, even though they tried to put us on the white supremacist enemy lists. They tried so many ways to set us up with prison gangs and stuff like that.

But part of the deal is sometimes in prison it's not a good idea to come in with a high-publicity profile. If you're just an individual and you get a lot of spectacular news, you get a lot of people not liking you just for being in the news. Prison's a petty-assed place when you really get down to it, in a lot of ways. I could give you a balance sheet with a lot of cool things and a lot of fucked-up things. Basically that's the deal with prison. I don't mean to denigrate prisoners, generally I'm for almost all of them because locking human beings up isn't my thing. I'm not for that, there's other remedies to putting people in cages.

They just made it so much easier for us. In 1974, 1975, 1976, the things that we did to defend ourselves were often cutting-edge things; we could try stuff because we didn't have anything to lose. In the beginning, they weren't cutting us any breaks; our offers were life without parole. They tried to give us the death penalty when there wasn't even a death penalty right at that moment. They were trying to figure out ways to do that, but they couldn't. Then, luckily, when we got busted, the legislature was already in the process of passing a new sentencing law, which totally benefited us. We went from ten-to-life in all of our cases to fixed terms because of a change in the law, not because of anything we did. If it was about us, it never would have happened. But we just rolled along with the tide, which really benefited us totally.

We used all these things to our advantage just to fuck with them and make it hard for them, and it worked out because we picked up on how the criminal justice system works a lot quicker than the average person does. But we were all older too. I had two university degrees already by that time. All of us have been to college somewhat, except for [SLA member Donald] DeFreeze, so we were quick studies on how to challenge the criminal justice system.

We were active. Russ, me, and Geronimo were the voices of unity and reason. I didn't go to prison to radicalize the prisons. First of all, I'm a white dude; I'm not running anything in there. I'm not really with any of the white dudes. They'd have to be radical white guys like me. There were a few of those guys. There were some guys that left the Aryan Brotherhood. They had a lot of swastikas and ink all over their bodies, but now they were allied more with the Blacks than with the racist whites.

In the hole at San Quentin, the yard was a segregated situation. The Blacks had their own yard, but the BGF [Black Guerrilla Family] ran it.[7] There were some cats on the yard like Geronimo, who weren't in the BGF and who'd been in the [Black Panther] Party, and he was one of the guys training the BLA originally, who could be independent. But that always was an issue. Gangs want you to be in their gang; they need bodies. So, somebody like Geronimo, not being in a gang, he had to be concerned about treachery just like we were. Our yard group was me and Russ, the two SLA guys, and then the Aryan Brotherhood (AB) and the Mexican Mafia were on one yard together.[8] So, their enemies were our allies. There was a gang from El Paso called the Texas Syndicate (TS), which was mostly locked up in the hole at San Quentin because there were fewer members than the guys from Southern California.[9] We were even an international yard; we even had one

---

7. The Black Guerrilla Family is a Black prison-based organization started by imprisoned intellectual George Jackson in 1966 in San Quentin prison in California. The BGF remains fairly prominent in prisons as of 2023, though is much less political than when initially founded.

8. The Mexican Mafia is a Mexican-American crime syndicate that originated in the 1970s and has become one of the most feared and most dangerous of those operating in 2023.

9. The Texas Syndicate is a Mexican-American crime syndicate established at Folsom Prison in California in 1978. TS is active both inside and outside of prisons, and its membership is primarily Mexican immigrants.

gnarly old Black guy who had killed a bunch of guys in prison and refused to join the BGF. So, everybody's afraid of him. But he told the organized Blacks to go fuck themselves. He was an independent, so we invited him to our yard so he could be outside. We took anarchists; we had an anarchist from Argentina who was a bit of a total lunatic. He tried to jump over the double fence to get in the yard just to have a talk with the Aryan Brotherhood because he wanted to convince them that they were wrong about racism. It was weird.

So, the difference between the first term and second term: The first term, it wasn't as crowded, didn't have as many people. Second term, it was horrible. It was during the peak of mass incarceration, before they started changing a little bit. It was very overcrowded. Three guys in triple bunks, and shit like that in dorms. I was always in more-restricted housing during my second term. I always had higher custody because of my background, but it also afforded me to have single cells almost the whole first term, for almost eight years. Single cells were not uncommon when there were only twenty thousand guys in the system. Back then there were just eleven institutions [in California]. They built like twenty more within the next twenty years. So, the second time around, there were no programs. I was lucky to get a job, and then that ended too. I was there during the time they fired prisoners from prison jobs. Then most people were just locked down all the time; it was just horrible. No school, and it was really hard to do self-study. You couldn't even work that out.

They tried to make it hard for me, and there were several years when I didn't know if I was going to make it through the next day, but I did. Overall, I was pretty lucky a lot of the time, and it was good to have a solid reputation. We made so much noise that it was not lost on anybody in the prison who the fuck we were. I wasn't really a targeted person. The only times I ever got really close to having to defend myself seriously, somebody always intervened and told the dumbasses to back off, that it was not in their interest to do that. Without me even asking, without me even doing anything. Really, I shouldn't ever have gotten through this. But it helped because there were a lot of people who admired me. Here's the thing, remember this: we didn't get paid. We didn't do this for money. The prisoners think we're insane. And in prison, you don't fuck with crazy people. Crazy people you leave alone because you never know what they're going to do. So, we got labeled as crazy people because we didn't do it for money. Most of us got killed. It could have been way worse, and it just wasn't because things fell into place. I don't want to ever do it again; it was horrible in so many ways. It's mostly lonely in there, but loneliness just makes you aspire to get out.

It was horrible the second time. Thank god I only had a fixed term; I didn't have to go to the board or anything. I was going to get out. The prisons were overcrowded, prisoner politics were gone, and it was like all for one and one for one. The guys like me, they just kept to themselves; they didn't make any effort to try to change it. It was too daunting. As soon as somebody stepped up, they got stabbed, they got narked. It was horrible.

I had to keep my independence, and that was hard. I got to Solano after being locked down for a couple weeks while they tried to figure me out. I got on the yard, and right away I ran into two guys I'd been in with twenty years earlier. They were lifers, and they were African American. They're doing indeterminate life, and they're still there two decades after I'd left. They've got nobody advocating for them, and they've got shitty lawyers doing their parole hearings that they don't choose or can't afford. After kicking it with them for an hour catching up, I was told I couldn't hang with the Blacks.

I think what shocked me the most was how many rats there are and how many untrustworthy prisoners and collaborators there are. It was worse the second time around. Before I went to prison, I had this notion that there was a certain amount of honor among convicts. But there really isn't, because these guys are desperate. A lot of cats in the underworld have gotten by talking with the man every time they get busted. Out of thousands of cases I've worked on, I swear I've only had a couple of clients who just said, "Take me to my cage, fuck you, I'm not talking to you." Everybody thinks they can say something to get out of jail. It's unusual for people not to cooperate. That's what I learned, and it was reaffirmed when I became an investigator. Fortunately, when we were forming the SLA, we had contact with convicts, but none of the convicts knew what we were up to (unless we were planning to bust a certain guy out). They didn't know about the SLA; they were as shocked as everybody else. They didn't have anything to do with the formation of it or anything. They had influences on some of our perspectives, and we had their backs in any way that we could, but we didn't trust them. They were in prison. They had a reason to cooperate, and if we'd have been in that kind of situation with them, we'd have probably been busted right away.

The thing about prison, there are no whodunits in prison. In prison everybody knows who committed any murders. You pretty much know in the beginning who's probably responsible just based on who the victim is. But it's not unusual for gangs to contract with their enemies to make it look like their enemy did something rather than themselves when they're trying to rub out one of their own. There's all kinds of treachery that goes on when dope is involved and certain payments are made.

If you've got any kind of organizational abilities, you could organize a prison to be a place where people get on with their lives, where all this internecine bullshit is not even happening, regardless of politics. If they're trying to lower the population in prisons, they get bogged down with trying to figure out which so-called nonviolent offenders they want to let out. To be honest with you, many of those guys are not the ones who I'd immediately choose to get out of prison. I would let the guys who have done a bunch of time for murder out first. In fact, you'd be better off in the community if the killers came home and moved into your neighborhood rather than the nonviolent offenders because many of the nonviolent offenders are addicted to narcotics, and they're fucking professional thieves. Meanwhile, the guys that have been convicted of murder, most of them have done one murder in their fucking life, and it was some kind of crime of passion. Now they've had years to introspectively go over all this shit in their mind, and the only way they can get out is to take programs and get their life together.

I don't support endless punishment. I don't support caging most humans. If you've got time to get a vocation, to maybe finish some of your education if they have these kinds of programs, that's all it takes. You don't need a whole bunch of prison time. I don't even know if you need *any* prison time on most crimes. Guys are doing way too much time in there, and most of the shit they did was when they were young, and now they're older, and they're not that guy anymore. Most people, if they have been to prison or even done a little time, they would come away thinking most people don't need to be in there. They need to be out here getting their lives together, and they need to have had opportunities to do that while they were in prison, which they used to do, and it can be done again.

Politics and Prison Dynamics

I never had to do anything I regretted. I usually struggled to calm shit down, and that usually worked. Generally, here's what I find: psychopaths like violence, but really most people would just like to avoid it, and people avoid violence like crazy inside prison. You'd be surprised. When you consider who's in prison and what violence they may have committed in their lives, the amount of violence in prison isn't all that remarkable compared to the violence in the streets. So what I found is, if there are other remedies to solving conflicts without violence, prisoners are happy to do that because it makes their lives easier. Violence on the street you can escape from; in prison you've got to stay there in the middle of it.

There's so much racism, obviously. You've got blood feuds that go back all the way to the middle 1960s and beyond. It's complicated, but, generally speaking, I find that guys are able to accept, maintain, and sustain much better living circumstances given the opportunity. It's not human nature to be violent; it's survival to be violent. A lot of times you don't have to go there. It's helpful when there's people like myself, Russ Little, Geronimo Pratt, who were good at calming shit down, figuring out ways to make everybody happy. How does everybody come out of this whole? It's the whole restorative concept.

We learned really early, because we had a lot of connections, that it was possible to elevate your quality of living in prison by using your head, without compromising your principles. You had to figure out who to talk to among the convicts to get jobs somewhere. And, back then, prisoners ran the prisons, basically. They had all the jobs. The prison wouldn't run without the prisoners. So there was a lot of supervision, but there weren't that many guards. Not like now.

In a lot of the places, there was an effort on the part of the different racial groups to keep shit down because it just made it impossible to make a living, or to get visits or to do what you wanted to do. Usually the violence was stuff that was well earned by the victim and contracted. Say the whites didn't want to kill one of their own, or not be known to have killed their own guy, they may contract with some other group to do it to make it look like they did it. But they didn't lock everybody down back then. They didn't use collective punishment as much. There weren't mass riots, per se. Occasionally, there was some race drama. I remember right after I got to San Quentin, in the honor unit in San Quentin, a bunch of bikers (could have been Hells Angels but it could have been some other biker gang) attacked some guys from the Nation of Islam, and four white guys got killed. They started it, and they got killed, and the Black guys that they suspected to be involved, they went to the hole. That was the kind of people who I was around. But they didn't lock down the whole fucking prison forever. They might lock down that unit for a while until they figured it out, but it wasn't like all this mass shit going on. Usually there was always some kind of logical reason why shit would happen. It wasn't on the mass scale that it became later.

Usually the people who like to talk a lot of shit about rats and pedophiles and rapists in the prison are usually those people you need to look at as being one of those people. That's creating an illusion because you're worried about yourself. It's mostly treacherous; all that shit about *omertà*. We had issues with gangs that emulated gangsterism. All for one and one for all. Gang leaders often cooperated with the guards and administration if they got a benefit (i.e., dope).

I was very clear, and everybody knew what my politics were. But the thing that saved me from being killed was that I was generally respected by most other prisoners for sticking to my principles and not aligning with any gang. We're all here. We're in the same gang basically, whether we like it or not. They're the ones that are keeping us here; we aren't keeping each other here. There's way more of us than there are of them.

But when it comes to fighting for our rights and our privileges and making what they call privileges our rights, that's our fight. There are some people on the outside that help us, but if we're not unified on these issues inside. . . There's more unification now than before, but it's flimsy. We do things differently here: we don't have special prisons for political prisoners. We dump all our political prisoners in with everybody else. It would have been easier for us if we had our own unit just for political prisoners. That would have been great—simpler and easy. We probably would still have some drama because we'd have commies and nationalists and anarchists, this and that. They're not on the same page most of the time. That was our whole point: trying to get everybody to come together made sense.

I learned this early: I don't need any more fucking enemies. I've already got enough with the administration and guards, and a few of these nuts that don't like the fact that I had Black comrades. Too fucking bad. I'm not changing that for you. I don't care. I'm not going to live here knowing that I compromised those politics just because you guys outnumber me. Even though I was on my own, a gang of one, I got a lot of respect for that.

The first time I was in general population, they threw me in with a bunch of Black guys, thinking I was going to get my ass kicked. It was funny, I mean, one of the guys in my tank was a guy I used to visit at San Quentin. And he's one of the leaders of the BGF. It always turned out easy for me; it was always serendipitous for me. I had good luck. At the bleakest times when some crazy shit happened, I'd get my ass saved, without even having to compromise a principle. I never had a fight in twelve years. Imagine that. And mostly in general population.

Regarding violence from deputies and guards, for me it only happened in the jails but not in prison. I stopped fighting with them by that time. I got tired of that shit. I always got beat up. Many years later, I've had guards ask me if I remember them. I'd say no and they tell me, "I got paid a lot of money after we beat your ass because we all claimed injuries. We all said we got beat up by the SLA!"

If I were Black, I'd be dead. I wouldn't have made it to prison. No question about it. It's phenomenal how that works because it wasn't like we had fans in the criminal justice system at all. They hated our guts and tried to kill us various times. It's just hard when you got all this notoriety, you know, they'd think, "I'm going to lose my job if I get caught." They always had to rely on other prisoners to try to do it for them. I had plenty of enemies among the racists, but in general the prisoners weren't my enemies. I wasn't about that, and I had a history of not being about that. So smart people got it; some dumbasses didn't.

Russ, me, Geronimo Pratt, we were among a handful of people in the hole at the San Quentin Adjustment Center. And Jalil Muntaqim, he was my next-door neighbor. I was with him in the Alameda County Jail and also in San Quentin for a while. The BLA and us, we were comradely. They were the most political of the Blacks. They weren't in the BGF. They weren't a prison gang. They were ex-Panthers who got kicked out of the party by [Huey] Newton back in 1969 or 1970 and eventually formed the BLA. Nuh [Washington] wasn't with us. They had some separate cases. I was never with Nuh, but he was with Joe at Folsom, however. But we were with the cats that got arrested in New Orleans, who shared the hole at LA County with Joe Remiro, me, and Emily for a while. It was Herman Bell, John Bowman, and Ray Boudreau.[10] We got a chance to meet each other for the first time while doing time, since they were operating on the East Coast and we were on the west coast. These cats knew that we formed at a time, we kind of jumped off somewhat prematurely, but it was largely to kind of open another front since they were the ones getting attacked the most. Blowing up bathrooms and shit in Washington, DC, wasn't getting the fucking FBI off the Panthers at all. So, we decided okay, let's get their attention, and we did. And they appreciated that, so they always had our back. We were always cool with them. It was a perfect match because they respected us because they knew we were putting it all on the line, that we were probably going to die. So, they respected that shit, and we got along just fine. The second time I did time was at Solano. None of the Panthers I used to know were there ever. I was pretty isolated. I met a couple guys I trusted. One is the cat from Venceremos who was with me, Bob Seabock.[11] He had been in prison for a long time when they were accused and convicted of killing a prison guard.

I corresponded with people, though, including Ed Mead. He's a fantastic one. He'll go down in my memory as one of the all-time greatest, most interesting guys. He did all kinds of radical shit, man. Ed Mead was state-raised, started out, I think, parlaying car thefts into life sentences, almost. Even before he got political, he was a bit of a rebel. It was always hard for him to go along with the program. But he did a bunch of time and got out right around the time all this stuff was jumping off, and he actually came down to the Bay Area trying to find us, to sign up, which was impossible by then. By the time I'm busted, [Ed and members of the George Jackson Brigade were] busted for a bank robbery up in Seattle, and we started corresponding. He'd done time all over, in Alaska and all kinds of fucked-up places. He'd done a bunch of time at McNeil Island and Walla Walla [both in Washington State]. So, he gets sent back to Walla Walla essentially doing life in the state prison and thirty-five years in federal prison. So Ed and I corresponded, and the

---

10. Herman Bell, John Bowman, and Ray Boudreau were members of the San Francisco 8.

11. Venceremos was a revolutionary organization active in the Bay Area in the late 1960s and early 1970s. Members were primarily Chicano and advocated armed self-defense, community education, and prison reform, amongst other things. Seabock was a Venceremos member who received a life sentence after being convicted of a 1972 murder of a prison guard.

thing about Ed that was really fascinating to me was, they got busted in this bank robbery, they got convicted of murder of a comrade who was killed by the police, so they got a vicarious liability homicide for that, which gave them life in state prison, and back then there was no murder statute in the federal system.

So, Ed Mead goes back to prison at Walla Walla. His comrades were a number of women, some lesbians. His politics were thoroughly anti-sexist and so forth, imagining what that might be like in 1975. Ed was not a half-stepper or a pretender. So, he gets to Walla Walla, and he has at least one comrade with him; I think it was Mark Cook. Anyway, so they're there, and some other guys get into reading political theory, and Ed was a big proponent of that. He was writing publications from inside. He formed this group called Men Against Sexism. And he came out as a homosexual, but I think he was just bullshitting, you know what I mean. I don't know if it's real or not; maybe he's bisexual, I don't know. The point is, he pointed out "I'm homosexual" to say we're going to protect anybody that people are pressuring for sex. All you have to do is come with us and we will protect you, and if they keep fucking with you, we're going to blow them up in their cell. Well, they all ended up in the hole, obviously, because of all this drama that had commenced. But I thought that was the boldest move of anybody I've ever heard of. That is really putting it out there in a prison setting. He's one of the more interesting cats that I've ever come across, for sure.

Corresponding with people made it easier, and it helps to have friends. If you're isolated, it's really a challenge. It's hard to do; you have to clique up almost to save your own ass. But I didn't have to do that. I saw right away how you get respect in prison without challenging anybody's manhood. I already had a good reputation with most people. It's like at least this guy had something to believe in. When people operate on their beliefs, no matter what anyone says, they get respect for that. When they don't back down, when they stick with the politics, in spite of being captured or whatever. I never presented a defeated individual. Some of it is just general male machismo. But the one thing I was never going to do if I was captured, which I didn't expect to happen, was to put a coat over my head. I think the first picture of me is me being dragged into the courthouse for my first appearance. There's a great photo of me cuffed in the front with my raised fists. I needed people to feel positive, and I always felt like I had a reputation to uphold, which was another thing. But I was good with groups in prison, the anarchists in particular. I got letters from all over the world from comrades.

It's hard to do time without becoming an abolitionist. I am not a supporter of locking people in cages.

Looking Forward

I was privileged: I always had visitors, I always had money, and I had people supporting me from all over the world both times I was imprisoned. My family never had to do shit for me. I had other people handle that. I had people sending me books, and I just mostly read books and wrote letters.

Outside support is invaluable. I got involved in prison support early on. I didn't communicate with prisoners or visit prisons until I got to California, but that was just a few years before all the SLA drama jumped off. I got hooked up with certain guys in prison. We got selected to go see certain people because most of us were white and most of them were not. So that's already an issue. You just can't send any old motherfucker that the guy can't relate to. It has to be somebody that's fairly conscious already. You're taking a risk; you're trying to build trust. But when you're in prison, you don't have much choice if you don't have family or friends outside visiting you.

Support's everything, man. I was extraordinarily privileged to have lots of it. We had so much support that we sent people to help other guys who had none. For instance, when the [National Lawyers] Guild came out with that "No Lawyers for the SLA," Stuart Hanlon, who was a young, brand-new lawyer at the time—in fact, he was finishing up his third year when the Guild came out with that—he immediately got involved in helping Joe and Russ, volunteering to work on their case for free as an intern.[12] And they told him that we really appreciate it, but you need to go see Geronimo Pratt because he needs somebody like you right now. So, he ended up working with Geronimo for twenty-seven years and eventually got him out. We had the privilege of being able to send people to help other people because we knew how important it was. We had people knowing what was happening

---

12. Stuart Hanlon is a radical attorney based in San Francisco who has defended former BLA political prisoner Geronimo Pratt, as well as former members of the SLA.

to us, and it was getting out, it was being published in the underground newspapers every day. So, you could find out what really happened in court. And we were our own lawyer, so we were getting lots of visits, and you could come talk to us, and we would help folks know what was happening to us. We were in the most privileged of positions, considering how it is for most folks fighting cases and doing time.

The government was too nervous to do to us what they'd already done to some others, like George Jackson. Or like they did to the RAF in Germany. When they tried to kill us, when they killed everybody [in the SLA safehouse] in LA because it was thought that Hearst was actually in the house, that really did it for Randolph Hearst trusting the FBI.

To fight for ourselves, as the SLA did, being abandoned by the left, the organized left, was hard. They had the leaders, the main Marxist-Leninists of the left, denouncing us, from Dennis Banks and Russell Means, the AIM leadership, to Angela Davis and Bruce Franklin.[13] They got all these people to denounce us and try to get us to release her [Patty Hearst]. We were kind of the bastard stepchildren of the left for a while. But it actually worked to our advantage because people that helped us, they didn't give a shit about politics. It was solidarity. And it didn't hurt us that they'd [the government] murdered six of our comrades already, and people had seen it on TV. That was to let people know that this is what we're going to do to you if you get out of line. Do this radical shit, and this is what happens. That was not lost on folks. I've even had two prison guards, two Black guys, come up to me and thank me and say "if you need anything, let me know because I was a little boy standing in line for food, and I appreciate all that you did."[14] It's not lost on all kinds of folks.

A lot of things have happened over the years that have changed, little things here and there. It used to be that prisoners had no voice. You had

13. Dennis Banks and Russell Means were Indigenous rights activists and leaders in the American Indian Movement. Angela Y. Davis is a prominent educator, activist, and former political prisoner who has advocated for liberation struggles around the world. H. Bruce Franklin is a scholar and activist who was involved in the Revolutionary Union and Venceremos, was terminated from Stanford University due to his antiwar protesting, and has always been an advocate for the incarcerated.

14. In February 1974, the SLA demanded that the Hearst Corporation undertake a massive food distribution program for people in need throughout California as a precondition for the release of the kidnapped heiress, Patty Hearst.

to write a book in prison, which was not easy to do, and get somebody to publish it in order to have a voice. And those people got jumped on; they got blocked at every turn. It took a movement, a minority prison movement, to have an impact. It's daunting because the average person thinks everybody in prison is some psychopath because all they ever know about is the most heinous of all crimes, and so everybody is a heinous criminal. To be able to enhance the voice of people in prison, so people can understand it without them getting locked up themselves, is a daunting task. And I've always been about that. That's why I chose to be a criminal defense investigator. That was the best thing I could do to help people, but it's on a small scale; I'm helping one person at a time stay out of prison.

Talk to somebody who's been there recently that's knowledgeable. Get a bead on it. I've often thought about getting paid a lot of money by white-collar criminals to help people learn about doing time. I don't see it as a money-making thing, though. I see it as a nonprofit kind of deal where everybody has access to it and they don't have to pay a lot of money to find out how to navigate prison. I think that's important, and I wouldn't mind doing it. For somebody like me to school a person who's about to go to prison on how to navigate prison is theoretically good for prisons too, because I'm trying to tell people how to get through prison without drama. Those of us who were political, more times than not, we would keep the drama down, and everybody would be satisfied. We weren't working with the man, because they need the drama to control us. They like the drama because they can lock us down, and they don't have to work as hard. Most people don't understand how this really works. It's counterintuitive since most prisoners don't want drama; they'd rather have their normal routine.

I did my time and kept my mouth shut. But I didn't keep my mouth shut when there were injustices going on. I stepped up on that, and I wasn't silent. I always advocated for prisoners and always tried to make our lives better in any way that I could. I figured the better it was for us, the more peace we would have. I came out with less enemies than I went in with, so I figure that's good.

I don't encourage anybody to learn what I learned the way I learned it. I don't want anybody to go to prison. More times than not, people who go to prison come out better than they were, if they set their minds to that. Some people are just so locked out of the economy that they'll never be able to be anything but a criminal of some kind. The options are not there. That's the deal. It's really not simple to deal with. If you give people opportunities to learn new things and get an education, they're captive audiences. Prison is so boring and fucked up, getting a chance to get a decent education, even online, would be something people would jump at, especially when they know they're getting out, and they're not being kept in there forever and ever and ever. We could have a prison system just like some of these European countries. And why not?

Jaan Laaman

Jaan Laaman was a member of the United Freedom Front who spent over four decades in prison. The group known as the Ohio 7—Jaan, Patricia Gros Levasseur, Barbara Curzi-Laaman, Carol Saucier Manning, Tom Manning, Ray Luc Levasseur and Richard Williams— were working-class revolutionaries charged with actions against US military facilities, recruitment centers, and corporate headquarters. These actions were done in solidarity with the people of South Africa and Central America, who were bearing the brunt of US imperialism. Jaan spent just over forty-five years in prison—thirty-seven years of which were spent in the federal system for his actions with the UFF— before being released on parole in May 2021. Jaan served time in various state prisons (including Attica immediately before the rebellion in 1971) and numerous federal prisons during his more than four decades of incarceration.

Prison Life

In 1972, I was captured and taken to trial for some anti–Vietnam War activities, specifically for bombing a Nixon reelection headquarters and the Manchester police headquarters. These were late-night actions targeting property only, not humans. Back then, New Hampshire was the first state to hold primary elections. It was the beginning of the presidential election season, and Nixon came up to Manchester, New Hampshire, to open up his first national reelection headquarters. He was met with a peaceful protest of over three thousand people—not just student activists and radicals but parents with little children were all marching. The newspapers directly quoted Nixon saying he did not want to see any antiwar protesters. So they ordered the cops to beat the people off the streets, even though they had a permit.

In the process, there was a young woman—hippie girl, as they were often called back then—a sixteen- or seventeen-year-old girl who was pregnant and was hit in the stomach by a police club and fell to the ground and aborted her fetus right there in the middle of the street. So, three days later, police headquarters was bombed, and Nixon's reelection headquarters was bombed. Unfortunately, I was arrested for that shortly thereafter, myself and another sister, and we were sent to prison. I did about seven years on that situation. I was originally given twenty years, but then I won an appeal, and I did almost seven years and got out in 1978.

As a youth, at first I lived in Boston, but then I spent a lot of my teenage years growing up in Buffalo, New York. Around seventeen, I was arrested for assault, kind of a fight with some guy—there was no political aspect to it or anything, and I did about twenty months in prison in New York State. In fact, it was there in New York State, as an eighteen-year-old in the prison system in 1966 and 1967, that I first started to develop any kind of consciousness about anything besides cars and girlfriends and hanging out on the corner—which, as a young teen, that's where my mind was at mostly. So, I started developing some political consciousness.

I got out at the beginning of 1968, and at first I went to Cornell, and then I went to the University of New Hampshire. Naturally, I was politically active in SDS, the Students for a Democratic Society, and antiwar activities and so on. When Kent State happened, there was a nationwide strike of students and young people across the country.[1] Literally, most universities and colleges were shut down. Hundreds and hundreds, at least, of high schools were also involved in it and were shut down. So, we shut down the University of New Hampshire, and the year ended with the school shut down. I was one of the leaders of the SDS chapter up there, and I got notified that my scholarship had ended. Not that it was being taken away for any political reasons but

---

1. The Kent State massacre was the killing of four unarmed Kent State University students and the wounding of several others by the Ohio National Guard on May 4, 1970. The students were protesting the expansion of the Vietnam War.

that it was being ended. So I went back to New York, and, when I went back to my old neighborhood, I saw lots and lots of activities going on.

Back when I was in SDS, we were working with the Black Student Union up there, and they were associated with the Black Panther Party. So we had contacts and coordinated activities and worked with both of them and the Puerto Rican independence movement, the Young Lords, things like that.[2] So when I got to Buffalo, I was surprised and pleased to see that there was both a Panther presence and a Young Lords presence in the city. There were also young people, mainly affiliated with the University of Buffalo, doing activism and organizing on the streets. So I got involved in that, especially in my own neighborhood, where a lot of the younger kids knew me. In that kind of neighborhood, if you'd done a little time in prison, people thought that you were someone that they should listen to. So, I went there and started telling them about revolution and the freedom struggle, of course.

We were quite successful in building some good multinational unity among the youth in the different neighborhoods and from different backgrounds. And, of course, also keeping up with the antiwar work. There was a big antiwar demonstration in Buffalo, and I spoke at the demonstration. It wasn't a spontaneous demonstration—there were permits, and there was a rally and all that. I spoke there, and about two days later I was arrested by the parole authorities because I was still on parole from the original youth act thing. I was arrested for public speaking in a public area, and I had five or six months left on the original youth sentence. So I was sent to Attica for public speaking in a public area, and I did about five months there as well.

That was before the [Attica] uprising.[3] And as I say to people often—totally seriously, not trying to sound like a wise guy or something—the reason why I'm here speaking to you is because I was released before the Attica uprising happened. I was released in May [1971], and in September

2. The Young Lords were a militant Puerto Rican independence party prominent in New York City and Chicago in the late 1960s and early 1970s that sought Puerto Rican self-determination and an end to US occupation of the island. They engaged in daring offensives and takeovers to highlight the oppression that Puerto Ricans and other communities continue to face.
3. The Attica Prison uprising occurred from September 9 through September 13, 1971, when prisoners took over part of the yard, held guards hostage, and demanded prisoners' rights and improved conditions. The prisoners were met with brutal and murderous violence from armed guards and police, resulting in authorities murdering thirty-three prisoners and ten of the guards who were being held hostage. This remains one of the most infamous prison uprisings in the US.

[1971] the Attica uprising happened. I'm sure that I wouldn't be here speaking today if I had been there because people were randomly shot and killed, but people were also targeted and executed! This has been proven. In particular, Sam Melville—a man I was very close to while I was in Attica—was seen alive by reporters and the negotiating committee, but after the uprising was put down by the cops and the prison guards, by gunfire, basically.[4] They just shot, wounded, and killed lots of people. But Sam was seen alive afterwards when they were clearing the yard one-by-one of individuals. People up and down the hallway who were part of this outside negotiating committee said, "Oh, there's Sam, he's here. He made it. He made it." Two days later, the county coroner up in western New York state released a list of all the people that were shot and killed, and Sam Melville was on that list.

Sam and I were close comrades when I was there. I mean, I wasn't there for a long time, but from the first day we met each other we were close. I, of course, knew who he was and had known about him and heard about him before. I told him about myself, as an SDS activist and all that. We just spent our time, when we had it, in the yard on a daily basis, talking, hanging around, and doing some political work together.

Of all the political prisoners I've met, from all the different areas of struggle and movements and so forth—the Black liberation struggle, the Puerto Rican independence struggle, Native American struggles for sovereignty and independence, the antiwar struggle, the anti-imperialist struggle, the labor movement, and also, in more recent years, the ELF and ALF, the animal rights and earth protectors, all these people, certainly the antifascist kids and all that—the one thing everybody knew and lived by and continued their life by was that being in captivity was a terrible thing. The busts, the specifics, the trials and impacts on families and friends, and all the rest of it are all serious, harsh, hard things. Being captured and then being thrown into captivity was just another front in the struggle. It didn't end the commitment, the need for, the desire to, or the urgency for activism and activity just because you were behind a prison wall. If anything, the need was there

---

4. Sam Melville was an anti-imperialist and antiwar militant who was responsible for several strategic and symbolic bombings in and around New York City in 1969. Due to an FBI informant, Melville was arrested and ended up at Attica Prison, where he was murdered by guards following the prisoner uprising in September 1971. There is a collection of his letters called *Letters from Attica* (Chicago Review Press, 2022).

even more because now you're also combining just pure survival struggle to stay alive.

Coming into the prison, first and foremost, certainly you had to get your bearings and see who's there, what's up, and all the rest of it. It's like you find yourself in another place and ask yourself, "How do we continue to struggle here?" When I left being a student in New Hampshire and went back to Buffalo and started doing community street organizing, many things changed, but the work and the commitment to the struggle and to the need for it wasn't impacted at all. Going in, the captivity was exactly the same situation.

I have never met one comrade yet who coming into prison somehow broke them or made them question who they were and what they were or the need to do the things they had been doing and that still needed to be done. It became a question of how do I continue to struggle here, and how do I survive here? What level of activity, what level of security, and just survival do I have to act on? And all those things, of course, change between being in captivity and not. But the basic need and continuation of activism as a freedom fighter, as a person involved in the freedom struggle, that always remains the same.

So the question becomes, What can I do here? What's most needed to be done here, and how can I be helpful in that? Who are the other people that I'm working with, and what are the other forces involved (besides, obviously, the enemy, the cops, the guards, the fascists)? Of course, when we're speaking about the reality of the prison struggle—certainly in this country, but also around the world—we're talking about fascism. We're not just talking about different rules but open fascism in and under what we all understand as a white supremacist, ideologically based, capitalist, and, more and more so, police state. The prison system is the harshest and most extreme part of that.

We [the United Freedom Front] were captured in November 1984. At that time, the underground movement in this country had been quite active and varied, from the Black Panther Party and the Black Liberation Army to other formations and anti-imperialist forces like the United Freedom Front, Red Guerrilla Resistance, the Puerto Rican independence movement, the FALN and Los Macheteros, various native struggles and issues. AIM, of course, was always a major organization, although they were not a clandestine organization.⁵ Underground activism had been not only prevalent but [also] significant from the middle to late 1970s through the middle of the 1980s, at least. So, one of the unfortunate realities was that there were quite a few underground revolutionary guerrillas in captivity.

When we were first captured, shortly afterwards, all my comrades, men and women, were sent to MCC New York in Manhattan, the federal pretrial detention place. It was a big high-rise, twenty-story building with cages built one on top of the other. At the time we were there, the New York 8 was there, Joe Doherty was there (the IRA man for whom Reagan changed some laws so he could be sent back to England), BLA people, FALN people, Macheteros people, they were all there.⁶ So, naturally, if we didn't know each other from previous places and times and struggles, we certainly knew each other there. It didn't matter what organization you were from, captured guerrillas always function and relate to each other as close comrades across the board and set up whatever structure might be needed to do the necessary things that had to be done. At MCC they put us in the highest security cellblock, and that's where they kept all the other guerrillas too. So, they put us all together, and that's the good part of it.

My codefendants and I went to trial for about five years, so that was kind of a drawn-out process. We weren't always at MCC, but wherever we were, in most cases, there were other political prisoners there too on other cases. So, there was always that. Once the trials finally ended, they dispersed us out to various federal penitentiaries. I, for example, got sent out to Leavenworth out in Kansas. When I got out there, I was greeted by people like Sundiata Acoli, Leonard Peltier, Bill Dunne. I mean, there were about a dozen political prisoners who had been there for quite a while. So, naturally, first and foremost, I stepped in with them, and they helped me acclimate to what's up, gave me a pair of sneakers and whatever else I might have needed to survive. Actually, because of my own history too, I ran into

5. The Red Guerrilla Resistance was a name used by people affiliated with the United Freedom Front and other militants to take credit for specific bombings carried out in the spring of 1984.

6. The New York 8— Lateefah Carter, Coltrane Chimurenga, Omowale Clay, Yvette Kelly, Colette Pean, Viola Plummer, Robert Taylor, and Roger Wareham—were Black revolutionaries arrested in New York City in October 1984. Together they faced over seventy-two conspiracy charges and were the first people held under the new federal Preventive Detention Law (No Bail Act). They were acquitted of all charges in August 1985.

other people who I [had] met in prison before, nonpolitical people, mob dudes and such.

You know, it's a shocking experience. After a while, it becomes the reality, and everything real in the streets becomes the unreal thing. It's a shocking reality. The cops, of course, hate you to some extent at least. They always have at least some concern and worry about political prisoners—maybe not fear but always concern and worry. And other prisoners kind of look at political prisoners a little differently, like, "Well, these guys are not just out there trying to make a dollar, selling some crack or robbing a bank. But they do stuff that is as serious as any other bank robber might do" and so on. So there was a certain amount of not really interest but a little curiosity about us, and they looked at us as pretty serious people and not someone to be checked and seen what they could get away with. Not that most people, even in prison, would do that, but there certainly are some that would. So, I never had a real problem entering a place and getting my feet on the ground and learning the ropes about that specific joint.

Being in captivity sucks, totally and fully. But that's not the point. The point is to keep up the struggle. The point is to do every day whatever the plan and strategy is to further the advancement of the freedom struggle. That's the point. If you have to do it within a not very nice environment, so be it. It's very important to deal with the physical reality of yourself—both as a person in captivity being held there by people who hate you and would just as soon kill or harm you as not—and the whole prison system and the guards. Also other people—everything from people with emotional problems, and there's certainly a lot in prison, and white supremacist elements and so forth.

So, the idea of maintaining yourself in a fit condition—because the food is bad, healthcare is impossible if it even exists—so you have to keep yourself together. You have to keep your physical self together, as well as your spirit, your mind, together. And they go hand in hand, as a matter of fact, because the more you are physically fit, and even beyond that just basic fitness, the more balance you have between head and mind, between body and mind, that helps as well.

So part of the regimen and routine of every prison I was ever in—and that includes many, many years of being locked up in control units or solitary confinement units where any movement is very restricted and impossible, really—you might get out for sixty minutes a day, five days a week or something like that; the rest of the time is spent in the cell. You have to figure out what to do, and that means different workouts, if you can. I used to be a runner (I've kind of got not-great knees these days, so I'm not running). But if I was in [general] population, that meant running, and that always meant some kind of daily workout routine.

They got rid of all the weights in the federal system years and years ago. But pull-ups, chin-ups, push-ups, different kinds of stretches and things like that. I found yoga to be really good, and I was teaching yoga classes inside the prison. You need to keep yourself physically fit and ready. That also helps with the overall mental outlook on things and your day-to-day life. So, that's real important. Staying focused on the struggle, keeping yourself fit, keeping your body and mind in balance, and you have to work on that every day.

No, I never lost hope. I mean, I never assumed that I would necessarily get out of prison alive, although my focus every day was to make sure I did. But inside you're always susceptible to illness, and then COVID hit, or any number of other possibilities. You just may not get to the end. You may not walk out that door. I didn't have a pessimistic attitude or think I'm probably going to die here. I did have a feeling like I'm going to get out of here, I will get out of here. And also, in particular, all my codefendants, at a certain point, were released. Except, of course, two of my codefendants, Richard Williams and Tommy Manning, who both died in captivity. So, I saw both the people who got released, which was most of us, and people who did not make it out. Those were the realities. I always had in my mind that I would get out. But if that was not to be the case, it wasn't something that disabled me mentally or physically. It just would be the reality.

I was always happy when I saw comrades—whether Ohio 7 comrades or other political prisoners—leave prison. When the Puerto Rican independence people, the FALN people, got released by Clinton in 1999, I was in Leavenworth at the time with Luis Rosa, a good comrade of mine.[7] We used to work out together and do all kinds of things together. He left that one morning after they were given their pardons, and that was certainly a wonderful day. So, those I think were certainly moments that you can think back on and reflect on.

---

7. Luis Rosa is a Puerto Rican freedom fighter who was a political prisoner for over thirty years due to sedition charges for his involvement in the FALN.

For the last four or five years that I was in captivity, my official job in the prison was teaching yoga classes in the recreation department. We pretty much set it up so we could do what needed to be done, and the cops didn't interfere with it. At the end of a good workout, I would teach and show and encourage the other men there to sit back and do a little sitting and meditating. In the course of doing that, even within that ugly, nasty prison situation, there was that moment of relaxation after a good, serious, nice workout. Just kind of clearing your mind, breathing, letting go of the ugly reality. Not letting go like it's gone, but letting go by not letting it harm you at this moment, right now, right here.

So there were many, many small, daily, but useful and powerful moments of being able to be yourself and maintain yourself. One of the things that you have to watch out for in captivity—certainly as a political prisoner but any prisoner, for that matter—is to not get overwhelmed by anger, by hatred, or by fear. Any of these things, not only are they harmful to you in the physical sense, but you yourself then become a tool of the harm that's being done to you. So you have to work against it. Don't be the tool that harms yourself. In fact, if anything, try to be the tool or the person or use the method that even within a very negative situation, you can breathe, you can let your body be as healthy as possible, under those conditions.

So that became almost a daily thing that I did, especially the last ten, fifteen years, I was more focused on things like that. And that's very important. It's very useful. It's very necessary. Even though physically you maintain yourself, you protect yourself, you continue to do your work—all good things—but it starts to hurt your spirit or your essence of who you are and how you feel and how you think and how you see and relate to other people. As much as possible, even in a very negative situation, you have to stay human, you have to stay as a human being in touch with humanity and the world, because that's really what the freedom struggle is all about. We're trying to allow people—the human race, poor and exploited and oppressed people—the ability to live positive and healthy and happy lives. So, in the process of doing that, in any situation, you've got to find ways to do that for yourself as much as possible.

But as far as physical activity goes, my basic point—and I would tell everybody this—the first point is always protect yourself. It doesn't matter who or what, whether cops or other prisoners, whatever. Always protect yourself, first and foremost. Beyond that, try to use your brain as much as possible. Try not to get into a situation that will, for sure, only harm you, even if physically you get through it. Eric King, a good young comrade of mine, is going to trial in Colorado next week [Eric King went to trial in Colorado in March 2022 and was found not guilty of assaulting a guard]. Three cops and a lieutenant assaulted him, and he's going to trial for assaulting a lieutenant. Those kinds of situations when you come into physical contact, conflict, or combat with an enemy inside a prison, you always have to protect yourself, but it's always going to come out against you in terms of rules, laws, more time, and all the rest of it.

On the family side, of course, when you're in captivity for decades, you lose family, and that certainly happened to me, as well as comrades and people you know. I mean, that's the reality. Whenever it happens, I think of my two comrades: my partner Richard, one of my oldest friends and comrades in this world, who died in 2005. And then Tommy Manning, who died in 2019. These were brothers, these were comrades, these were fellow guerrilla fighters of mine, and I miss them today, I miss them a lot. It's just hard, and it's just a reality that people—because of the bad food and horrible, horrible medical care—are dying every day in prison. People are dying in the US every day in prisons. And that includes good comrades and political prisoners. The worst situation of all, of course, is my son. My son died while I was in prison, back in 2011, and that's the worst part of it all.

The quality inside prisons got worse. I was in the federal system. In 1984, we got captured, and toward the end of 1988 I finally wound up in the system after the trials. It was that era, then and for the next ten years at least, when they were building prisons every month somewhere, and, as soon as the prison was opened, it was packed. It was the whole attack against the Black community, using crack and drugs and all that. Things in prison got worse on every level because more people were being thrown into already overcrowded prisons.

I mean, prison was never okay, but the overcrowding was nuts. Even as they were literally building prisons every month, new prisons were opening up for several years in a row. There were always more people they were trying to pack in than they actually had cells for. So double-celling, triple-celling, all kinds of different things, which makes the day-to-day reality of being in captivity even worse than just the fact of being there. So they got worse.

Along with everything else, food declined, and that was never okay to begin with. Medical care was always a big question too, and it just got worse and worse. I mean, every level from dental to medical. People died because they couldn't get *basic* care in time. So, yeah, things got worse.

I personally saw and/or was close to (not eyewitness saw, but I was nearby) many, many, many terrible things. Assaults by guards on people, beatings, people dying because medical didn't even respond to an emergency situation. Death and even murder and literal hunger. No medical care when a little medical care would have saved a life. I saw a lot of that at every prison I was in.

I'm certainly proud and glad, even more than being proud, of the assistance and support that I was able to provide for comrades that allowed them to get out of prison, other political prisoners at certain times. Oftentimes we had to do different things to make that all happen. I'm certainly very, very glad to see that support, and I'm proud of being able to provide what support I could.

I did certain things myself too. Way back in the 1980s and 1990s, there were still some programs that were available in the federal system, so I completed a couple of BA degrees and things like that. I was always happy to get that and proud to be able to do it. My mother was still alive at that time, and she was very happy, and that's always a good thing to make your mother happy.

Just on an individual level—and this is true especially with younger prisoners, sometimes with political prisoners—to be able to give them some guidance or advice as far as how to do the bid, not to let it eat you up, not to be consumed by that anger and hatred and so on. To do positive for yourself, which included things like let's go work out tomorrow morning and the day after and each day afterwards. Or let's come to the yoga class because it's not just for women out there. When I first started yoga class in prison, people said, "My wife does yoga out in the streets. This is a penitentiary. We don't do yoga here." And I'd say, "Yeah? Well I'm going to do some yoga here, so come on and check it out." Oftentimes, because it was me teaching the class and inviting them, they came, and then, next thing you know, we had twenty or thirty people in classes every day, sitting there meditating and getting the benefit of that. So I'm glad to have not only done that for myself but to have been able to give that opportunity to other people as well.

Politics and Prison Dynamics

Not to sound too righteous or something, but if there's an ethical point, an ethical principle, I mean, if it's real, if it's there, if it means something to you, you can't really go against it, you can't violate it, you can't disregard it. There were situations that developed in prison—and this continues today, and it's always there. Of course, society as a whole, an oppressive, capitalistic society, survives because its victims are kept at each other's throats or at least kept distrusting and disliking each other. That's the way oppressive societies operate and survive.

Certainly, in prison, in that environment and situation, that's taken up to even higher notches than we see outside. And what that means is, first and foremost, white supremacy–based racism, racial hatred against various people of color, or territorial beefs. We can't relate, we can't work together, we can't do something. That's the way the prison system operates. It keeps people at each other's throats, keeps people fighting each other, keeps them thinking more about each other than about the man that's locking the door on them every night. So, fighting against that is always a constant and ongoing struggle. I mean, that never ended.

Even if a certain situation would develop in a certain cellblock, in a certain prison, and you overcame that, people will get moved around, or new people will come in, and it's the same thing over and over again. So it was very important to have ongoing lines of communication, and that included what I consider really enemy elements, Ku Klux Klan types, Nazis, and these kinds of people. Now the individual white person who was identified as a Nazi, they might have some avenue or potential to question their thoughts. The ideology itself, and the structure that comes from that ideology, organizations, gangs and so forth, there's nothing to do with that, except make sure it doesn't harm anybody or you, or be the least disruptive of ongoing positive prison struggle and prison organizing.

The way I always tried to frame it was, first and foremost, we're all convicts. It doesn't matter what town you come from, it doesn't matter what race you are, doesn't matter what gang you're in, because all those divisions are the divisions that the cops use to keep us at each other's throats so they can keep all of us oppressed. Now, sure, they might give you and your gang a little extra leeway, let you sell drugs next month, but then two months from now they're going to come after you. They're going to take you to court, they're going to lock some of your guys up and give them more time. They're going to play that game of trying to pit one against the other. So, that was always something that had to be put out, put forth. There were times when convict unity was stronger and more understood, and there were times when it wasn't.

I was in conflict with guards pretty much every day. But in terms of physical conflict, as much as possible, that doesn't result in a winning situation. What I did for myself, my basic bottom line, and what I told everyone else I know and work with, is always defend yourself. There's just no two ways about it—always defend yourself. In most cases, not coming to a physical confrontation, whether with guards or other prisoners, is always the better solution than getting into that conflict. I'm not trying to sound like a tough guy or something, but my own situation, because I did always work out and I have been a martial artist my whole life and so forth, people looked at me as not necessarily being an easy situation if they came into conflict with me. Also, I always had other political prisoners and/or comrades that were close to me, and I was close to them. And that's important in prison, not to allow the cops themselves or some other prison element to isolate you. Especially negative, bullying, fascist elements, they're looking for some easy way to get to their goal or get over. And if they figure that it's not going to be easy or they might not even be able to do it, they probably won't.

Racism in prison is horrible, just like in society as a whole, but in prison it's more raw. In a way, prison in America is life in America—white supremacy and racism against people of African descent and other people of color and other nationalities. I mean, there was a time when the Irish were hated, not that long ago even. That's always been the method by which the system is able to maintain the divide and conquer. Racism in prison is more raw, more ugly, more present, in my experience certainly, than anywhere else on the streets of America. That is the reality; that's the bottom line.

Now within that reality, we have to figure out how to work, how to not only maintain and stay safe, but [also] how to advance the struggle. Even reformist issues like on the streets, same thing in prison. Sometimes you have to unite people just to make the food better because it's so bad. Sometimes you have to employ work strikes and different things like that around whatever issues, medical, food, or whatever. You have to find ways to deal with and talk to other people, other elements within the prison population, including white gangs or other types of gangs, nationalities and so forth.

A lot of prisons run by the home-boy system, like if you're from Boston, Boston is your homies. If you're not in an actual gang, then you relate to your hometown group and pretty much stand with them. Political prisoners are probably the exception because we relate to people from our hometown and so forth, but everybody knows that we stand uniquely on our own, always against the cops and always trying to do something that needs to be done.

Within the context of being in prison—and being in prison a long time (but even if it's not for a long time)—the best experiences and the best times are when you're with the people who you're close to, that you like, you admire, you might love, you certainly respect, and from whom you seek guidance and advice, and for me those have always been political prisoners. In my life, it's always been that. There was Leonard Peltier and Sundiata Acoli, Sam Melville and Eric King, Jamil Al-Amin, and many, many others.[8] Some, I'm glad to say, a good number, have actually gotten out. Some have passed. But those brothers, those comrades, were always my closest people and the people that made my days better—because we were there together, even in that ugly situation.

But I would say too that there's other people beyond the political prisoners whom I've met and befriended and been befriended by. I mean, I was cool with literally thousands of people inside over the years, but hundreds and dozens of people on a regular basis. But then some people—even in the prison situation, just like on the streets—sometimes you just make a friend. And I do have a small number of people like that, who weren't considered political prisoners initially, whom I consider good friends. Most are still locked up, but some have gotten out, and I was really happy to see that.

As much as possible, figure out ways to do at least some work in coordination and solidarity with each other. It's very important for the political prisoner inside, but it's also important for the struggle outside because the prison struggle is part of the overall struggle. Also, I mean, let's just look at

8. Jamil Abdullah Al-Amin, formerly known as H. Rap Brown, a civil rights and Black Power activist who was active with both the Student Nonviolent Coordinating Committee (SNCC) and the Black Panther Party, was given a life sentence in Georgia in 2000 for the death of a sheriff. As of 2023, he remains imprisoned.

our own lives and realities. If you're going to be involved in political struggle out in the streets, some of you all are going to get locked up. That's just the way it's going to be. So, that communication and contact is really important.

I was in the control unit in Massachusetts at Walpole for six years. That was permanent confinement that lasted six years. Five days a week we'd get out for ninety minutes a day—we'd have time to take a shower, do a little exercise, sometimes you could use the phone for about fifteen minutes—and then back to the cell. That was it. Five days a week of that. The other two days a week you were locked in twenty-four-hours a day. I never went outside—never got any fresh air or saw the sun for over six years. This was in the early 2000s.

On the whole, never stop being what you are: a revolutionary, a freedom fighter. You're captured, this is the front you find yourself in. You've got to stay healthy, you've got to stay positive, you've got to stay active. You can't let the circumstances that they put you in stop that, because if they do, then they've won. I never thought that I should let them win—being in prison/captivity is not the point—the point is to keep on struggling and being a freedom fighter—a revolutionary! A slogan I have long said applies: "Freedom is a constant struggle!"

Looking Forward

Outside support is very, very important. I mean, I can't say enough about it. It's crucial. Without outside support, they would get away with doing a lot worse and even deadly things to people. Harmful things. Things that don't have to happen do happen because they think they can get away with it. So, outside support, knowing a political prisoner has got outside support, is a way of holding back the ugly and even deadly hand of the state, even just a little bit.

Outside support in terms of political prisoners themselves is also very important. Dealing with that reality is very real. How do you go on, day to day, month to month, years or decades? A big part of that is knowing that you're still connected to that overall struggle, that there are people out there. They know your name, they know your situation, they support you, even to the extent of sending fifty bucks a month, like the Partisan Defense

Committee did for years, for example, and ABC and so forth.[9] Knowing that the people are there supporting you like that, as well as the actual support, both of those are very, very important.

So outside support, in terms of holding back the hand of the state is one thing. Actual social, political, and financial support to the person in captivity is also just as important. Also, this isn't some kind of welfare organization or something; both sides benefit from it. Gaining the experience, maybe even wisdom, of that person in captivity—and all that they've been through before they were captured, since, and so forth—will probably strengthen the organization and the people outside, as well. So it works both ways, but it's very crucial.

It's important to not let people fall through the cracks. There's some people who are more well known, maybe they've been active longer, but there's other people, and newer people, and we can't let anybody fall through the cracks. There are different kinds of people in jail for specific things, and they have supporters, and then there are political prisoners who have different circles of supporters. More unity and more knowledge and unity between the outside supporters—animal rights people here and anti-imperialist people here—more knowledge and support and contact is important.

Writing to political prisoners is a good thing. Just make contact. They don't have to write you back, but leave the door open. Throw out some ideas and leave the door open. If you're part of a political formation of some kind, make some outreach not only to political prisoners but [also] to other organizations that support political prisoners and see what's up, see where you might work together with them, see where they're really looking for certain kinds of support. I think those methods not only work but could [also] be very important.

Always protect yourself, first and foremost. The reality is: here you are. Whatever appeal you may have, stay on it. But don't let the reality of being in prison overwhelm you. By that, I mean not just maybe you are depressed or feel bad, but also sometimes people don't even do much drugs and then come into prison and start doing a lot of drugs because the reality is just kind of hard to handle. So, don't let that reality impact you or make you do

---

9. The Partisan Defense Committee (PDC) is a nonsectarian legal and social defense organization that champions cases and causes that are often political in nature.

negative things that are only going to harm you more. It's not going to help you, getting high and then getting busted and then maybe getting more time or going to the SHU, all the hassles you could get from the people who sell you the drugs and all the rest of it. Stay away from all that and look at the reality of where you are and figure out what you can do. Especially as an activist, I thought, what can I do and what should I be doing to continue my support of, and [be] part of, activism that is so important, if not key, to my whole life?

Jake Conroy

Jake Conroy is a longtime animal rights activist who was sentenced to four years in prison for his involvement in the Stop Huntingdon Animal Cruelty (SHAC USA) campaign. Jake has been involved in various forms of activism since the mid-1990s, working on campaigns both local and international. The SHAC 7, as he and his codefendants became known, were tried as domestic terrorists for running a website and supporting controversial tactics and ideologies. Jake served his four-year sentence in FCI Victorville and Terminal Island prisons, both in California. Since his release, he has remained tirelessly committed to the struggle on many fronts. He is currently the host of the *Three Minute Thursdays* show on his Cranky Vegan YouTube channel and is cohost of *Radicals and Revolutionaries*, an oral history podcast about direct action movements.

Prison Life

I don't think there's anything that you really can do to fully mentally prepare yourself for going to prison. We [SHAC 7 defendants] had that nine months of lead-up time of house arrest [before entering prison]. That was really helpful. I wrote people who were incarcerated for activism and exchanged letters and just asked as many questions as I possibly could. Like, How do I carry myself? What should I expect? What are the politics? We would exchange dozens of pages of letters back and forth just to hopefully become prepared and have some sort of understanding of what I was getting myself into. I also watched a lot of prison documentaries. On MSNBC there was *Lockup*, the show where they would go inside of a California State Prison for a month. God, what a terrible idea that was, watching those things. So, as stupid as it sounds, I watched a lot of that stuff.

But when you get there, everyone's experience is going to be different. Even if you're in the same facility, it's going to be completely different. So, you can do your best to prepare yourself mentally, physically, emotionally; sorting your relationships and your friendships before you go in. But at the end of the day, you're going to be hit with so many unknowns and so many variables and things that you just never could have possibly prepared yourself for, and you're really going to be tested as an individual—and as an activist and as a human—in such big ways that there really isn't any preparing for that.

The routine portion wasn't that difficult for me. I'm kind of a creature of habit; I just do the same things over and over again in life anyways. But I was not prepared for the culture. I'd known a little bit about what I was getting into in terms of a political climate on the inside. But it's a world I just had never been a part of before, and it wasn't something I was prepared for. That was hard to get my head wrapped around. I was lucky because I had a little bit of leeway to learn the ropes of what this particular prison was going to be like and what was expected of me and figure out how to balance that without getting attacked. And so, in that sense, I was lucky. But the first several months were pretty hit or miss, literally, in terms of "how am I going to survive this?"

I always say that if you have to go to prison, go to Terminal Island. It's the crown jewel of the West Coast and the federal system. Without people knowing what Victorville was like, it might sound weird to hear that Terminal Island is great, but it really was in comparison. Victorville is a four-prison complex. They have two medium security prisons, a penitentiary, and a women's camp, and it's in the Mojave Desert, so you're in the middle of absolutely nowhere. Everything's brown and gray dirt and concrete. There are no plants. There are no colors. Literally, you wear brown and gray. Really the only colors you see are on the TV, in magazines, in photos, that type of thing. From a sensory perspective, that's what you are given, brown and gray. It may sound kind of silly, but that really wears on you as a person. Just the physical structures and makeup of the prison wears on you.

There were fights and beatings pretty much every single day. There were stabbings, there was gang warfare, there were racial riots somewhat regularly. You were on twenty-four-hour lockdown a bunch. Then there was this whole kind of culture of how you carry yourself as an inmate. And if you don't carry yourself like that, you'll get the shit kicked out of you. You might get told, if you're lucky, "Hey, don't do that again." But, the reality is, if you fuck up too many times, five guys will throw you to the ground and kick your face in with steel-toed boots, which is what happened pretty regularly. As someone who is not interested, obviously, in gang politics or race politics, that's not something I involved myself in. It was difficult to walk that line of, "I'm not going to compromise my beliefs and my feelings, but also I don't want to get the living shit kicked out of me."

You really have to have that balance between your own personal safety and your personal politics. I got really lucky because I was able to walk that line. I think I was able to do that in a way where I didn't really compromise myself, but I also didn't get hurt. I think that was because I had a very interesting and unusual case, and once people got an opportunity to learn what I was about, people respected that, and I was able to get a lot of respect from a lot of different communities there. That allowed me to engage in a life that I wanted to lead as opposed to being bullied into something that I didn't want to be a part of.

When you go into prison, there's a handful of things that make you stick out, and if you're the oddball in prison, then you are a target. That means you might be extorted for money, you might be extorted for commissary, you might get the crap beat out of you so that you'll get extorted for protection, you might just get rolled off the yard, meaning they'll beat the living hell out of you until the prison determines it's not safe for you to be on that prison yard and they put you in solitary confinement and ship you off somewhere else. So, as someone who came in as a person swimming in this giant 2X orange jumpsuit and I self-surrendered—which is something you don't normally do at Victorville, rather it's a place you get sent to as a punishment—so that's a red flag to a lot of inmates. I walk in, and they're like, "What are you in for?" I say I'm in for protesting, and they're, like, "No you're not. Who are you?" It makes it a very volatile situation. The first few months were probably the most intense of my time there because people didn't know who I was. They couldn't determine if I was a snitch or a child molester or someone whom they could just beat the shit out of and take everything. They wanted answers, and I had to buy myself time in order to answer those questions honestly and in a way that they would believe me. I got lucky because I managed to get that time, when a lot of people don't, simply by having a couple guys take pity on me and negotiate that time for me.

So, when I moved from Victorville to Terminal Island, that world of inmate culture and inmate politics just didn't exist anymore. It's a low security prison where a lot of people are there for white-collar crimes. Businesspeople with some shady tax dealings, a lot of cops were doing time there, a lot of child molesters, a lot of snitches were doing time there. In a way, it was an uncomfortable place to be in terms of not trusting anyone there. I don't want to be around cops; I don't want to be around child molesters or snitches. And there's only a handful of people who have come from other places like Victorville. In a way, I felt more comfortable with, for lack of a better term, felons and convicts as opposed to white-collar criminals. So that was weird. But from a physical perspective, being on a yard that has grass and a grass soccer field and a basketball court—and since you're literally on an island, you're ten feet from the ocean instead of in the middle of a sea of sand. You can see dolphins and sea lions and birds, and there are flowers and trees in the yard. That was such a massive breath of fresh air. As silly as it sounds, it was life-changing for me.

But the government made it very difficult for me to do my time, and they did that intentionally. I really thought I was going to leave this world of activism behind—you know, Jake Conroy, the activist—and just go into prison and do my time as 93501-011. But the government was like, "No, we're going to continue to harass you." And so they made it very difficult for me to get mail and really difficult for me to send mail. All my mail was monitored. So, instead of mail arriving in three or four days, it took three or four weeks. At one point they told me I'm writing too many letters, so if I want to receive all my mail on time, I need to stop writing so many letters. Essentially they were saying to stop communicating with your friends and family if you want to hear from them. They were recording all of my phone calls onto a computer and monitoring everything I was saying.

They would not approve any of my visitor applications. When you're in prison, you have to send an application to your friends and family. They fill out the application and send it back to your case manager or your counselor and they determine whether that person's going to come and visit you or not. They can't really deny family, but all my family lived three thousand miles away on the other side of the country, so it wasn't very feasible for them to come very often. They would occasionally allow one or two friends, but for the most part, across the board, all my friends were denied visiting access, including my girlfriend at the time, whom I had to fight really hard to get approved. I did manage to figure out a workaround, and I got an old high school friend of mine to be approved to come visit, and she visited me. Then within a couple of weeks, the FBI showed up on her doorstep, wondering how she got permission to visit me, what she was doing, how she knew me. They visited her at home, visited her at her workplace, wanting to know what we talked about, things like that.

They put me on a high-visibility inmate watch list at Victorville where they said I was in the top ten inmates in terms of creating a security threat. I was a high risk. There were about 1,300 inmates at Victorville, and there's about ten of us who were on this special "red card." They called it the red card program, high-visibility inmate, where they said we were security threats. Primarily the people who were on that list were people who had escaped from prisons in the past. Of course, that was not me; I'd never been to prison, nor have I attempted an escape. There were actually people who tried to escape while I was at Victorville and they didn't get put on the red card system, so I didn't know what was going on.

What the red card system meant was that every two hours I had to report to a correctional officer, a cop, starting at 6:30 in the morning when they unlocked my cell door to 8:30 at night when they locked us back in. So, every two hours I had to go to a cop and essentially tell them that I had not escaped from prison yet. That was now my job to make sure that I remained.

The crappy thing about it was I had to check in with an officer and then the officer would have to get on a landline—he couldn't call from his radio or a cell phone—and call the main control center and be like, "Conroy's still here." And these cops, if they're hanging out with their buddies and are not going to walk to their office and call from a landline, so they forget. Then they blast your name over the whole prison intercom system, "Conroy, report to the nearest staff member." Then you've got to go find them again to ask them to call you in. And if they don't, and they think you've escaped, they'll recall the whole yard. They'll pull 1,300 people off the yard from their jobs, from rec, from the chow hall, and put them into the cells and count them all. If I had not escaped, then I would get put in solitary confinement as a punishment, indefinitely. So, I had that threat of solitary time hung over my head every two hours for twenty-five months. That was really stressful.

So, all those things combined give me that sense of like, "Fuck, this is so hard." I don't mean to say that lightly, like, "Prison's hard." But they really went out of their way to break me down. Prison in itself is designed to destroy you as a human being and crush you. But they seemed to be putting extra pressure on me because of my political beliefs and my case.

At the same time, you're dealing with all the stuff that's going on outside of prison. You know, your relationships, your friendships, your parents. My sister got married when I was in prison. My brother had his first child when I was in prison. I was trying to maintain a relationship. That is really difficult when you can only talk fifteen minutes at a time on the telephone and it's costing you sixty cents or whatever a minute, eighteen dollars for a phone call or something ridiculous. There are times when all those things were kind of compounded and crushed into one. You're not getting your mail, you're not getting any visits, you have solitary hanging over your head, you're in a tough spot with your girlfriend, you're missing your sister's wedding, and you're like, "Fuck, this is awful. This is not the way people should have to live their lives." And I say that recognizing I also had a lot of privilege, right? I'm a cis white guy in a prison for four years. There were people in there who were doing decades and had been forgotten about, and they never got letters, they never had a visitor, they didn't have family to talk to on the outside. So I say all these things with a grain of salt, but from my own personal experiences, yeah, it was incredibly difficult. Survivable, but incredibly difficult.

I tried to maintain my sense of self through the whole thing. I told myself, "You need to laugh or smile at least once a day." I had friends and I had people whom I enjoyed spending time with. In a sense, part of my program was hanging out with my friends, like I'd make sure I built that in. If you sit in your cell the entire time, one, you're going to become miserable, and two, you're going to look like the weirdo who is a target for violence or extortion. And so I made sure to go watch TV for an hour or hang out with my friends in their cells for an hour or share a meal or tell a joke or something like that. That was important to me.

Because I had that respect among all the communities within prison, I was able to have conversations with people who normally, under normal prison culture rules, I should not have been allowed to have. Having talks with folks about gang politics or drug dealing or prison politics, being able to ask questions and listen to people, I found incredibly cathartic. I found that a lot of people just wanted to be listened to, they wanted to come into my cell and shut the door—which you weren't supposed to do in terms of prison culture—and talk for an hour about, as an example, the trans person that was housed with us. They'd say, "I don't get it," and I would explain, "Well, this is why trans people deserve just as much respect as you and I do." How often do you have a conversation like that with high-level gang members from South Central about why we should respect trans people? Making those connections was really nice and important, I think, for everyone.

Or the guy who was embarrassed that he couldn't read, and he just wanted to come into my cell and shut the door and try to read something to me. And I would help him learn how to read, and that was really important. The fact that a lot of people put their trust in me to have private conversations in a place where normally, not only would it be frowned upon that the two of us were talking, but could have resulted in violence because the two of us were talking. For people to trust me like that, I think, made me feel good that I could be of some sort of help.

Then I always talk about letter writing. Receiving letters is such a big deal to an inmate. For me, every letter was an escape from prison. It allowed me to escape out of my cell and hear about your day and see a picture of your dog or the place you went camping or the food you were eating. I just wanted that escape. I was really lucky—when the government was not keeping my mail from me—I got letters every single day. Sometimes I got two or three, sometimes I got ten, sometimes I was getting like thirty or forty or fifty letters a day. And each letter was like an escape. So when I got a stack of twenty letters, I would just go into my cell and open up each one slowly, read the whole thing slowly and put it back in the envelope, and go on to the next one and just savor every letter.

People are always like, "Oh, when I write prisoners, I never know what to say." You don't have to say anything, just write about your day, write about anything. Those letters were such a—I hate to say a blessing, but they were, they were a blessing. They allowed me to survive. I sent them all home, and now, twelve years later, I still have boxes and boxes, thousands of letters in my storage unit because I just can't get rid of them because they mean so much to me.

But I think the most interesting thing about prison was the black market. You could literally buy anything you wanted if you had enough money. The interesting thing was seeing this weird formation of a micro-capitalist society and how it evolved in the prison. It used to be, cigarettes were the form of currency, and then, when smoking was banned in the federal system, it changed to postage stamps. When I was in, a postage stamp was worth twenty-five cents on the black market, and you could buy or sell anything you wanted. You could hustle for stamps, where you earn stamps, or you could buy stamps off inmates. If you could buy stamps off of someone or earn them, then you could do all sorts of weird things. So for me, a bit of my hobby was figuring out how I can make money (postage stamps) and what I could buy with them. Most people buy drugs and tobacco and alcohol and tattoos and gamble. Those things I was just not interested in at all.

But as a vegan, that's pretty much how I ate while I was in prison. I'm buying tofu and veggie burgers and fruit and vegetables and stuff with my postage stamps from people who worked in the kitchen. Then I ran a store out of my locker so that people in my unit, if they didn't have actual cash to buy things off the commissary but had postage stamps (because maybe they had a hustle), then they could come to me and buy things—coffee, sodas, tortillas, dehydrated beans, dehydrated rice, candy, peanut butter, things like that. Then I would take those postage stamps, and I would sell them. So people who needed postage stamps could come to me (or to other stores that were in the units), and I would sell books of stamps, which was twenty stamps for $5 apiece.

All that operates on credit. So, at the end of the week, it's, like, "All right, you bought $20 worth of postage stamps from me, so you need to buy this much stuff at commissary and pay me back that way." I was making about $100 to $200 a week for a year and a half—I would take that money, and with half of it I would use it to restock my store. The other half I would just use to buy food, like loads of fruits and vegetables. I became known as the guy who wanted all things produce. People wouldn't even wait for me to ask for it. They would just show up and say, "You want these apples?" I'm like, "Yeah, put them in my cell, and I'll shoot you some money."

[Prisons] just kept getting worse and worse and worse. A lot of programs were being taken away. The physical structures and what we were allowed to do kept diminishing and being taken away. I mean, it's different between the two prisons. The higher the security, the more likely they will just let you do whatever you want as long as you're not making them look bad or hurting one another. But it also seemed like they were going to provide you with a lot less to do. You were kind of left to your own devices, as opposed to the low [security prison], where there was more structure and opportunities in your day to day, but also the cops were much more likely to fuck with you. They knew they weren't going to be attacked by an inmate or caught up in a riot at a low, but that was a bigger risk at a medium.

Victorville was a newer prison. I think it was built in the late 1990s. There had already been a law passed that, for example, new prisons couldn't have weights, so we didn't have any weightlifting. Everything had to be body weight if you wanted to work out. You could run, but there wasn't a track; there was just a dirt path in the desert that you could run around. If they saw you doing pull-ups in the unit or on soccer goals on the yard, they would tell you to stop. People would make water bags—take garbage bags and fill them with water or sand, attach them to a broom, and do curls with them. But then the cops would come and pop them in your cell. They just didn't want you to do any upper body workouts, essentially because they didn't want you to be stronger than them.

That was a constant thing where they kept taking things away more and more. The rules were getting stricter. The violence was intensifying. Since I've left, I think Victorville has become a closed yard, meaning there's no open movements. Only certain units can go to the rec yard on certain days. There's never a point where the whole general population could be on the rec yard at the same time. So, in that sense, I think it got worse.

At Terminal Island at some point they just let all the grass die. Other prison administrations would come to see how Terminal Island was being run, and they would paint the grass to make it look like it was green to impress them.

The one interesting thing, though, was a change in the crack laws while I was in prison. There had been a lot of disparities between sentencing around crack versus cocaine. People who used and dealt cocaine were predominantly from white communities, and people who used or sold crack were predominantly from Black communities. But they're essentially the same drug; they're just cooked a little different. And people who were busted for cocaine got far less time than people who were busted for crack. That's just one example of how racist the prison industrial complex is, that two people essentially using or selling the same drug would be sentenced differently, almost entirely based on their race. For decades, there had been fights to change the racist crack laws. In 1995, there were some kind of famous prison riots that kicked off all over the country simultaneously, which I was told were called the "crack riots." That was in the 1990s when people just organized across multiple prisons to basically riot against the administrations and the staff. They ended up doing millions of dollars in damage.

I met a guy who came to Victorville in 2007. He called himself "Miami," and he and I used to play Scrabble a lot. He'd always tell me, "Don't get used to me being here." I was like, "Why?" And he said, "Because in 1995 I helped organize the crack riots, and they've put me on 'diesel therapy' ever since." What that means is, since it's the federal system, they can transfer you to any prison in the entire federal system around the entire country. When they don't like you, they put you on "diesel therapy," where every six months they wait for you to get settled in at a prison and start making friends, and then they ship you to a different prison. Then they wait for you to get settled, and right before you get settled they ship you to a different prison. And this guy had been moved every six months since 1995, so twelve years of him being shipped around because he helped organize those riots against the racist crack laws. And sure enough, in about four months, Miami was gone, and I never saw him again.

But that law started to be changed while I was at Victorville, if I remember correctly. All of a sudden, I had friends in there whose sentences went from twenty-five years to seven years and who had already served four years and were now eligible for halfway house in a year, as opposed to being eligible for a halfway house in twenty years. People's whole lives changed. It was amazing and heartbreaking to see all at the same time. So, there was a little hope in that, with enough political pressure and apparently prison riots and protests, we can get things changed. But what a nightmare—just in my unit alone of like 120 people, there were four or five or six Black guys who had their sentences reduced by a decade or two decades because the law was changed to reflect the fact that crack and cocaine should be sentenced the same. It was wild.

I think the thing that shocked me—and I hate to say it shocked me because it shouldn't shock anyone, but it did—was how implicit the government was in facilitating violence and segregation within the prison. Everything in Victorville was segregated by race, and a lot of that was because that's how the prisoners wanted it, or they were under the impression that that's how they wanted it. I think the prison-industrial complex recognizes that getting rid of this idea that you are a prison class, as opposed to segregated classes of people based on race or gang affiliation, benefits the government because when you're a prison class and you're all one, then you recognize the oppression that you're under much more clearly, and you also see who's responsible for it much more clearly. And the prison-industrial complex doesn't want that, obviously.

And so they facilitate this segregation. They facilitate the process of keeping us all separated and giving the impression that we are the ones who are making that happen. From little things—like you're not "supposed to cell with someone that isn't in your race." So, as a white guy, I was expected to be in a cell with a white person. If they put me in with a person of color, then I was supposed to refuse. And if I refused, I'd be sent to solitary. But if I didn't refuse and I celled up with someone who was a different race than my own "people," they would beat the shit out of me for being a race traitor or some bullshit like that. So the prison would facilitate this by saying, "Okay, we'll make sure we put you in with a white guy."

The chow hall was also segregated, but not by the government; it was the inmates doing it, like these are the white tables, these are the Black tables, these are the Sureños tables, these are the Norteños tables, so forth and so on.[1] But the prisons encourage it, they allow it, and they facilitate it. That facilitation even goes as far as riots.

So if there's a riot, then you're expected to show up for it. It's like an event on the yard. And so, if this group of people are going to riot against this group of people, and you are categorized as one of those groups, and you don't show up, then they'll stab you when they come back and find out you didn't go out to the yard. It's like, on this day the white guys are going to riot against this group of people. And it's not really a secret. There's like six

---

1. The Sureños and Norteños are Mexican American gangs prevalent in Southern California and Northern California, respectively. The Norteños are affiliated with the Nuestra Familia while the Sureños are affiliates of the Mexican Mafia.

hundred people who are all going to beat the living hell out of one another on the rec yard at 8:00 p.m. on a Tuesday night. And so the 8:00 p.m. move comes, and six hundred people all walk out to the recreation yard, when usually everyone's coming back in. And while this is happening, I'm just thinking the guards have got to know this is going to happen. The prison can't possibly be okay with this happening. And so you get out to the rec yard, and everything's fenced in—the rec yard is divided up into three areas, two softball fields and a soccer field, and each is fenced in with doors and everything—and you go through what's called a metal shack, which is a metal detector. There's like six hundred guys going through this thing, and they're all setting the metal detector off. The guards are all there and SIS— which is the investigative wing of the prison, kind of like the FBI within a prison—and they're just standing there and they're just watching everyone go in and directing everyone to go to the south softball field. They're just facilitating this process, this riot. Then they move everyone into the soft-ball field, and they literally lock the door, and they stand back, and they say, "Have at it, go beat the shit out of each other."

And it was awful. It was unreal. I'd never seen anything like that before. There's helicopters flying around. All the cameras on all the buildings are pointed at the softball field, and there's six hundred guys in there and maybe four shot callers (leaders of the groups) who are trying to work it out so we don't have to beat the holy hell out of each other. And then there would be me probably just running away as fast as I could! "Don't hit me. I don't care about this stuff." It's terrifying. You're just sitting there waiting for these shot callers to sort out the politics because two white guys bought heroin off these other guys and didn't pay the $3,000 bill and checked themselves into solitary confinement instead so they wouldn't have to pay, and the people come to the white guys saying you owe us $3,000. The white guys say, "It's not our problem. You shouldn't have given them $3,000 of heroin on credit." So it's like, "Well, all right, let's riot. We're going to wipe all the white guys off this prison yard." It's like two hundred white guys and four hundred guys in this other group. And I'm thinking, "I'm not going to get the shit kicked out of me for a bad heroin deal." But the alternative is, stay in your unit. And after the riot, they are coming back for you with shanks and padlocks on the end of belts. True story. So you have to decide which could potentially have the worse outcome. But anyways . . .

But the government just facilitates this whole process. Luckily that riot didn't happen; they sorted it out. But at other times, there were big riots. When there's a riot, they lock everyone in their cells on lockdown for twenty-four hours a day until the shot callers from both groups can sort out the politics and then agree that they won't riot. And then they let you all out. And the government facilitates all of this: they're taking the shot callers, who are the prison-wide inmate leaders, they're taking the leaders within the units, called the unit reps who are also inmates, and bringing them in and allowing them to have meetings and talk about this stuff.

In this particular riot, they couldn't sort through their differences so we were on lockdown for seven weeks in our cells without being let out at all. The prison administration had to bring leaders from other prisons over to Victorville, either permanently or temporarily, to get the yard under control. And that was done by the administration removing and replacing shot callers that would keep better control of their inmates.

There was a point where the shot caller for the white guys got hooked on heroin and the cops facilitated that guy getting the shit kicked out of him. So, a bunch of guys jumped the shot caller and beat the shit out of him in front of the cops, and the cops threw them all in the SHU, and then they let the guys that beat him up out a day later, even though they're supposed to do thirty days. Then the cops brought two white guys over from the penitentiary to the medium to be the new shot callers, to run the yard. The facilitation process that they participate in to keep this segregation, essentially to keep this warfare going, is just unreal.

I think I've made it through prison with a little bit of dignity and humility. I don't want to say, "Oh, I helped a bunch of people," but I was able to befriend people and have important conversations with people and just listen to people in a way that I don't think often exists in prison. And that felt important to me. Being able to have those conversations—being able to show that we don't have to be this segregated group of people, we can do it with dignity and respect for ourselves and for each other—I think was important. Even if it was just important to me that that's how I spent my time in prison. And if that rubbed off on other people, I don't know. I hope so.

Politics and Prison Dynamics

There is this expectation that you are part of this, for lack of a better word, group based on your race. So, as a white guy who's not affiliated with any white power groups, obviously, you're automatically lumped in with the general "white guy" group. So there were all these general groups of people, and then within those groups, there were smaller groups or gangs. There were Independent Skins, there were Warhammer Skins, there was the Aryan Brotherhood, there was Dirty White Boys.[2] There were the Bloods and Crips, and among the Crips there was the Grape Street Crips.[3] Then the Sureños had 18th Street and MS-13 and all these other subsets of gangs, for lack of a better term.[4] So there was an expectation that if you are white you ride with the white guys; if you're Black you ride with the Black guys; et cetera. Then you're broken down into smaller groups called cars. And I just didn't give a shit about any of that stuff. I was opposed to it.

And, again, all prison situations are different. All prisons are different. So, this isn't going to apply to everyone's experience. But from my experience in Victorville, if you didn't participate in that to a certain degree—participating in the culture and the inmate rules and expectations—then you would get the shit kicked out of you. And I'm not talking about someone giving you a little punch. I saw guys get thrown to the ground and get their faces kicked in with boots on, guys with their lips hanging off of their faces being dragged away by cops with trails of blood because they changed the channel in the TV room without permission. Literally guys fighting over whether to watch a cowboy movie or the morning news, and twelve hours later this guy's getting dragged off the yard with his lip hanging off his face. So, you have to figure out pretty quickly which battles you want to fight.

When there are situations where you have to show up, whether that's for a riot or for a fight or whatever, you have to show up. And if you don't—I saw

---

2. The Independent Skins, the Warhammer Skins, and the Dirty White Boys are white supremacist, violent gangs that are prevalent in US prisons.

3. The Grape Street Crips are a subset of the Crips (Community Revolution in Progress) which are active in the Watts neighborhood of Los Angeles.

4. Mara Salvatrucha, or MS-13, originated in Los Angeles in the 1970s and 1980s to protect immigrant populations from other local gangs. MS-13 is known to be quite violent and is prevalent in many US prisons. The 18th Street gang is a rival of MS-13 and is also based in Los Angeles and prominent in many US prisons.

people get stabbed because they didn't show up. Do you roll the dice and decide not to go out to the prison yard because there's potentially going to be a riot, and I'll definitely get stabbed when it's over, one way or the other? Or do I go out to the prison yard, hope it doesn't jump off, and, if it does, then just try to run away from people and hope you don't get caught up in it? I don't know. It's hard, it's really difficult. I think people on the outside like to say, "Well, you shouldn't do this, or you should do this." But you have no idea what it's like until you are in there.

As someone who was in there, I didn't know what it was going to be like. It was a situation where it was so fluid and volatile that you just never knew what was going to happen. One day you're buddies with someone, and the next day someone's coming up to you saying, "He got the shit kicked out of him for not falling in line, and you might want to say goodbye to him because he's not going to be here in the morning. He's going to get thrown in solitary or the hospital once the cops see how bad it is." And I'd ask, "How bad is he?" And the guy says, "Well, you're not going to recognize him—his eye is hanging out of his head." What do you do in those situations?

I was able to buy enough time in the beginning of my prison sentence to learn what I could and couldn't get away with and get enough respect that most people just gave me a pass. So, 95 percent of the time I didn't have to go along with a lot of the stuff that was happening, and I got really lucky for that. I think that was part of the respect that I got, part of the people I befriended, not just white guys but people from all the different communities in prison. And so I got a lot of passes.

But, yeah, there are times when, if someone needs to "be disciplined," meaning get the shit kicked out of them for falling out of line, your unit rep just says, "Okay, you, you, and you go beat that guy up, smash him." And there were a couple of times when he said, "Okay, Jake, you got to go." And I had to figure out a way not to do it. It's hard. So I'd reply, "I'm the scrawny vegan guy. If I were to hit someone, I probably wouldn't hurt them. I wouldn't be teaching them a lesson." Then the unit rep would say, "Yeah, you're right, Jake. Good lookin' out."

So I had to think fast—sometimes I would get into a political discussion about the broader politics of it all, and sometimes I just had to come up with a fast excuse. I'm lucky that the one or two times that happened, it wasn't because someone changed the TV, it was because the guy was a snitch or something. But, yeah, you're forced into these situations, and there's no good way out of it. So you just really hope for the best. Like I said, 95 percent of the time I got really lucky. I didn't actually have to be involved in it. But I saw it every single day, and it was awful.

The conflicts I was personally involved in, I had that respect where I had people who were higher up on the food chain that I was friends with that were like, "No, that's not going to happen." In the beginning, I had a lot of white power guys coming up to me saying, "Hey, let's hang out. Let's go to the yard. Let's do this. Let's do that." I'm like, "No, I'm not fucking with you guys. Go away." So that caused conflict, and then they started picking on me a lot when I first got there, calling me names. It gets dangerous. It gets dangerous quick. You can either go hang out with a bunch of assholes with swastikas and lightning bolts tattooed all over them, or you tell them to fuck off and they beat the living shit out of you. For me, I was like, "I'm not going to hang out with those people. They can go fuck themselves." So that became volatile pretty quickly.

I was lucky in the fact that there were a couple of guys who realized I wasn't your usual inmate, and they took me under their wing and learned about my case. We would walk around the rec yard for days and days, for hours every day, and I would tell them about my case and who I was and what I was about. They really schooled me in terms of what is expected of you, what you should do, what you can't do, and how to get around it. They really taught me a lot. They went back to those white power dudes and said, "Hey, this guy's not a child molester, he's not a snitch, he took his case to court" (which no one ever does, so I got a lot of respect for that). So they told them to leave me alone, and they did.

After that, I had enough friends, and friends in the right places, that if someone's fucking with me then they're going to fuck with them. They had my back, which was pretty cool. And that got me out of pretty much every other situation I got put into.

I think it's an intense world. As a white person living in the United States, I'm not on the receiving end of racism and don't see it so overtly like I did in prison. In there, it's white guys walking around with Hitler tattoos and swastikas and lightning bolts and it's n-word this and n-word that. It's just a very volatile situation where people are just ready to attack at any moment. I feel like that level of hate and racism just feels so much more intense, and it's so much more in your face. And obviously those types of emotions and feelings and experiences happen outside of prison as well, to people every single day. But maybe because it's such close quarters and you're just living literally on top of one another. It just feels like a powder keg that's waiting to blow. It feels so much more heightened. It was just a different experience for me, and I'm not really sure how to express that properly.

I definitely got strange looks from some of the people in my car because I played in the soccer league (I think there were three white guys in a league of about 150 people), I ran a store from my cell that sold to everyone (something that was frowned upon by some), I shared food and meals with Black guys (an act by a white guy that was not "permitted"), hung out in cells of other races, generally things that a lot of people in my car were not cool with. But again, I had friendships with and respect from the right people, and they would let me do as I pleased.

When I arrived at Victorville, John Walker Lindh was there, but he was put in solitary confinement. He was like the "American Taliban." He was there, but he got picked on so much that they put him in solitary. Then, when I came in, I was classified as a domestic terrorist by the BOP. So they were really concerned that I was next, like people were going to come after me, like they did John Walker Lindh. That didn't happen. But that was what they were warning me about, saying, "Oh, you're going to get the shit kicked out of you because you're a terrorist" type of thing.

But that hype, in a way, helped me. I think most people didn't understand why I was on this high-visibility list. I had to say I'm an "ecoterrorist." It's how I actually got a lot of the respect that I had because people were like, "Who's this kid on the red card system? Did you escape from prison?" No. "Where did you do time before?" I've never done time before. "Why are you on this thing?" Because they have me as a domestic terrorist. "What are you in for?!" And then I would say I'm in for protesting. "What do you mean?" And then that was how I got an opportunity to talk to people about my case because that's when people would become really interested in it and invested in the story.

I think I got people to think differently about things, for sure, whether that was animal rights or radical activism or just thinking about general politics. And I talked about trans and gay issues and things like that with people. There would be people who were doing a lot of drug dealing and stuff like that, and I'd ask them if they ever thought about taking some of that money and reinvesting it in their community, like buying bikes for kids or building a playground. They said they'd never really thought about that, but they were super interested in conversations about what that would look like. Stuff like that. Whether that had an influence on anyone, I don't really know, but I think just having those conversations felt important.

I think just having conversations with people, listening, is something that a lot of inmates don't experience. People who would just genuinely listen to them—understand them or take the time to understand them, and do the same, to tell them stories and have them listen and understand you—it felt like a beautiful thing to me and felt really important. Some of those people whom I befriended I'm still friends with today. I keep up with them, and they're all doing really interesting things, including activism supporting people who are being released from prison. I don't know if that had anything to do with me, but it felt important.

There was one instance that I always think about. There was a guard in the visiting room, and he was a real piece of shit. Everyone called him Alabama State Trooper because he looked like a good old boy from the South. A big goatee, always had dip in his mouth, just a scary-looking dude. He went into the visiting room and just treated people with so much disrespect. That was the one place—you're with your family, you're with your friends or with your kids, your parents—and guards knew you treat people with respect in there. You treat the visitors with respect, you treat the inmates with respect. It was the one place where the inmates became who they actually were on the outside. To see these hardened inmates crying as their kid runs over and gives them hugs. You just don't disrespect that space. And this guy, he was a monster. He would yell at your kids, getting in the inmates' faces, he was awful. He put a friend of mine in solitary confinement because he said that when he kissed his wife, which was allowed, it was too long and that he was being passed drugs that he swallowed. So they put him in a dry cell for a week, where there's no toilet, no sink. You have to defecate into a bucket so they can look through it and make sure there are no drugs in it, which, of course, there weren't. A bunch of people in my unit decided this wasn't okay and we needed to do something about it.

So myself and a couple other guys—including my friend that had his sentence reduced by like fifteen years when they changed the crack laws—decided to ride up on the warden and do something about this. When organizing it, we said, "We need to make sure we have people from all the different communities, all the different races, represented." So, we went to all the different groups of people in our unit and got everyone together, like a delegation of ten guys. And we all walked down to the main line at lunch, where all the administrative people line up and you can ask them questions. So we all roll down there together—people from all different races and backgrounds and gangs together, which is an unusual thing to see. And everyone's looking at us and we're forming this line-up of ten people rolling up to the main line. There's the warden standing there, an Iraq veteran who didn't dress in a suit but wore his desert camos even though he was in a prison. There's the assistant warden, the lieutenants, and SIS; all kind of sidled up to form their line. And we just walked up to them, and we didn't really have a plan. This guy Dre addressed the warden and said, "We've got a problem." The warden said, "What's the problem?" Dre said, "It's in the visiting room." And the warden said, "I know all about the problem. We're going to take care of it."

We didn't plan for that, so it was like . . . well, what do we do now? And Dre said, "All right, I hope it gets taken care of real soon." And the warden said, "Understood." And then we all just kind of backed away and went about our business.

Sure enough, the next week Alabama State Trooper was taken out of the visiting room, and then a week later he was taken out of the compound. He wasn't in the prison anymore. That was a big win. Ten inmates came together and recognized the idea of being a prison class, and together rolled up on the administration in an intense prison and said, "You need to take this cop out, otherwise you're going to have problems." And they did it! It's a real testament to what can happen if we do away with racial politics, gang politics, and fight back. It was a small-scale thing for us, but it was important. We felt that we were being disrespected and our family and friends were being disrespected, and we stood up to it, and we won.

The lockdowns were awful. We had a bunch of them because there were a lot of riots. So every time there's a riot, or if there's a fight that involves two different races or two different groups of people, they would lock you down as well. Even if it was just like a one-versus-one. You're usually locked down for like three or four days. If there's a riot, you might get locked down for two or three weeks. For the big one that they couldn't negotiate an end to, we were locked down for seven weeks. You are locked in your cell twenty-four hours a day. You can't get commissary, so you get three meals a day pushed through the flap in the door, and they're bag lunches.

As a vegan, that became impossible because you could have a cheese sandwich or you could have a sliced meat sandwich. Then you had an apple that was covered in the juice that dripped off the deli meat. You had some powder to put in water to make a juice and maybe a bag of chips or something.

So the food was really difficult. I barely ate for seven weeks. You know lockdowns are coming, so I'd have a lockdown stash. Basically a box under my bed with an extra jar of peanut butter or a box of granola or some chips, books that you haven't read, paper and pen, that type of thing, so when you get locked down for a week or two, you have the food there for you and things to keep yourself occupied. Eventually on that long one, I ran out of food, so I stopped eating for a few days.

When you're locked down for like two weeks and you're by yourself, it's amazing how fast you start talking to yourself. For me, I just started having conversations with myself and yelling to my friends in the other cells. But most of the time you're like, "Am I talking to myself out loud, or am I talking to myself in my head?" I think back, and I don't know how I did that. It was awful. You didn't get let out.

I got lucky because my friend was the head cook in the kitchen, and, when everyone's on lockdown, the cops suddenly are responsible for feeding everyone, as opposed to when the inmates work the kitchen. So, they're making 1,300 bag lunches three times a day, and they quickly were, like, "We're not doing this anymore." So they started pulling some of the main kitchen staff out of the cells and making them work making the bag lunches. And my buddy Dave, he knew I was out of peanut butter, which was my only source of food. For three days I didn't eat, and he had stolen all these little ketchup pack-sized peanut butters. He stuck them in his boots, and he ran up to my cell and just started throwing all the peanut butter packets under the door, one after the other. It was a lifesaver. The cop kept yelling at him to get away from the door, and he just said, "I got you, Little Buddy." He used to call me Little Buddy because he was this huge ex–football player, this massive dude. We got out a week later, but he really saved my life. To big Dave Waller, wherever he is, he saved me.

It's easy to look back and wish I had done things differently, but the reality is that survival comes first—physical and emotional. But I wish I did more activism while on the inside. I wish I had organized more. I look at political prisoners in the past who were in much harsher conditions than me, and they were doing incredible work while locked down. And I would have liked to have put more of an emphasis on my time trying to change and organize my environment.

I think the hard part of looking back, and more so for those on the outside looking in and assessing someone else's time, is that you never know how hard it is unless you're there. It's easy to judge someone for how they did their time. It's easy to write someone off because they didn't do their time the way you think they should. And even as someone who is formerly incarcerated, it's easy to look back and say, "I should have done that differently."

But the reality is, unless you are there, you don't know how hard it was. I still look back and think, "How in the hell did I get through some of those situations?" I don't know how I didn't get really hurt. How I didn't end up in solitary longer. How I managed to get away with what I did. I don't know how I managed it. But I did.

Looking Forward

Prisoner support was important to me. I got a lot of inspiration from the Black Panther Party and the Black Liberation Movement, the American Indian Movement, things like that. When I first got involved in activism there were, and continue to be still, loads of political prisoners from the 1960s and 1970s and 1980s. That's kind of how I got more schooled in terms of what prisoner support looks like. Decades later, a lot of these folks still have amazing support. There just weren't a lot of animal rights prisoners at the time when I got involved—I think there was only one in the US. But as the campaigning and the movement got a little more radical, and the SHAC campaign started, the one that I was in prison for, there were a lot more people going into prisons and jails for it. So, we did a lot of prisoner support that way.

I also helped start a magazine called *Bite Back*, which was an animal liberation, direct action magazine.[5] We did a lot of prisoner support that way. So, it was interesting to be on the receiving end of it after being on the other side for so long and realizing you can talk about why it's important to write prisoners and support them, but until you are receiving that support you just don't understand how critical it is. I still stress that as much as I can: support political prisoners. Everyone in there is stuck in an absolutely miserable situation. I can't tell you how many people would say, "Hey, can you get me a pen pal? Can you get me someone to write?"

People who have nobody—who have been in there for ten or twenty years, and their family has forgotten about them, or their parents have died, or their brothers and sisters don't have time anymore to support them, and they don't have any friends anymore because they've been in prison for years—and just a letter made people's eyes light up. It's just unreal how desperate people are for any sort of interaction with someone that isn't another inmate or a cop. So, write political prisoners. It doesn't have to be about politics. It can just be something as mundane as "this is what I ate for dinner, what I did on my walk, or I went camping this week."

I always say, one of my favorite people I wrote back and forth with must have had one of those "100 great conversation starters" books. Every letter, she would write me a "desert island" type of question. What would be your three favorite books on a desert island? Then I would spend the whole letter writing back my answers and why and getting really detailed. Then at the end, I would write her a similar question, and then she would get it and write me back pages of why she would pick what she chose. And we wrote for years that way, and we never really talked about anything political. Nothing really intense. It was just a nice escape. I'd spend twenty minutes reading her letters, and I would spend an hour writing her back. That was an hour and a half of my day that was like an escape—from just one letter—and it made me happy. It kept my brain engaged, kept me thinking, kept me thinking about things going on outside prison.

The world goes on without you when you're in prison. It goes on without you really fast, and it's hard to keep up with it. And I think letters and support are really important. But political prisoner support isn't just letters.

---

5. *Bite Back* is a magazine started in 2002 to give voice to activists who choose to break the law to help animals and to feed an animal rights movement hungry for news about nonviolent direct action.

People need books. Having books inside was great for me to be able to read but also to interact with other inmates because they didn't have access to these books, and they wanted them. I started a lending library out of my cell because I got so many books. I had a big crate of books, and when lockdowns were coming people would run up to my cell trying to get books. I'd just be passing out books before they locked us in our cells. So, that was really important. And just having money on commissary. Like I said, people had to run hustles to have postage stamps to be able to buy necessities like beans and rice. People need money on their books in order to buy food and toiletries and clothing so that they can take care of themselves and have that sense of self while there. So I really encourage people to write a letter, send a book, do a fundraiser, send some cash, whatever you can do to support activists or people in prison.

There are lots of things you can do [to prepare for prison] but nothing really that can get you ready for it, full stop. I think talking to other political prisoners, people who have been on the inside, is really important. I think realizing that everyone's experience is going to be completely different and that every prison is completely different, but you can still get the general sense of what's to come. If you've been found guilty but haven't been sentenced, you can figure out what level security you're going to be sent to using the point system that they have in the federal system. So you can figure out roughly if you're going to be in a camp, a low, a medium or a high [security]. Then when you're sentenced, you can often request the judge to send you to a certain prison. So, doing a little bit of research about that might be helpful if you know you're going to go in.

It sounds really stupid, but, if you're an activist, organizing your own political support is helpful. Make book lists, make a list of things you like and things that you don't like that people can write you about. When you figure out what prison you're going to be sentenced to, you can start sending yourself things to that prison like a day or two before you get there, like money on your books. In Victorville, inmates made you show your paperwork to make sure you weren't a snitch or a child molester. So sending that stuff to yourself before you go in is really important so you have that paperwork immediately because if you take a long time to show that paperwork, they immediately assume you're hiding something. That was something I did that I think really helped out.

And sort through your relationships. I think that's really important too. Whether that's a partner or your family or your close friends, just having an understanding of what you're hoping for out of those relationships I think is important. They're difficult conversations to have, but I think that peace of mind can make a big difference.

Prison is a scary place. Being incarcerated is tough. It's often romanticized in political circles—doing time for your cause. But it's a very real and potentially volatile situation that shouldn't be taken lightly. And it's something you should really process and think about before you engage in your activism and not when you're sitting in the back of a cop car. Have those big conversations with your friends and your comrades. Do real-world risk assessments. Don't be afraid to say no.

But also don't be afraid to say yes. If we are going to change the world, we have to fight hard, dream big, and we are going to have to take risks. But those risks can be mitigated when we are better informed about all the potential outcomes. Be informed, be courageous, and keep fighting.

Marius Mason

Marius Mason is a transgender environmental and animal rights activist, anarchist, and artist currently serving a twenty-two-year sentence for an action in the name of the Earth Liberation Front in which no one was harmed. In 1999, he set fire to a lab at the University of Michigan that was conducting research on genetically modified organisms (GMOs). After Marius's husband turned state's evidence, Marius pleaded guilty and was given an extremely long sentence with a "terrorism enhancement." Marius came out as transgender in 2014 and is believed to be the first person in the Federal Bureau of Prisons to begin therapy to transition from female to male. He and his supporters also initiated the annual International Day of Solidarity with Marius Mason and All Long-Term Anarchist Prisoners on June 11.

Prison Life

> "Much as I long to be out of here, I don't believe a single day has been wasted. What will come of my time here, it is too early to say. But something is bound to come of it."
>
> —Dietrich Bonhoeffer[1]

---

1. Dietrich Bonhoeffer (1906–1945) was a German theologian, pastor, and ardent antifascist during the Third Reich. He was imprisoned by the Gestapo after being convicted in a plot to assassinate Adolf Hitler, and he was hanged on April 9, 1945.

This quote showed up in a book that we were assigned to read for my trauma group, Resolve. While the conditions during the now almost fourteen years in prison [as of 2022] have not been anywhere near as dire as they were for Bonhoeffer or [that] my own grandfather endured while they were imprisoned by the Nazis, there has been enough hardship that has made it more difficult to glean the lessons that incarceration can bring.

Being "put aside" for so long has its own cruelties, even without the addition of starvation or torture that the victims of concentration camps surely suffered. While I have been away, a good friend committed suicide, and another died waiting for a kidney donation. My youngest child suffered and struggled with addiction and almost died—and then heroically recovered and triumphantly graduated from college. I have missed sharing in my eldest child's graduation from Oxford and from attending his marriage. Most painfully, I was not able to be with my mother as she contracted cancer and succumbed to the illness in terrible pain. Not being with family and friends to be present for their pain and joy is its own kind of torture.

But I still agree that my time has not been wasted here and that I've tried to embrace my opportunity to do support for my fellow prisoners to the best of my ability. Sometimes the support is very simple, just an application of the anarchist principle of mutual (and material) aid. Books, shoes, stamps, cough syrup, aspirin, hats, gloves, scarves, warm weather and cold weather clothes, as well as vegan food—whatever is needed and can be shared. It is an opportunity to talk about philosophy and how society could be organized on such different principles, which are always meaningful conversations filled with good humor and a minimum of moralizing.

Sometimes just being a sympathetic elder, to listen and to empathize and counsel, is a timely support to someone who may have burned some bridges with their own parents. I try to share this walk with my fellow prisoners, since we are in the same circumstances now and have life experiences to share as well. As a recovering alcoholic, I have been glad to be in recovery groups with folks inside and to be there when they are having tough times. As a survivor of trauma, I have been proud to be a support to others who have also been through events that shaped and twisted them—and to be present as they share their stories of trauma in order to heal.

But, most of all, it has been my honor and my privilege to be a trans elder who can be an encourager and support to the many young trans folks and nonbinary folks whom I have met in prison, to help them connect with resources and to give them the space to ask questions and to sound out how they want to navigate the issues around coming out in prison. It can be a very loaded question, as prison can be a very unstable and sometimes violent environment for nonconforming folks.

For several trans folks I met, they had not made a decision to begin their transition before they began serving their sentences. Fortunately for them, the policy concerning trans medicine has been changing to become more accessible since I first came to the BOP in 2009. There was a landmark case in 2013 that made it possible for a trans person to pursue a medical transition in a federal prison, even if they had not been diagnosed with gender dysphoria and prescribed hormones before beginning their sentence. This change in policy made it possible for me to do what I had not thought possible until my sentence would end in 2030.

Even so, it was still initially a long and frustrating process, full of fits and restarts, interviews and questionnaires with psychology and medical staff. My own process took two years, but a trans woman friend of mine had begun her request almost fourteen years earlier, and she was granted the right to transition only a few months before me! So definitely an improvement.

The Transgender Policy Manual came out in 2016, and that helped to clarify a number of social and medical issues. It directed staff to use preferred pronouns and to change some of the policies about body searches—but there were definitely loopholes and misuse of the language. Things changed with the Trump administration; there was a discontinuity in care, and it became a lot harder for folks to begin the process. However, the fortunate ones who were already in transition were not prevented from continuing in most of the cases I was aware of (though I heard of two trans men in Carswell who were—but they were leaving the system).

The Biden administration made efforts to reinstate the earlier policy and to expand some of the language protecting the social rights of trans inmates. And most recently, to explicitly talk about affirmation surgeries—which was what so many folks I knew were concerned about, though not everyone wants to transition in this way. The new policies have also reaffirmed prisoners' right to be designated to a facility of their chosen gender, though there are some hoops to jump through for that too.

I have met many trans women prisoners who have found that being in a women's facility was much better for them psychologically and much safer physically, as they experienced less harassment by other prisoners and staff and were far less likely to be molested. Several of the trans women that I have met here at a male facility feel they must be very guarded about expressing their gender identity as a safety precaution.

My experience of being designated to a male facility has been, overall, a huge opportunity to socially transition, and I feel like it has gone better than I had feared. I had certainly been told some really intimidating stories about what I could expect, and fortunately that has not been what I found here. There have been some awkward and shaming moments around strip searches and how they were conducted, around medical trips and some shower stalkers, but that has now ceased, and it feels like there is a better reception for me here with both staff and prisoners.

I have also had to navigate religious issues concerning my gender as a practicing Jew. Fortunately, my congregation here, despite being predominantly Orthodox, has also been very inclusive and welcoming. I have been really grateful to these men; to be able to learn from them and to pray with them has been an unexpected blessing.

I have also been able to continue with my vocational education as an HVAC [heating, ventilation, and air-conditioning] tech. The first four months of this class, I was at the female prison at FSL Danbury, which is just across a parking lot from the men's facility, FCI Danbury. There have been several breaks in the class meeting because of the many COVID lockdowns we have experienced in the past two years. But the class continues, and I was able to move from the female class to the male class here.

Politics and Prison Dynamics

The difference in what is available for the women and what is made available for the men is like night and day. This is not because of our instructor, who is a real advocate and champion for equality and access for all genders. I have been so appreciative and grateful for his inclusion of me in the men's class and how he has been really supportive and helpful at every step of this process. It is more the BOP that decides what resources are allocated and where. The BOP has given the men's class so many more teaching materials and space to do this class that it is hard for our instructor to try to create parity between the classes.

But it is really in this class setting that I am forced to confront the differences in my own background, having been raised as a woman, with that of my male counterparts. Here I notice the differences in acculturation in what skills are shared from generation to generation of men, as in tool use and apprenticing as machines are repaired and taken apart. I really feel the lack of experience. So I am always trying to play catch up and hoping to learn quickly. It has been a humbling experience, as I am also a small guy and no spring chicken. Oftentimes, I am trying to see a demonstration and can only see the backs and butts of the guys who crowd around in front and are wider and taller than I am, blocking any meaningful view. So, I resort to my diagrams and try to figure stuff out.

Even so, the time here has helped me to work out how I relate to men as a man, both in my unit (which is a programming unit for folks who have some skills deficit, either physical or emotional issues, along with peer mentors) and on the compound generally. I feel like this place has taught me things I could have not learned anywhere else, and it has been great to be relating to others as my genuine self, as just me and no masks.

I am encouraged that both trans and cis people that I have met have felt like they can ask any question they feel concerned with so that we can have honest conversations that might contribute to a better understanding between all genders on the continuum. And if COVID ever takes a break for long enough, there could be a transgender support group that will meet and help folks who identify as such to support each other and discuss issues as they come up. I have been able to preview the material developed by the special populations coordinator here, who will be the staff person supporting this group, and the material seems helpful. The trans women I have met here all seem to think that it would be a good thing for them to be able to support each other and connect. I have not met any other trans men here, but maybe now that I have been able to make it here a year without any scandals (good grief!), there might be others who will come.

There was supposed to be a meeting about my medical request for affirmation surgery, in line with the new policy that the BOP has adopted for the transgender inmate population. But it may not be able to happen, as with the COVID lockdown and as a precaution for the safety of staff, there may not be a way for us to meet this September [2022] to mark my year of living in my gender at a male facility. We will see how this evolves, but they know here unequivocally that I am adamant in my desire to continue my transition medically and surgically, with both "top" and "bottom" surgery. I even had a conversation with a regional doctor who came here to help with our beleaguered medical department about specific surgeries and how they might be accomplished (all at once, in steps, specific phalloplasty procedures). So that was hopeful, but it has been a long, long road, and, as I said, I am not a spring chicken anymore.

Looking Forward

It has been an interesting bid, and I have learned a lot about other people and about myself. There has been pain, and I have witnessed some terrible things that people do to each other when they are in pain. I have met some fascinating and worthy people and also a few jerks. It is all too easy to get lost in here, to drift in the waves of how things run in prison and to lose track of the world outside. But it has helped a lot to feel connected and a part of the community of resistance that links so many of us together through the outreach of some powerful individuals who make such a difference. Please know that your words matter when you write a letter to a prisoner—you send a literal lifeline to someone who might drown otherwise. Thank you for sending that hope and strength through these steel bars.

Bill Dunne

Bill Dunne is an anarchist political prisoner who was sentenced to ninety years in 1979 for the attempted liberation of comrades from King County Jail in downtown Seattle. During the escape, a shootout occurred, and Bill and two of his comrades were arrested. In 1983, Bill tried to escape from USP Lewisburg and was sentenced to an additional fifteen years. He spent seven and a half years imprisoned in the notorious control units at USP Marion and has been incarcerated at dozens of federal prisons and county jails. Bill was denied during his first parole hearing in 2014. He has been a GED teacher for the majority of his four decades of imprisonment, helping hundreds if not thousands of people complete their General Educational Development tests.

Prison Life

I did not find it hard to adapt to prison routine, structure, or culture, either as a social prisoner or as a political prisoner. It was what it was. It beat the county jail, at least for people of sound mind and body and perhaps a modicum of social skills. As to culture, one learns how far one can push the limits one feels particularly oppressed by—which always entails the occasional mistake—without being destructive to one's self, one's social infrastructure, and one's desire to expand the limits, which exist in every social situation. For example, I saw a lot of "SWP" around when I entered the California system. I wondered why I had not heard of so many comrades being imprisoned in my dalliance with the Socialist Workers' Party. I finally couldn't contain myself and said to one large, heavily tatted driver of big iron on the iron pile who sported a sizable SWP on a huge pectoral, "Hey Comrade! Socialist Workers' Party!" Well, I was quickly disabused of the notion that I was backstroking through a friendly sea of the people.[1] But even little worker bees like me and my comrades of circumstance, wild and crazy as we didn't feel like not being, could demand some respect, even from rhinoceri.

There have been times in prison that have been better, even if I don't know that I could say that any one such period was the best time. Early in my bit, while I was incarcerated in the Washington State Penitentiary, also known as Walla Walla after the nearby town and "the Walls" for the even nearer walls around the joint, many comrades shared my confinement and from many different fronts in the struggle. My codefendant was already there and introduced me to many other political and radicalized social prisoners.

Everyone was active in various ways: cultural pursuits, political publications, and even radio programs, interactive mutual aid, and engagement between proponents of different perspectives, and—of course!—resistance to our collective and individual oppression. The state permitted conjugal visits, and during this period my partner and I created a beautiful daughter, probably the most significant thing I'll ever do. But that era came to an end when the agency of repression decided our practice of the struggle was accomplishing too much and banished my codefendant, a number of others, and me into internal exile in the federal prison system (and in some state prison systems).

Another such relatively better period was during my first stint at USP Leavenworth in Kansas and for the same reasons: many good comrades, progressive activity, and the attendant feeling of place and connection and the ability to do something with them. Nor are such relatively better times necessarily periods of months or years. They may be fleeting and transitory: an evocative smell, playing a close game of handball or pinochle with friends, a good study group with comrades, a legal discussion with fellas

---

1. The Socialist Workers' Party (SWP) is a US-based communist party focused on solidarity work, which was formed in the 1930s after splitting with the Communist Party USA. In this instance, however, SWP refers to Supreme White Power, a slogan that originated in the California prison system.

who know of what they speak, being gone into a good book, article, letter, et cetera.

I do not recall having lost hope while inside. Indeed, I can't really think of a situation in which I would be inclined to give up, giving up being more or less synonymous with having lost hope in my mind. When I feel violated, sick, in pain, unproductive, dissatisfied, alone, there are always ways to seek to alleviate the discomfort. Resistance and escape are always good tactics. If afflicted with a mental pain, I seek to address its cause. If it is something I cannot fix, I try to escape from the pain by distracting myself from it as the psycho-scar forms. The body can carry on with a lot of wear and even altered abilities, and so can the mind.

I have lost people dear to me, both fellow prisoners and people outside. And it is not only via death. Every time a friend or comrade is transferred, a hole is blown in the body of one's life. The world we experience is conditioned by the people in it. The injury of losing any of those people may be physical, emotional, intellectual, psychological—and no such injury can be entirely one and none of the others. It may be traumatic, as deaths of close people always are. Or the loss is ameliorated by being more gradual, with declining contact because the relationship was built on things that don't convey well via writing or phone conversations (if the transfer is to the other side of the razor wire), or because it is a slow loss as the relationship recedes because its participants lack the skills to maintain it. Sometimes the relationship is preserved as in amber into a hard little rock of consciousness and the relationship may ebb and flow like the tide but will endure. Other relationships in which physical presence never played a role, of course, persevere. Mostly one just has to let the hole heal, to extend the tendrils that form one's social infrastructure in other directions so their dendrites can lace over the hole with a network of new connections. And our people always live in our minds and influence us through the lines of our mental programs they wrote: that is the afterlife. That is why we say "¡Robin Doe, Presente!" when we honor them.

The quality of life in prisons has absolutely deteriorated, and markedly. After pushing fifty years of incarceration and sampling the many prisons I've been to, I can categorically say that in all respects, with the possible exception of cell size. When I began this bit, the food was generally relatively good, nutritious, and enough, even for bigger guys; medical and dental care were adequate; educational programs were many and diverse; and connection to the community via cultural and interest programs and broader visiting opportunities were promoted.

Now the food is considerably worse: inadequate in palatability, nutrition, and quantity. Having to get by without being able to supplement from the commissary is a rough row to hoe—and is used as a punishment despite rules prohibiting using food as a punishment. Medical and dental services have deteriorated to the point of being life-threatening. Prisoners' complaints about serious medical needs are blown off, ignored, or unreasonably delayed. Written sick-call requests here are discarded; the warden claims this is according to "BOP procedures" but doesn't elaborate. In fact, destroying these records is to prevent the generation of records memorializing prisoncrats' deliberate indifference to prisoners' serious medical needs. Access to the administrative remedy system has become exceedingly difficult, and requests are frequently not answered or "lost"—again, to avoid creating records of malfeasance. Undermining access to grievance procedures thusly makes staff members feel unaccountable and that they can get away with anything in their behavior toward prisoners and without doing their jobs properly—or at all.

Education is starved for resources. Pencils, paper, folders, and books are in short supply. Vocational programs are rare and very basic. Cops are too lazy to run the apprenticeship programs that are already approved. Verily, the Federal Bureau of Prisons (BOP) is even failing (refusing?) to implement even the tiny Trump-era reforms in the First Step Act mandating educational programs to reduce prisoners' risk of recidivism and shorten their sentences marginally.

Ventilation doesn't work in many cells. Clothing has deteriorated from military surplus with frequent underwear and linen exchanges to junky, mostly polyester, UNICOR-made, low-quality uniforms and marginal underwear of similar provenance or industrial seconds or thirds. Recreation is artificially limited, especially if one has a job—of which there are never enough to go around. In the name of security, prison officials have reduced and continue to reduce connection to the community by cutting visiting and making it more restrictive, attacking mail with ever more new and more onerous rules—apparently toward banning physical mail, as is already done in some prisons. Events with outside groups, such as religious, entertainment, motivational, and other community groups, have virtually disappeared. I could continue, but books could undoubtedly be written on this subject.

The thing that has shocked me the most inside is the crazy sentences that are broadcast like confetti in the name of justice for minor to non-offenses, like drug crimes, mere possession of weapons, and illegal reentry into the US. The increasing unwillingness of the legal system to do anything about these draconian sentences—verily, to not make them worse—is also shocking. This slide into reaction is not in the name of law and order, though that is the gloss put on reactionary attitudes toward crime the harshness represents. A large part of that attitude is scantily clad racism and classism.

The idea of a "correctional" system has dissolved into a system to control poor and oppressed communities—not least by maintaining a huge gulag archipelago should any organized movement for redistribution of the social wealth become threatening to the ruling class. When I came into the system, there were around twenty-three thousand federal prisoners. That system would have had a hard time absorbing the Muslim men rounded up in the immediate aftermath of 9/11. By 2001, it could swallow such numbers without a burp.

What I was prepared for the least was the business fascistification of the prison population itself. In the early 1970s to the late 1980s, while there were sundry sorts of white supremacists and capitalist roaders in the mix, there were many left-wing and leftist political prisoners and many social prisoners attracted to or already holding more communitarian ideas. This was likely the legacy of the prison reform movements of the late 1960s, early 1970s, and the fact that society generally held a more "we the people" attitude engendered by the New Deal and its progeny and had not been so heavily indoctrinated with individualistic and capitalistic notions. But I digress. Nowadays, leftists are few and far between; there are many more reactionaries, everything has a price, prisoners steal from each other, and collaboration with the enemy in various ways is not only okay but even commendable. Fox TV and its fascistic, condescending, mendacious commentators and editorial policy can frequently be seen on TVs stationed in the units as pacifiers—and prisoners of all races watching them!

I try to avoid being self-congratulatory and prideful about constructive activities I undertake. I do them because they are correct things to do—I can do them, therefore I have an obligation to do them. One must struggle in whatever community one finds oneself in the ways of which one is capable. The revolution will not make itself! That said, I think I have done good work as a GED teacher and law library clerk for the last twenty-five years. All of my comrades in confinement are class brethren and a few sistren who need to know how to read and write and cipher at least a bit, whether they know it or not. So I provide the service for both the class and the individuals here who comprise it. And I sit with prisoners on suicide watch during their times of diminished capacity, because I think they would prefer me to a cop. I also think that I've done some decent legal work that has at least slowed the roll of the empire over the remaining residue of rights we, the people, retain. And I have thrown down a bit of propaganda in my time that, I think, has preserved some knowledge that may otherwise have been lost, and passed on a few ideas worthy of consideration.

Politics and Prison Dynamics

I have had conflicts with other prisoners and with staff. Fortunately, many more with the latter. With prisoners, I try to make it an issue between individuals rather than some matter of principle regarding whatever group with which that prisoner may be associated. With staff, I tend to do the opposite: point out that prisoners in my situation and the rank and file staff members have more in common with each other than with the executive staff. Of course, I can't make that argument with the executive staff, with whom most of my beefs have been. With prisoners, all of my conflicts have worked out well. With staff, not so much. Those have resulted in about sixteen years of SHU (hole) time out of the last forty-two, plus fifteen years added to my sentence.

Yes, unfortunately, racism does thrive inside prisons. I sit in the white section in the chow hall here because I am objectively white and cannot sit elsewhere without joining a gang or religion whose principles I cannot share. In Walla Walla, there was a no-flesh eaters area in the chow hall where we got our food that was not segregated, and I sat there because I do not eat meat. I have been in places where white groups have claimed governance over white prisoners and authority to prescribe rules for whites. I make a point to tell members of such groups that I am an independent, that I didn't sign up for any group, and that, as a result, I had no "shot caller" and was not under anyone's authority (except the swine, whose authority is backed by guns).

I make the same argument to friends and acquaintances who may feel pressured by behavioral prescriptions by gang members or other authoritarians. I try to promote the view that we are all the prisoners and the only relevant distinction is between "us" and "them," them being the agents of repression who keep us all together. Plus, I find that the close quarters of prison and prisoners' very visible collective oppression make social and group distinctions difficult to maintain. We live and interact so closely that only the densest cannot see that asshole nature is an individual, not a group, characteristic and that fulfilling one's human needs requires that interaction.

I spent ten years in USP Marion when it was a lockdown joint. When I first went, the program was 23/7 lockdown. While I prefer the additional increment of freedom of a general population, I did not do bad time at USP Marion.

The first time I went, I did seven years. The process started when I got pinched in the vocational welding shop at USP Lompoc with a pair of exercise grips I had a fella in the machine shop make for me. My right hand had lost some strength and function from nerve damage done by a police bullet through my right arm. Hand-strengthening exercise grips were banned at USP Lompoc, but they had previously been permitted, and existing ones had been grandfathered in. I didn't think it would be a big deal, but the fella in whose booth I got pinched had escaped from McNeil Island (then a federal prison) like twenty years earlier. The tower guard who shot at him sixty-two times and missed was then warden at USP Lompoc—and had been waiting for a get-back for the "talking to" he undoubtedly got for his marksmanship, not to mention the laughing at. Hence, even though I took the beef, we were both found guilty of possession of escape paraphernalia by the Institution Disciplinary Committee (how a mild steel device that opened when squeezed could be wire cutters was never explained). We were both trundled off to USP Marion as a result.

When I arrived at Marion, the program was 23/7 lockdown; by the time I last left, it was about 21.5/7 lockdown. After the TV wore out (about a month) and talking to the fellas on either side and above or below also wore out (interest renewed with moves, but I'm not a big long-distance talker), my world became my cell, ameliorated by brief conversations during tier time [brief periods of time when people were let out of their cells to talk to others on their tier or wing]. But it was a cell full of doors. All I had to do was open the cover of a book and I could slip out. I did a lot of writing there too, occasional articles, the *Marionette/Prison News Service* (a publication published monthly in Canada) and a lot of letters. I also took about a dozen correspondence courses. I got most of my workout in the cell and finished up with a run and some pull-ups or other calisthenics on the tier, a little conversation, and then a shower. I learned something about the law, amongst other things, and developed some skill at filing administrative and court documents. I met some cool people and some knaves. And I remained more or less sane.

Keeping myself occupied and entertained kept me from dwelling on the isolation and confinement. The consciousness that the only thing we truly control in life is the attitude with which we address our circumstances. Just spacing off into the woods some distance outside a dirty barrel and screened window from a closely circumscribed reality, an evocative sound or smell or sight might pull a transporting association unbidden from the recesses of my mind. But do I let it break me down in a sense of loss and self-pity or updraft me into a vision of future deeds presaged by that prompt? Do I greet the curmudgeon with a smile and a bright word or just keep on steppin'? Do I interpret an ambiguous comment cordially or defensively, happily, or angrily? Is the glass half full? All of those choices are within my power, and the upside choices have always worked best for me. So the swine could never really get to me in a strategic sense—tactically, sure, but never strategically. And, indeed, they taught me to amuse myself.

Marion-style lockdown differed from the "normal," mainline, general population in that it was a much less social place. Prisons are generally intensely social. In lockdown, however, one is thrown much more onto one's own devices. There are no jobs or programs or congregate activities with which to while away time that is not externally occupied. General population life is going to work, the chow hall, the yard, the school, the hobby shop, or just hanging out on the tier sharing a few TVs or the phone or email lines or tables, and games with others for whom there are not enough jobs or inclination to do them. Interactions over various things that are less important than the interaction itself—the human connection—absorb a lot of time.

If I could go back and do it again, I would be more disciplined about educating myself and seeking out those other prisoners with whom I could share learning in the spirit of mutual aid. Lots of people find a physical work-out partner (a relationship hard to maintain), but few seem able to maintain that within the razor wire. I would try all of those harder.

Looking Forward

Outside support is always important because it allows a fella to see which way the wind is blowing and try to trim the sails of the struggle to best advantage. Such support may also provide a modicum of protection; it gives prisoners a degree of visibility that makes them less prone to victimization by official skullduggery—and even just neglect or deliberate indifference to prisoners' needs or circumstances. And, no, I have not always felt supported because my politics have not always been compatible with or popular in the quarters doing much of the supporting. But so it goes: the struggle ebbs and flows and eddies in unpredictable ways. Prisoner supporters should know—and I think they do for the most part—that political prisoners seek to be more involved in the struggle from which they have been isolated. They are generally not merely looking to pass the time but to contribute something more than they can inside and alone.

Political prisoners generally would feel much more supported if the movement for the most equitable social reality were large and strong and thus capable of wringing concessions from the status quo—such as releases of comrades who are old and sick and no threat to anyone or anything to which they are not still a threat (and maybe more so) from inside. To be sure, outside supporters have been able to accomplish such victories, but more needs doing.

A stronger movement would also be better able to pry prisons open to programs for prisoners generally and to engage with the community toward reintegrating them now through such programs rather than isolating them into a divergent community of criminality. Such a movement would shine a sanitizing light of public scrutiny on atrocious conditions, such as inadequate medical and dental care, education, recreation, et cetera. A bigger, more dynamic movement would be more able to involve prisoners in their struggles. Riders of the revolutionary road (and the right seeks not revolution but reaction) must be able to involve people to the levels of their commitment and ability. And each one must teach one. And each one must wear many hats, even if they don't all fit well. And each one must stay on the road even when she/he/they must suffer the slings and arrows of the outrageously fortunate. All these and the other slogans can be better practiced within and by a more vibrant movement. And each one must practice mutual aid. And since prisoners are almost exclusively the class brethren/sistren/themren of the people on our side of the barricade, creating opportunities for them strengthens the movement and diminishes the legitimacy of the apparatus.

Another support for prisoners would be confronting the prison-industrial complex, not only rhetorically or generally but [also] on a more granular level. The complex's denizens seek to cater to prisoncrats' desire to drive down the cost of incarceration by selling them substandard products prisoners must use. Well, those people and the prisoncrats themselves live in our communities too. Campaigns or mere events or encounters against exploitative businesses and the people behind them (and promoting progressive ones) not only shine disinfecting light into the dirt done in dark concrete corners of the gulag archipelago and the financing thereof, [they] diminish the influence and attractiveness of the apparatus of repression. Managers, manufacturing workers, delivery people, warehouse workers, et cetera, don't want to be associated with feeding prisoners food marked "not for human consumption" and other abuses. And prisoncrats don't like to be called out for their perfidious practice, especially in public and by people against whom they can't easily retaliate. People on our side of the barricade need to develop both economic and political influence and not merely wallow in "anti." Doing so requires both individual and collective action, especially considering that the targeted entities will sometimes push back.

I do think prisoners today are at least more or less united in opposition to the prison system. "Fuck the feds!" is sported on more than a few tattoos. Some prisoners may pay lip service to "programming" and the notion that they are being rehabilitated (or something) in an effort to take advantage of the attendant opportunities and or benefits, but the opposition is still there. I don't hear any prisoners extolling the virtues of state prison systems either, except comparatively, as in this one is better than that one (but not good), with few exceptions.

What prisoners need is to overcome their factional divisions in order to act on that unity. They need to put aside the racism, regionalism, sexism, car-ism (which I distinguish from gangsterism because gangs are not all bad, just like any other culture). Perhaps the commonality of opposition to the agency of repression and its owners will help in that regard—will help people recognize that we have more in common than at odds and that we can accomplish things with that commonality we cannot with division. Perhaps that commonality with respect to prisons will show us that the contest is between oppressed and oppressors, and we all need to get all of the oppressors out of our game so we can build that unity against the prison-industrial complex out across all the fronts of the struggle. That's how we can get the boot off all our necks.

To people coming into prison today, I would say, "Don't waste your time! Just because you'd rather be doing something else doesn't mean there's nothing to do!" Take what courses may be available on how to do things in the real world. We have to support ourselves and our movement's activities. Many prisons still have apprenticeship programs that allow people to fall out with a journeyman's (that's still what it's called, but maybe participation by a few more women and gender nonconformists toughened by the rigors of life with big bro could change that) certificate. Such skills allow people on our side to draw resources from the other side. Be supplied by the enemy. With that also comes access to the means of production and increased capacity to form collective living and working situations not only to survive but to prefigure the institutions of the future society we will build. There are also certificate and other programs. Even if the institution offers only junky courses, they beat a blank and may serve as interest inventories that show people in which direction they can move most effectively.

Even if one's confinement institution offers no worthwhile learning, there are places that help prisoners get books on various areas so prisoners can do their own studying. Book sources may also be able to connect prisoners with people knowledgeable in the subject. Plus, one does have an obligation to maintain the tools of the struggle: learning to do new things or just understand them is working out for the mind. The mind will get soft and lazy and wear just like the body if it is not active. Plus, having all the information one may think he/she/they need in one's hand via phone is no substitute for knowledge in the head. What's out there in the ether can't cruise one's neural pathways and cross-fertilize at a hundred billion intersections in that mental highway system with innumerable bits and bytes also itinerant between one's ears.

Be social. Don't hide who you are. You have not only a right to your identity but [also] an obligation to represent it. Just don't be an asshole about it. There are plenty of shiny needles (and a few rusty ones!) in the prison haystack. Among them there is a wide array of knowledge that isn't taught in any course. And there are always opportunities to sell the revolution car. Nor have connections ever hurt anyone. It is better to have friends in low places than no friends at all. One can't just put everyone sentenced to prison on "criminal" status and write 'em off as irrevocably damaged or flawed. No one thinks their action that brought them to prison was a crime at the time they did it. Most members of the "criminal element" didn't either. Some still don't and never will. The same act may be done from a position of principle (or illness or mistake) or may be spawned by depravity. While some actions are inherently criminal, others depend on motivation. Hence, it is apparent that determining the knavery of someone whose actions resulted in prison is subjective. We thus might not like all of the positions or past practice of those with whom we struggle, but sometimes the best comrade is the one you have.

Stay active. Get what recreation and education you can. Some of us are differently abled than others, but everyone has something they can do to build themselves into better physical and emotional health. Maintaining the tools of the struggle includes the most basic one: the meat machine and its operating system.

Remember that the only thing we absolutely control in life is the attitude with which we confront the conditions that confront us. A smile is always better than a sneer. The glass is always half full. The sun always shines after a storm. We will win.

Oscar López Rivera

Oscar López Rivera is a Puerto Rican freedom fighter and community activist who was imprisoned for nearly thirty-six years due to sedition charges for his involvement in the Fuerzas Armadas de Liberación Nacional Puertorriqueña, a clandestine paramilitary organization fighting for Puerto Rican independence. Arrested in 1981, López Rivera remained incarcerated in several of the highest-level prisons in the country before his sentence was commuted in January 2017 by outgoing President Barack Obama. He published the book *Between Torture and Resistance* (PM Press, 2013).

Prison Life

I was in prison just short of thirty-six years—thirty-five years, eleven months, and seventeen days. I was housed at various prisons, among them USP Leavenworth, UPS Marion, Florence ADX, and USP Terre Haute. I also spent a short amount of time at the Metropolitan Correctional Center in downtown Chicago awaiting trial.

I was mentally prepared. I never felt that I would have to ask for support once I went to prison. I was always supported; never once did I arrive at a prison and not feel supported and respected. I made a deal with myself that I was going to come out of prison with energy intact and my mind clear.

Basically, most of my happiest moments were when my family would come and visit me, when my friends would come and visit me. Mostly, when people would come and engage in conversations with me.

I learned how to paint inside; I became a fairly good artist inside. Also, I did a lot of artwork for other things, and at the same time I was a teacher for inmates who did not speak English. The prison made it easy because they needed someone who could do artwork. It forced them to give me the kind of treatment I deserved to have; the amount of time that I needed, they gave to me.

I lost many members of my family [while I was imprisoned], and it was very difficult and very painful for me. Sometimes I found out days later about the conditions of my family, so it was always very painful and very difficult.

At first I thought [the quality of life inside] would get a little bit better, but when the prisons got privatized that changed a lot. Some of the inmates I knew who were fairly good people, once they put them out of the prisons they could not deal with the experience. Some of them went through very difficult experiences that no inmate should ever have to go through.

I never thought that I was not prepared. I think that I told myself when I arrived at the first prison that I would walk out alive and stronger. I was told when I arrived at the first penitentiary that I would be dead by the time I finished my sentence. That did not happen.

Politics and Prison Dynamics

One of the first real hard moments was when twenty-two prisoners who had been condemned to death were brought into the holding penitentiary that I was in. I knew some of these guys, and, when they came in, I knew they were going to be killed. I think that was one of the hardest experiences for me.

I never had conflicts with inmates while in prison. On the contrary, I think that inmates were always very helpful to me. I cannot complain about any experience with inmates. We exercised, the yard, the educational part, which was all very, very important. There were a few hard moments with the staff, especially the ones who mistreated me. There was one moment when I was taken out of the cell and put in the hole, and then, when I returned, all my written materials were underwater, my photos were underwater, other materials were disappeared. When I asked the staff, they said the FBI must have done it. When I confronted the FBI, they said they had nothing to do with it.

I never faced racial violence in prison. On the contrary, I had the opportunity—always, whenever something was going to happen—that I could
intervene and make sure that nothing would come up, but that the end result
was a positive result. I think that I had enough experiences on the streets in
Chicago to bring a difficult situation to a peaceful conclusion.

I have done time with members of the Ohio 7, I have done time with
Fernando González Llort of the Cuban Five, some of the Palestinians, with
Sundiata Acoli and with Leonard Peltier, to name a few.[1] Those experiences
were mutually beneficial.

Looking Forward

Outside support is very important. I believe that all inmates should receive
support from families and friends because this is what is needed most—that
they feel they have access to the outside world, not just being in a cell feeling
so miserable. As long as people from the outside go to them and help them,
it is a very different environment.

I did feel supported in prison! My family was there, my friends were
there, people from throughout the world were there. I think that I was very
fortunate to have been supported not only by Puerto Ricans but [also] by
people all over the world. This contributed to helping me feel that I was
ready for the outside world. The outside world plays a crucial role if their
goal is to make that person be more human instead of the opposite.

I would definitely tell [people facing prison time today] to be prepared
mentally and physically and to take advantage of what is offered to them.
I think that there are things that can be advantageous to the inmate who
comes in with nothing, nothing at all.

I think that the conditions are not that good. I think that there's this
whole system of hatred toward inmates. The prison system itself has a
responsibility to help a person be as human as possible. This way they can
help their communities and be an asset when they come out.

---

1. The Cuban Five were five Cuban intelligence officers—René González, Fernando
González Llort, Antonio Guerrero, Gerardo Hernández, and Ramón Labañino—who were convicted of espionage and held in US prisons from 1998 until their eventual releases in 2013 and 2014.

Afterword

Support Political Prisoners

As was said so often in the pages you just read, it is vital that we support the political prisoners of our liberation movements. Providing support builds bridges across and through prison bars, giving those locked inside a connection to the outside world. Your support matters.

Get involved. Write to a political prisoner—a simple letter provides a needed escape. Visit them in prison. Ask what a political prisoner needs and do what you can to help them. Offer them support.

Visit the NYC Anarchist Black Cross website (nycabc.wordpress.com) and learn more about those currently imprisoned for political reasons. Buy a Certain Days: Freedom for Political Prisoners calendar (certaindays.org). Visit your local Books Through Bars group and send books to those incarcerated (booksthroughbarsnyc.org/resources). Join your nearest Anarchist Black Cross group (abcf.net). Visit rattlingthecages.com to learn more.

Glossary

Below is a list of groups, organizations, people, and publications mentioned in these pages. Following that is a list of prison terminology and a list of all prisons, jails, and other carceral facilities mentioned in this book.

Groups and Organizations

The **American Indian Movement (AIM)** was founded in Minnesota in 1968 to address police brutality, poverty, and violence and discrimination against Native communities. They organized for treaty rights, self-determination, and the reclamation of tribal land. AIM activists organized and advocated on behalf of Indigenous communities and led provocative marches and occupations in the early 1970s. The group met fierce resistance from local and federal law enforcement agencies and COINTELPRO operations. **Dennis Banks, Russell Means**, and **Leonard Peltier** are organizers connected to AIM who are mentioned herein. See more about Peltier below.

The **Anarchist Black Cross (ABC)** is an anarchist political prisoner support federation dating back to Russia in the early twentieth century and popularized in Europe in the late 1960s. ABC chapters began to appear in the US in the mid-1980s, providing support to political prisoners from the liberation movements of the 1960s and 1970s. Find an ABC chapter or start one near you.

The **Animal Liberation Front (ALF)** is an international direct action movement that operates clandestinely in support of animal liberation and against animal cruelty. In the early 2000s, numerous people were arrested and imprisoned for actions done in the name of the ALF and the ELF, a time often referred to as the Green Scare (alluding to the Red Scare and fear of communism in the 1950s). **Jake Conroy** and **Andy Stepanian** are former political prisoners connected to the ALF who are mentioned herein.

Anonymous is a decentralized hacktivist collective that started in the early 2000s and has targeted corporations, governments, institutions, and individuals for their lack of transparency and their criminal and immoral conduct. **Jeremy Hammond** is a former political prisoner connected to Anonymous who is mentioned herein.

The **Aryan Brotherhood (AB)** is a neo-Nazi prison gang known to be violent and white supremacist in their actions. The AB has members inside and outside of prisons across the United States.

The **Black Guerrilla Family (BGF)** is a Black prison-based organization started by imprisoned intellectual **George Jackson** in 1966 in San Quentin prison in California. The BGF remains fairly prominent in prisons as of 2023, though it is much less political than when initially founded.

The **Black Liberation Army (BLA)** was an underground revolutionary Black nationalist organization in the 1970s and 1980s that fought back against the institutional racism and violence of the US government. The BLA was both feared and pursued by law enforcement agencies across the country. **Jihad Abdulmumit, Sundiata Acoli, Ashanti Alston, Kuwasi Balagoon, Herman Bell, Joe-Joe Bowen, Robert Seth Hayes, Teddy "Jah" Heath, Maliki Shakur Latine, Jalil Muntaqim, Sekou Odinga, Geronimo Pratt, Kojo Bomani Sababu, Assata Shakur, Russell Maroon Shoatz,** and **Albert Nuh Washington** are current or former political prisoners connected to the BLA mentioned herein. See more about Abdulmumit, Acoli, Balagoon, Odinga, and Shakur below.

The **Black Panther Party (BPP)** was a militant vanguard organization formed in 1966 to protect and advance Black lives. They engaged in self-defense tactics, initiated community survival programs "pending revolution," and were met with constant attack by local and federal law enforcement agencies and COINTELPRO operations. BPP chapters were prevalent around the world in the late 1960s and early 1970s. **Mumia Abu-Jamal**, **Jamil Abdullah Al-Amin** (formerly known as **H. Rap Brown**), **Veronza Bowers, Jr.**, **Elaine Brown**, **Eddie Conway**, **Eddie Ellis**, **Fred Hampton**, **Bobby Hutton**, **George Jackson**, **Huey P. Newton**, **Ed Poindexter**, and **Bobby Seale** are former members of the BPP mentioned herein. See more about Abu-Jamal, Jackson, and Newton below.

The **Bloods (Brotherly Love Overcomes Overrides and Destruction)** and the **Crips (Community Revolution in Progress)** were formed in Los Angeles, California, in the late 1960s and early 1970s, as youth community organizations turned street gangs. Members of both continue to be targeted for imprisonment.

Books Through Bars (BTB) are informal groups that send free books and information to incarcerated people. Find a BTB group or start a books to prisoners group near you. See the Afterword.

The **Catholic Worker** movement was started by **Dorothy Day** and **Peter Maurin** in 1933 as autonomous groups of nonviolent adherents around the world living in accordance with the teachings of Jesus Christ and participating in civil disobedience to bear witness to state violence. **Martha Hennessy** and **Elizabeth McAlister** are Catholic Workers and former political prisoners who are mentioned herein. The Plowshares movement includes both individuals and philosophies from the Catholic Worker movement (see more about the Plowshares movement below).

COINTELPRO (Counter Intelligence Program) was an illegal and top-secret government counterintelligence program that was most prominently orchestrated by the FBI from the 1950s through the 1970s to discredit, neutralize, and eliminate subversive individuals and organizations. Numerous activists and organizers were discredited, imprisoned, or killed as a result of COINTELPRO operations.

The **Crips (Community Revolution in Progress)**—see **Bloods (Brotherly Love Overcomes Overrides and Destruction)**

Critical Resistance was founded in 1997 and has worked ever since to eliminate the prison-industrial complex (PIC), seeking to build an international movement to end the PIC by challenging the belief that caging and controlling people makes us safe. Critical Resistance is a national grassroots organization that has chapters across the United States.

Direct Action was an underground group of five anarchists in Canada during the early 1980s. Once arrested for their bombings and other actions, the Squamish Five served various prison sentences. **Ann Hansen** is a former political prisoner connected to Direct Action who is mentioned herein.

The **Earth Liberation Front (ELF)** is an international direct action movement that operates clandestinely in support of the earth and against the exploitation and destruction of the environment. **Daniel McGowan, Bill Rodgers**, and **Rebecca Rubin** are former political prisoners connected to the ELF who are mentioned herein.

The **Front de libération du Québec (FLQ)** was a militant Québecois independence group that carried out several actions throughout the 1960s and into 1970.

The **Fuerzas Armadas de Liberación Nacional Puertorriqueña (FALN)** was a clandestine paramilitary organization that fought for Puerto Rican independence in the United States from 1974 until 1983, when the majority of its members were imprisoned. *Independentistas* was a term used to describe Puerto Rican independence fighters. Sixteen FALN members were imprisoned in the early 1980s, and fourteen received clemency from outgoing president Bill Clinton in 1999. **Oscar López Rivera** was the last FALN member released from prison after a commutation from outgoing president Barack Obama in 2017. **Adolfo Matos, Dylcia Pagan, Carmen Valentín Pérez, Oscar López Rivera, Alicia Rodriguez, Lucy Rodriguez, Luis Rosa, Alejandrina Torres**, and **Haydee Torres** are former political prisoners connected to the FALN who are mentioned herein.

The **George Jackson Brigade (GJB)** was a guerrilla underground organization based in the Pacific Northwest in the mid-to-late 1970s. Members were racially and sexually diverse and carried out symbolic bombings in solidarity with national and international liberation struggles. The group was named after George Jackson (see more below). **Janine Bertram, bo brown, Mark Cook, Therese Coupez**, and **Ed Mead** are former members of the GJB who are mentioned herein.

The **Hells Angels Motorcycle Club (HAMC)** is a nationwide outlaw motorcycle organization founded in 1948. Known to be involved in organized crime, the Hells Angels are often violent and racist in their actions.

The **Incarcerated Workers Organizing Committee (IWOC)** is a prison-led section of the Industrial Workers of the World (IWW) that works to abolish prison slavery and fights to end the exploitation of incarcerated workers.

The **Irish Republican Army (IRA)** was an Irish paramilitary organization that fought for a united Ireland. Their battles with the British state were most intense in the 1970s and 1980s, a period commonly referred to as the Troubles. **Joe Doherty** was a political prisoner connected to the IRA who is mentioned herein.

The **Jericho Movement** was founded in 1998 to raise awareness and seek the freedom of US-held political prisoners. Its founding followed a national march on the White House in spring 1998, called by political prisoner **Jalil Muntaqim**.

The **Ku Klux Klan (KKK)** is one of the oldest and most notorious white supremacist groups in the United States. Members of the KKK are prominent in the prison system among white prisoners and guards alike.

Los Macheteros, or the **Boricua Popular Army**, was a clandestine paramilitary organization based in Puerto Rico that struggled to achieve freedom for the island's people. **Filiberto Ojeda Ríos** is a former political prisoner and founder of Los Macheteros who is mentioned herein.

May 19th Communist Organization was a revolutionary anti-imperialist organization dedicated to acting in solidarity with and following the leadership of national liberation movements inside the borders of the United States and around the world. The name refers to the birthdays of Malcolm X and Ho Chi Minh and the date of the death of José Martí. May 19th worked with Black, New Afrikan, Puerto Rican, Mexicano/Chicano, South African, Palestinian, and other groups fighting to free the land and for independence and socialism, and analyzed the United States as being a white, settler-colonialist state. The group organized white people to join in anti-imperialist solidarity in a number of projects, including the John Brown Anti-Klan Committee, and in support of political prisoners.

The **MOVE** organization was founded in Philadelphia by John Africa in 1972 as a spiritual, back-to-nature group with a revolutionary ideology. MOVE faced police abuse from the start, and nine of its members spent decades imprisoned as political prisoners before seven of them gained their freedom. Two MOVE members—Merle and Phil Africa—died while in prison.

The **New Afrikan Black Panther Party (NABPP)** was founded in Virginia prisons around 2005, with Kevin Rashid Johnson and Shaka Zulu (or Zulu Sharod) as its founding members. The group was active in the 2016 US prison strike. Johnson split from the original NABPP in 2020. **Kevin Rashid Johnson** is a politicized prisoner connected to the NABPP who is mentioned herein.

The **Plowshares movement** consists of Christian pacifists who protest against nuclear weapons and war. The name refers to the prophet Isaiah who said that swords shall be beaten into plowshares, and adherents are influenced by the Catholic Worker movement. Many Plowshares activists are jailed for their civil disobedience. **Jackie Allen, Clare Grady, Sister Anne Montgomery, Kathleen Rumpf,** and **Suzanne Schmidt** are former political prisoners and Plowshares activists who are mentioned herein.

The **Prairie Fire Organizing Committee (PFOC)** was a revolutionary anti-imperialist organization active from the mid-1970s to the mid-1990s. They were an aboveground affiliate of the Weather Underground Organization (WUO), and their name comes from the 1974 WUO manifesto *Prairie Fire*. The PFOC focused primarily on international solidarity with people's movements in Nicaragua and El Salvador and support of the Puerto Rican Fuerzas Armadas de Liberación Nacional Puertorriqueña.

The **Puerto Rican independence movement** consists of Puerto Ricans and their supporters who struggle to realize a free and autonomous Puerto Rican homeland. **Oscar Collazo**, **Andrés Figueroa Cordero**, **Lolita Lebrón**, **Rafael Cancel Miranda**, and **Irvin Flores Rodríguez** (together known as the Puerto Rican Five) are former Puerto Rican political prisoners who are mentioned herein.

The **Red Army Faction (RAF)** was a West German underground and anti-imperialist organization active from the early 1970s through the late 1990s. The majority of the founding members died tragically while in police custody.

Release Aging People in Prison (RAPP) is a New York-based advocacy and education organization created and led by formerly incarcerated people that works to free incarcerated elders. RAPP was founded by two former political prisoners, **Kathy Boudin** and **Laura Whitehorn**, and **Mujahid Farid**, a former jailhouse lawyer and cofounder of the Prisoner Education Project on AIDS with **David Gilbert** and **"Papo" Nieves**.

The **Republic of New Afrika (RNA)** was a Black nationalist organization founded in 1968 in part based on the teachings of Malcolm X. The RNA has had many prominent members and seeks to establish a Black-majority country in what are now the five southern states of Louisiana, Mississippi, Alabama, Georgia, and South Carolina. **Dr. Mutulu Shakur** is a former political prisoner connected to the RNA who is mentioned herein. See more about Shakur below.

The **Revolutionary Army** was a militant Bay Area underground group founded in the early 1970s by **Willie Brandt**, **Wendy Yoshimura**, and others. They planted bombs and planned other actions to protest the Vietnam War, and members sometimes worked in solidarity with the SLA.

Running Down the Walls (RDTW) is a 5k noncompetitive run/jog/walk/ roll held annually since 1999 to raise awareness and funds for political pris- oners currently held in North American prisons. Outside participants run/ jog/walk/roll in solidarity with those participating behind the bars. It is orchestrated by the Anarchist Black Cross. Find one or start one near you.

Students for a Democratic Society (SDS) was a predominantly white student-activist organization that rose rapidly in membership between 1960 and 1969 before splintering. SDS advocated New Left ideas, an end to the Vietnam War and US imperialism, Black Power, and the adoption of "partic- ipatory democracy" on the home front.

The **Symbionese Liberation Army (SLA)** was an underground paramilitary organization founded by an escaped Black prisoner, **Donald DeFreeze**, and white coconspirators in the Bay Area in the early 1970s. Their most widely publicized action was the kidnapping of media heiress Patty Hearst. The majority of the original members were murdered by the Los Angeles Police Department (LAPD) and the FBI in a massive attack in Los Angeles in 1974. **Bill Harris**, **Emily Harris**, **James Kilgore**, **Russ Little**, and **Joe Remiro** are former political prisoners connected to the SLA who are mentioned herein.

The **United Freedom Front (UFF)** was a group of working-class revolution- aries who engaged in armed struggle against US imperialism in solidarity with freedom struggles in South Africa, Palestine, and throughout Central America in the 1980s. Actions done by some of these same people during the 1970s were done in the name of the Sam Melville–Jonathan Jackson Unit. **Sam Melville** was a political prisoner who was murdered in the aftermath of the September 1971 Attica uprising. **Jonathan Jackson** was murdered in an attempted kidnapping at the Marin County Courthouse in August 1970 in an attempt to free his brother, politicized prisoner **George Jackson**. **Jaan Laaman**, **Ray Luc Levasseur**, **Tom Manning**, and **Richard Williams** are former political prisoners connected to the UFF who are mentioned herein.

Venceremos was a revolutionary organization active in the Bay Area in the late 1960s and early 1970s. Members were primarily Chicano and advocated armed self-defense, community education, and prison reform, among other things. **Bob Seabock** was a Venceremos member who received a life sentence after being convicted of a 1972 murder of a prison guard.

The **Venceremos Brigades** are an international solidarity effort first orchestrated between SDS and the Cuban government in 1969. Volunteers labor alongside Cuban workers as an act of solidarity to combat US embargoes.

The **Victory Gardens Project** (**VGP**) was formed between political prisoner **Herman Bell** and outside supporters in rural Maine as a mutual aid project of growing and distributing organically grown produce in oppressed communities and providing political prisoner education.

Water Protectors are activists and organizers who defend the earth's water and respect all that it enables. This movement blossomed at Standing Rock in 2016 when Indigenous communities and activists from around the world gathered to protest construction of the Dakota Access Pipeline. **Rattler** and **Jessica Reznicek** are current or former political prisoners connected to the movement of Water Protectors who are mentioned herein.

The **Weather Underground Organization** (**WUO**), an offshoot of SDS, was a militant clandestine organization that carried out bombings of corporate and government targets throughout the 1970s in solidarity with Third World communities inside and outside of the United States.

Whistleblowers are individuals who expose the corrupt or malicious internal actions of a public or private organization, government, or entity, leaking information thought to be pertinent to the general public. **Daniel Hale** and **Chelsea Manning** are current or former political prisoners that engaged in whistleblowing who are mentioned herein.

The **Young Lords** were a Puerto Rican independence party prominent in New York City and Chicago in the late 1960s and early 1970s that sought Puerto Rican self-determination and an end to US occupation of the island. They engaged in daring offensives and takeovers to highlight the oppression that Puerto Ricans and other oppressed communities continue to face.

The **Zapatista Army of National Liberation (EZLN)** is an Indigenous paramilitary organization based in Chiapas, Mexico, that opposes globalization, capitalism, and neoliberalism. The Zapatistas released their first public communique on January 1, 1994, the same day that the North American Free Trade Agreement (NAFTA) came into effect. **Oso Blanco** is a current political prisoner who helped support the EZLN and is mentioned herein.

People

Jihad Abdulmumit spent twenty-three years in prison as a political prisoner for his involvement with the Black Liberation Army. Since his release from prison, Abdulmumit has served as chairperson of the National Jericho Movement.

Mumia Abu-Jamal is a journalist, author, and former member of the Black Panther Party who has been imprisoned since 1981. His death sentence was overturned in 2001, but supporters have been advocating for his release from prison ever since. As of 2023, Mumia remains in prison. He has written numerous books and essays while confined to his cell.

Sundiata Acoli is a former member of the Black Panther Party and the Black Liberation Army, and a former New York Panther 21 defendant, who was a political prisoner from 1973 until he was paroled in 2022 after forty-nine years at the age of eighty-five. He was a codefendant of **Assata Shakur**.

Kuwasi Balagoon was an anarchist and lifelong activist who was involved with the Black Panther Party and the Black Liberation Army. He was a defendant in the infamous New York Panther 21 case, he escaped from confinement numerous times, and he was imprisoned from 1981 until his death of pneumocystis pneumonia, an AIDS-related illness, in 1986 at age thirty-nine. There is a collection of his writings called *Soldier's Story: Revolutionary Writings by a New Afrikan Anarchist* (PM Press, 2019).

Silvia Baraldini is an Italian activist who supported Black liberation and Puerto

Rican independence and was imprisoned in the United States in 1982 for grand jury resistance and aiding in the prison escape of **Assata Shakur**. After being transferred to Italy in 1999, Baraldini was released from prison in 2006.

The **Cuban Five** were Cuban intelligence officers—**René González, Fernando González Llort, Antonio Guerrero, Gerardo Hernández**, and **Ramón Labañino**—who were convicted of espionage and held in US prisons from 1998 until their eventual releases in 2013 and 2014.

The **Holy Land Foundation Five (HLF 5)** are former leaders of a Dallas-based Muslim charity (the Holy Land Foundation) who were unjustly convicted in 2009 of funneling millions of dollars to Palestinian militants. They are **Mufid Abdulqader, Shukri Abu Baker, Ghassan Elashi, Mohammad El-Mezain**, and **Abdulrahman Odeh**. The five were given sentences of between fifteen to sixty-five years in prison.

George Jackson was serving a sentence of one year to life in California state prisons when he joined the Black Panther Party and cofounded the Black Guerrilla Family in the late 1960s. He wrote two highly publicized books while incarcerated—*Soledad Brother: The Prison Letters of George Jackson* and *Blood in My Eye*—and garnered international support prior to being killed by guards in a supposed escape attempt in 1971.

Huey P. Newton was a Black revolutionary and writer who cofounded the Black Panther Party in 1966. He spent time in and out of jail due to his politics, and he was a target of the FBI's COINTELPRO. Newton was murdered in Oakland in 1989 by a member of the Black Guerrilla Family.

Sekou Odinga was formerly a member of Malcolm X's Organization of Afro-American Unity (OAAU), the Black Panther Party, and the Black Liberation Army and spent thirty-three years as a political prisoner. He was released from prison in 2014.

Leonard Peltier is a Native American activist who has been wrongly imprisoned since 1977 for his involvement in a shootout with FBI agents on the Pine Ridge Reservation in South Dakota. He is a member of the American

Indian Movement, and he remains imprisoned as of 2023. He wrote the book *Prison Writings: My Life Is My Sun Dance* (St. Martin's Griffin, 2000).

The **Resistance Conspiracy Case** started in 1985 when seven anti-imperialist activists were charged with bombing military and corporate targets in the United States throughout the early 1980s. Those charged were **Alan Berkman, Timothy Blunk, Marilyn Buck, Elizabeth Duke, Linda Evans, Susan Rosenberg**, and **Laura Whitehorn**. Six of the seven did various amounts of time in prison, most of the time in solitary confinement, though all are all out of prison now. Marilyn Buck died in 2010, weeks after being granted medical release.

The **San Francisco 8** were former members of the Black Panther Party who were arrested in 2007 in connection with the 1971 murder of a San Francisco police officer. **Herman Bell** pled guilty to involuntary manslaughter and **Jalil Muntaqim** pled no contest to conspiracy to commit voluntary manslaughter, though all eight of the defendants suffered tortuous conditions during their confinement.

Assata Shakur is a former member of the Black Panther Party and the Black Liberation Army who was imprisoned from 1973 until 1979, when she escaped from prison, and was later given political asylum in Cuba. She wrote the book *Assata: An Autobiography* (Lawrence Hill Books, 2001).

Dr. Mutulu Shakur has been active in the struggle for Black liberation his entire adult life and has been imprisoned since 1986. He was involved with the Republic of New Afrika and also practiced acupuncture to provide healing to oppressed communities. Denied parole ten times, Shakur was finally released in 2022 after being given just months to live due to late-stage cancer. Shakur died in July 2023, a free man. Free the land!

Russell Maroon Shoatz spent forty-nine years in prison for his involvement with the BLA and the Black Liberation Struggle before gaining his freedom in 2021. Twenty-two of those years were spent in solitary confinement. Maroon died of cancer less than two months after his release, after suffering years of medical neglect in prison. His collected writings were published as *Maroon the Implacable* (PM Press, 2013).

Publications

4strugglemag was a joint project between anti-imperialist political prisoner **Jaan Laaman** and organizers with the Montreal and Toronto Anarchist Black Cross, publishing writings by political prisoners, prisoners of war, social prisoners, and their friends and families.

Bite Back is a magazine started in 2002 to give voice to activists who choose to break the law to help animals and to feed an animal rights movement hungry for news about nonviolent direct action.

California Prison Focus is the newspaper of a grassroots organization with the same name that works to abolish the California prison system in its present condition, with a focus on ending long-term solitary confinement.

The Certain Days: Freedom for Political Prisoners Calendar Collective was formed in 2001 and creates the annual *Certain Days: Freedom for Political Prisoners* calendar to raise awareness and funds for North American political prisoners. Certain Days was originally cofounded by New York state political prisoners **Herman Bell**, **David Gilbert**, and **Robert Seth Hayes**, and their outside supporters. The three founding members were all released from prison as of 2021, though **Xinachtli**, a current inside collective member, remains imprisoned as of 2023.

Fire Ant is a publication focused on spreading the words of anarchist prisoners, generating material solidarity for them, and fostering communication between anarchists on both sides of the walls. Fire Ant Collective members included here are **Michael Kimble**, **Eric King**, **Marius Mason**, **Jennifer Rose**, and **Sean Swain**.

Hard Crackers is an online and print publication that is guided by the principle that in ordinary people there resides the capacity to escape from the mess we are in, and it is committed to documenting and examining their strivings to do so.

Love and Rage began in 1989 as an anarchist newspaper and became a network of local collectives of anarchists and antiauthoritarians in the early 1990s.

Prison Legal News is a monthly periodical that has been reporting on criminal justice issues and prison litigation since its founding in 1990. Founded by **Ed Mead** and others, *PLN* is the longest running newspaper produced by and for current and former prisoners in the US.

Prison News Service: A Bulldozer Publication/The Marionette was a prominent prisoner-led abolitionist paper during the 1980s and 1990s. *The Marionette* was edited solely by **Bill Dunne** from prison.

Wildfire was a newsletter focusing on solidarity with US anarchist prisoners, support for prison rebellion, and antiauthoritarian struggle against prison.

Glossary of Prisons and Prison Terminology

Generally speaking, jails are short-term local facilities that incarcerate those recently arrested, those awaiting trial or sentencing, or those with relatively short sentences (generally a year or less). In the Federal Bureau of Prisons (BOP), jails are commonly called detention centers. Compounds are also facilities known to hold incarcerated individuals for short-term periods of time. Prisons, on the other hand, are state- or federally managed facilities that imprison those who have been convicted, with separate prisons for different security levels. In addition to these separate and often distinct federal, state, and local carceral systems, there is also a vast private, for-profit prison system that operates and maintains jails, prisons, and other facilities across the United States through contracts with local, state, and federal government agencies.

Prison Terminology
ADX, commonly called **Florence AdMax**, or **ADX Florence**, refers to United States Penitentiary, Administrative Maximum, a super-maximum security male facility in Florence, Colorado. Opened in 1994, this supermax

prison houses a few hundred people in constant control unit confinement with extremely limited communications with the outside world.

A **bit** or **bid** refers to an inmate's sentence, as in "doing a bit [of time]."

A **car** is the group or clique that one "rolls" with and allies oneself with. This is generally based on race, geography, or political affiliation.

Communication Management Units (CMUs) are specially designated control units established at USP Marion and FCI Terre Haute. Restrictions are more severe in these units than in regular solitary confinement facilities. The USP Marion CMU was in operation from 1983 to 2006; the Terre Haute CMU opened in 2006.

Control units are long-term administrative solitary confinement facilities— either wings within prisons or entire prison facilities, like USP Marion, since reclassified as a medium security prison, or Florence AdMax.

A **cop-out** is the filing of an Inmate Request to Staff form.

Correctional officers (CO) is another name for a prison or jail guard or staff member paid to maintain control over those imprisoned at a given facility.

Double-cell housing refers to two prisoners being held in a cell meant for one. This is often done because of overcrowding but also for punishment or to incite conflict.

The **FBI Gang Unit**, also known as the **Violent Gang Task Force**, pursues "violent gangs through sustained, proactive, coordinated investigations to obtain prosecutions on violations such as racketeering, drug conspiracy, and firearms violations," according to the FBI website. It is known to engage in extreme violence, both inside and outside of prisons.

General population, gen pop, or **GP**, sometimes called the **mainline**, describes where the majority of prisoners are housed, as opposed to segregated housing or solitary confinement.

K2, or **spice**, is a synthetic marijuana with effects that can be more unpredictable and dangerous than cannabis. The prevalence of K2 in prisons has increased, leading to increased scrutiny, mail restrictions, and conflict.

A **kite** is a message or note that is secretly passed between prisoners or between prisoners and guards.

Residential Drug Abuse Program (RDAP) is a Federal Bureau of Prisons approved program of therapy related to substance abuse. Reduced sentences are often offered to incentivize prisoners to participate in RDAP.

Sensitive Needs Yard (SNY) is a California Department of Corrections and Rehabilitation (CDCR) designation, codified in 2022, for "incarcerated people who have safety concerns regarding living on a General Population (GP) yard."

A **shot** is a written documentation of an infraction or a physical altercation given to a CO. This is referred to as being "written up," and multiple shots can impact someone's record while incarcerated.

Solitary confinement—variously called administrative segregation, the hole, the box, Secure Housing Units (SHU), Administrative Segregation Units (ASUs), Intensive Management Units (IMU), Security Threat Group Management Units (STGMU), Special Management Units (SMUs), et cetera—implies that a prisoner is held in a single cell, often for twenty-three to twenty-four hours per day (for months, years, or even decades on end), with no contact with anyone else.

A **special investigative supervisor (SIS)** works in the Bureau of Prisons to investigate alleged criminal matters and present them to the warden for referral to outside agencies for prosecution.

UNICOR, or **Federal Prison Industries, Inc.**, was established in 1934 as a prison labor program for those incarcerated within the Federal Bureau of Prisons.

List of prisons, jails, and other detention facilities mentioned in this volume

These are just a few of the carceral institutions in the United States. According to the Prison Policy Initiative, in 2023 there were 1,566 state prisons, 98 federal prisons, 3,116 local jails, 1,323 juvenile correctional facilities, 181 immigration detention facilities, and numerous other facilities meant to hold people against their will.

International facilities
Grand Valley Institution for Women (GVI), a female facility operated by the Correctional Service of Canada in Kitchener, Ontario. The prison was opened in 1997 to replace the Prison for Women (P4W), and as of 2010 GVI is the only federal women's prison in Ontario.

Prison for Women (P4W), a former maximum security female facility operated by the Correctional Service of Canada in Kingston, Ontario, operational from 1934 to 2000.

Private facilities
Citrus County Detention Facility (CCDF), a mixed security male facility operated by CoreCivic and located in Lecanto, Florida

CoreCivic, previously the **Corrections Corporation of America (CCA)**, is the second-largest private corrections company in the United States. It has managed and operated over sixty-five state and federal prisons and detention centers since its founding in 1983.

Federal facilities
Federal Correctional Institution, Danbury, a low security male and female facility with an adjacent minimum security prison camp and a nearby low security facility, Federal Satellite Low (FSL) Danbury, in Danbury, Connecticut

Federal Correctional Institution, Dublin (previously called Pleasanton), a low security female facility in Dublin, California

Federal Correctional Institution, Englewood, a low security male facility with an adjacent minimum security prison camp in Englewood, Colorado

Federal Correctional Institution, Marianna, a medium security male and female facility with an adjacent minimum security satellite camp in Marianna, Florida

Federal Correctional Institution, Sandstone, a low security male facility in Sandstone, Minnesota

Federal Correctional Institution, Talladega, a medium security male facility in Talladega, Alabama

Federal Correctional Institution, Terminal Island, a low security male facility in Los Angeles, California

Federal Correctional Institution, Terre Haute, a medium security male facility with an adjacent minimum security satellite camp in Terre Haute, Indiana

Federal Correctional Institution, Victorville, two medium security male facilities in Victorville, California

Federal Medical Center, Carswell, an administrative facility for female prisoners requiring medical or mental health care with an adjacent minimum security satellite camp for female prisoners in Fort Worth, Texas

Federal Medical Center, Lexington, an administrative facility for male or female prisoners requiring medical or mental health care with an adjacent minimum security satellite camp for female prisoners in Lexington, Kentucky

Federal Prison Camp, Alderson, a minimum security female facility in Alderson, West Virginia

Guantánamo Bay Detention Camp, a military prison first opened after the September 11, 2001 attacks, located at the Guantánamo Bay Naval Base in Cuba

Marine Corps Brig, Quantico, a Level 1 military prison facility at Marine Corps Base Quantico in Quantico, Virginia

Metropolitan Correctional Center, Chicago, a mixed security male and female prison in downtown Chicago, Illinois

Metropolitan Correctional Center, New York, an administrative security male facility in downtown Manhattan, New York

Metropolitan Detention Center, Brooklyn, an administrative security male and female facility in downtown Brooklyn, New York

United States Penitentiary, Administrative Maximum, also called Florence AdMax, or ADX, a super-maximum security male facility in Florence, Colorado

United States Penitentiary, Alcatraz Island, commonly called The Rock, a former maximum security facility and US Army military prison, operated from 1934 to 1963, located in San Francisco Bay, California

United States Penitentiary, Atlanta, a low security male facility in Atlanta, Georgia

United States Penitentiary, Leavenworth, a medium security male facility with an adjacent minimum security satellite camp in Leavenworth, Kansas. There is also a United States Disciplinary Barracks, a military facility, located at Fort Leavenworth, Kansas

United States Penitentiary, Lewisburg, a medium security male facility with an adjacent minimum security satellite camp in Lewisburg, Pennsylvania

United States Penitentiary, Lompoc, a medium security male facility in Lompoc, California

United States Penitentiary, Marion, a medium security male and female facility with an adjacent minimum security satellite camp in Marion, Illinois. USP Marion was originally built in 1963 to replace the maximum security federal prison on Alcatraz Island, and it was the first prison to be a "control unit prison," meaning all prisoners are regularly held in solitary confinement. The USP Marion CMU was in operation from 1983 to 2006

United States Penitentiary, McCreary, a high security male facility in McCreary County, Kentucky

United States Penitentiary, Tucson, a high security male facility with an adjacent minimum security prison camp in Tucson, Arizona

State facilities

Alexandria Detention Center, commonly called Alexandria City Jail, a mixed security male and female facility in downtown Alexandria, Virginia

Allegheny County Jail, a mixed security male and female facility in downtown Pittsburgh, Pennsylvania, originally built in the 1880s

Arizona State Prison Complex – Florence, commonly called Florence State Prison, a mixed security facility in Florence, Arizona

Attica Correctional Facility, a maximum security male facility in Attica, New York

Auburn Correctional Facility, a maximum security male facility in Auburn, New York

Baltimore City Detention Center, formerly the Baltimore City Jail, a male and female facility in downtown Baltimore, Maryland

Bedford Hills Correctional Facility, the largest women's prison in New York, a maximum security female facility in Bedford Hills, New York

Brushy Mountain State Penitentiary, a former maximum security male facility in Petros, Tennessee, operational from 1896 to 2009

California Institution for Men, California, commonly called Chino, a mixed security male facility in Chino, California

California Medical Facility, commonly called Vacaville, a mixed security male facility in Vacaville, California

California State Prison Solano, a medium security male facility in Vacaville, California

Camden County Sheriff's Office, a male and female county jail in Woodbine, Georgia

Clinton Correctional Facility, commonly called Dannemora, a maximum security male facility near the Canadian border in Dannemora, New York

Cook County Jail, a mixed security male and female jail in Chicago, Illinois

DC Central Detention Facility, commonly called the DC Jail, a mixed security male and female facility in downtown Washington, DC

Deuel Vocational Institute, sometimes called Tracy, was a male facility operational from 1953 to 2021, near Tracy, California

Eastern Correctional Facility, sometimes called Napanoch, a maximum security male facility in Napanoch, New York

Elmira Correctional Facility, commonly called The Hill, a maximum security male facility in Elmira, New York

Folsom State Prison, California's second-oldest prison, a mixed security male and female facility in Represa, California

Grady County Jail, a mixed security male and female facility in Chickasha, Oklahoma (often used as a transport facility for federal prisoners being transferred between prisons)

Great Meadow Correctional Facility, commonly called Comstock, a maximum security male facility in Comstock, New York

High Desert State Prison, a high security male facility in Susanville, California

Howard County Detention Center, commonly called the Howard County Jail, a male and female facility in Ellicott City, Maryland

Kern Valley State Prison, a maximum security male facility in Delano, California

King County Adult Detention, sometimes called King County Jail, a mixed security male and female facility in downtown Seattle, Washington

Los Angeles County Men's Central Jail, a male and female facility in Los Angeles, California

Maine State Prison, a maximum security male facility in Thomaston, Maine

Mansfield Correctional Institution, a mixed security male facility in Mansfield, Ohio

Massachusetts Correctional Institution – Cedar Junction, formerly named MCI – Walpole, a maximum security male facility in Walpole, Massachusetts

McNeil Island Corrections Center, formerly a federal prison from 1875 to 1981, a former medium security male facility on McNeil Island, Washington, operational from 1984 to 2011

Onondaga County Justice Center, a maximum security male and female facility in Syracuse, New York

Pelican Bay State Prison, a supermax male facility in Crescent City, California

Rikers Island, a mixed security complex of ten jails, housing male and female prisoners, in the East River in New York City

Rockingham County Jail, commonly called the Brentwood House of Correction, a male and female facility in Brentwood, New Hampshire

Sacramento County Jail, a male and female facility in Sacramento, California

Salinas Valley State Prison, a maximum security male facility near Soledad, California

San Quentin State Prison, California's oldest prison, a mixed security male facility, with the state's only death row (and largest death row in the United States) in San Quentin, California. San Quentin's infamous "Adjustment Center" is part of its death row.

Shawangunk Correctional Facility, commonly called "the Gunk," a maximum security male facility in Wallkill, New York

Southport Correctional Facility, a supermax male facility in Southport, New York

Sybil Brand Institute, a former female jail facility operational from 1963 to 1997 in Monterey Park, California

Tennessee State Penitentiary, a former high and medium security male facility in Nashville, operational from 1898 to 1992

Washington State Penitentiary, commonly called Walla Walla, a mixed security male facility in Walla Walla, Washington

Wende Correctional Facility, a maximum security male facility in Alden, New York

William C. Holman Correctional Facility, a maximum security male facility in Atmore, Alabama

William E. Donaldson Correctional Facility, a maximum security male facility in Bessemer, Alabama

William G. McConnell Unit, a high security male facility in Beeville, Texas

CONTRIBUTOR BIOS

Josh Davidson is an abolitionist who is involved in numerous projects, including the Certain Days collective that publishes the annual *Freedom for Political Prisoners* calendar and the Children's Art Project with political prisoner Oso Blanco. Josh also works in communications with the Zinn Education Project, which promotes the teaching of radical people's history in classrooms and provides free lessons and resources for educators. He lives in Eugene, Oregon.

Eric King is a father, poet, author, and activist. He is a political prisoner serving a ten-year federal sentence for an act of protest over the police murder of Michael Brown in Ferguson, Missouri, in 2014. He is scheduled to be released in 2024. He has been held in solitary confinement for years on end and has been assaulted by both guards and white supremacists. King has published three zines: *Battle Tested* (2015); *Antifa in Prison* (2019); and *Pacing in My Cell* (2019). His sentencing statement is included in the book *Defiance: Anarchist Statements Before Judge and Jury* (2019).

Angela Y. Davis is Professor Emerita of History of Consciousness and Feminist Studies at UC Santa Cruz. An activist, writer, and lecturer, her work focuses on prisons, police, abolition, and the related intersections of race, gender, and class. She is the author of many books, including *Angela Davis: An Autobiography* and *Freedom Is a Constant Struggle*.

Sara Falconer is a writer, editor and digital strategist who works with nonprofits. She has been creating publications with prisoners since 2001. Sara lives with her awesome family in Hamilton, Ontario—the traditional territories of the Erie, Neutral, Huron-Wendat, Haudenosaunee, and Mississaugas.

AK PRESS is small, in terms of staff and resources, but we also manage to be one of the world's most productive anarchist publishing houses. We publish close to twenty books every year, and distribute thousands of other titles published by like-minded independent presses and projects from around the globe. We're entirely worker run and democratically managed. We operate without a corporate structure—no boss, no managers, no bullshit.

The **FRIENDS OF AK PRESS** program is a way you can directly contribute to the continued existence of AK Press, and ensure that we're able to keep publishing books like this one! Friends pay $25 a month directly into our publishing account ($30 for Canada, $35 for international), and receive a copy of every book AK Press publishes for the duration of their membership! Friends also receive a discount on anything they order from our website or buy at a table: 50% on AK titles, and 30% on everything else. We have a Friends of AK ebook program as well: $15 a month gets you an electronic copy of every book we publish for the duration of your membership. *You can even sponsor a very discounted membership for someone in prison.*

Email **friendsofak@akpress.org** for more info, or visit the website: **https://www.akpress.org/friends.html**.

There are always great book projects in the works—so sign up now to become a Friend of AK Press, and let the presses roll!